The Contemporary Writer

Second Edition

The Contemporary Writer

Second Edition

A Practical Rhetoric

W. Ross Winterowd

University of Southern California

HARCOURT BRACE JOVANOVICH, INC.

New York   San Diego   Chicago   San Francisco   Atlanta
London   Sydney   Toronto

For the magnificent Grahams

ISBN: 0-15-513726-3

Library of Congress Catalog Card Number: 80-83162

Printed in the United States of America

Picture Credits

Preface

The response of teachers and students to the first edition of this book has been gratifying. Both instructors and students seemed to find *The Contemporary Writer: A Practical Rhetoric* engaging, effective, and conceptually rich. In this thoroughgoing revision I have retained the strengths of the original but have put greater emphasis on the "practical" part of the subtitle, aiming the revision at today's students.

Three features of the new edition should enhance its value for those students.

First, the book contains a minimum of "talking about" writing and a maximum of *showing how to write*. For example, although it is important to *tell* students about the virtues of unity and coherence, the purpose of a composition text, after all, is to show them *how to* write unified, coherent essays and paragraphs. An analogy can be quite useful here. A course in music appreciation is very different from a workshop in conducting; the workshop shows students how to *produce* satisfying music, whereas the music appreciation course teaches them how to *listen* and why the music is satisfying. Of course, this book fosters an appreciation of good writing, but beyond that, it is oriented toward performance.

The second feature derives from the first: this book contains a great number of exercises. The instructional method of *The Contemporary Writer* is both "deductive" and "inductive"—which is to say, a principle is first explained and then immediately demonstrated in an exercise. The exercises, then, are not only for reinforcement and review, but are an integral part of instruction. Again, the emphasis is on performance—on *doing*, not "talking about."

The third feature of this edition lies in the structure of its chapters, which are carefully planned to move from a basic level to a more sophisticated one. The essentials of a concept or skill are presented first; then variations and refinements are introduced. (Chapter 4, "Developing Ideas: The Paragraph," is a good example.) This method of development should make the book useful to a wide range of students—those who are moving toward sophistication in their writing, as well as those who need the basics.

This book contains a rich array of prewriting techniques. Response to the "Discovering Ideas" chapter of the first edition was overwhelmingly favorable. This revision builds on that success by increasing the range and usefulness of methods of analysis and comprehension—of solving problems and generating content.

The writing instruction in the book is based on the simple but crucial notion that a *writer* conveys *meanings* and *intentions* through *language structures* to an *audience* of readers. The concept of audience permeates the book.

To a great extent, differences in audience determine content and style. Thus, the concept of audience has a major influence on how one teaches self-expressive writing (as in the journal); explanatory, exploratory, and scientific writing (as in a set of directions, a speculative essay, or a research paper); persuasive writing (as in an advertisement or an editorial); and such other forms of writing as the critical essay or business letter. Learning all these forms can be of inestimable value to students during their careers in college and afterward in the broader world of business and society.

In this revision, the chapter on writing poetry and fiction has been deleted, on the assumption that students will have ample opportunity to express themselves imaginatively if they maintain a journal throughout the course and follow the suggestions in the second chapter.

A new chapter has been added that may prove of great practical interest. Betty P. Pytlik, an instructor of business and technical communication, has prepared a chapter on business writing that covers job search letters, resumés, letters to and from business concerns, and interoffice memoranda. Not only will students find this chapter extremely useful, but, we believe, they will also find it interesting and challenging.

Traditional material on sentences, with the customary full quotient of exercises, appears in the Appendix, where it is readily available for use throughout the semester at the discretion of the instructor. This unit also includes an entirely new section on readability, which might well be one of the most important features for some students whose prose is "fluent" but hard to read.

In sum, *The Contemporary Writer* covers the whole range of written composition, from the intensely personal and private to the most impersonal and public. And it contains full instruction in all the subprocesses of composition, including revision.

While I have wanted the new edition to be effective and practical, I have also tried to make it humane and interesting—a "real book." The ability to write is not merely utilitarian, in the narrow sense of communicating with the world "out there"; it is also a powerful way of dealing with the inner world of aspirations, feelings, values, identity, imagination.

At its best moments, this edition reflects the intelligence, craftsmanship, and taste of my editor, Sidney Zimmerman. His meticulousness and his care not only in adjusting the whole tone of the book but in helping, sometimes forcing, me to get my ideas straight have saved me from varying degrees of embarrassment.

The results of the excellent work of Carolyn Viola-John, my copy editor, are evident in these pages. I thank her for her care and sensitivity.

My old friend Cele Gardner is working on the project, and this heartens me, for she is admirable in every respect.

My thanks to Drake Bush for his confidence and guidance, and to Nina Indig, Stephen Saxe, and Richard Lewis for the care and attention they gave to producing the book.

The list of friends and colleagues who have influenced this edition is a long one, and, rather than name a few, I shall thank them collectively for their help and support.

But I wish to extend special thanks to two colleagues: Professors James Kinney of Virginia Commonwealth University and Walt Klarner of Johnson County (Kansas) Community College, both of whom provided intelligent and extremely helpful reviews of the manuscript.

As for Norma, she's still speaking of islands.

W. Ross Winterowd

Contents

The Writing Process

The *Contemporary Writer* is essentially a book about problem-solving. Writing tasks can be viewed as a series of problems to be solved, problems that range from a concern with words ("What word will best convey my meaning here?") to the structure of the whole piece ("How can I most effectively organize this essay?"). The best writer is the one who has available the widest variety of solutions for the problems of writing.

You can view *The Contemporary Writer* as a guide to more effective writing. Performance—that's the key word! When you have understood what some books say, when you have learned the materials that they contain, those books have served their purpose, for they have taught you *about* a subject. To be successful, *The Contemporary Writer* must go one step further: after you have understood what the book is *about,* you must be able to use these concepts to help you *perform* more effectively as a writer. This is essentially a *how to* book. For this reason, the exercises are important. Winning Saturday's game is the objective of tennis players; hours of practice provide the skills for them to win. Without practice, they might understand tennis thoroughly, but they would not be able to play effectively.

A MAP OF THE BOOK'S TERRITORY

As a beginning, let's sketch out a map of the problems that a writer encounters. The chapters following this will fill in the details.

For purposes of this map, we will divide the total writing process into four sections: *prewriting, writing, rewriting,* and *editing.*

PREWRITING

Before actual composition begins, there is always a period of getting ready, and this period can be a few moments, a few hours, days, weeks, or even years. Consider the problems involved in this prewriting stage of composition.

Finding a Usable Topic

Suppose that you are assigned to write a theme on the subject "writing," certainly a massive idea, a territory that covers everything about writing: its history, the different kinds of writing, the techniques of various writers, the uses of writing in an age of electronics, and so forth. You must boil this vast subject down into a *topic* that you can handle. If you do not do so, your teacher's comment will probably be something like this:

> Your paper is far too general; you have attempted to cover too much territory. Narrow and focus your subject.

Your topic should deal with ideas that interest you and that will interest and inform a reader. In the following chapters, you will learn many techniques for finding such topics.

Exercise

Suppose that you have been asked to write a paper about "Writing." How would you go about finding a usable topic in that vast subject? The following simple steps show you *one* way to solve the problem of deriving a topic from a large subject.

1. On a sheet of scratch paper, list as many of your own ideas (or questions) about *writing* as you can think of. The more specific the ideas are, the better. Your list can contain single words, phrases, sentences, and groups of sentences. If you spend fifteen or twenty minutes, you should be able to fill the page with ideas.

Write down everything that you think of. At this stage of the game, no idea is silly or useless.

2. From your list, choose three or four ideas that particularly interest you. Underline them.

3. Now ask yourself these questions about each of the underlined ideas:

Do I know enough about this idea to write an informative paper on it?

Will what I have to say interest my readers?

Why will the readers be interested in my topic?

4. From the three or four ideas that you have underlined, choose the one that is best suited to your interests and knowledge and that will also interest and inform your readers.

You can use this simple technique to find a topic. Notice: in choosing a topic, you have considered both your interests *and* those of your readers.

If you have trouble getting your list started, you can continue from the following suggestions:

"The misery of writing"
"I don't see why freshman English is needed."
"Spelling"
"What can I use writing for in the world outside of school?"

Discovering Ideas

In general, ideas about any subject come from two sources: (1) your own experience and knowledge; (2) research sources (such as libraries, interviews, laboratories, and so on). Therefore, you need ways of discovering what you already know about your topic and also ways of discovering what you need to find out through research.

Suppose you choose as your topic "the misery of writing"—and writing does involve misery; it's just plain hard work to get ideas successfully down on paper. You are interested in why writing is such an agonizing process for you. You know that it is, but you don't have a clear understanding of *why*. You know there's a *problem,* but you don't understand that problem very well. Your purpose is to explain the problem to yourself and then to your readers.

If your paper is not filled with pertinent, original ideas, your teacher's comment might be something like this:

Your paper lacks originality of thought; I learned very little from it.

Exercise

One way to discover ideas that will help you understand any problem is to ask yourself a series of questions and answer them. Some of the answers will come from your own knowledge and experience; others will come from research. Here is a series of questions that you can ask yourself:

1. Do my personality and background contribute to the problem? (For example, how much and what kind of writing instruction did you receive in high school? Are you a person who likes activities such as sports rather than thinking and writing, or a person who likes the precision of math better than the open-endedness of writing?)
2. Is the problem influenced by time and place? (How about the pressure of deadlines? Trying to work in the dorm? Other demands that college life puts upon you? Other ideas?)
3. Can the problem be broken down into parts? How do the parts work together?

Does this simple method of discovering ideas work? Try it.

Use "the misery of writing" for your topic, or, if you prefer, choose another topic. At the tops of three separate sheets of paper, write the questions. Feeling free to jump from one sheet to another, jot down ideas until you have filled all three sheets. Some of your ideas may be questions themselves.

Then think about the following three questions:

1. Did the answers to the questions provide you with insights concerning your topic? What ideas did you discover?
2. Were any of the ideas that you wrote down questions themselves? How would you go about answering these questions? Through research? Through further questioning?
3. Did the answers to your questions give you enough material to make you feel you have the basis for a theme? Explain.

Defining Your Audience

If you forget your readers, you run the risk of boring or baffling them. Suppose, for instance, that you are an expert in the field of semantics (the science of meanings). If you are writing for someone who knows nothing about the field, you will need to be very basic, explaining the most simple concepts; if you are writing for another expert, your paper will be uninformative, boring, and actually useless if you dwell on the basics, which your expert reader already knows.

One important principle to keep in mind is this: your writing should be informative. If the reader gets no new information from the paper, he or she will be bored; if the paper is too complicated for the reader, he or she will be frustrated.

Your readers, like you, are individuals, with their own values and beliefs. If you were writing a paper to be read by the Young Americans for Freedom on your campus, you would be foolish to start with the statement: "Political conservatives are unintelligent and don't understand the needs of modern society."

Every decision you make when you are writing must take your readers into account. One physician writing for other physicians can use medical terminology freely; but when writing for nonphysicians, he or she must choose other vocabulary or make an effort to explain the technical terms. In short, the writer must attempt to understand and to write "for" the reader.

If you forget your audience when you are writing, you could well receive a comment such as the following:

> Everything in this paper is true enough, but why should your ideas interest me? Unfortunately, I learned nothing from the paper and, therefore, was not interested in it. While the paper might be of great interest for other readers, you wrote it for me, and, to be honest with you, you completely missed the boat.

Exercise: Understanding Readers

Assume that the readers for a piece of your writing are the members of your class. You can begin to define their needs by asking and answering the following questions. (Write your answers on a sheet of paper.)

1. What values and beliefs do the members of my audience share?
2. What backgrounds do the members of my audience have in common? Educational? Social? Economic? Ethnic?
3. How much can I expect the members of my audience to know about my subject?

Defining Limitations

To state the point most simply, circumstances dictate that certain things must or must not be done in a given piece of writing. Libel laws are one obvious limitation: you cannot publish falsehoods about another person. Rules of decency in some circumstances prevent the use of profanity. The writing assignment itself imposes limitations. If the assignment asks you to "compare and contrast," you are not free to use any other means of development.

No less real are the limitations of time and place. Tahitians would probably not be interested in a well-written, powerful argument for repeal of the Twenty-First Amendment to the Constitution. The amendment was repealed in 1930, so the issue is dead; prohibition in the United States could hardly ever have been an issue in most other places, particularly Tahiti.

Exercise

Suppose that your composition teacher has given you the following assignment: "Contrast your use of spoken language in these three situations: in class discussions, in serious conversations with close friends, and in casual conversations with strangers." Through answering the following questions, you can develop a sense of the limitations that you would have to work under.

1. Limitations of the assignment
    What does the assignment ask for? What limitations does the subject itself impose upon what can be written?
2. Limitations of time and place
    Is my subject timely? How can I manage my time so as to complete the assignment before the due date? Does place have any influence on my subject or my handling of it?
3. Limitations of language
    What language is appropriate to my subject and my audience?
4. Limitations of purpose
    What is the purpose of my writing? How will this purpose affect my handling of the subject? Am I trying to inform, amuse, or persuade?

Think about these questions, and discuss them.

Prewriting: Summary

The general "map" of prewriting has now been sketched. The major problems that a writer encounters in the prewriting stage of composition are those that involve

Finding a usable topic
Discovering ideas concerning that topic
Defining the audience
Defining limitations

Later chapters in the book will help you develop many solutions to these problems.

However, no one should believe that the prewriting stage of composition is as clear-cut and simple as our discussion so far might have implied. It is obvious that in some senses prewriting goes on simultaneously with writing. As I think about what I am doing at this very moment, I realize that I am thinking slightly ahead, knowing the points that I want to make, but not sure just how I want to make them and not able to know until just the moment before they are to be made. Therefore, I use prewriting techniques moment by moment as I struggle to convey my ideas to you, my readers, within a whole web of limitations.

Experienced writers, of course, do not pause continually and go through a series of routines to discover ideas. Having mastered the skill of dealing with their subjects—much as a good tennis player has mastered the skill of the game—experienced writers can often solve their problems quickly and almost automatically. They do not have to pause continually to think about what to do next.

Through practice, everyone can develop the skills necessary for writing, and a large portion of this book is intended to help students develop those skills. Perhaps learning to play the harmonica is a good comparison: at first, one must consciously *think* about when to inhale and exhale and when to tongue; every note is produced through conscious effort, and the performance is halting, difficult for the performer and painful for the audience. But gradually this conscious knowledge about how to play the harmonica becomes automatic. At this point, the harmonica player can begin to think about whole phrases or whole melodies, without concentrating on the mechanics of producing a single note, even though those mechanics make the whole performance possible.

The goal of this book is to give you greater ability as an accomplished performer in the written expression of ideas.

WRITING

The object of all prewriting is, of course, to produce writing—an essay, report, story, description, argument, letter, piece of dialogue, set of instructions—that is successful in terms of the writer's *purpose* and *audience*.

One way to think of the writing process is to break it down into its major units, the kinds of "chunks" that the writer must be able to produce in order to be successful: *sentences,* which go together to make up coherent *paragraphs,* and paragraphs that make up coherent *essays.*

Therefore, we can say that the major problems in the writing process are

1. producing effective sentences;
2. constructing paragraphs;
3. creating a coherent overall form for the essay.

Traditionally, these problems are called "sentence structure," "paragraph development," and "organization."

There are other interesting problems that we will explore in this book: *tone,* which is the "voice" that your reader perceives in what you write; *figurative language,* such as metaphor and irony; *informal logic,* or "good reasons" for the reader to agree with what you say; and many other important concerns. For the time being, in this overview, this "map" of the writer's problems, let's think about the three basic problems: sentence structure, paragraph development, and organization.

Sentence Structure

A *sentence* is sometimes defined as "the expression of a complete idea," and that definition is helpful as far as it goes. In the following sentence, we feel that we have a complete idea because we know who did *what, with which,* and *to whom.*

Mary bopped Jerry with a frying pan.

But notice that in the following sentence, we seem to have two ideas:

Grabbing the frying pan, Jerry clobbered Mary.

The two ideas are

Jerry grabbed the frying pan.
Jerry clobbered Mary.

In other words, in the second sentence, two ideas that could be expressed in two separate sentences have been expressed in one sentence.

The language gives us many ways to put ideas together into one sentence, and the writer who cannot use these *sentence combining* devices will have major problems.

Think of a harmonica player. If the player must think about every note—whether to blow or suck, how to tongue—it is unlikely that he or she will ever be able to play a whole tune, for concentration on each separate note must be so intense that the whole piece can never emerge except haltingly and choppily, unsuccessfully as a piece of music.

Such is the case with writers: they must automatically and unconsciously be able to use the sentence structure of the language to put their ideas down in a fluid, coherent way. Lack of sentence sense (or "syntactic fluency," as it is called) makes the whole writing process halting and difficult for the writer and the finished piece ineffective and difficult for the reader. Therefore, to write successfully and easily it is necessary to gain the ability to use sentences. The writer who is not fluent with sentences has a "stutter" that must be overcome.

Compare the following passages:

> Three passions have governed my life. They are simple. They are overwhelmingly strong. One is the longing for love. Another is the search for knowledge. The third is the unbearable pity for the suffering of mankind. These passions have blown me hither and thither, in a wayward course, over a deep ocean of anguish. They are like great winds. This ocean of anguish reaches to the very verge of despair.

> Three passions, simple but overwhelmingly strong, have governed my life: the longing for love, the search for knowledge, and the unbearable pity for the suffering of mankind. These passions, like great winds, have blown me hither and thither, in a wayward course, over a deep ocean of anguish, reaching to the very verge of despair.
>
> —Bertrand Russell, *Autobiography*

I think everyone agrees that the second passage is easier to read than the first; it also sounds more intelligent, more mature, even though the basic ideas in both passages are the same.

If Bertrand Russell had been confined to the kinds of sentences

THE AUTOBIOGRAPHY OF BERTRAND RUSSELL   Bertrand Russell, Vol. 1 (London: Allen & Unwin, 1967). Reprinted by permission of the publisher.

that appear in the first passage, it is safe to say that he never would have been able to write his autobiography, for this passage "stutters."

If you had written a theme containing only sentences like those in the first passage, it is likely that your instructor would have written a comment like this:

> Because your sentences are choppy and immature, your paper is hard to read.

Exercise

1. Use the *model* sentences as guides for combining the *exercise* sentences into one sentence like the model.

a. *Model*   Typewritten essays, which are easier to read than handwritten ones, often receive high grades.

   Exercise   Low calorie soft drinks don't cause tooth decay. Low calorie soft drinks are not healthy.

b. *Model*   Bertrand, the most ambitious young man in my class, wants to be the captain of a freighter.

   Exercise   Maria is studying to be a psychiatrist. She is one of the most intelligent of my friends.

c. *Model*   Not wanting to hurt Clyde's feelings, Luisa didn't mention the missed appointment.

   Exercise   Natasha reminded Ivan of his promise. She thought he might forget it.

d. *Model*   The campers having pitched the tent and started a fire, Bert prepared the evening meal.

   Exercise   The passengers had evacuated the flaming wreck. The crew of the plane hurriedly escaped.

e. *Model*   Cool in the evening, but extremely hot during the day, the Mohave Desert is a land of extremes.

   Exercise   The river changes dramatically from season to season. It is roily during the spring runoff. It is crystal-clear in midsummer.

2. Using any techniques that you want to, combine the following groups of sentences into one complete sentence.

a. Gregory was an athlete. He was good at all sports. He liked tennis best.

b. Gloria enjoys art. She is a sensitive, intelligent person. Her favorite art form is sculpture. She spends many hours in the County Museum. In the County Museum, she enjoys the sculpture exhibits.

c. The Hessians roared down the freeway. The Hessians are a motorcycle club. They frightened the other motorists. They frightened the other motorists with their darting in and out of traffic.

d. Herb wanted to travel during the summer. He took a job at a taco stand. The stand was near his home. The owner was a friend of his mother's.

e. Our fathers brought forth on this continent a new nation. They brought it forth four score and seven years ago. It was dedicated to a proposition. The proposition was that all men are created equal.

By now, you should have demonstrated to yourself that you—that everyone—can develop sentence skills. You should be aware that these skills are absolutely necessary, for without them, the writer does not have the fluency needed to create essays—or other whole pieces—that "hang together" and convey ideas effectively. In later sections of this book, you will have the chance to practice and improve your sentence skills.

Paragraph Development

A paragraph indentation is a signal to your readers: it tells them that you have set this chunk of your writing off for special attention, and, that being the case, the indentation tells them that for some reason you view this chunk of writing as a complete unit. Paragraphs, of course, may be short (even, at times, as short as one word), or they may be very long; but, in any case, paragraphing gives your readers important clues to the way you are developing your ideas.

To demonstrate to yourself that paragraphing is extremely important for readers, just think of how difficult it would be to read this book if there were no paragraph indentations, if all the pages were merely solid blocks of sentences, not grouped according to any purpose or plan. The book would be very difficult to read and understand.

So, just as writers need to develop sentence fluency, they also need to gain fluency with paragraphing.

In other parts of this book, we will explore the uses of paragraphs, their different varieties, and ways of developing them. For now, it is enough to understand that one problem the writer needs to solve is developing the ability to use paragraphs effectively.

The basic kind of paragraph gives *details and explanations* concerning a more *general idea*. The paragraph is adequately developed when enough details are given to *support* the general idea. Many paragraphs move from general statements to more and more specific details, as is the case with the following example:

> Going to work and back, shopping, dropping people off, picking them up, occasionally a ride purely for pleasure—this is the sort of driving many of us do much of the time.
>
> And with fuel prices being what they are, an increasing number of us are seeking small, front-wheel-drive economy sedans for this purpose.
>
> A good choice too: These cars tend to be fuel- and space-efficient, relatively inexpensive to own and operate, and they're often fun to drive as well.
>
> Thus the rationale for this comparison test: Assemble a collection of small fwd cars, and evaluate them in the manner a prospective buyer would like to, head to head in ordinary driving as part of daily routine.
>
> —"Nine Front-Wheel-Drive Sedans," *Road and Track*

Suppose you were writing the essay from which this example was taken, and suppose that your paragraphs looked like this:

> The Datsun 310 is a combination of ostentation and dullness. It didn't fare very well in our ratings.
>
> The Fiat Strada is roomy, comfortable and stylish, but it didn't win many hearts in the personal preference poll.
>
> Fast, fun, functional, but not terribly well finished sum up the Ford Fiesta.
>
> The Honda Civic is an entertaining car, but it's beginning to show its age.
>
> Stylish, quick, with a novelty value all its own, the Plymouth Champ finished second in the overall ratings.
>
> Despite an excellent point total in the cumulative ratings, the Horizon was no one's first choice in personal preference.
>
> A charming Gallic personality says it all for the Renault Le Car.
>
> "Pity the poor Subaru," said one of our staff. "I've heard its reliability and longevity are exemplary, but I haven't the patience to experience them."
>
> Still efficient, still entertaining, but suffering from Americanization, the Volkswagen Rabbit won the cumulative ratings portion by a hair.

Which is the top of the pack? This depends on precisely what you're looking for in a small fwd car.

—Adapted from "Nine Front-Wheel-Drive Sedans"

Your instructor's comment would probably be something like this:

Your paragraphs need development. You must supply examples and data, backing for your claims. Your essay lacks necessary detail.

Exercise

One way to develop paragraphs is simply to give examples. For instance:

Topic	In spite of their disadvantages, large cities are good places to live.
Example	Metropolitan areas have museums, symphony orchestras, theaters, and other cultural institutions.
Example	Every major American city has professional sports teams, giving fans a chance to attend football, baseball, and basketball games.
Example	If you happen to like dining in exotic restaurants, small towns are not for you, because big cities have all kinds and varieties of eating establishments, cheap and expensive: Thai, Chinese, Korean, German, Italian, French, Roumanian, Arabic—you name it.

Develop the following "essay" by supplying two, three, or four examples for every paragraph:

Everything considered, it is better to live in a small town than a big city.
However, small town life does have its disadvantages.
If one wants the best of both worlds, a suburb might be the most logical choice.

Organization

In some ways, organization is the most difficult problem writers must face. Composing would be easy if it were a clear-cut process: first, decide what you want to say; second, plan the order in which you want to say it; third, say it. But we know that most writing (and speaking) is not that easy, not that clear-cut, not that neat. The writer grapples with ideas during the writing process and often learns about his or her subject as the writing goes on. Changes of mind, shifts of intention, discoveries, disappointments, inability to "get it into words"—all of these factors make rigid, neat preplanning difficult, if not impossible, for most writers most of the time.

For five years, I have been gathering evidence on how students actually write, and I have found that few successful writers use formal, detailed outlines. With some students, the outline is a bother at best and a severe hindrance at worst; others cannot begin the actual process of composition until a detailed outline has been completed.

However, there are some very simple and straightforward principles of organization that can be learned and applied. Once these techniques become intuitive and automatic for the writer, he or she will begin to modify and adapt them, will develop the same natural, organic fluency in organization that can be developed in sentence structure and paragraph construction.

If a piece of your writing is unorganized or disorganized, the comment is likely to be something like this:

> You need to reorganize this piece so that the parts come in a logical sequence. The order that you have given the parts confuses the reader.

Exercise

A quick demonstration of a useful principle of organization is difficult, for when we speak of "organization," we have long pieces of writing in mind. One does not think of organization in terms of sentences or paragraphs, but rather in terms of sequences of paragraphs.

Nonetheless, here is one example of a series of "rules" that could help you organize some pieces of writing.

1. In the first paragraph, state and explain your thesis or topic.
2. In the second paragraph, state and explain or illustrate one aspect or feature of your thesis or topic.
3. In the third paragraph, repeat the process, focusing on another aspect of your topic.
4. In the fourth paragraph, repeat the process again, focusing on a third aspect of your topic.
5. In the fifth paragraph, state and explain a conclusion based on paragraphs 2, 3, and 4. Make certain it is logical to begin this

last paragraph with the word "therefore," which will demonstrate that you have actually come to a conclusion.

Discuss the advantages and disadvantages of such organization.

It must be stressed that "rules" for organization such as the ones above have limited usefulness and that they will often produce mechanical, awkward organization. The point right now, however, is that there are principles of organization that one can learn, though most of these principles are more complicated (and often more useful) than the series of "rules" set forth in the exercise.

Writing: Summary

This section—like that on prewriting—has been extremely general, merely a survey of problems which, as the book progresses, will be handled in more and more detail. Nonetheless, it is true to say that the writer expresses ideas (attitudes, values) in sentences, shows sentence groupings through paragraphing, and creates coherence or organization by the way the paragraphs relate to one another in the essay: sentence structure, paragraph development, organization.

REWRITING

All writers do some *re*writing; most writers do a great deal of it.

What do we mean by "rewriting"? Rewriting is the process of making *deletions, additions, rearrangements,* and *substitutions.* When one rewrites, one makes significant changes in the paper. Rewriting should not be confused with *editing* (which will be discussed in the next section of this chapter), for by "editing" we mean "cleaning up the manuscript": punctuating correctly, eliminating misspellings, making sure that verbs agree with their subjects, and so on.

When we rewrite, we can

Delete
Add
Rearrange   } *words   phrases   sentences   paragraphs   sections*
Substitute

Skilled writers are "fluent" rewriters; they learn what operations will bring each piece of writing into the most effective form for the intended audience.

Exercise

Rewriting sentences, paragraphs, or whole essays is made easier if we think of the four processes: *deletion, addition, rearrangement, substitution.*

I. *Delete* unnecessary words from the following sentences. For example:

 a. The president who is the head man of our college will resign next year.
   The president of our college will resign next year.

 b. We gave a donation of five dollars to the library.
   We gave five dollars to the library.
   or
   We donated five dollars to the library.

Now do it yourself.

1. The boat which was just coming into the harbor listed heavily to starboard.
2. The last person at the end of the line could not buy a ticket.
3. The news of Alvin's death made me sad and melancholy.
4. The cardiologist doctor who treats my uncle's heart condition told him to lose twenty-five pounds.
5. On a cloudy day with no sunshine, we began our hike up the John Muir Trail.

II. *Add* details to the following sentences. For example:

 a. The student's hair hung over his collar.
   The student's greasy hair hung over his frayed collar.

 b. The dog loped across the field.
   The dog, an Irish setter, loped easily across the field, stopping occasionally to sniff at a gopher hole, zigzagging his way toward the lake.

Now, it is your turn.

1. The man entered the room.
2. The Sears Tower in Chicago is the world's tallest building.
3. Americans are becoming more and more football crazy.
4. My neighbor rebuilt a 1931 Packard.
5. Roses are red.

III. *Rearrange* the following sentences, but do not make them ungrammatical or change their basic meanings. Here are some examples:

a. My family drinks tea for breakfast every morning of the year.

Every morning of the year, my family drinks tea for breakfast.

or

For breakfast, my family drinks tea every morning of the year.

or

For breakfast every morning of the year, my family drinks tea.

b. It is strange that bacteria cause disease.

That bacteria cause disease is strange.

c. I want some chocolate ice cream.

What I want is some chocolate ice cream.

or

Some chocolate ice cream—that's what I want.

Now, you try it.

1. The councilperson decided to run for mayor at the very last minute.
2. It is well known that cigarette smoking is unhealthy.
3. I like music.
4. In the afternoon, the Schultzes often take a walk.
5. An expert on nematodes, the professor was often called upon as a consultant by various farm groups.

IV. Make one or more *substitutions* in the following sentences, but do not change the basic meaning. For example:

a. The young dog barked with pain when I accidentally stepped on it.

The puppy yelped with pain when I accidentally stepped on it.

b. On his wrist he wore a watch that shows the time by a series of numbers, not by hands that go around a dial.

He wore a digital wristwatch.

Now, you find substitutions.

1. The young cat made a noise when I petted her.
2. When Uncle Charlie kicks the bucket, I will inherit his stamp collection.
3. Matilda uses a little gizmo with numbered keys and a lighted dial to figure up her bills.
4. "I completely disagree," said Max angrily.
5. Knowing that the class would wait patiently, the professor dawdled.

Many writers do most of their rewriting at the same time they are writing, changing sentences and substituting words, crossing out some paragraphs and putting others in, making notes for rearranging paragraphs and sections of their manuscripts—and the result, of course, is that the first drafts are very messy, with crossouts, interlinear insertions, and marginal notations. (In fact, I do a great deal of my rewriting in this way, scratching out one word or sentence and then adding another, substituting one paragraph for another, and so on, forging ahead briefly with my writing, and then circling back to do more or less extensive rewriting, so that often when my very messy first draft is finished, I have done a great deal of the necessary rewriting; but invariably, after the first draft is completed, after I can see the "whole thing," I do further rewriting.)

Other writers do almost no rewriting until they have finished the first draft, after which they are likely to get out the scissors so that they can actually rearrange parts of their manuscripts.

In any case, it is not unusual for at least two drafts to precede the final one: a very rough first draft, a rewritten second draft, and a final edited draft.

EDITING

Many students think the whole process of revision is merely editing, correcting spelling and other "surface" errors, such as the following:

PUNCTUATION

Incorrect   The battle was lost however the war was won.

Correct   The battle was lost; however, the war was won.

VERB AGREEMENT

Incorrect   The members of the home team usually *has* the advantage.

Correct   The members of the home team usually *have* the advantage.

PRONOUN REFERENCE

Incorrect   Mary told Sally that she must leave immediately. [Does "she" refer to "Mary" or to "Sally"?]

Correct   Mary told Sally to leave immediately.
                 or
                 Mary told Sally, "I must leave immedi-
                 ately."
                 or
                 Sally must leave immediately, Mary told her.

But as the section on rewriting tried to demonstrate, revision includes much more than mere "error" correcting.

However, if you are a bad editor, if you don't know how to use punctuation or the grammar of the language, you definitely have a problem, for most readers insist that the niceties of editing be observed in writing. It is just a fact of life that most readers will devalue—will not respond favorably to—writing that is full of mechanical errors.

Therefore, it is extremely important that you learn to edit: your audience demands it of you.

If you lack editing skills, your instructor's comment may be something like this:

Your paper is riddled with mechanical errors. Even though your ideas are interesting, most readers would distrust what you say because of the way in which you say it. In other words, your errors detract from what you are trying to convey to a reader.

THE COMPOSING PROCESS

Our general "blueprint" of the composing process has identified *prewriting, writing, rewriting,* and *editing,* each with its special problems. As was said earlier, some writers carry out all four operations either sentence by sentence or paragraph by paragraph, whereas other writers have clear-cut stages of prewriting, writing, rewriting, and editing. The goal of the student is to learn to do all four operations efficiently and effectively.

However, the discussion of "stages" of writing and the problems involved in each stage has, to a certain extent, oversimplified the whole process of composition, which is, after all, one of the most complicated activities that any human can perform. Since we have gained a simplified view of the composing process, we are now ready to think about some of the complications.

When you write anything, there is, of course, you the *writer,* and often you may be writing only for yourself: class notes that only you will see, a private diary, scribbles that help you solve a problem. If this kind of writing (for yourself) satisfies you and serves your purposes, it is successful.

Since the purpose of most writing is to communicate with *readers* (or perhaps only one reader), the whole matter becomes more complicated, for the reader does not know what is in the writer's mind and may not even know the writer. In general, the reader must rely totally on the written text for meaning. So the writer must think about the reader's needs, interests, personality, values.

The fact that you are trying to let a reader know what you mean is one complication of the whole composing process, which can be shown this way:

WRITER ⟵————————————⟶ READERS

For skilled writers, their readers are always present, looking over their shoulder as sentences and paragraphs tumble onto the page.

The writer is writing *for* the reader *about* something; there is *content* or subject matter for the writing, and the content itself creates problems. If the subject of the writing is controversial (abortion, mercy killing, legalization of drugs), the writer, with the reader in mind, must proceed cautiously, being careful not to overstate the case, making certain that the evidence is convincing. Or suppose that the writer sets out to prove a point through the use of facts; in this instance, the nature of a "fact" becomes extremely important: Is it accurate? Is it complete? Is it up-to-date?

Writers, then, must think not only about their readers, but also about their content. So we can add another word to our diagram.

CONTENT

WRITER ⟵————————————⟶ READERS

Suppose that the writer knows everything there is to know about dictionaries. This knowledge would make up the content of his writing. The reader wants to learn about dictionaries. The writer could start making a list of facts about dictionaries, writing down ideas as they occurred to him. This list, however, would have no structure, no organization, and as a result, the reader would not know which subjects belonged together. The list would not be effective in presenting content to the reader. The list needs to be organized, arranged in some kind of meaningful order, with adequate explanations. Thus, with all writing *structure* is important for two reasons: (1) it organizes information for the reader, and (2) it helps the writer to gain the effect that he or she wants. (Mystery stories are structured to keep readers in suspense until the very end. The writer does not want to give away the information about "who done it" until near the conclusion. Scientific reports are structured so that readers can learn the results or conclusions immediately, before entering into the details which are presented in the "body" of the report. The writer of a scientific report does not want to create suspense in the reader.) We now have another term for our diagram of the composing process:

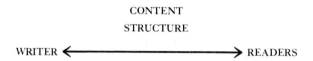

CONTENT

STRUCTURE

WRITER ⟵————————————⟶ READERS

But the content and the structure of writing always appear in a *medium,* a word which is now common, as when people talk about television as an electronic medium. So medium means nothing more than the form of communication. A magazine is a medium, as is a newspaper or a book.

Some examples will illustrate the importance of medium. (1) William Nolen, a nationally known physician, recently wrote an article on heart disease for *McCall's Magazine,* a popular journal. The fact that he was writing for that medium influenced what he could say and how he could say it. *McCall's* obviously would not publish a technical article on a medical subject, but if Dr. Nolen had been writing for the highly respected *New England Journal of Medicine,* the piece would have been quite different, for it would be aimed at experts in the field. (2) If you were writing a speech to be delivered orally, you would need to give more examples to illustrate your points, and you would need to develop your ideas more slowly, for the oral medium is harder to follow than the written. (3) In some of your classes, your teachers may demand that your research papers follow the organization and footnote and bibliography forms of papers that are published by scholarly journals in the various fields: sociology, history, literature, and so on. In these cases, media will be influencing your writing. (The plural of *medium* is either *media* or *mediums*!)

So we can now expand our diagram of the composing process:

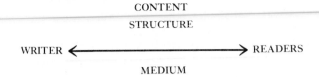

Finally, every piece of writing demands language choice or *style*. If your purpose is to explain, as clearly as possible, how to get to your home, you will use one kind of style, but if you want to describe the beauty along the route to your house, you will use quite another. So we can add a final term to our diagram of the composing process: style.

These elements are not separate and distinct, but influence one another at every point in the composing process. There is an all-at-onceness about them. Suppose that you (writer) decide to compose an essay about the high prices and bad food in the college cafeteria (content), to be published in the school magazine (medium), to influence your fellow students (readers), using sarcasm (style) to make your point. As you can see, each element must be adjusted to the rest. The fact that you have chosen as your medium the school magazine means that you cannot become libelous in your attempt to be sarcastic. (You might say that the cafeteria manager is a misplaced garbage collector, but you cannot state that he or she is an embezzler unless you have sound evidence to support that accusation.)

Since most of your readers will be familiar with your subject matter (content), you will not need to give extensive background on location and so on. (But you will need to give all of the details about prices, perhaps doing some comparisons between prices in the cafeteria and in other eating places.) You can choose many structures for your piece. For example, you might start with the general statement that the prices in your college cafeteria are far too high and then go on to analyze that statement and give examples and data to support it, or you might give data about the cafeteria and then conclude that prices are too high.

Problems of *content, structure, medium, style,* and *readers* guide the composing process, and as a preview to the rest of this book, we might look at some of these problems:

Content
> Reliability? Adequacy? Timeliness? Appropriateness? Fairness? Interest value? Pertinence?

Structure
> Coherence? Inductive ordering (from the specific to the general) or deductive ordering (from the general to the specific)? Special forms, such as scientific reports? Value of unusual organization? Structural requirements of the medium?

Style
> Appropriateness to subject? To medium? To readers? Accuracy? Clarity?

Readers
> Knowledge of the subject? Interest in the subject? Values? Prejudices? Purposes for reading the piece? Relationship to the writer?

The composing process is a complicated drama, the writer adjusting his or her composition according to the interrelated demands of content, structure, medium, style, and readers.

Exercise: For Discussion

1. Carefully reread the paragraph on page 21 beginning "But the content and the structure of writing always appear in a *medium*. . . ." and the paragraph following it, which begins "Some examples will illustrate the importance of medium." The intention of the paragraphs is to explain the nature of medium. Is the content sufficient to accomplish the purpose? If not, why not? What methods of development are used to explain the concept "medium"?

2. I have carefully planned the structure of this book, and I consider the first chapter to be extremely important in that overall plan. Now that you have read the first chapter, why do you think I chose the structure that I did? What was my purpose? Explain your reasoning.

3. *The Contemporary Writer* is a textbook. What influence do you think that medium had on the style and structure of the book? Do you find things in this book that you would not find in other kinds of books? What are they, and why were they included?

4. What would have been the effect on you, the reader, if the book had been written in a "flowery," poetic style? Would the style have detracted from the purpose of the book? Explain. Do any aspects of the style annoy you? Explain.

5. The following is Tom Wolfe's account of how he came to write the book *The Kandy-Kolored Tangerine-Flake Streamline Baby*.[1] Read this selection, and discuss in detail what you learned about the composing process from it.

I don't mean for this to sound like "I had a vision" or anything, but there was a specific starting point for practically all of these stories. I wrote them in a fifteen-month period, and the whole thing started with the afternoon I went to a Hot Rod & Custom Car show at the Coliseum in New York. Strange afternoon! I was sent up there to cover the Hot Rod & Custom Car show by the New York *Herald Tribune,* and I brought back exactly the kind of story any of the somnambulistic totem newspapers in America would have come up with. A totem newspaper is the kind people don't really buy to read but just to *have,* physically, because they know it supports their own outlook on life. They're just like the buffalo tongues the Omaha Indians used to carry around or the dog ears the Mahili clan carried around in Bengal. There are two kinds of totem newspapers in the country. One is the symbol of the frightened chair-arm-doilie Vicks Vapo-Rub *Weltanschauung* that lies there in the solar plexus of all good gray burghers. All those nice stories on the first page of the second section about eighty-seven-year-old ladies on Gramercy Park who have one-hundred-and-two-year-old turtles or about the colorful street vendors of Havana. Mommy! This fellow Castro is in there, and revolutions may come and go, but the picturesque poor will endure, padding around in the streets selling their chestnuts and salt pretzels the world over, even in Havana, Cuba, assuring a paradise, after all, full of respect and obeisance, for all us Vicks Vapo-Rub chair-arm-doilie burghers. After all. Or another totem group buys the kind of paper they can put under their arms and have the totem for the tough-but-wholesome outlook, the Mom's Pie view of life. Everybody can go off to the bar and drink a few "brews" and retail some cynical remarks about Zora Folley and how the fight game is these days and round it off, though, with how George Chuvalo has "a lot of heart," which he got, one understands, by eating mom's pie. Anyway, I went to the Hot Rod & Custom Car show and wrote a story that would have suited any of the totem newspapers. All the totem newspapers would regard one of these shows as a sideshow, a panopticon, for creeps and kooks; not even wealthy, eccentric creeps and kooks, which would be all right, but lower class creeps and nutballs with dermatitic skin and ratty hair. The totem story usually makes what is known as "gentle fun" of this, which is a way of saying, don't worry, these people are nothing.

So I wrote a story about a kid who had built a golden motorcycle, which he called "The Golden Alligator." The seat was made of some kind of gold-painted leather that kept going back, on and on, as long as an alligator's tail,

[1]Tom Wolfe, *The Kandy-Kolored Tangerine-Flake Streamline Baby* (New York: Farrar, Straus & Giroux, 1965). Copyright © 1963, 1964, 1965 by Thomas K. Wolfe, Jr. Copyright © 1963, 1964, 1965 by New York Herald Tribune, Inc. Reprinted with permission of Farrar, Straus & Giroux, Inc.

and had scales embossed on it, like an alligator's. The kid had made a whole golden suit for himself, like a space suit, that also looked as if it were covered with scales and he would lie down on his stomach on this long seat, stretched out full length, so that he appeared to be made into the motorcycle or something, and roar around Greenwich Village on Saturday nights, down Macdougal Street, down there in Nuts Heaven, looking like a golden alligator on wheels. Nutty! He seemed like a Gentle Nut when I got through. It was a shame I wrote that sort of story, the usual totem story, because I was working for the *Herald Tribune,* and the *Herald Tribune* was the only experimental paper in town, breaking out of the totem formula. The thing was, I knew I had another story all the time, a bona fide story, the real story of the Hot Rod & Custom Car show, but I didn't know what to do with it. It was outside the system of ideas I was used to working with, even though I had been through the whole Ph.D. route at Yale, in American Studies and everything.

Here were all these . . . *weird* . . . nutty-looking, crazy baroque custom cars, sitting in little nests of pink angora angel's hair for the purpose of "glamorous" display—but then I got to talking to one of the men who make them, a fellow named Dale Alexander. He was a very serious and soft-spoken man, about thirty, completely serious about the whole thing, in fact, and pretty soon it became clear, as I talked to this man for a while, that he had been living like the *complete artist* for years. He had starved, suffered—the whole thing—so he could sit inside a garage and create these cars which more than 99 per cent of the American people would consider ridiculous, vulgar and lower-class-awful beyond comment almost. He had started off with a garage that fixed banged-up cars and everything, to pay the rent, but gradually he couldn't stand it anymore. Creativity—his own custom car art—became an obsession with him. So he became the complete custom car artist. And he said he wasn't the only one. All the great custom car designers had gone through it. It was the *only way. Holy beasts!* Starving artists! Inspiration! Only instead of garrets, they had these garages.

So I went over to *Esquire* magazine after a while and talked to them about this phenomenon, and they sent me out to California to take a look at the custom car world. Dale Alexander was from Detroit or some place, but the real center of the thing was in California, around Los Angeles. I started talking to a lot of these people, like George Barris and Ed Roth, and seeing what they were doing, and—well, eventually it became the story from which the title of this book was taken, "The Kandy-Kolored Tangerine-Flake Streamline Baby." But at first I couldn't even write the story. I came back to New York and just sat around worrying over the thing. I had a lot of trouble analyzing exactly what I had on my hands. By this time *Esquire* practically had a gun at my head because they had a two-page-wide color picture for the story locked into the printing presses and no story. Finally, I told Byron Dobell, the managing editor at *Esquire,* that I couldn't pull the thing together. O.K., he tells me, just type out my notes and send them over and he will get somebody else to write it. So about 8 o'clock that night I started typing the notes out in the form of a memorandum that began, "Dear Byron." I started typing away, starting right with the first time I saw any custom cars in California. I just started recording it all, and inside of a couple of hours, typing along like a madman, I could tell that something was beginning to happen. By midnight this memorandum to Byron was twenty pages long and I was still typing like a maniac. About 2 A.M. or something like that I turned on WABC, a radio station that plays rock and roll music all night long, and got a little more manic. I wrapped up the memorandum about 6:15 A.M., and by this time it was 49 pages long. I took it over to *Esquire* as soon as they opened up, about 9:30 A.M. About 4 P.M. I got a call from Byron Dobell. He told me they were striking out the "Dear Byron" at the top of the memorandum and running the rest of it in the magazine. That was the story, "The Kandy-Kolored Tangerine-Flake Streamline Baby."

What had happened was that I started writing down everything I had seen the first place I went in California, this incredible event, a "Teen Fair." The details themselves, when I wrote them down, suddenly made me see what was happening. Here was this incredible combination of form plus money in a place nobody ever thought about finding it, namely, among teen-agers. Practically every style recorded in art history is the result of the same thing—a lot of attention to form, plus the money to make monuments to it. The "classic" English style of Inigo Jones, for example, places like the Covent Garden and the royal banquet hall at Whitehall, were the result of a worship of Italian Palladian grandeur . . . plus the money that began pouring in under James I and Charles I from colonial possessions. These were the kind of forms, styles, symbols . . . Palladian classicism . . . that influence a whole society. But throughout history, everywhere this kind of thing took place. China, Egypt, France under the Bourbons, every place, it has been something the aristocracy has been responsible for. What has happened in the United States since World War II, however, has broken that pattern. The war created money. It made massive infusions of money into every level of society. Suddenly classes of people whose styles of life had been practically invisible had the money to build monuments to their own styles.

6. Examine the purposes for which you write. (To use your imagination in poems or stories? To explain something to others? To give your opinions on a subject? To argue for or against something?) Do you ever write for "impractical" purposes, just to express yourself (as in a private diary)? Why, or why not?

7. Discuss your own reactions to and problems with writing assignments that you receive in all your classes, not just English. Would you work better if you were allowed to choose your own subjects and if you were not forced to meet deadlines? Explain.

8. Suppose that you know the details concerning a particularly grisly murder and that you plan to write an account of it. What will be the limitations if

   a. you are doing a report for a daily newspaper?
   b. you decide to write it up for a "scandal sheet"?
   c. you have a contract to dramatize the event for television?
   d. you use the subject for an English theme?

9. The following selection talks about some powerful limitations that are imposed on users of language, either written or spoken. Read the selection carefully, and discuss its ideas concerning limitations.

THE COMPOSING PROCESS 27

Why Do Some Dialects Have More Prestige Than Others?

In a specific setting, because of historical and other factors, certain dialects may be endowed with more prestige than others. Such dialects are sometimes called "standard" or "consensus" dialects. These designations of prestige are not inherent in the dialect itself, but are *externally imposed,* and the prestige of a dialect shifts as the power relationships of the speakers shift.

The English language at the beginning of its recorded history was already divided into distinct regional dialects. These enjoyed fairly equal prestige for centuries. However, the centralization of English political and commercial life at London gradually gave the dialect spoken there a preeminence over other dialects. This process was far advanced when printing was invented; consequently, the London dialect became the dialect of the printing press, and the dialect of the printing press became the so-called "standard" even though a number of oral readings of one text would reveal different pronunciations and rhythmic patterns across dialects. When the early American settlers arrived on this continent, they brought their British dialects with them. Those dialects were altered both by regional separation from England and concentration into sub-groups within this country as well as by contact with the various languages spoken by the Indians they found here and with the various languages spoken by the immigrants who followed.

At the same time, social and political attitudes formed in the old world followed to the new, so Americans sought to achieve linguistic marks of success as exemplified in what they regarded as proper, cultivated usage. Thus the dialect used by prestigious New England speakers early became the "standard" the schools attempted to teach. It remains, during our own time, the dialect that style books encourage us to represent in writing. The diversity of our cultural heritage, however, has created a corresponding language diversity and, in the 20th century, most linguists agree that there is no single, homogeneous American "standard." They also agree that, although the amount of prestige and power possessed by a group can be recognized through its dialect, no dialect is inherently good or bad.

The need for a written dialect to serve the larger, public community has resulted in a general commitment to what may be called "edited American English," that prose which is meant to carry information about our representative problems and interests. To carry such information through aural-oral media, "broadcast English" or "network standard" has been developed and given precedence. Yet these dialects are subject to change, too. Even now habit patterns from other types of dialects are being incorporated into them. Our pluralistic society requires many varieties of language to meet our multiplicity of needs.

10. Everyone has sudden breakthroughs in knowledge, moments when, almost in a flash, something becomes clear—the reasons for some action of a friend, the solution to a mathematical problem, the under-

standing of a joke or a riddle. Think of a time when you had such a breakthrough, and be prepared to discuss it, either orally or in writing. What was the nature of the problem? What seems to have been the clue that gave you the insight? What was the nature of the insight?

11. Without any attempt to organize, just as they pop into your mind, write down all of the details that you can think of concerning a favorite relative. Think of looks, speech, actions, mannerisms, mode of dress. Don't merely say, "My Uncle Clayton has gray hair," but give details about that hair: "My Uncle Clayton has silvery gray hair, combed straight back in a pompadour and cascading down the back of his neck over his collar."

12. Discuss your use of outlines. Do you prepare a detailed outline before you begin to write? Do outlines help or hinder your composing? Why? What did you learn about outlining in your high school English courses?

13. In a panel discussion, a group of talented screenwriters discussed their methods of composing. Gloria Katz and Willard Huyck outline scenes on three-by-five cards and then arrange these scenes into the sequence they want. The cards serve as the "map" to guide the writers through their first draft of the script. After they have produced a first draft, they revise, often doing five or six complete versions. David Ward thinks his whole story through, working out every detail, before he sets pen to paper. Once he has the whole story in mind, he writes the script, and his revisions are minor. John Milius thinks of a character or a situation and begins to write. He says that the ending of his script is as much a surprise to him as he hopes it will be to the audience.

In your own words, summarize what the above paragraph tells you about planning a composition.

The Journal

JOURNAL writings can be compared with practice sessions on a musical instrument or in a sport. Practice is essential, but you gain applause for the real performance before an audience, and you win the championship in a real game. The journal is important—just as practicing an instrument or a sport is—but you will not be judged on your performance in the journal, even though your friends or your instructor may want to read your entries.

Sometimes it is well to state and underscore the obvious: first, a writer is a person who writes, and your journal gives you the opportunity of becoming a writer without risking failure; second, the more you practice writing, the easier that skill will be for you. The advice, then, is this: write in your journal every day, and write a lot each time. This chapter will help you develop ideas for and approaches to journal writing.

As an object, your journal can be a spiral or looseleaf notebook, a manila folder for keeping pages together, a file in your desk, a box to contain three-by-five or four-by-six cards.

The content of your journal will be your own writings of various kinds and on various subjects: jotted-down ideas that have occurred to you, descriptions of scenes that have impressed you, narrations of events, poems, wordplay, thinking-in-writing, even doodles.

The journal has an important use that is related to the way the mind seems to work. It has been well documented that original thinkers go through certain fairly clear-cut stages in the process of solving intellectual problems.

First, they get an idea or hunch; or they recognize some problem that has not been clearly seen before. This is the stage of *formulation*. Second, they *prepare* to deal with the idea or problem (research, thought, questioning, etc.). If the breakthrough of understanding does not come during this period of conscious work, thinkers enter the third stage: they turn away from the idea or problem; they stop making a conscious effort to achieve a breakthrough. However, the subconscious mind continues to work on the problem, even though the conscious mind is focused elsewhere. After this period of *incubation,* the fourth stage often comes about in the form of a sudden breakthrough, an *inspiration* about the idea or problem. The final stage, then, is one of *verification:* developing, explaining, or testing this inspiration.

How does all of this relate to journal writing? If you record ideas and impressions in your journal, the very act of writing them down has forced you to *formulate* them. You can then use your journal to record further ideas, to carry on a dialogue with yourself about your subject, to refine and redirect your ideas and hunches. The journal, then, is useful in preparing to write anything: an essay, a story, a novel, a scientific report. Having formulated your ideas, and having prepared to deal with them in "public" writing, you have probably started the process of incubation.

The stage of verification comes about when you say to yourself, "Now I'm ready to begin the 'real' piece of writing"—whatever that may be.

One successful writer keeps a massive journal, into which he enters all sorts of information about his subject. When he finally gets ready to write, he can often say, "The essay is already 'written.' Now it only needs typing." What he means is this: using his journal, he has done such thorough work in formulation and preparation that he knows quite well what he wants to say. This particular writer spends three-fourths of his time with the journal and one-fourth in the actual writing of the first draft of the piece.

Exercise: Starting Your Journal

Start your journal right now!

On the first page, write this question: *What changes would I make in my present life if changes were possible?*

Now begin to jot ideas down, in no particular order or form. These ideas can be words, phrases, declarative or interrogative sentences, or paragraphs.

To get a start, you can simply ask yourself five questions, the answers to which will give you material for writing:

1. What changes would I make in my own personality, appearance, or habits?
2. Where else would I prefer to be? Where would I move to?
3. What would I need in order to make those changes? More money? Plastic surgery? Better will power? More time? Help from others?
4. Why should I want to make the changes?
5. What would be the final result if I made the changes?

DEVELOPING JOURNAL ENTRIES

The exercise that you just completed may or may not have been productive for you. You may have gained insights that you would like to set forth in a short (or long) essay, but if the work led to nothing, you should not be discouraged, for that is the nature of the journal: many of your entries will not "pay off" in the sense that they give you materials for public writing. It is an excellent bet, though, that many of your entries through the weeks and months will result in usable ideas and materials.

In this chapter, you will find several warming-up exercises: suggestions for developing journal entries. These exercises are planned not only to stimulate journal writing, but also to begin illustrating some principles about writing in general; therefore, you probably ought to work with each of the exercises. On the other hand, you should not view the exercises and suggestions in this chapter as limits on the quantity of your journal writing or on the kinds of entries you make. *It's your journal!* In it, you can write as much as you want of any kind of writing you choose whenever you desire.[1]

Abstract-Concrete Sentences

From the comic strip *Peanuts* come such sentences as this one: "Happiness is a warm blanket." The noun "happiness" is *abstract:* one cannot see, touch, taste, smell, or hear "happiness," for it is a

---

[1] For many of the concepts in this chapter, the author is indebted to D. Gordon Rohman and Albert O. Wlecke, whose 1964 study *Pre-Writing: The Construction and Application of Models for Concept Formation in Writing* (East Lansing: Michigan State Univ. Press, 1964) was a significant effort to reestablish invention within composition pedagogy and theory.

concept, not a physical object. On the other hand, "blanket" is a *concrete* noun: one can see and touch blankets, or taste, smell, and even hear them for that matter. The basic formula for a "Peanuts sentence," then, is this:

Abstract Noun	is	Concrete Noun
Love		a red *rose*.
Jealousy		a *monster*.
Democracy		the *sound* of many voices.

Knowing involves both the concrete and the abstract. For example, you can't see, touch, hear, smell, or taste "love," for it is an abstract concept, but you can learn about love by seeing and hearing a mother with her baby. The mother and baby would be concrete instances of a loving relationship, but are not the abstract concept "love."

As convincing research demonstrates, some writers work very well with abstract concepts, but find it difficult to get down to concrete experience, whereas other writers are extremely skilled at conveying the concrete and specific, but find it almost impossible to get beyond this realm into that of the abstract concept or generalization.

The "Peanuts sentence" is good practice for writers because it does explain the *abstract* in terms of the *concrete*. The sentence "Happiness is a warm blanket" defines the abstract concept of happiness in terms of something that we might experience with our senses; we get the *image* or "picture" of a blanket; we know how a blanket feels, its soft fuzziness and warmth; we might even associate a smell or a sound with the blanket.

The abstract-concrete sentence forces us to jump from one kind of knowing—that of abstract concepts—into the knowing that is based on the senses, and the result can be heightened awareness, greater interest, new insights. (As we shall see presently, the joining of abstract and concrete nouns in a sentence is the basis for some kinds of *analogy,* and analogy is a powerful tool for thinking and for explaining.)

Here are the rules for composing abstract-concrete sentences in your journal:

First, choose an abstract noun such as *success.*
Second, define it in terms of the concrete.

Your definition can be a concrete noun with its modifiers:

Success is a big red *"100"* at the top of a midterm exam.

It can be a word-group describing an event:

Success is *harvesting the first tomato in August.*

It can be a concrete noun and its modifiers, followed by a word-group that gives further explanation:

Success is *the contented sighs of your guests after they've finished the meal that you spent all day cooking.*

Here are a few more examples of abstract-concrete sentences:

Laziness is pajamas, B.O., and a two-day beard.
Vacation is Uncle Eldon, a boat, a fishing rod, and a cold beer.
Failure is succumbing to the temptation of chocolate cake when you're on a diet.
Failure is a blank page.
Failure is a crumpled sheet in the wastebasket.

Exercise

I. The following list gives *abstract nouns* on the left and *concrete nouns* on the right. Without advance thought, make random combinations of abstract with concrete nouns and add any modifying words or word-groups that you desire. Write these sentences in your journal, and then think about and discuss the questions that follow the list.

Abstract	Concrete
authority	zygote
barbarity	YWCA
contentment	xenophobe
diplomacy	whip
efficiency	vegetable
falseness	umiak
greed	tree
health	sonic boom
industry	root
joy	quicksand
knowledge	potato
loneliness	oboe
majesty	nurse
narcosis	mountebank
obligation	lion

1. Some of your combinations probably seemed *not* to make sense to you—in other words, to result in nonsense sentences. (For ex-

ample, here is a combination that, from my point of view, results in nonsense: "Efficiency is a sonic boom.") Why did these combinations result in nonsense?

2. Since everything in the universe is like everything else in *some* way—though that way might be obscure—finding the points of similarity between *efficiency* and *vegetable* might give at least some minor insights into or understanding of the concept "efficiency." What did you learn, if anything, from the nonsense sentences that this exercise generated? What ideas did the nonsense sentences stir up in your mind?

3. The exercise undoubtedly generated some sentences that you feel are meaningful. What insights did these sentences give you? Explain.

II. Abstract-concrete sentences are good journal material. With practice, you can become a real master at writing these sentences. Start now! In your journal, write ten of them.

Analogy

The analogy, an extremely useful device for thinkers and writers, is simply the comparing of an unknown or imperfectly known thing or concept to something that is known. (In a way, the abstract-concrete sentence is an analogy.) Suppose that I want to explain the *Readers' Guide to Periodical Literature* to someone who has not used it, but who does understand how to use a card catalogue in a library. The analogy would be this:

The *Readers' Guide* is an index of articles published in generally nontechnical magazines, such as *Time* or *The Atlantic*. It is like the card catalogue of a library. The card catalogue lists books by (1) their authors or editors, (2) their titles, and (3) their subjects. The *Readers' Guide* has the same listings for magazine articles (in alphabetical order, of course).

When Einstein wanted to explain nuclear fission to nonscientists, he used the analogy of the rich man and his sons.

What takes place can be illustrated with the help of our rich man. The atom M is a rich miser who, during his life, gives away no money (*energy*). But in his will be bequeaths his fortune to his sons M' and M", on condition that they give to the community a small amount, less than one thousandth of the whole estate (*energy or mass*). The sons together have somewhat less than the father had (*the mass sum M′ + M″ is somewhat smaller than the mass M of the radioactive atom*). But the part given to the community, though relatively small, is still so enormously large (*considered as kinetic energy*) that it brings with it a great threat of evil. Averting that threat has become the most urgent problem of our time.

—Albert Einstein, Out of My Later Years

Here is a somewhat more complicated example. To explain Freudian theory, the American psychologist Jerome Bruner draws an analogy between that theory and drama:

Freud's is a theory or a proto-theory peopled with actors. The characters are from life: the blind, energic, pleasure-seeking id; the priggish and punitive super-ego; the ego, battling for its being by diverting the energy of the others to its own use. The drama has an economy and a terseness. The ego develops canny mechanisms for dealing with the threat of id impulses: denial, projection, and the rest. Balances are struck between the actors, and in the balance is character and neurosis. Freud was using the dramatic technique of decomposition, the play whose actors are parts of a single life. It is a technique that he himself had recognized in fantasies and dreams, one he honored in "The Poet and the Daydream."

—Jerome S. Bruner, "Freud and the Image of Man"

As you can see from the three examples above, analogy is a good way to explain things and ideas.

Exercise

In your journal, write an analogy by which you explain something to any person of your choice (a friend, your instructor, a relative, the president of the United States). You must choose a thing to be explained that your intended reader does not yet understand (fully at least), and you must use the familiar or well known as the basis for your analogy. You can choose a concrete object (such as a complicated instrument), a process (such as registering in college), or a concept (such as honesty).

Outrageous Analogies

In a later chapter, we will find that analogy is one of the devices of argumentation, for we can convince our readers of a point of view by drawing analogies, and we have already seen that analogies are very useful devices for explanation. When analogies are used either for argumentation or for explanation, writers must be cautious, making sure that the analogy is not false or overextended. (A false analogy compares two things which, *in the context of the argument,* are not comparable; an analogy which is overextended carries the comparison too far.) At present, however, we are not concerned with the validity of analogies, only with their use as stimulants to thinking and as devices for language play—which is precisely why this section is titled "Outrageous Analogies." One should not feel that the ideas and exercises necessarily create *valid* analogies; the purpose is to create interesting analogies that will stimulate thought, insight, and imagination.

In writing an outrageous analogy, one describes a common activity in terms of another common activity: driving a car in terms of brushing teeth, keeping a journal in terms of tending a garden, snoozing in terms of chewing gum. For example, the following outrageous analogy describes the activity of *reading* in terms of *fishing.* Notice that the beginning is an abstract-concrete sentence.

> Meaning is a trout that keeps the reader ever alert, casting his attention into riffles of words in the hope that meaning will rise for a strike. Warily, meaning sulks beneath a large rock, undulating in the current of the sentences and the paragraphs, ignoring cast after cast by the fisherman. Then suddenly it flashes into view, arcing above the surface and engorging the lure. After a careful battle, the fisherman slips the meaning-trout into his creel, and in the evening he fries the catch in butter and eats it with gusto.

This brief passage can stir up many interesting ideas, can make you ask important questions about reading, questions that you probably would not have asked without the stimulus of the analogy. For example:

1. Where does the meaning lurk? In the individual words? In the sentences? In the paragraphs?
2. Which leads to this big question: What is *meaning?*
3. Why is it that meaning sometimes eludes us?
4. Why is it that meaning sometimes flashes into view, almost as if the reader had received a sudden inspiration?

5. How is meaning stored in memory?
6. How is meaning used?

And the list of questions could go on and on. I merely want to point out that analogies—outrageous or not—produce ideas. And outrageous analogies are fun to create.

Exercise

In your journal, write at least two outrageous analogies. If you have trouble, here are some steps toward creating interesting samples:

1. Choose two activities with which you are thoroughly familiar (for example, driving a car and baking a cake).
2. List the steps or parts of each activity.

Driving a car	Baking a cake
fastening seat belt	reading recipe
starting engine	assembling ingredients
activating left turn signal	heating oven
putting car in gear	mixing ingredients
pulling into traffic . . .	baking . . .

3. Use terms and suggestions from the second column to describe the first process.

When you drive a car, the best recipe for a safe trip is to fasten the seat belt immediately. You can cook up a successful trip if you'll carefully assemble the ingredients before you start baking. You need a key, a gas pedal, a gearshift lever, and a steering wheel. First, insert the key into the starter switch and turn, at the same time mixing in carefully a slight depression of the gas pedal so that . . .

(Corny? Yes! Certainly! But in writing for the journal—since it is actually writing for oneself—anything goes. And, in fact, it did take some ingenuity to describe driving a car in terms of baking a cake.)

The Meditation

The word "meditation" as it is used here has nothing to do with any religion or with any mental discipline such as yoga; it means only the systematic construction of an imaginative experience. For our purposes, then, the meditation is a way of stimulating and guiding the imagination.

It goes without saying that meditation takes place in a quiet, comfortable spot at a time when the meditator is calm and relatively at peace.

The kind of meditation that I am suggesting as a stimulus to writing depends heavily upon one's ability to imagine scenes and actions, for it involves creating or re-creating an event. In this kind of meditation, the meditator is a dramatist, and the meditation itself is the drama that he or she creates.

All forms of drama (stage, television, or film) have certain elements in common.

First, there is *scene.* All actions take place in a scene that is represented in detail or that the viewer must imagine, for dramas can take place on bare stages.

Second, there are *characters:* the hero or heroine and others.

Third, there is *plot,* and plot consists of the actions that occur and the reasons or motives for these actions. Thus, plot consists of *actions* plus *motives.*

In constructing the drama of your meditation, you will create a detailed scene; into that scene you will put yourself as the central character, and you may add one or two more characters; the character or characters will do something, perform some action, simple or elaborate, for some reason.

Exercise

1. Prepare yourself for fifteen to thirty minutes of intense meditation. Choose a quiet spot where you won't be disturbed, and make yourself comfortable. Get settled, and then close your eyes.

2. Make your mind as completely blank as possible.

3. Within the empty stage of your mind, construct a scene, not a general scene, but one that is specific. What are the three or four most important objects in the scene? What colors appear? What would the textures be if the objects were touched? Are there any sounds? Smells? (When you construct your scene, you should do a sense inventory, registering sights, sounds, smells, tactile feelings, even tastes.)

4. Put yourself in the scene. What exactly do you look like? How are you dressed? Are you wearing perfume or shaving lotion? How does your skin feel? What is the texture of your clothing? What colors stand out? If you wish, you can add one or two other characters.

5. Have your main character (yourself) do something. If there are

other characters, involve them in the actions. *Imagine the actions in detail, not in general.* If your main character walks across a room, picks up a newspaper, and begins to read, supply all of the details: the manner of walking, sounds, hand movements, etc.

6. Supply or explain the motives for the actions. If you already know why your character or characters do what they do, explain. If you do not know, invent motives, and explain them.

Your meditation having ended, record it in your journal, capturing as many of the details as possible. You supplied a great many details for your meditative drama; try not to lose any of them as you record that drama.

If you feel the urge or the need to write an autobiographical narrative, the meditative technique just outlined will help you immensely. The exercise above *constructs* a drama; using the same techniques to recall something that has happened to you will *reconstruct* that event. What you find here is just exactly the difference between fiction and history: fiction portrays possible worlds that have not and probably never will come into actual being; history portrays worlds that have existed. The writing of both history and biography demands imagination. We have used meditation as a stimulus to the imagination.

REASONS FOR KEEPING A JOURNAL

We have explored several kinds of journal entries, intended largely as warming-up exercises, language games, and the like: the abstract-concrete sentence, analogy, outrageous analogies, and meditation. If there is one lesson to be learned from these techniques, it is this: *writers must provide specific, concrete details even when dealing with abstract subjects.*

The journal serves as a bridge between the writer's private world of thoughts, feelings, and intuitions and a reader or group of readers who might possibly be interested. That is to say, journal entries are practice sessions in the writing game, but some of them can also serve as the bases for public writing. In fact, a good journal will have all sorts of entries in it, reflecting all of the various purposes for writing.

The following sections of this chapter, arranged according to purposes for writing, will give you further ideas about the kinds of entries you can make in your journal.

Self-Expression

We often use language merely for self-expression, "to get something off our chests," to let off steam, to release the internal pressure that silence creates. When you stub your toe on a chair at night and curse a blue streak, you are using language self-expressively—not to convey information, not to convince anyone of anything, but merely as a safety valve.

Under the self-expressive motive, we can classify any kind of writing which is for *the writer him- or herself*. Self-expressive writing is reflexive; writer and reader are one and the same.

One kind of self-expressive writing is the *interior monologue,* in which you attempt to record your thoughts just as they come. The best interior monologue will give you a sense that your thinking has been recorded almost as if by tape. Sounds easy, doesn't it? Just turn on the thoughts and let the writing flow. But thoughts come rapidly, and they are often vivid with images; writing is a slow process, and images are difficult to capture in words.

As you might guess, examples of interior monologues are hard to find, for writers do not publish them but often use them as sources of ideas for public writing. Even if we did have an example, it would be difficult to understand because the writer records the interior monologue for him- or herself, not for readers.

Perhaps the following entry from Allen Ginsberg's *Indian Journals* will give you a sense of what one kind of interior monologue sounds like, but you should not be troubled if you don't understand everything Ginsberg says.

Friday 13 July 1962

Top floor Hotel Amjadia Chandy Chowk & Princep St. Calcutta: looking out the barred window at sunset & the clouds like a movie film over the sky with cheap red paper kites fluttering over the 4 story roofs against the mottled green & orange mists of maya—down for a cup of tea, the sloppy Moslem waiters barefoot & bearded in black-edged white uniforms—the clang of rickshaw handbells against wooden pull staves—bells under hand cars—slept all afternoon after the M last night and visit to doctor this morning—worm pills—& read Time & Newsweek & Thubten Jigme Norbu's autobiography—constantly the unnoticed details of the going universe outside the room where in heat & sickness & lethargy Peter & I drowse & read & browse & sleep—Now it's dark evening time and the reality of the thousand barefoot street vendors & car honkers outside visible from both windows downstairs as I sit leg folded under me in bed—Peter wakes half asleep—"my arm's falling apart" I massage it it's asleep & feels dead & sweaty—neon lights in the porcelain & dish store downstairs—half a dozen streetlights dot-burning the picture—looks like Lima Chinatown 2 years ago—most cars speeding by have red tail lights—nasal beggar or vendor voices—the fan whirling overhead for the last 12 hours—Everything random still, as any cut up. Burroughs it's already a year still haunting me. I slept all afternoon & when I woke up I thought it was morning, I didn't know where I was. I had no name for India.[2]

Exercise: Writing an Interior Monologue

In your journal, write an interior monologue. Here is some advice for accomplishing that:

1. Be as honest as you can.
2. Forget about all reality except that which is in your own mind; this is the source for your material. Get that material from *introspection*—from thinking about your thinking.
3. Disregard structure (organization). The thoughts as they occur to you provide their own organization, and if you tamper with that, you are falsifying.
4. Use whatever language (style) you think best suits your purpose, the only restraint being this: if you want someone else to read your monologue, you must at least be intelligible.
5. Since the primary audience for your interior monologue is you yourself, you can forget about making adjustments so that your readers will like what you say; they must take you on your own terms.

Exposition

Writing is most often used to *explain, demonstrate,* and *explore* ideas. Such writings are called *exposition* or *expository writing,* and they deal with reality or with what we take to be reality. In later chapters, we will discuss the different varieties of expository prose (explanatory; exploratory; and scientific, which demonstrates ideas), but for the moment it is important to understand the most significant difference between self-expressive and expository writ-

[2] Allen Ginsberg, *Indian Journals* (San Francisco: Dave Haselwood Books and City Lights Books, 1970), pp. 42–43. Copyright © 1970 by Allen Ginsberg. Reprinted by permission of City Lights Books.

ing: *expository writing is intended for an audience, for a reader, or group of readers.* This means that *content* must be adequate and interesting; *structure* must be clear and logical; *style* must be appropriate.

If self-expression is the most *private* kind of writing, then exposition is the most *public.* And that being the case, one might ask what place exposition has in a journal, which, after all, is not intended for the public. The answer to that question is this: the journal is a good place to begin pieces of writing that finally might be developed for an audience.

When you make an expository entry in your journal, you will be thinking about a possible audience other than yourself, and this projected or possible audience will lead you to make certain adjustments even in your journal entry. For example, your style will probably be more formal than in self-expressive writing, you will clarify details and amplify points, and you will begin to think about the most effective structure. In short, when you write exposition in your journal, it will be as if an imagined reader were peeking over your shoulder, trying to read and understand what you are writing.

From Journal to Exposition

Let's look closely at a dramatic example of how an expository entry in a journal can serve as the basis for a larger piece of more public writing. Henry David Thoreau's journal entry for July 6, 1846, reads as follows:

> I wish to meet the facts of life—the vital facts, which are the phenomena or actuality the gods meant to show us—face to face, and so I came down here. Life! who knows what it is, what it does? If I am not quite right here, I am less wrong than before; and now let us see what they will have. The preacher, instead of vexing the ears of drowsy farmers on their day of rest at the end of the week,—for Sunday always seemed to me like a fit conclusion of an ill-spent week and not the fresh and brave beginning of a new one,—with this one other draggletail and postponed affair of a sermon, from thirdly to fifteenthly, should teach them with a thundering voice pause and simplicity. "Stop! Avast! Why so fast?" In all studies we go not forward but rather backward with redoubled pauses. We always study *antiques* with silence and reflection. Even time has a depth, and below its surface the waves do not lapse and roar. I wonder men can be so frivolous almost as to attend to the gross form of negro slavery, there are so many keen and subtle masters who subject us both. Self-emancipation in the West Indies of a man's thinking and imagining

provinces, which should be more than his island territory,—one emancipated heart and intellect! It would knock off the fetters from a million slaves.

This journal entry of some 240 words served as the basis for a long passage in *Walden,* Thoreau's classic book:

I went to the woods because I wished to live deliberately, to front only the essential facts of life, and see if I could not learn what it had to teach, and not, when I came to die, discover that I had not lived. I did not wish to live what was not life, living is so dear; nor did I wish to practice resignation, unless it was quite necessary. I wanted to live deep and suck out all the marrow of life, to live so sturdily and Spartan-like as to put to rout all that was not life, to cut a broad swath and shave close, to drive life into a corner, and reduce it to its lowest terms, and, if it proved to be mean, why then to get the whole and genuine meanness of it, and publish its meanness to the world; or if it were sublime, to know it by experience, and be able to give a true account of it in my next excursion. For most men, it appears to me, are in a strange uncertainty about it, whether it is of the devil or of God, and have *somewhat hastily* concluded that it is the chief end of man here to "glorify God and enjoy him forever."

Still we live meanly, like ants; though the fable tell us that we were long ago changed into men; like pygmies we fight with cranes; it is error upon error, and clout upon clout, and our best virtue has for its occasion a superfluous and evitable wretchedness. Our life is frittered away by detail. An honest man has hardly need to count more than his ten fingers, or in extreme cases he may add his ten toes, and lump the rest. Simplicity, simplicity, simplicity! I say, let your affairs be as two or three, and not a hundred or a thousand; instead of a million count half a dozen, and keep your accounts on your thumb nail. In the midst of this chopping sea of civilized life, such are the clouds and storms and quicksands and thousand-and-one items to be allowed for, that a man has to live, if he would not founder and go to the bottom and not make his port at all, by dead reckoning, and he must be a great calculator indeed who succeeds. Simplify, simplify. Instead of three meals a day, if it be necessary eat but one; instead of a hundred dishes, five; and reduce other things in proportion. Our life is like a German Confederacy, made up of petty states, with its boundary forever fluctuating, so that even a German cannot tell you how it is bounded at any moment. The nation itself, with all its so called internal improvements, which, by the way, are all external and superficial, is just such an unwieldy and overgrown establishment, cluttered with furniture and tripped up by its own traps, ruined by luxury and heedless expense, by want of calculation and a worthy aim, as the million households in the land; and the only cure for it as for them is in a rigid economy, a stern and more than Spartan simplicity of life and elevation of purpose. It lives too fast. Men think that it is essential that the *Nation* have commerce, and export ice, and talk through a telegraph, and ride thirty miles an hour, without a doubt, whether *they* do or not; but whether we should live like baboons or like men, is a little uncertain. If we do not get out sleepers, and forge rails, and devote days and nights to the work, but go to tinkering upon our *lives* to improve *them,* who will build railroads? And if railroads are not built, how shall we get to heaven in season? But if we stay at home and mind our business, who will want railroads? We do not ride on the railroad; it rides upon us. Did you ever think what those sleepers are that underlie the railroad? Each one is a man, an Irishman, or a Yankee man. The rails are laid on them, and they are covered with sand, and the cars run smoothly over them. They are sound sleepers, I assure you. And every few years a new lot is laid down and run over; so that, if some have the pleasure of riding on a rail, others have the misfortune to be ridden upon. And when they run over a man that is walking in his sleep, a supernumerary sleeper in the wrong position, and wake him up, they suddenly stop the cars, and make a hue and cry about it, as if this were an exception. I am glad to know that it takes a gang of men for every five miles to keep the sleepers down and level in their beds as it is, for this is a sign that they may sometime get up again.

Why should we live with such hurry and waste of life? We are determined to be starved before we are hungry. Men say that a stitch in time saves nine, and so they take a thousand stitches today to save nine to-morrow. As for work, we haven't any of any consequence. We have the Saint Vitus' dance, and cannot possibly keep our heads still. If I should only give a few pulls at the parish bell-rope, as for a fire, that is, without setting the bell, there is hardly a man on his farm in the outskirts of Concord, notwithstanding that press of engagements which was his excuse so many times this morning, nor a boy, nor a woman, I might almost say, but would forsake all and follow that sound, not mainly to save property from the flames, but, if we will confess the truth, much more to see it burn, since burn it must, and we, be it known, did not set it on fire,—or to see it put out, and have a hand in it, if that is done as handsomely; yes, even if it were the parish church itself. Hardly a man takes a half hour's nap after dinner, but when he wakes he holds up his head and asks, "What's the news?" as if the rest of mankind had stood his sentinels. Some give directions to be waked every half hour, doubtless for no other purpose; and then, to pay for it, they tell what they have dreamed. After a night's sleep the news is as indispensable as the breakfast. "Pray tell me any thing new that has happened to a man any where on this globe,"—and he reads it over his coffee and rolls, that a man has had his eyes gouged out this morning on the Wachito River;

never dreaming the while that he lives in the dark unfathomed mammoth cave of this world, and has but the rudiment of an eye himself.

For my part, I could easily do without the post-office. I think that there are very few important communications made through it. To speak critically, I never received more than one or two letters in my life—I wrote this some years ago—that were worth the postage. The penny-post is, commonly, an institution through which you seriously offer a man that penny for his thoughts which is so often safely offered in jest. And I am sure that I never read any memorable news in a newspaper. If we read of one man robbed, or murdered, or killed by accident, or one house burned, or one vessel wrecked, or one steamboat blown up, or one cow run over on the Western Railroad, or one mad dog killed, or one lot of grasshoppers in the winter,—we never need read of another. One is enough. If you are acquainted with the principle, what do you care for a myriad instances and applications? To a philosopher all news, as it is called, is gossip, and they who edit and read it are old women over their tea. Yet not a few are greedy after this gossip. There was such a rush, as I hear, the other day at one of the offices to learn the foreign news by the last arrival, that several large squares of plate glass belonging to the establishment were broken by the pressure,—news which I seriously think a ready wit might write a twelvemonth or twelve years beforehand with sufficient accuracy. As for Spain, for instance, if you know how to throw in Don Carlos and the Infanta, and Don Pedro and Seville and Granada, from time to time in the right proportions,—they may have changed the names a little since I saw the papers,—and serve up a bull-fight when other entertainments fail, it will be true to the letter, and give us as good an idea of the exact state or ruin of things in Spain as the most succinct and lucid reports under this head in the newspapers: and as for England, almost the last significant scrap of news from that quarter was the revolution of 1649; and if you have learned the history of her crops for an average year, you never need attend to that thing again, unless your speculations are of a merely pecuniary character. If one may judge who rarely looks into the newspapers, nothing new does ever happen in foreign parts, a French revolution not excepted.

What news! how much more important to know what that is which was never old! "Kieou-he-yu (great dignitary of the state of Wei) sent a man to Khoung-tseu to know his news. Khoung-tseu caused the messenger to be seated near him, and questioned him in these terms: What is your master doing? The messenger answered with respect: My master desires to diminish the number of his faults, but he cannot accomplish it. The messenger being gone, the philosopher remarked: What a worthy messenger! What a worthy messenger!" The preacher, instead of vexing the ears of drowsy farmers on their day of rest at the end of the week,—for Sunday is the fit conclusion of an ill-spent week, and not the fresh and brave beginning of a new one,—with this one other draggletail of a sermon, should shout with thundering voice,—"Pause! Avast! Why so seeming fast, but deadly slow?"

Shams and delusions are esteemed for soundest truths, while reality is fabulous. If men would steadily observe realities only, and not allow themselves to be deluded, life, to compare it with such things as we know, would be like a fairy tale and the Arabian Nights' Entertainments. If we respected only what is inevitable and has a right to be, music and poetry would resound along the streets. When we are unhurried and wise, we perceive that only great and worthy things have any permanent and absolute existence—that petty fears and petty pleasures are but the shadow of the reality. This is always exhilarating and sublime. By closing the eyes and slumbering, and consenting to be deceived by shows, men establish and confirm their daily life of routine and habit every where, which still is built on purely illusory foundations. Children, who play life, discern its true law and relations more clearly than men, who fail to live it worthily, but who think that they are wiser by experience, that is, by failure. I have read in a Hindoo book, that "there was a king's son, who, being expelled in infancy from his native city, was brought up by a forester, and, growing up to maturity in that state, imagined himself to belong to the barbarous race with which he lived. One of his father's ministers having discovered him, revealed to him what he was, and the misconception of his character was removed, and he knew himself to be a prince. So soul," continues the Hindoo philosopher, "from the circumstances in which it is placed, mistakes its own character, until the truth is revealed to it by some holy teacher, and then it knows itself to be *Brahme*." I perceive that we inhabitants of New England live this mean life that we do because our vision does not penetrate the surface of things. We think that *is* which *appears* to be. If a man should walk through this town and see only the reality, where, think you, would the "Mill-dam" go to? If he should give us an account of the realities he beheld there, we should not recognize the place in his description. Look at a meeting-house, or a court-house, or a jail, or a shop, or a dwelling-house, and say what that thing really is before a true gaze, and they would all go to pieces in your account of them. Men esteem truth remote, in the outskirts of the system, behind the farthest star, before Adam and after the last man. In eternity there is indeed something true and sublime. But all these times and places and occasions are now and here. God himself culminates in the present moment, and will never be more divine in the lapse of all the ages. And we are enabled to apprehend at all what is sublime and noble only by the perpetual instilling and drenching of the reality that surrounds us. The universe constantly and obediently answers to our conceptions; whether we travel fast or slow, the track is laid for us. Let us spend our lives in conceiving then. The poet or the artist never yet had so fair and noble a design but some of his posterity at least could accomplish it.

Let us spend one day as deliberately as Nature, and not be thrown off the track by every nutshell and mosquito's wing that falls on the rails. Let us rise early and fast, or break fast, gently and without perturbation; let company come and let company go, let the bells ring and the children cry,—determined to make a day of it. Why should we knock under and go with the stream? Let us not be upset and overwhelmed in that terrible rapid and whirlpool called a dinner, situated in the meridian shallows. Weather this danger and you are safe, for the rest of the way is down hill. With unrelaxed nerves, with morning vigor, sail by it, looking another way, tied to the mast like Ulysses. If the engine whistles, let it whistle till it is hoarse for its pains. If the bell rings, why should we run? We will consider what kind of music they are like. Let us settle ourselves, and work and wedge our feet downward through the mud and slush of opinion, and prejudice, and tradition, and delusion, and appearance, that alluvion which covers the globe, through Paris and London, through New York and Boston and Concord, through church and state, through poetry and philosophy and religion, till we come to a hard bottom and rocks in place, which we can call *reality*, and say, This is, and no mistake; and then begin, having a *point d'appui*, below freshet and frost and fire, a place where you might found a wall or a state, or set a lamp-post safely, or perhaps a gauge, not a Nilometer, but a Realometer, that future ages might know how deep a freshet of shams and appearances had gathered from time to time. If you stand right fronting and face to face to a fact, you will see the gun glimmer on both its surfaces, as if it were a cimeter, and feel its sweet edge dividing you through the heart and marrow, and so you will happily conclude your mortal career. Be it life or death, we crave only reality. If we are really dying, let us hear the rattle in our throats and feel cold in the extremities; if we are alive, let us go about our business.

Time is but the stream I go a-fishing in. I drink at it; but while I drink I see the sandy bottom and detect how shallow it is. Its thin current slides away, but eternity remains. I would drink deeper; fish in the sky, whose bottom is pebbly with stars. I cannot count one. I know not the first letter of the alphabet. I have always been regretting that I was not as wise as the day I was born. The intellect is a cleaver; it discerns and rifts its way into the secret of things. I do not wish to be any more busy with my hands than is necessary. My head is hands and feet. I feel all my best faculties concentrated in it. My instinct tells me that my head is an organ for burrowing, as some creatures use their snout and fore-paws, and with it I would mine and burrow my way through these hills. I think that the richest vein is somewhere hereabouts; so by the divining rod and thin rising vapors I judge; and here I will begin to mine.

Discussion

In building his journal entry into a passage for his book, what changes does Thoreau make? You can ask yourself these questions (1) What is *added?* (2) What is *deleted?* (3) What is *rearranged?* (4) What *substitutions* seem to have been made? For example, in the journal Thoreau says,

> Even time has a depth, and below its surface the waves do not lapse and roar.

In *Walden,* Thoreau transforms this somewhat bare metaphoric idea:

> Time is but the stream I go a-fishing in. I drink at it; but while I drink I see the sandy bottom and detect how shallow it is. Its thin current slides away, but eternity remains. I would drink deeper; fish in the sky, whose bottom is pebbly with stars.

The first entry is saying something like this: below the surface of time in which we live, with its momentary turmoil, lies the endless calm of eternity. The passage in *Walden* tells us that time is shallow and passing, like the brook that one fishes in. When one looks at the sky, "whose bottom is pebbly with stars," one senses eternity.

Considering the Audience

As we have seen, the audience for self-expressive writing is the writer him- or herself, but the audience for exposition is some other person, perhaps a friend or relative or even a teacher, but possibly a reader or group of readers the writer will never meet. (Instructions for assembling bicycles, newspaper editorials, essays in magazines such as *Harper's* or *The New Yorker* or *Popular Mechanics,* scientific reports, letters to business firms—these are just some examples of expository writings for which the audiences of readers cannot ordinarily be precisely defined.) Because the purpose of exposition is to convey information or deal with ideas as efficiently as possible, the writer must take care: anything that distracts the reader from the ideas or content will undermine the purpose of the writing.

For eksample. There is certain convenshuns that most readers of eksposition agree on—convenshuns of spelling. Punctuation. Verb agreement. And others. If the riter. Violates these here convenshuns? the reader is distracted from content. When you rite exposishun you should assume that your reeder will be annoyed if you don't follow the "rules" that are generally agreed upon.

In other words, the common errors in writing are bad because they distract readers and thus keep writers from achieving their purposes in exposition. When you write exposition, you are entering into a contract with your reader or readers: you agree to present your ideas or information as clearly and completely as possible.

Exercise

The audience for the following exercises is a group of intelligent adults whom you don't know. (Stated another way: you assume that what you write is intended to be read by intelligent, educated strangers.)

1. Write a set of instructions for getting from one place to another: from the airport to your home; from the entrance of a building to a precise spot in that building; from one city to another. . . .

After you have written your set of instructions, show it to a classmate and ask if he or she thinks the instructions are clear and complete. What is lacking? What problems does your reader find in your instructions? (Your reader should pretend that he or she is a complete stranger to you.)

2. Regarding some topics, we simply don't know what to think; we haven't reached a conclusion; we haven't achieved understanding. Writing is a good way to define such problematic situations. Choose an idea or topic that troubles you, and in a journal entry explore it for your intelligent, unknown audience. The topic could be a decision that you finally must make (the choice of a major, whether or not to get married), a concept that you do not fully understand (capital punishment, the reason for general education requirements at your college, a current fad or craze), some habit or compulsion of your own (biting your nails, procrastination, a phobia).

Again, have a classmate—who takes the role of an intelligent stranger—criticize your entry.

3. You have solved some problems on the basis of evidence that you feel is conclusive. The "facts" of the case speak for themselves. (For example, scientific experiments are attempts to establish conclusive evidence for a hypothesis.) In a journal entry, outline such a problem, explain your conclusion, and present the data that is the basis for that conclusion.

This entry need not be long or complicated. For example, Jones has a problem: his car won't start. He removes the battery and takes it to a garage for testing. He finds that the battery is not low and reinstalls it in the car. Again, he tries to start the auto, with immediate success. Since he had tightened the connections when he put the battery back in, he concludes that the problem was a bad connection which the reinstallation has remedied.

The problem you choose may be this simple or much more complex. In any case, get a reaction from a classmate (in the role of intelligent stranger). Is your outline of the problem clear and adequate? Is your conclusion reasonable? Have you presented enough evidence?

In the first exercise of the group above, you were explaining, that is, giving a set of instructions. As a writer, you were implying to your reader that you were an "expert" whose information could be relied on. Your relationship with your reader was that of an "authority" who had the knowledge to convey a given body of useful data. When you convey information—such as a set of instructions—you would be puzzled if your reader questioned the veracity of your writing. For example, if I gave instructions for getting to my home from downtown Los Angeles, I would be puzzled if my reader asked me, "How do you know?"

In the second exercise, you were exploring a problem, in effect saying to your reader, "Here is something that puzzles me. Follow along, and see if my problem interests you too. I have no answers, but I do have some interesting ideas." In a sense, your reader becomes a coexplorer.

In the third exercise, you were saying that the evidence is adequate to convince your reader that your solution is valid. You were not "arguing" a point; you were merely presenting the data that led you to your more or less certain conclusion. In effect, you were saying, "All reasonable people would reach the same conclusion that I have."

In these three exercises, you have written *explanatory, exploratory,* and *demonstrative* (or *scientific*) prose.

Discussion

Discuss the following questions:

1. In explanatory writing, what is the relationship of the writer with the reader?
2. In exploratory prose, what is the relationship of the writer with the reader?
3. In demonstrative or scientific prose, what is the relationship of the writer with the reader?

Persuasion

Persuasive writing has two general characteristics, among others. First, it is action-oriented, intended to make readers do something: buy a product, vote for a candidate, give up smoking.

Second, the audience is most often rather clearly defined. There is a world of difference between writing a clear set of instructions for planting a vegetable garden and persuading one's brother to follow those instructions.

Like demonstrative or scientific writing, persuasion uses data, and embedded in the persuasive piece are explanations and even exploratory passages, but the overall purpose remains this: to convince a given audience to take some action.

Discussion

Carefully read and think about the advertisement on page 52, and then answer the following questions:

1. What kind of audience is the advertisement intended for? How do you know?
2. What is the purpose of the advertisement?
3. What information does the ad contain, and how does that information serve this purpose?
4. What explanations are necessary for the purpose to be fulfilled?
5. What devices does the ad use to appeal to its audience?
6. Do you feel that the ad is convincing? Why, or why not?
7. Explain any improvements that you could make in the ad.
8. In general, how does this piece of persuasive writing differ from explanatory, exploratory, and demonstrative prose?

Practice

1. In your journal, write a brief advertisement for some product, and aim your ad at a particular audience: teenagers, your classmates, college professors, surfers, wealthy people. Be prepared to discuss the ways in which you tried to make your ad appealing to your chosen audience.

2. Just for fun, try writing one of the following ads: (a) One to be placed in the *Journal of the American Medical Association,* selling bubble gum to physicians; (b) One to be placed in *Field and Stream,* convincing hunters that civilians should not be allowed to own firearms; (c) One intended for *Motor Trends,* arguing that the U.S. Government should take over all automobile production and produce only one model, a sensible, economical, completely safe vehicle; (d) One for *Playboy,* attempting to convince readers to abstain from drinking alcohol. (If none of the above appeals to you, invent your own situation for an impossible ad.)

3. Think of something that you want a friend or relative to do for you. Write a letter convincing that person to do what you want.

52

Discussion

In general, what did you do to make your ads and your letter appeal to their audiences? Think especially of language choice, your attitude as reflected in the ad, your selection of data and suppression of certain points.

Freewriting

In this chapter so far, you have encountered a variety of suggestions for journal entries: the abstract-concrete sentence, analogy, outrageous analogies, meditation, self-expression, three sorts of exposition, and persuasive pieces. There is no reason, however, that your journal entries should be confined to or structured by these suggestions. You can use your journal for freewriting—simply letting words, phrases, and sentences tumble out onto the page, one after another, unplanned, spontaneous, with no obligation to make sense or be coherent.

Freewriting can be compared to the warming-up exercises that athletes perform; freewriting limbers up the muscles of your mind, gets you in the mood, undams the stream of language.

Here is a bit of practical advice: if you have mental writer's cramps, merely sit down with your journal and start entering words in it, just as they pop into your mind; don't think even about sentences necessarily, but fill a complete page of your journal with spontaneously discovered words. There is a good chance that this uncontrolled, effortless writing will begin to assume a direction that you can follow.

Practice

In your journal, make three columns of words, starting at the top of the first column and going to the bottom of the page, then completing the second and third columns in like manner. Now look over these lists of apparently unrelated words. Can you see that some of them make groups of related meanings or fields? And do these related groups give you any ideas for paragraphs (or even short essays) about a subject? If so, write the paragraph or short essay.

SUMMARY

This chapter has made the point that the journal is a useful instrument for writers. It provides a way to practice the skill of writing without the threat of failure; it is an excellent "idea bank"; for many writers, the journal is a source of great pleasure, a place in which can be recorded the thoughts, experiences, and emotions that are important to them.

The chapter has also introduced three basic kinds of writing: self-expression, exposition, and persuasion. In the discussion of these three modes, one point was made over and over again: a sense of audience is crucial to the writer. And a second point ran through much of the chapter: the need for concreteness.

It is simply a fact that a great many—and perhaps most—writers keep some kind of journal. For beginning writers, the journal is an important tool, but often it can give them pleasure as well.

Discovering Ideas

AMONG composition teachers there is a standing joke about the first theme assignment of the fall semester. The unimaginative teacher, so the story goes, assigns this topic: "What I did during my summer vacation." And the equally unimaginative student sweats and struggles for hours, after which agony, he or she is able to write nothing more than

> During my summer vacation, I visited Tibet. It was an interesting trip.
> We saw many strange sights, and we enjoyed the Himalayas.
> I hope to return to Tibet some day.

Every time you take a vacation trip, you are flooded with new experiences—sights, tastes; people, architecture; landscape, climate; customs, art; sounds, smells. And yet, it would probably be somewhat difficult for you to write a satisfactory essay about your trip. First, you would need to "sort out" the experiences in your own mind, and you would need to make some effort to recall significant details. Second, there are probably data about the journey that you would need to look up. How much did the trip cost? What is the population of a city that you visited? What is the height of a mountain that you climbed? If you were on a cruise ship, how many other passengers were on it with you? And so on.

If you were to write a satisfactory essay about the trip, you would need *content* or subject matter. And there would be two sources for this content: your own memory, and such references as books, encyclopedias, and so on.

But notice this, for it is an important point: when you first decide (or are required) to write about your summer vacation, *you will probably not immediately know what information you will need.* You must have a way of opening your subject up, of discovering the ideas and data that relate to it, of learning just exactly what you do and do not know about the subject, and of defining your attitude. As a writer, you need a great many details at your fingertips.

Any writing task begins with this huge problem: discovering things to say about the subject. Even if you know your subject thoroughly, you probably need techniques to "retrieve" that knowledge from your memory and to put it into some kind of structure.

All of this can be stated in another way: the writer needs to develop versatility in thinking; that is, he or she needs ways to view the subject from different angles, to "take it apart" and see what makes it tick, to find various ways of understanding and explaining it.

Exercise: Angles of Vision

Think of a trip that you have taken—to a different part of your city, to another city, to another continent. Compare that trip with

1. a pilgrimage to a holy place
2. a battle
3. an athletic contest
4. trying to thread a piece of fuzzy yarn through a small needle
5. a dream
6. life
7. a rotten apple
8. a civic organization such as the Rotary Club
9. swimming
10. painting pictures

The purpose of this exercise is to demonstrate that different—and even strange—angles of vision on your subject often help you discover new ideas about it. When you change perspectives, you discover ideas.

Be prepared to discuss how each of the comparisons helped you define your attitude toward the subject and discover new ideas. (If some of the comparisons seem too farfetched, think them over again, for it is exactly these farfetched perspectives that sometimes give writers new ideas about their subjects. Note also that the farfetched comparisons are very much like the "outrageous analogies" on pages 36–37.)

DISCOVERY PROCEDURES

This chapter will deal with a number of *heuristics,* and a heuristic is nothing more than a technique for discovering ideas or finding solutions to problems. (The word "heuristic" is one that you should know, for it is used often in fields such as psychology, mathematics, and philosophy. In this book, however, the term *discovery procedure* will be substituted for "heuristic.")

"I'm stuck" is one of the writer's most common complaints. "I just don't know what to say about this subject." Discovery procedures are intended to help writers overcome this *stuckedness.* They can be used to develop content or subject matter for writing.

Before we begin, five *important* points must be made.

First, the discovery procedures in this chapter will become increasingly more complicated; we will start with the simple and move toward the complex.

Second, these procedures seem to relate to personality or mental style. Some people just naturally take to certain methods of developing subject matter and find them immediately valuable while other methods always seem cumbersome, more bother than they're worth. (That's why this chapter contains so many.) You should try to understand all of the procedures that will be presented, but it is unlikely that you will find all of them equally useful.

Third, there are no rules for the use of these procedures. Results are all that count. Therefore, you should never argue about a procedure itself but should always focus on results. If the procedure helps you discover ideas, then it is successful.

Fourth, some procedures for discovering subject matter work better with certain topics than with others. For example, some of the methods explained in this chapter are particularly valuable when you are trying to understand and compose an essay about a piece of writing (poem, essay, story, etc.), but others are not as useful for this purpose.

Fifth, as you become familiar with a procedure, it will tend to "disappear." That is, you will no longer think about the procedure itself, for it will become part of your equipment for thinking, and you will automatically apply its principles.

The result of the chapter should be this: after you have worked with the procedures in it, you will find it easier to discover important, interesting ideas about your topic; you will be a more fluent prewriter.

Brainstorming

To explain how brainstorming works, we must find a subject of general interest, one that everyone in a college or university knows something about. As our case in point, we will choose the college cafeteria.

Now then, we have a problem: we must write up a set of recommendations for improving the cafeteria—lowering prices, improving the quality of food, speeding up service.

Exercise: Practice and Explanation

The *problem* is to discover recommendations for improving the cafeteria. The solution procedure that we will use is brainstorming.
"Rules" for brainstorming:

1. Choose someone to record all of the ideas, either on paper or on the blackboard (preferably on the blackboard).
2. Everyone in the class should state as many ideas as possible. You will find that the ideas your classmates suggest will give you hints for further ideas.
3. *No idea can be rejected.* The purpose of brainstorming is to discover as many ideas as possible. It is important not to judge the ideas during brainstorming, for some that appear to be the silliest may well turn out to be the most useful.

Try brainstorming on the problem of the cafeteria.
Now discuss the following:

1. On the list, are there ideas that you yourself would not have thought of?
2. Do any of these ideas seem especially valuable? Why?
3. In the process of brainstorming, did any of the ideas that others brought forth suggest new ideas to you? Explain.
4. Did the brainstorming give you a new perspective on the problem? Explain.

5. Using the ideas developed in brainstorming, could you perhaps write an essay recommending improvements in the cafeteria? Explain.

A Structural Approach: Finding Alternatives

As you have seen, brainstorming is a discovery procedure that is largely unstructured, but most such procedures do have a structure, and, as we will find, that structure can be very useful.

In the first variation on brainstorming,[1] one first lists the attributes (features, characteristics) of a thing or concept and then under each attribute lists alternatives. For example, one attribute of the cafeteria may be that food is served on china plates, which are expensive, easily broken, and hard to wash. But there are alternatives or different methods of serving food; thus, one would list

CHINA PLATES

metal trays

paper plates

plastic dishes

serve only food
    that doesn't
    need dishes,
    such as sandwiches

have customers
    bring their own
    dishes

Again, we need a problem as an example. Suppose you want to recommend changes that will improve one of your classes. You will list the attributes of the class (which you might find through brainstorming), and below those attributes, you will list alternatives (which you might also find through brainstorming). After you have made your lists, combine the attributes in many ways, choosing one from the first list, another from the second list, and so on, to see if you come up with a new kind of class that you could recommend.

This process is easier to demonstrate than to explain, and a demonstration follows. (Notice that some of the ideas in the lists

---

[1] From James L. Adams, *Conceptual Blockbusting: A Guide to Better Ideas* (San Francisco: W. H. Freeman, 1974).

appear silly. However, as in brainstorming you should record every possible idea, for you can discard those that don't turn out to be useful.)

PROFESSOR LECTURES	MEETS THREE DAYS A WEEK	NINETY-MINUTE SESSIONS
small-group discussions	one day a week	flexible time period
question-answer sessions	every day	longer time
videotapes	occasionally, when something special is to be covered	shorter time
no lectures, only readings and conferences	never	five-minute break after forty-five minutes
give credit by examination, with no class meetings	continually	

ONLY TWO EXAMINATIONS	TERM PAPER	150 STUDENTS IN CLASS
daily quizzes	no papers	break class into smaller sections
no examinations	frequent short papers	accept more students into class
only final	several major papers	many small-group sessions
hour exam every week	oral reports	hire more teachers
grades by lottery		

LECTURES DIFFICULT TO HEAR	WRITING ON BOARD HARD TO SEE	GOALS NOT DEFINED
microphone	slides	state goals
voice lessons for teacher	posters	keep students confused
keep down noise in room	films	handout stating class objectives
get a hearing aid	colored chalk	
have teacher use sign language	larger handwriting	

Here are two of the possible combinations that can serve as starting places to draw up a set of recommendations:

1. Question-answer sessions   meeting occasionally   longer time   no examinations   oral reports   accept more students into class   voice lessons for teacher   colored chalk   handout stating class objectives
2. give credit by examination   never meet   require frequent short papers   accept more students into class   state goals   (In this run through the alternatives, I happened to choose "never meet"; therefore, questions about length of class sessions, difficulty in hearing the professor, and inability to read what is written on the board were eliminated.)

Just for fun, we might go through the process once again, this time with a completely zany problem. (Because the problem is zany, the result could possibly be a humorous theme.)

Suppose that we are the members of the board of directors and are the owners of the Acme Marshmallow Company. Every cent we have is invested in the business, and two thousand workers and their families depend on us for their livelihoods, but our sales are sinking rapidly, from 100,000,000 bags of marshmallows sold in 1973 to only 10,000,000 bags in 1980. Clearly, we must take immediate action, else our fortunes will be lost and thousands of families will be destitute.

The chairperson of the board, infinitely resourceful and persuasive, proposes that we develop totally new kinds of marshmallows that will allow us to increase our sales to their former levels. To come up with ideas, we use the brainstorming variation illustrated in the lists on page 62.

The first pass through the lists has yielded a marshmallow that is

animal shaped
polka-dotted
tart
crunchy
fortified with Geritol
better packaged
chocolate coated
free of charge
mysterious

More passes will yield different kinds of marshmallows.

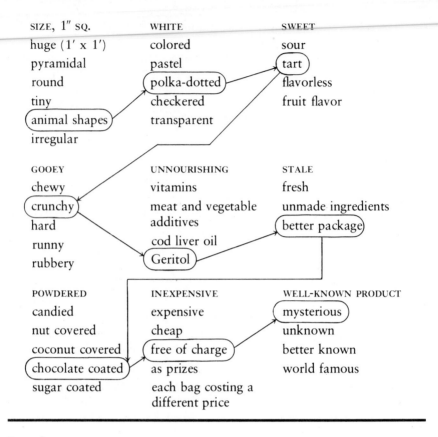

SIZE, 1″ SQ.	WHITE	SWEET
huge (1′ x 1′)	colored	sour
pyramidal	pastel	tart
round	polka-dotted	flavorless
tiny	checkered	fruit flavor
animal shapes	transparent	
irregular		

GOOEY	UNNOURISHING	STALE
chewy	vitamins	fresh
crunchy	meat and vegetable additives	unmade ingredients
hard		better package
runny	cod liver oil	
rubbery	Geritol	

POWDERED	INEXPENSIVE	WELL-KNOWN PRODUCT
candied	expensive	mysterious
nut covered	cheap	unknown
coconut covered	free of charge	better known
chocolate coated	as prizes	world famous
sugar coated	each bag costing a different price	

Exercise

The class should agree on an *abstract* subject: the kind of education offered by your college or university; the lifestyle of the typical student; American democracy; relationships between faculty and students in your college or university. (You may want to use brainstorming to come up with a subject that interests everyone in the class.)

Your problem is this: to discover ways in which your subject (e.g., faculty-student relationships) can be improved.

The solution procedure is this:

1. Through brainstorming, discover as many attributes of the situation as you can.
2. Through brainstorming, discover as many alternatives to those attributes as you can.
3. Make several passes through the alternatives to discover new forms of the situation.

Then discuss the following questions:

1. Do any of the new forms that you discovered seem to be reasonable? Which ones? Why?

2. Did the solution procedure give you new insights into your subject? What were they? Explain.
3. Did the solution procedure develop enough ideas to serve as the basis for an essay on your subject? Could you explain in general what direction your essay should take?

Clustering

A useful variation on brainstorming is called "clustering."[2] Suppose your problem is this: in your English class, you have been assigned to write a paper on your own composing process—on the way you write.

In class discussion, you can find the key ideas about the composing process. For instance, one class found that the key ideas on the subject were (a) feelings about writing, (b) "props" (such as snacks and music), (c) writing the first draft, and (d) rewriting. Once they had agreed on these key ideas (and there could have been more), they started the process of clustering by making the following diagram on the blackboard:

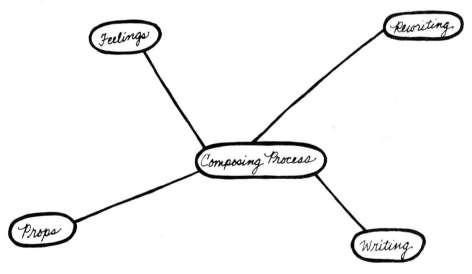

The next step is to come up with ideas suggested by the key ideas. For example, if the idea "feelings" suggests terror to a member of the class, then "terror" will be added to the clusters. As the brainstorming goes along, more key ideas can be added. The point is that one idea suggests another, and the clustering begins to

[2] The technique was developed by Gabrielle Rico.

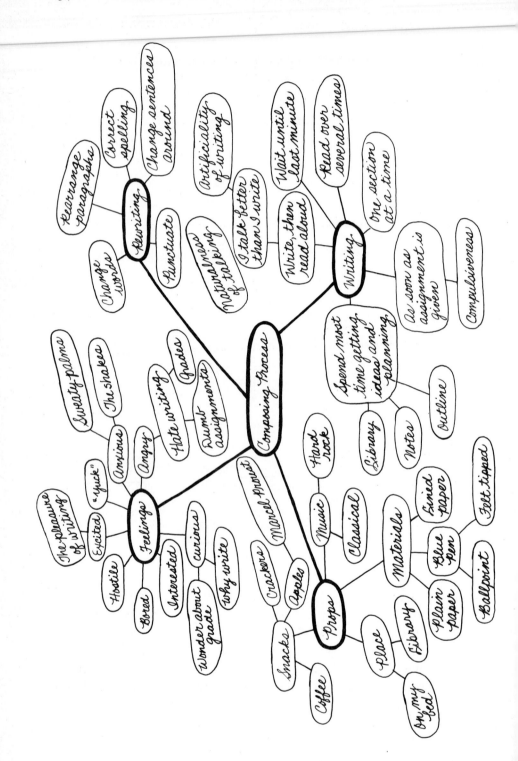

show the relationships among ideas, as the diagram on page 64 illustrates.

You can use clustering as a class activity or when you are alone in your room, trying to think of ideas to write about.

Exercise: Clustering

Use clustering to develop ideas concerning this topic: how to prepare for a test.

QUESTIONS LEADING TO NEW IDEAS

The following list of questions can be applied to any subject, concrete or abstract.[3] It could be useful in helping you discover ideas about any of the subjects we have talked about so far: your summer vacation, the cafeteria, the college class, the marshmallow, or your composing process. Here is the list:

Put to other uses?
New ways to use as is? Other uses if modified?

Adapt?
What else is like this? What other idea does this suggest? Does past offer a parallel? What could I copy? Whom could I emulate?

Modify?
New twist? Change meaning, color, motion, sound, odor, form, shape? Other changes?

Magnify?
What to add? More time? Greater frequency? Stronger? Higher? Longer? Thicker? Extra value? Plus ingredient? Duplicate? Multiply? Exaggerate?

Minify?
What to subtract? Smaller? Condensed? Miniature? Lower? Shorter? Lighter? Omit? Streamline? Split up? Understate?

[3] In Adams, from Alex Osborn, *Applied Imagination,* 3rd ed. (New York: Scribner's, 1963).

Substitute?

Who else instead? What else instead? Other ingredient? Other material? Other process? Other power? Other place? Other approach? Other tone of voice?

Rearrange?

Interchange components? Other pattern? Other layout? Other sequence? Transpose cause and effect? Change pace? Change schedule?

Reverse?

Transpose positive and negative? How about opposites? Turn it backward? Turn it upside down? Reverse poles? Change shoes? Turn tables? Turn other cheek?

Combine?

How about a blend, an alloy, an assortment, an ensemble? Combine units? Combine purposes? Combine appeals? Combine ideas?

Exercise: Checklist for New Ideas

1. The checklist for new ideas is especially valuable when you are rewriting papers. Almost every question can give you an idea for a change or a new angle of attack on your subject.

Use the checklist to plan the rewriting of a paper you have already completed—and discuss the changes you would make.

2. In discussion with your classmates, choose a problem that is common to all of you: saving energy, developing efficient study habits, amatory relationships, getting the most for your money. Apply the checklist for new ideas to that problem to see if you can arrive at any insights or at reasonable solutions.

Note: If some of the questions in the list do not seem to apply to the problem, forget them and go on to others. You can always come back to the questions you have skipped.

Who-What-Where-When-Why-How

One of the best known and most widely used discovery procedures is a series of questions: *who? what? where? when? why? how?* This method for discovering subject matter has been useful for newspaper reporters, who must give complete accounts of human events.

The list is not as simple as it might appear, however. If the questions are answered superficially, the procedure will be unproductive, resulting in undeveloped reports such as the following:

who?	Bert Simmons
what?	spilled acid on his hand
where?	in the chemistry lab
when?	this morning
why?	because he was careless;
how?	he overturned a bottle filled with acid.

And yet, if one asks the questions seriously, deeply, probingly, interesting things begin to happen. Let's think about what the six questions imply in regard to the little event that is reported above.

who?	What kind of person is Bert Simmons? Is he typically slipshod and careless? What is his relationship to me? How much does he mean to me? Why?
what?	What are the details of the action? Did Bert scream with pain? Did the acid damage the lab? What were the reactions of the onlookers? Did someone call a doctor?
where?	What is the lab like? How does it look? Smell? How do I feel about it? How does Bert feel about it?
when?	Why is the time important? Was Bert sleepy and not alert? Was this the usual time for lab work? Why was or was not this the usual time for lab work?
why?	What were the circumstances? Was Bert angry or worried? Was the lab equipment faulty? Does Bert seem to be self-destructive? Did anyone else have an influence on the mishap?
how?	In detail, what happened? Was there anything strange or unusual about the event? Do such things often occur in the lab? Was Bert paying attention to instructions? Was he following lab rules?

Of course, the number of questions that could be generated is endless. The original questions are just probes to get the inquiry under way.

This method is excellent for gathering ideas concerning events. You can use it not only to gain understanding of your immediate experiences but also to analyze and understand current events in the news as well as happenings in history. It is also an excellent guide to understanding what you read, whether poetry, fiction, or "fact."

Note: as with all discovery procedures, you should write down the ideas that this one generates. *All of the ideas.* When you are gathering subject matter for writing, you should not judge the validity or even the sanity of the ideas you discover. When you begin to choose and assemble your ideas for writing, you can discard those that are illogical or beside the point.

Exercise: Questioning

1. Get a copy of a current issue of your local newspaper, and analyze the lead story for the day. Point out the details of *who? what? where? when? why? how?* that the writer has included in the story. Are you satisfied with the information the story supplies? What more do you want to know that the story does not supply?

2. As a class activity, choose a recent event on campus: an election, a rally, an athletic event, a change in college rules or regulations. Now use the questions to discover information and ideas concerning that event.

3. Your problem now is to explain the traditional ballad "Barbara Allan." As a group activity, use the questions to see if you can gain an understanding of the poem.

Barbara Allan

It was in and about the Martinmas time,
  When the green leaves were a-falling,
That Sir John Graeme, in the West Country,
  Fell in love with Barbara Allan.

He sent his men down through the town
  To the place where she was dwelling:
"O haste and come to my master dear,
  If ye be Barbara Allan."

O slowly, slowly rose she up,
  To the place where he was lying,
And when she drew the curtain by,
  "Young man, I think you're dying."

"O it's I'm sick, and very sick,
  And 'tis all for Barbara Allan."
"O the better for me you'll never be,
  Though your heart's blood were a-spilling.

"O dinna ye mind, young man," said she,
  "When ye was in the tavern a-drinking,
That ye made the healths go round and round,
  And slighted Barbara Allan?"

And slowly, slowly rose she up,
  And slowly, slowly left him,
And sighing said, she could not stay,
  Since death of life had reft him.

She had not gone a mile but two
  When she heard the dead-bell ringing,
And every stroke the dead-bell gave,
  It cried Woe to Barbara Allan!

"O mother, mother, make my bed!
  O make it soft and narrow!
Since my love died for me today,
  I'll die for him tomorrow."

The Pentad

The *Pentad*[4] is a set of five categories that may at first seem very much like the questions in the last section but, as you will discover shortly, it has significant (and useful) differences. In *A Grammar of Motives,* Kenneth Burke explains that in order to understand any human action—anything that people do, say, or think—you need relatively complete answers to the following questions:

Act	What was done?
Agent	Who did it?
Agency	By what means or with what was it done?
Scene	Where and when was it done?
Purpose	Why was it done?

As with the six questions, the answers to these five questions can be superficial (and therefore useless), or they can be thorough and penetrating (and therefore useful).

Some comments on the terms of the five categories will help you understand why it is different from the other questions.

Act. People perform acts. When a rock falls off a cliff, a *motion,* not an act, has occurred. Therefore, the term *act* focuses

---

[4] Developed by Kenneth Burke, *A Grammar of Motives* (Berkeley: Univ. of California Press, 1969).

sharply on the human situation. Furthermore, acts are motivated; there is a human reason for them. When I blink my eyes, I am not performing an act, but a motion, for there is no motive, only physiological reflex. When I chew on the end of my pencil, I may be performing an act—there may be some psychological reason for what I'm doing—but I may simply be performing a meaningless motion. When I shout "Watch out!" to a person who is about to step in front of a car, I am performing an act that can be analyzed in human terms.

Agent. This term names the doer of the action. Unlike the *who* of the six questions, *agent* implies a relationship between the act and the doer of the act.

Agency. We can interpret this word very broadly. Here are some possibilities. (1) Agency can be language, as the agency for a warning is the sentence "Look out!" or as the agency for "Barbara Allan" is the language that the poet chose. (2) Agency can also be some kind of instrument, as is the case with the murder weapon in a detective story. (3) Agency can be logic, as when I convince you of my point of view through the use of logical argumentation. (4) In the case of an article or book, the agency can be the publisher. The agency can also be the pen or pencil with which you write. In short, agency can be anything whereby acts are brought into being.

Scene. You can broaden or narrow this term at will. For instance: the seconds during which you read these words; the week in which you read them; the year; the century. The place where you sit as you read these words; the building; the city; the country. But you need not interpret scene literally. It can also be, for instance, the ethical, economic, or political context of an act, as the scene in which the Constitution of the United States was written was the "Age of Enlightenment" or the "Age of Reason," and it is unlikely that the Constitution could have been produced in a different sort of "scene." In terms of plays and movies, scene is very important: Dracula strikes on foggy nights; tragedy usually does not occur on sunny spring days.

Purpose. Apparent purpose is not always real purpose. The real purpose of a patent-medicine ad is to sell products, not to cure illnesses. To understand any speech or writing, you must find out the purpose behind it—and that applies to individual sentences, as well as to essays, novels, and so on. For example, if an instructor says to his students, "I promise you that you'll study for this class," we cannot really understand what he means until we know whether he is threatening or promising.

Practice: The Pentad

The following brief items are from the "Newsmakers" section of *Newsweek* for March 13, 1978.[5] They will serve as a first demonstration of the usefulness of the Pentad.

1. In regard to the following item, ask as many questions and record as much information as you can about the *agents* involved. Then be prepared to discuss whether or not this in-depth probing of the agents gives you insights into or ideas about the piece.

Had Richard Nixon recruited David Frost to help edit the Nixon memoirs? So said The New York Trib in a front-page "exclusive," and it was true—after a fashion. However, the Frost who was penciling at San Clemente wasn't the dapper British TV celebrity but a bespectacled, goateed, and somewhat rumpled publishing executive from Brooklyn who has been getting double takes at his name for years. Frost heads a three-man editing team sent to California by Nixon's publishers, Grosset & Dunlap, last July for an eight-week editing job. Eight months later, they are still ensconced in the San Clemente Inn.

In a conference room only a few hundred yards from Casa Pacifica, and next door to the fallen President's own team of writer-researchers, Frost and his staffers tackle material that has been dictated by Nixon to his writers and polished into prose. Said co-editor Nancy Brooks: "This is Nixon's 'Roots'—where he came from, what his growing up was like." Rigidly chronological and not focused on Watergate, it begins with Nixon's birth "in the house my father built" and ends on Aug. 9, 1974, the day he resigned. Revisions since publication of H. R. Haldeman's "The Ends of Power," Brooks said, have been "negligible." As for blockbusters, "there are a lot of little things, but no one big thing," claimed indexer Bob Daugherty. If Nixon knows who "Deep Throat" is, he's not saying. Nor is he using the book to charge that he was hounded from office: "There's very little vindictiveness," said Daugherty. Added Brooks: "He's attempting to describe what he did and why he did it." In the end, Frost surmised, readers will be surprised at how "personal and candid" Nixon can be. Summed up Daugherty: "I don't think anyone will have a radically different profile of him. You will have more sympathy for him, but I don't think you change your evaluation of him as a person or as a President."

2. What influence does *scene* have on your understanding of the following item?

As Revlon's "Charlie" girl, model Shelley Hack is trailing the scent of success. But as No. 3 in the Perfume War behind Catherine Deneuve (Chanel) and Margaux Hemingway ("Babe"), she was stuck with an implacably wholesome image. So the long-stemmed beauty started a small skirmish by posing with a decidedly un-"Charlie" look. "Hot stuff, huh?" she grinned. "I do try to be well-rounded." Hack's act has always varied: a Smith College graduate, she studied archeology in Australia, hitchhiked through Bora-Bora and now prefers the quiet life on her farm in upstate New York—where she raises flowers—to the swinging social scene in the city. "I don't see myself as the next Cheryl Tiegs or Farrah Fawcett-Majors," she explained. "My main concern is being an actress." To date, she landed a walk-on in "Annie Hall" and a leading role in "If Ever I See You Again." But others see Shelley up there with the supermodels, and Columbia Pictures has decided a pinup poster is in order. Her spokeswoman shrugged, "Why not? It's a good gimmick. If it's cute and sexy, you'll buy it, right?"

3. Now focus on the act itself. What significance does the act reported in the following piece have? (Is the act somehow like a ritual or ceremony? Does it have political implications? Or is it merely an ordinary, everyday event?)

It was not the pomp, or the power, but the sheer pleasure of playing for his biggest fan that drew the private Vladimir Horowitz to a rare White House recital on the 50th anniversary of his American concert debut. And the President was wowed. "He's never played better," Jimmy Carter told violinist Isaac Stern after the most glittering cultural event yet staged during Carter's tenure. "Incredible," Stern agreed. Before a select audience of 200 guests—and millions more who watched the recital later on public television—Carter hailed the Russian-born pianist's "fearless expression of emotion." The White House has been host to "a lot of great people," said Carter, "but never a greater man or a greater performance." Afterward, Horowitz got his chance to return the compliment. Was he really the "true national treasure" that Carter claimed? "If he says so, I have to agree," Horowitz chuckled. "He is the judge." And he added, "The President knows his music very well."

4. Think about and discuss *purpose* in the following piece. Remember that many acts have several purposes and that a purpose is seldom uncomplicated.

It was billed as an evening of "Birds, Beasts and Flowers," performed by a royal thrush. To celebrate International Wildlife Year, Monaco's Princess Grace returned to her native land for a ten-day series of poetry readings. Hours before her appearance at Pittsburgh's Carnegie Hall, Grace nervously downed lemon and honey to soothe a cold. But sharing the stage with actor Richard Pasco of the Royal Shakespeare Company, she flawlessly recited two hours of verse, over 60 selections that included Keats's "Ode to a Nightingale," William Blake's "The Tiger" and Sandburg's "Blossom Themes." To nearly 2,000 fans, the onetime Academy Award winner was poetry in motion, but "I'm not taking up my career where I left off," Grace insisted. That was in a 1952 New York production called, appropriately, "To Be Continued."

5. In order to gain the full meaning of the following item, we must understand the *agencies* involved. What are they? Why do they give the piece meaning?

"You know what they say," twanged Nebraskan Henry Fonda: "It's not how good you are, it's how long you last." Over four decades, Fonda had proved himself both the Galahad and the grand old man of American cinema, portraying such folk heroes as Abe Lincoln, Mister Roberts, Wyatt Earp and Tom Joad. Last week, before a star-studded audience at a Beverly Hills dinner, the 72-year-old actor got what he richly deserved: a Life Achievement Award from the American Film Institute. (CBS will air the tribute as a special on March 15.) In his speech of thanks, Fonda recalled his boyhood feuds with his father over acting. Finally, after viewing Henry in a local play, his father cut short a critical sister with a sharp rebuke: "Shut up, he's perfect." Echoing, Fonda told daughter Jane's critics: "Shut up, she's perfect." The silver-haired Fonda was reminded that despite 80 screen appearances, he had never won the coveted Oscar. "I voted for you," assured buddy Jimmy Stewart, whose own "Philadelphia Story" triumphed over Fonda's 1940 classic, "Grapes of Wrath." "Of course," ribbed Jimmy, "I also voted for Alf Landon, Wendell Willkie and Thomas Dewey."

So you can view the Pentad as a series of questions that will give you a way to begin understanding and discussing any human act. And the five categories are also useful for discussing works of literature:

> Act = *plot*
> Agents = *characters*
> Agency = *medium* (film, book, etc.), *genre* (play, poem, story), and *style* or *language*
> Scene = *scene* (setting; time and place)
> Purpose = *motivation* (why the characters do what they do)

You might want to turn back to the ballad of "Barbara Allan" and reconsider it from the standpoint of the Pentad.

By a very simple maneuver, you can make the categories more complicated, but also more penetrating, more powerful. You can consider any one term from the standpoints of all the others. This will give you twenty *ratios*, each implying a question. The Pentad itself implies only five master questions.

In the following, *agent* is considered from the standpoint of the other four terms:

Ratios	*Questions*
agent-scene	What does scene reveal about the agent(s)?
agent-agency	What does agency reveal about the agent(s)?
agent-act	What does act reveal about the agent(s)?
agent-purpose	What does purpose reveal about the agent(s)?

Exercise: Ratios of the Pentad

Construct the rest of the ratios, and state the questions that these ratios imply.

The following is an article from the October 6, 1979, issue of *TV Guide*. Read the article, and pay close attention to the kinds of questions that the five categories can develop concerning it (pages 78–79).

Words Take the Place of Blood

Richard C. Hottelet

Each fall, from our CBS booth, we watch the members of the human family come together for three months in the UN General Assembly. They are all sizes, shapes, colors and conditions but this is the one place on Earth where they meet as political equals. Some, of course, are more equal than others. Others behave as though they were.

Over the past 20 years, the opening spectacle has become more colorful—more men and women in national dress—togas of kente cloth from Ghana, shorts and feathers from Swaziland, saris and sarongs mixing amiably. Many know each other from earlier Assemblies and other meetings through the year. Their camaraderie is genuine—but there is less to it than meets the eye. Getting below the bright holiday surface and staying with the often shabby political reality is the reporter's everyday job.

Never has there been nor is there likely to be another United Na-

WORDS TAKE THE PLACE OF BLOOD   Richard C. Hottelet, *TV Guide*, 6–12 Oct. 1979, pp. 2–6. Reprinted with permission from *TV Guide*® Magazine. Copyright © 1979 by Triangle Publications, Inc., Radnor, Pennsylvania.

tions General Assembly like the one that convened in New York in September 1960, my first year as CBS's UN correspondent. History crackled in the great blue-and-gold Assembly chamber. Nikita Khrushchev brought all the leaders of the Soviet bloc. The non-aligned came in force: Nehru, Tito, Nasser, Indonesia's Sukarno and Kwame Nkrumah of Ghana, not to mention Fidel Castro. President Dwight Eisenhower spoke for the United States, Prime Minister Harold MacMillan for Britain.

Khrushchev came to cheer decolonization—and to whip it to a headlong pace. The Assembly—the admission that year of 17 new member states, former colonial territories, had brought its membership to 99—declared that no colony could be denied independence because it was politically, economically or socially unprepared. Today the UN has 151 members. The politics of economic development, the struggle between the haves and have-nots, has been added to the East-West and regional rivalries that shape the world. In 1960 that explosive mixture produced one of the UN's most melodramatic scenes, starring Khrushchev, his hammering fists and his old brown shoe.

Khrushchev's pounding on his desk was not low comedy. His disruptive intervention set severe limits to the UN's peacekeeping powers in the Congo and destroyed Dag Hammarskjold politically long before he died in a plane crash the following year. But the volatile Soviet leader rose to new histrionic heights when a Filipino speaker demanded that any discussion of imperialism deal also with the Soviet empire and its subject peoples. Khrushchev obviously felt that his and all his friends' drumming fists could not adequately answer such an outrage. He took off his shoe and pounded on his desk. To stop the ensuing pandemonium, Assembly president Frederick Boland of Ireland adjourned the session with such vigor that he broke his gavel.

Khrushchev's shoe was unforgettable. Unfortunately, it remains so only in memory. The TV networks had not activated their cameras in the booths overlooking the Assembly hall. The UN's own cameras did not catch the performance; whether they were being discreet or just slow will never be entirely clear. There is no filmed record.

Other climaxes were recorded. Adlai Stevenson cornered Russia's Valerian Zorin at the height of the Cuban missile crisis in 1962, and offered before the Security Council to wait "until hell freezes over" for Zorin to deny that Moscow was placing nuclear missiles in Cuba. Zorin demurred and Stevenson produced the photographic evidence.

Henry Cabot Lodge rebuffed Soviet charges of aggressive U.S. espionage after the U-2 was shot down on its way across the Soviet Union in 1960 and an RB-47 was brought down off the Soviet Arctic coast. Lodge showed the Security Council a large carved wooden seal of the United States, a gift to the U.S. Ambassador in Moscow from workers who had decorated the embassy residence. It contained a bug that for quite a while beamed to the secret police, the KGB, every word spoken in the Ambassador's study.

A broadcast journalist works with deadlines as sharp and pitiless as a guillotine. For everything less than the most urgent information, 30 seconds late is too late altogether. How often have we cursed a long-winded speaker's delaying a Council decision until it just missed the *CBS Evening News*. American politicians have learned to pace themselves to prime time. Foreigners have not. Some of them speak mainly for the written record, where the timing hardly counts. Others speak, apparently, just to hear what they have to say. The result can be excruciating in many ways. Toward the end of the Six Day War, when Syria, in utter defeat and fearing even the fall of Damascus, frantically urged the Council to order a cease fire, Saudi Arabia's Jamil Baroody held up the proceedings with one of his endless, pointless statements. The Syrian Ambassador approached apoplexy. The Israeli army advanced on the Golan Heights. When the Council finally acted, one Arab ambassador told us sourly, "Baroody was the equivalent of two Israeli divisions."

Looking back, 1967 marks a turning point in UN coverage. From then on, the support and sympathy that had characterized American public opinion since the UN was created at San Francisco in 1945 seemed to turn to cynicism and contempt. People forgot that it was not set up as a world government. It has no power to pass laws, let alone enforce them. The UN was meant to be a forum where controversy may—but need not—lead to consensus. It is an instrument for the world community to use when it agrees to do so. Given the foibles of the human race, this happens seldom—and then, not tidily. By 1967, the UN was manifestly no longer the Western club that did what the West thought was right.

It also seemed unable to act in the general interest. For example, when Secretary General Kurt Waldheim, after the massacre of Israeli athletes at the Munich Olympics, put terrorism on the General Assembly's agenda, he hit a stone wall. One man's terrorist is another man's freedom fighter.

The bitter fact that the clash of political interests has kept the UN from doing anything at all about most of the nearly 150 wars the world has seen since 1945, or about the massive violations of human rights acted out every day—most recently against the Vietnamese boat people—leads many to write the organization off as useless and hypocritical. The American public, which tends to regard both national and international politics as a spectator sport, simply turns away from what it does not like. One classic example—when the Arabs ganged up against Israel in UNESCO several years ago, people stopped buying UNICEF Christmas cards, confusing the initials of the two totally different UN agencies.

A widespread conclusion that the UN is largely irrelevant has reduced interest in what happens there. Coverage has fallen noticeably in the American press, both print and broadcast. Many major newspapers have shut their UN bureaus. TV and radio network correspondents have a harder job competing for air time, especially as the national audience concentrates more on domestic headaches. Going to the mat with the producer, who functions as the editor in the TV scheme of things, to get an additional 30 seconds to explain a point or to retain 15 seconds of text that is hard to cover with pictures has become increasingly arduous.

In itself, the UN is not a picture story. The scene at the Security Council table or in the General Assembly hall is always essentially the same. It draws its power from what is said and done, how and by whom—on camera. Seldom, if ever, is there an occurrence that speaks for itself. Crisis can electrify the formal proceedings—the Middle East wars, conflicts in Asia and Africa, the Cuban missile showdown and the Soviet invasions of Hungary and Czechoslovakia. Personalities command attention—a recent example being the emotional resignation speech by Andrew Young, the first American UN Ambassador to resign over policy differences with his Government.

However, without the visible crisis or the colorful visitors, it can be agonizingly difficult—or impossible—to get time for the slow-moving, complex, inconclusive story that is the UN. The UN reporter, competing with the latest inflation or energy bulletin from Washington, loses the toss when, asked what the latest resolution means concretely, he is forced to admit that its practical effect is hard to gauge.

Compressing and clarifying without distorting and oversimplifying is the constant challenge. Meeting it within minutes or seconds can be downright harrowing. There are other hazards. Like a surgeon, a reporter must care enough about each case to give it the necessary thought and effort; but not so much as to become emotionally engaged. No matter that he has opinions; he cannot espouse causes or identify with one party. To get the information he needs from Arabs and Israelis, Greeks and Turks, Russians and Chinese, not to mention any number of other sensitive egos, they must all believe that however annoying the reporter may be, he is honestly trying to be impartial.

Some difficulties that an outsider might envisage do not really exist. In this Tower of Babel on the East River, there is no language barrier. Everyone understands what is said. If people choose to call each other liars or to harp on opposite sides of an issue, it is for political reasons. The reporter's game is to trace the reasons.

National customs and diplomatic protocol are no impediment. Ambassadors are not more likely to be stuffed shirts than are bankers or businessmen. Getting along with them requires only the kind of courtesy and consideration it takes to deal amicably with any stranger. In fact, the varied cast of characters is part of the attraction of this world theater. You see that human intelligence knows no color bar. Some of the brightest and nicest men and women come from remote lands and (to us) exotic cultures.

The UN remains a mirror of the world. Everything is here: truth and falsehood, noise and silence, success and failure for the observer to sort out. It is usually more a detective yarn for the ear than a cut-and-thrust drama played out for the camera's eye. But, all the great elements of conflict are present, except that—and this may be the UN's saving grace—words that do not kill take the place of blood.

Agent(s)-Scene(s)

The article says that in the scene of the United Nations, representatives meet as political equals, even though some are more equal than others. What effect does that equality have on UN negotiations? On the world and its politics in general? What effect does the scene—for instance, the lengthy speeches that take place in it—have on the broadcast journalist?

What are some of the advantages of the scene?

What are the nonexistent difficulties that outsiders imagine? How does this information influence your judgment of the scene?

Can the scene be compared to others? Which ones? What are the results of the comparisons?

Agent(s)-Acts

What are some of the specific acts that the author describes?

Why does he describe these acts?

What acts do the members of the UN seem unable to perform?

Why?

What kinds of acts is a reporter at the UN forced to perform? How does the author describe the act of reporting?

Agent-Agencies

What effects do the broadcast media, particularly TV, have on UN reporters?

Do any of the agents discussed in the article use particular agencies to make their points? What is the effect?

How would a newspaper report on the UN differ from a

TV report? What could a writer accomplish that a TV reporter could not?

Agent(s)-Purpose(s)

Why did Hottelet write the article?
What do you learn about the purposes of members of the UN?
Why do you think members of the UN are so cordial to one another, almost as if they were members of a club?

These are only some of the items that the four ratios can generate concerning the article and its subject. You could undoubtedly add many items to the lists. The important thing to notice is this:

1. Some of the items generated were nothing more than the "facts" that appeared in the article. The Pentad or categories, like any other discovery procedure, serve to call your attention to the "facts" of the case, information that is right before your eyes, but that you might overlook.
2. Some of the items probably were bits of information that you had already stored in your mind. A discovery procedure serves to probe your memory, bringing forth knowledge that you already have.
3. Some of the items were questions that could be answered through (a) further thought or logic, or (b) research.

Each time you switch to a new ratio, you get a slightly different angle on the subject, a new perspective that is likely to produce ideas, and that, after all, is the purpose of a discovery procedure: to get you out of your tunnel vision and to make you see your subject from many different perspectives.

Exercise: The Pentad Again

1. The twenty ratios of the Pentad or five categories imply these five questions:

   a. What can I learn about the *act* through considering agent, scene, agency, and purpose?
   b. What can I learn about the *agent* through considering act, scene, agency, purpose?
   c. What can I learn about the *scene* through considering act, agent, agency, purpose?

d. What can I learn about the *agency* through considering act, agent, scene, purpose?

e. What can I learn about the *purpose* through considering act, agent, scene, agency?

To begin finding ideas for a paper concerning the United Nations, apply the five questions to "Words Take the Place of Blood" (pages 74–78). You can do this as a class activity or as an individual exercise.

2. Probably at some time in your college career, you will be asked to write an explanation of a piece of literature, and, as has been said, using the Pentad is an excellent way to get into a poem, story, or play.

"The Lottery," by Shirley Jackson, is an extremely popular and intriguing short story. Read this story—reprinted below—and use the categories to generate ideas that will explain the story's meaning.

First you can simply use the five master questions as a guide to understanding the "surface" of the story:

Act (plot): What happens?

Agents (characters): What sort of people are the characters?

Scene (scene): What is the scene?

Agency (form and language): What devices of narration and style does the author use?

Purpose (motivation): Why do the characters do what they do?

After you have scanned the story with help from the Pentad, apply the ratios, and then discuss the following questions:

a. What new insights, if any, did the ratios reveal?

b. Do you feel that you now know enough about the story to begin planning an essay on it? Explain.

c. Do the five categories and their ratios give you any ideas about how to organize your paper? Explain.

The Lottery

Shirley Jackson

The morning of June 27th was clear and sunny, with the fresh warmth of a full-summer day; the flowers were blossoming profusely and the grass was richly green. The people of the village began to gather in the square, between the post office and the bank, around ten o'clock; in some towns there were so many people that the lottery took two days and had to be started on June 26th, but in this village, where there were only about three hundred people, the whole lottery took less than two hours, so it could begin at ten o'clock in the morning and still be through in time to allow the villagers to get home for noon dinner.

The children assembled first, of course. School was recently over for the summer, and the feeling of liberty sat uneasily on most of them; they tended to gather together quietly for a while before they broke into boisterous play, and their talk was still of the classroom and the teacher, of books and reprimands. Bobby Martin had already stuffed his pockets full of stones, and the other boys soon followed his example, selecting the smoothest and roundest stones; Bobby and Harry Jones and Dickie Delacroix—the villagers pronounced this name "Dellacroy"—eventually made a great pile of stones in one corner of the square and guarded it against the raids of the other boys. The girls stood aside, talking among themselves, looking over their shoulders at the boys, and the very small children rolled in the dust or clung to the hands of their older brothers or sisters.

Soon the men began to gather, surveying their own children, speaking of planting and rain, tractors and taxes. They stood together, away from the pile of stones in the corner, and their jokes were quiet and they smiled rather than laughed. The women, wearing faded house dresses and sweaters, came shortly after their menfolk. They greeted one another and exchanged bits of gossip as they went to join their husbands. Soon the women, standing by their husbands, began to call to their children, and the children came reluctantly, having to be called four or five times. Bobby Martin ducked under his mother's grasping hand and ran, laughing, back to the pile of stones. His father spoke up sharply, and Bobby came quickly and took his place between his father and his oldest brother.

The lottery was conducted—as were the square dances, the teen-age club, the Halloween program—by Mr. Summers, who had time and energy to devote to civic activities. He was a round-faced, jovial man and he ran the coal business, and people were sorry for him, because he had no children and his wife was a scold. When he arrived in the square, carrying the black wooden box, there was a murmur of conversation among the villagers, and he waved and called, "Little late today, folks." The postmaster, Mr. Graves, followed him, carrying a three-legged stool, and the stool was put in the center of the square and Mr. Summers set the black box down on it. The villagers kept their distance, leaving a space between themselves and the stool, and when Mr. Summers said, "Some of you fellows want to give me a hand?" there was a hesitation before two men, Mr. Martin and his oldest son, Baxter, came forward to hold the box steady on the stool while Mr. Summers stirred up the papers inside it.

The original paraphernalia for the lottery had been lost long ago, and the black box now resting on the stool had been put into use even before Old Man Warner, the oldest man in town, was born. Mr. Summers spoke frequently to the villagers about making a new box, but no one liked to upset even as much tradition as was represented by the black box. There was a story that the present box had been made with some pieces of the box that had preceded it, the one that had been constructed when the first people settled down to make a village here. Every year, after the lottery, Mr. Summers began talking again about a new box, but every year the subject was allowed to fade off without anything's being done. The black box grew shabbier each year; by now it was no longer completely black but splintered badly along one side to show the original wood color, and in some places faded or stained.

Mr. Martin and his oldest son, Baxter, held the black box securely on the stool until Mr. Summers had stirred the papers thoroughly with his hand.

Because so much of the ritual had been forgotten or discarded, Mr. Summers had been successful in having slips of paper substituted for the chips of wood that had been used for generations. Chips of wood, Mr. Summers had argued, had been all very well when the village was tiny, but now that the population was more than three hundred and likely to keep on growing, it was necessary to use something that would fit more easily into the black box. The night before the lottery, Mr. Summers and Mr. Graves made up the slips of paper and put them in the box, and it was then taken to the safe of Mr. Summers' coal company and locked up until Mr. Summers was ready to take it to the square next morning. The rest of the year, the box was put away, sometimes one place, sometimes another; it had spent one year in Mr. Graves's barn and another year underfoot in the post office, and sometimes it was set on a shelf in the Martin grocery and left there.

There was a great deal of fussing to be done before Mr. Summers declared the lottery open. There were the lists to make up—of heads of families, heads of households in each family, members of each household in each family. There was the proper swearing-in of Mr. Summers by the postmaster, as the official of the lottery; at one time, some people remembered, there had been a recital of some sort, performed by the official of the lottery, a perfunctory, tuneless chant that had been rattled off duly each year; some people believed that the official of the lottery used to stand just so when he said or sang it, others believed that he was supposed to walk among the people, but years and years ago this part of the ritual had been allowed to lapse. There had been, also, a ritual salute, which the official of the lottery had had to use in addressing each person who came up to draw from the box, but this also had changed with time, until now it was felt necessary only for the official to speak to each person approaching. Mr. Summers was very good at all this; in his clean white shirt and blue jeans, with one hand resting carelessly on the black box, he seemed very proper and important as he talked interminably to Mr. Graves and the Martins.

Just as Mr. Summers finally left off talking and turned to the assembled villagers, Mrs. Hutchinson came hurriedly along the path to the square, her sweater thrown over her shoulders, and slid into place in the back of the crowd. "Clean forgot what day it was," she said to Mrs. Delacroix, who stood next to her, and they both laughed softly. "Thought my old man was out back stacking wood," Mrs. Hutchinson went on, "and then I looked out the window and the kids were gone, and then I remembered it was the twenty-seventh and came a-running." She dried her hands on her apron, and Mrs. Delacroix said, "You're in time, though. They're still talking away up there."

Mrs. Hutchinson craned her neck to see through the crowd and found her husband and children standing near the front. She tapped Mrs. Delacroix on the arm as a farewell and began to make her way through the crowd. The people separated good-humoredly to let her through; two or three people said, in voices just loud enough to be heard across the crowd, "Here comes your Missus, Hutchinson," and "Bill, she made it after all." Mrs. Hutchinson reached her husband, and Mr. Summers, who had been waiting, said cheerfully, "Thought we were going to have to get on without you, Tessie." Mrs. Hutchinson said, grinning, "Wouldn't have me leave m'dishes in the sink, now, would you, Joe?" and soft laughter ran through the crowd as the people stirred back into position after Mrs. Hutchinson's arrival.

"Well, now," Mr. Summers said soberly, "guess we better get started, get this over with, so's we can go back to work. Anybody ain't here?"

"Dunbar," several people said. "Dunbar, Dunbar."

Mr. Summers consulted his list. "Clyde Dunbar," he said. "That's right. He's broke his leg, hasn't he? Who's drawing for him?"

"Me, I guess," a woman said, and Mr. Summers turned to look at her. "Wife draws for her husband," Mr. Summers said. "Don't you have a grown boy to do it for you, Janey?" Although Mr. Summers and everyone else in the village knew the answer perfectly well, it was the business of the official of the lottery to ask such questions formally. Mr. Summers waited with an expression of polite interest while Mrs. Dunbar answered.

"Horace's not but sixteen yet," Mrs. Dunbar said regretfully. "Guess I gotta fill in for the old man this year."

"Right," Mr. Summers said. He made a note on the list he was holding. Then he asked, "Watson boy drawing this year?"

A tall boy in the crowd raised his hand. "Here," he said. "I'm drawing for m'mother and me." He blinked his eyes nervously and ducked his head as several voices in the crowd said things like "Good fellow, Jack," and "Glad to see your mother's got a man to do it."

"Well," Mr. Summers said, "guess that's everyone. Old Man Warner make it?"

"Here," a voice said, and Mr. Summers nodded.

A sudden hush fell on the crowd as Mr. Summers cleared his throat and looked at the list. "All ready?" he called. "Now, I'll read the names—heads of families first—and the men come up and take a paper out of the box. Keep the paper folded in your hand without looking at it until everyone has had a turn. Everything clear?"

The people had done it so many times that they only half listened to the directions; most of them were quiet, wetting their lips, not looking around. Then Mr. Summers raised one hand high and said, "Adams." A man disengaged himself from the crowd and came forward. "Hi, Steve," Mr. Summers said, and Mr. Adams said, "Hi, Joe." They grinned at one another humorlessly and nervously. Then Mr. Adams reached into the black box and took out a folded paper. He held it firmly by one corner as he turned and went hastily back to his place in the crowd, where he stood a little apart from his family, not looking down at his hand.

"Allen," Mr. Summers said. "Anderson . . . Bentham."

"Seems like there's no time at all between lotteries any more," Mrs. Delacroix said to Mrs. Graves in the back row. "Seems like we got through with the last one only last week."

"Time sure goes fast," Mrs. Graves said.

"Clark . . . Delacroix."

"There goes my old man," Mrs. Delacroix said. She held her breath while her husband went forward.

"Dunbar," Mr. Summers said, and Mrs. Dunbar went steadily to the box while one of the women said, "Go on, Janey," and another said, "There she goes."

"We're next," Mrs. Graves said. She watched while Mr. Graves came around from the side of the box, greeted Mr. Summers gravely, and selected a slip of paper from the box. By now, all through the crowd there were men holding the small folded papers in their large hands, turning them over and over nervously. Mrs. Dunbar and her two sons stood together, Mrs. Dunbar holding the slip of paper.

"Harburt . . . Hutchinson."

"Get up there, Bill," Mrs. Hutchinson said, and the people near her laughed.

"Jones."

"They do say," Mr. Adams said to Old Man Warner, who stood next to him, "that over in the north village they're talking of giving up the lottery."

Old Man Warner snorted. "Pack of crazy fools," he said. "Listening to the young folks, nothing's good enough for *them*. Next thing you know, they'll be wanting to go back to living in caves, nobody work any more, live *that* way for a while. Used to be a saying about 'Lottery in June, corn be heavy soon.' First thing you know, we'd all be eating stewed chickweed and acorns. There's *always* been a lottery," he added petulantly. "Bad enough to see young Joe Summers up there joking with everybody."

"Some places have already quit lotteries," Mrs. Adams said.

"Nothing but trouble in *that*," Old Man Warner said stoutly. "Pack of young fools."

"Martin." And Bobby Martin watched his father go forward. "Overdyke . . . Percy."

"I wish they'd hurry," Mrs. Dunbar said to her older son. "I wish they'd hurry."

"They're almost through," her son said.

"You get ready to run tell Dad," Mrs. Dunbar said.

Mr. Summers called his own name and then stepped forward precisely and selected a slip from the box. Then he called, "Warner."

"Seventy-seventh year I been in the lottery," Old Man Warner said as he went through the crowd. "Seventy-seventh time."

"Watson." The tall boy came awkwardly through the crowd. Someone said, "Don't be nervous, Jack," and Mr. Summers said, "Take your time, son."

"Zanini."

After that, there was a long pause, a breathless pause, until Mr. Summers, holding his slip of paper in the air, said, "All right, fellows." For a minute, no one moved, and then all the slips of paper were opened. Suddenly, all the women began to speak at once, saying, "Who is it?" "Who's got it?" "Is it the Dunbars?" "Is it the Watsons?" Then the voices began to say, "It's Hutchinson. It's Bill," "Bill Hutchinson's got it."

"Go tell your father," Mrs. Dunbar said to her older son.

People began to look around to see the Hutchinsons. Bill Hutchinson was standing quiet, staring down at the paper in his hand. Suddenly, Tessie Hutchinson shouted to Mr. Summers, "You didn't give him time enough to take any paper he wanted. I saw you. It wasn't fair."

"Be a good sport, Tessie." Mrs. Delacroix called, and Mrs. Graves said, "All of us took the same chance."

"Shut up, Tessie," Bill Hutchinson said.

"Well, everyone," Mr. Summers said, "that was done pretty fast, and now we've got to be hurrying a little more to get done in time." He consulted his next list. "Bill," he said, "you draw for the Hutchinson family. You got any other households in the Hutchinsons?"

"There's Don and Eva," Mrs. Hutchinson yelled. "Make *them* take their chance!"

"Daughters draw with their husband's families, Tessie," Mr. Summers said gently. "You know that as well as anyone else."

"It wasn't *fair*," Tessie said.

"I guess not, Joe," Bill Hutchinson said regretfully. "My daughter draws with her husband's family, that's only fair. And I've got no other family except the kids."

"Then, as far as drawing for families is concerned, it's you," Mr. Summers said in explanation, "and as far as drawing for households is concerned, that's you, too. Right?"

"Right," Bill Hutchinson said.

"How many kids, Bill?" Mr. Summers asked formally.

"Three," Bill Hutchinson said. "There's Bill, Jr., and Nancy, and little Dave. And Tessie and me."

"All right, then," Mr. Summers said. "Harry, you got their tickets back?"

Mr. Graves nodded and held up the slips of paper. "Put them in the box, then," Mr. Summers directed. "Take Bill's and put it in."

"I think we ought to start over," Mrs. Hutchinson said, as quietly as she could. "I tell you it wasn't *fair*. You didn't give him time enough to choose. *Every*body saw that."

Mr. Graves had selected the five slips and put them in the box, and he dropped all the papers but those onto the ground, where the breeze caught them and lifted them off.

"Listen, everybody," Mrs. Hutchinson was saying to the people around her.

"Ready, Bill?" Mr. Summers asked, and Bill Hutchinson, with one quick glance around at his wife and children, nodded.

"Remember," Mr. Summers said, "take the slips and keep them folded until each person has taken one. Harry, you help little Dave." Mr. Graves took the hand of the little boy, who came willingly with him up to the box. "Take a paper out of the box, Davy," Mr. Summers said. Davy put his hand into the box and laughed. "Take just *one* paper," Mr. Summers said. "Harry, you hold it for him." Mr. Graves took the child's hand and removed the folded paper from the tight fist and held it while little Dave stood next to him and looked up at him wonderingly.

"Nancy next," Mr. Summers said. Nancy was twelve, and her school friends breathed heavily as she went forward, switching her skirt, and took a slip daintily from the box. "Bill, Jr.," Mr. Summers said, and Billy, his face red and his feet over-large, nearly knocked the box over as he got a paper out. "Tessie," Mr. Summers said. She hesitated for a minute, looking around defiantly, and then set her lips and went up to the box. She snatched a paper out and held it behind her.

"Bill," Mr. Summers said, and Bill Hutchinson reached into the box and felt around, bringing his hand out at last with the slip of paper in it.

The crowd was quiet. A girl whispered, "I hope it's not Nancy," and the sound of the whisper reached the edges of the crowd.

"It's not the way it used to be," Old Man Warner said clearly. "People ain't the way they used to be."

"All right," Mr. Summers said. "Open the papers. Harry, you open little Dave's."

Mr. Graves opened the slip of paper and there was a general sigh through the crowd as he held it up and everyone could see that it was blank. Nancy and Bill, Jr., opened theirs at the same time, and both beamed and laughed, turning around to the crowd and holding their slips of paper above their heads.

"Tessie," Mr. Summers said. There was a pause, and then Mr. Summers looked at Bill Hutchinson, and Bill unfolded his paper and showed it. It was blank.

"It's Tessie," Mr. Summers said, and his voice was hushed. "Show us her paper, Bill."

Bill Hutchinson went over to his wife and forced the slip of paper out of her hand. It had a black spot on it, the black spot Mr. Summers had made the night before with the heavy pencil in the coal-company office. Bill Hutchinson held it up, and there was a stir in the crowd.

"All right, folks," Mr. Summers said. "Let's finish quickly."

Although the villagers had forgotten the ritual and lost the original black box, they still remembered to use stones. The pile of stones the boys had made earlier was ready; there were stones on the ground with the blowing scraps of paper that had come out of the box. Mrs. Delacroix selected a stone so large she had to pick it up with both hands and turned to Mrs. Dunbar. "Come on," she said. "Hurry up."

Mrs. Dunbar had small stones in both hands, and she said, gasping for breath, "I can't run at all. You'll have to go ahead and I'll catch up with you."

The children had stones already, and someone gave little Davy Hutchinson a few pebbles.

Tessie Hutchinson was in the center of a cleared space by now, and she held her hands out desperately as the villagers moved in on her. "It isn't fair," she said. A stone hit her on the side of the head.

Old Man Warner was saying, "Come on, come on, everyone." Steve Adams was in the front of the crowd of villagers, with Mrs. Graves beside him.

"It isn't fair, it isn't right," Mrs. Hutchinson screamed, and then they were upon her.

LANGUAGE FACTORS

At the end of the first chapter of this book (pages 19–23), we found that all communication in written language involves six factors: a writer, content or subject, structure, a medium, language, and readers. Thus, we had the diagram:

CONTENT

STRUCTURE

WRITER ⟷ READERS

MEDIUM

LANGUAGE

Used as a way to discover ideas, this framework develops some obvious questions: Who is the writer? What is the piece about? How is it structured? What is the medium? What is the style? Who are the readers? (For example, the *writer* composes an essay about the *subject* of noise pollution and *structures* the essay so that the first paragraph is a general outline of the whole essay; the essay is printed in the campus newspaper, the *medium;* the *language* (style) is straightforward and unembellished; the *readers* are the students and faculty at the writer's college.)

Perspectives on Writing

If the framework were only this, we would not be very interested in it, even though it does introduce concepts of *structure* and *audience,* which did not appear so forcefully in the Pentad. But if you'll think about it, this diagram has a very interesting feature. Viewed from the left-hand side (the writer's perspective), it is a summary of the problems that a writer must face: developing *content* and *structuring* the material, choosing an appropriate kind of *language* (style)—processes that are heavily influenced by *medium* and *readers.* It can be said, then, that the writer is working with a content-structure-medium-language-reader ratio. But the right-hand side of the diagram gives the reader's perspective, and we get a writer-content-structure-medium-language ratio.

From the reader's standpoint, here are some questions:

1. What do I need to know about the *writer* in order to understand the piece?
2. Is the *content* adequately developed and explained? Is the reasoning logical? Is the information accurate and complete?
3. What influence does the *structure* of the piece have on my understanding of it? How could it be better structured or organized?
4. What influence does the *medium* of publication have on the piece?
5. What is the nature of the language of the piece? What influence does that kind of language have on my understanding?
6. What biases, prejudices, emotional sets, past experiences, etc., influence my understanding of and reaction to the piece?

Note also that certain kinds of writing tend to make one factor more important than the others. In scientific writing, the *content* is most important, and we are most interested in its reliability and completeness; in poetry, the *structure* is often most important, for we are sometimes not so much interested in what the poem says (the information it conveys) as in the patterns of symbols and metaphors that give us the meaning; when we read autobiography, we might well be more interested in the *writer* than in other factors; persuasive writings often are aimed at special groups of *readers,* in which case, we might be more interested in the readers than in the piece itself.

A Close Look at a Piece of Writing

Here is a simple example of how language factors can serve to help us understand, analyze, evaluate, and discuss what we read.

Serving Caviar

Craig Claiborne

All caviar, whether fresh or pasteurized, should be served thoroughly chilled. To keep it cold, the serving bowl is usually embedded in ice.

With fresh caviar, many gourmets declare, no embellishments are necessary. They heap it on fresh toast—either buttered or dry—and relish it as is. Others demand a dash of lemon juice. Caviar is also superb, and obviously more economical, when served with blini, melted butter and sour cream.

Chopped hard-cooked egg yolk, chopped hard-cooked egg white and raw onion rings or chopped raw onion often are offered with both fresh and pasteurized caviar. They are particularly recommended with the pasteurized product.

For a delicious spread for buttered bread fingers, mix pasteurized pressed caviar with cream cheese and enough sour cream to make it of spreading consistency.

Fresh caviar is highly perishable and must be kept refrigerated. Never put fresh caviar in a home freezer; freezing ruins it.

Two beverages are eminently suited for service with caviar. They are chilled vodka and chilled dry champagne.

As readers, what do we notice about this piece?

The Writer

When we read some writings, such as journals or autobiographies, the personality of the writer is constantly with us, but it almost seems as if the writer of "Serving Caviar" has disappeared behind his subject matter and his style. Notice, for instance, that the first person personal pronoun *I* is not used, and the writer does not insert his own opinions and preferences into the discussion. In fact, he avoids "slanting" the discussion; we never know the way in which he prefers to have caviar served: "With fresh caviar, *many gourmets* declare, no embellishments are necessary" (emphasis added).

Another device the author uses to achieve this *impersonality* is a sentence form known as *passive voice,* in which the doer of the action is not the subject of the sentence. In the third paragraph, the author says *are offered* and *are particularly recommended.* Notice how the author suddenly appears when the paragraph is taken out of passive voice:

> I often offer chopped hard-cooked egg white and raw onion rings or chopped raw onion with both fresh and pasteurized caviar. I particularly recommend them with the pasteurized product.

Or look at this rewrite of the last paragraph:

> I particularly like two beverages with caviar. They are chilled vodka and chilled dry champagne.

In this example of expository writing, then, the reader is hardly aware of a writer. *Which is not to say that all expository writing is or ought to be impersonal.*

The Content

Anyone who reads "Serving Caviar" has, it seems to me, one overriding purpose in mind: to gain information about how to serve caviar. That is, the reader is interested in what we have been calling content, and the demands of the content control the piece. The little essay contains only about 170 words, but note the fullness with which it covers its topic. At least, the piece seems to leave no questions unanswered, and that is the best test of completeness. If you want a quick check on the completeness of your own essays, ask yourself if the reader might have any questions that you have left unanswered. Ask yourself if you have given enough detail to explain all the points that you introduce in your essay.

The Structure

The structure of the caviar piece is so simple as to need little comment. You could easily make an outline like this:

Serving caviar chilled
Serving fresh caviar
Embellishments for caviar, particularly pasteurized caviar
A caviar spread
Keeping fresh caviar
Beverages to serve with caviar

In most types of writing, organization is a major problem, one that is discussed in some detail in Chapter 5.

The Style

The style of the piece is simple and straightforward. There are no figures of speech. But notice how a few figures of speech would totally change the effect of the piece:

Caviar *is the tsar of hors d'oeuvres* and, whether fresh or pasteurized, should be served thoroughly chilled. To keep *the little black berries as fresh as dew,* the serving bowl is usually embedded in ice.

No improvement. In fact, the figurative language is totally out of place in the piece.

The sentence structure is easy and clear. After all, it makes sense to present simple concepts in uncomplicated sentences. Notice what happens to the tone of the second paragraph when the sentence structure is changed:

Many gourmets, heaping fresh caviar on fresh toast—either buttered or dry—and relishing it as it is, declare that no other embellishments are necessary, though it is also superb, and obviously more economical, when served with blini, melted butter and sour cream.

Again, no improvement. When the writing becomes ornate, with figures of speech and complicated sentences, the style and the subject clash. The successful writer learns to adjust style to subject.

The Readers

What about the audience for "Serving Caviar"? The very nature of the subject would indicate that the piece is aimed at a certain class; after all, only a small minority of the population wants to learn about serving caviar. But the author is not addressing anyone in particular. He is restrained and straightforward, aiming his message at those people who have the interest and the means to want to know about caviar.

Practice: Language Factors

The following marvelous passage is from *Roughing It,* by Mark Twain. Read *and enjoy* it first. Then apply the questions from the framework on page 87 to develop ideas for a discussion of the piece.

It was the end of August, and the skies were cloudless and the weather superb. In two or three weeks I had grown wonderfully fascinated with the curious new country [the Nevada territory], and concluded to put off my return to "the States" awhile. I had grown well accustomed to wearing a damaged slouch hat, blue woolen shirt, and pants crammed into boot-tops, and gloried in the absence of coat, vest, and braces. I felt rowdyish and "bully" (as the historian Josephus phrases it, in his fine chapter upon the destruction of the Temple). It seemed to me that nothing could be so fine and so romantic. I had become an officer of the government, but that was for mere sublimity. The office was an unique sinecure. I had nothing to do and no salary. I was private secretary to his majesty the Secretary, and there was not yet writing enough for two of us. So Johnny K—— and I devoted our time to amusement. He was the young son of an Ohio nabob and was out there for recreation. He got it. We had heard a world of talk about the marvelous beauty of Lake Tahoe, and finally curiosity drove us thither to see it. Three or four members of the Brigade had been there and located some timber-lands on its shores and stored up a quantity of provisions in their camp. We strapped a couple of blankets on our shoulders and took an ax apiece and started—for we intended to take up a wood ranch or so ourselves and become wealthy. We were on foot. The reader will find it advantageous to go horseback. We were told that the distance was eleven miles. We tramped a long time on level ground, and then toiled laboriously up a mountain about a thousand miles high and looked over. No lake there. We descended on the other side, crossed the valley and toiled up another mountain three or four thousand miles high, apparently, and looked over again. No lake yet. We sat down tired and perspiring, and hired a couple of Chinamen to curse those people who had beguiled us. Thus refreshed, we presently resumed the march with renewed vigor and determination. We plodded on, two or three hours longer, and at last the lake burst upon us—a noble sheet of blue water lifted six thousand three hundred feet above the level of the sea, and walled in by a rim of snow-clad mountain peaks that towered aloft full three thousand feet higher still! It was a vast oval, and one would have to use up eighty or a hundred good miles in traveling around it. As it lay there with the shadows of the mountains brilliantly photographed upon its still surface I thought it must surely be the fairest picture the whole earth affords.

We found the small skiff belonging to the Brigade boys, and without loss of time set out across a deep bend of the lake toward the landmarks that signified the locality of the camp. I got Johnny to row—not because I mind exertion myself, but because it makes me sick to ride backward when I am at work. But I steered. A three-mile pull brought us to the camp just as the night fell, and we stepped ashore very tired and wolfishly hungry. In a "cache" among the rocks we found the provisions and the cooking-utensils, and then, all fatigued as I was, I sat down on a boulder and superintended while Johnny gathered wood and cooked supper. Many a man who had gone through what I had, would have wanted to rest.

It was a delicious supper—hot bread, fried bacon, and black coffee. It was a delicious solitude we were in, too. Three miles away was a sawmill and some workmen, but there were not fifteen other human beings throughout the wide circumference of the lake. As the darkness closed down and the stars came out and spangled the great mirror with jewels, we smoked meditatively in the solemn hush and forgot our troubles and our pains. In due time we spread our blankets in the warm sand between two large boulders and soon fell asleep, careless of the procession of ants that passed in through rents in our clothing and explored our persons. Nothing could disturb the sleep that fettered us, for it had been fairly earned, and if our consciences had any sins on them they had to adjourn court for that night, anyway. The wind rose just as we were losing consciousness, and we were lulled to sleep by the beating of the surf upon the shore.

It is always very cold on that lake-shore in the night, but we had plenty of blankets and were warm enough. We never moved a muscle all night, but waked at early dawn in the original positions, and got up at once, thoroughly refreshed, free from soreness, and brim full of friskiness. There is no end of wholesome medicine in such an experience. That morning we could have whipped ten such people as we were the day before—sick ones at any rate. But the world is slow, and people will go to "water cures" and "movement cures" and to foreign lands for health. Three months of camp life on Lake Tahoe would restore an Egyptian mummy to his pristine vigor, and give him an appetite like an alligator. I do not mean the oldest and driest mummies, of course, but the fresher ones. The air up there in the clouds is very pure and fine, bracing and delicious. And why shouldn't it be?—it is the same the angels breathe. I think that hardly any amount of fatigue can be gathered together that a man cannot sleep off in one night on the sand by its side. Not under a roof, but under the sky; it seldom or never rains there in the summertime. I know a man who went there to die. But he made a failure of it. He was a skeleton when he came, and could barely stand. He had no appetite, and did nothing but read tracts and reflect on the future. Three months later he was sleeping out-of-doors regularly, eating all he could hold, three times a day, and chasing game over mountains three thousand feet high for recreation. And he was a skeleton no longer, but weighed part of a ton. This is no fancy sketch, but the truth. His disease was consumption. I confidently commend his experience to other skeletons.

I superintended again, and as soon as we had eaten breakfast we got in the boat and skirted along the lake-shore about three miles and disembarked. We liked the appearance of the place, and so we claimed some three hundred acres of it and stuck our "notices" on a tree. It was yellow-pine timber-land—

a dense forest of trees a hundred feet high and from one to five feet through at the butt. It was necessary to fence our property or we could not hold it. That is to say, it was necessary to cut down trees here and there and make them fall in such a way as to form a sort of inclosure (with pretty wide gaps in it). We cut down three trees apiece, and found it such heartbreaking work that we decided to "rest our case" on those; if they held the property, well and good; if they didn't, let the property spill out through the gaps and go; it was no use to work ourselves to death merely to save a few acres of land. Next day we came back to build a house—for a house was also necessary, in order to hold the property. We decided to build a substantial log house and excite the envy of the Brigade boys; but by the time we had cut and trimmed the first log it seemed unnecessary to be so elaborate, and so we concluded to build it of saplings. However, two saplings, duly cut and trimmed, compelled recognition of the fact that a still modester architecture would satisfy the law, and so we concluded to build a "brush" house. We devoted the next day to this work, but we did so much "sitting around" and discussing, that by the middle of the afternoon we had achieved only a half-way sort of affair which one of us had to watch while the other cut brush, lest if both turned our backs we might not be able to find it again, it had such a strong family resemblance to the surrounding vegetation. But we were satisfied with it.

We were landowners now, duly seized and possessed, and within the protection of the law. Therefore we decided to take up our residence on our own domain and enjoy that large sense of independence which only such an experience can bring. Late the next afternoon, after a good long rest, we sailed away from the Brigade camp with all the provisions and cooking-utensils we could carry off—borrow is the more accurate word—and just as the night was falling we beached the boat at our own landing.

SHIFTING PERSPECTIVES

The final procedure that we will deal with comes from *tagmemics,* a system for analyzing languages that is based on three questions: (1) In what ways does the unit (sound, word, phrase, etc.) differ from others in its class? (2) How much can the unit change and still be itself? (3) Where does the unit fit in its system? The questions, then, concern *contrast, variation,* and *distribution.* The following ways of viewing a subject (or shifts in perspective) are derived from that system. (At the end of this chapter, we will explore what is known as the *tagmemic grid* as a way of discovering ideas.)

Anything—concrete object or abstract concept—can be viewed from five perspectives, each of which will reveal a different aspect of the subject.

The Five Perspectives

The Los Angeles freeway system, for instance, can be viewed

1. *As an Isolated, Static Entity:* We ask, What features characterize it? We can draw a map of it; we can measure its total length; we can count the number of overpasses and underpasses. We can describe it in great detail. In fact, such a description could well demand a number of thick volumes. But the point is that we can view anything as an isolated, static entity and begin to find those features that characterize it.

2. *One Among Many of a Class:* We ask, How does it differ from others in its class? From this point of view, we would compare the Los Angeles freeway system with others like it. I, for instance, immediately think of the differences between the L.A. freeway system and the turnpikes of the East and Midwest.

3. *As a Part of a Larger System:* We ask, How does it fit into larger systems of which it is a part? The L.A. freeway system would be worthless if it did not integrate with national, state, and county highway systems; therefore, its place in these larger systems is crucial.

4. *As a Process, Rather Than as a Static Entity:* We ask, How is it changing? In regard to the L.A. freeway system, this question brings up the whole problem of planning for the future, which implies the problem of history, or how the system got to be the way it currently is.

5. *As a Closed System, Rather Than as an Entity:* We ask, What are the parts, and how do they work together? Now we are focusing on the L.A. freeway as a transportation system, each part of which must integrate and function with the whole.

That is one example of how the procedure works. You can ask the questions in any order, starting with any one of the five perspectives.

It might be interesting to see how many ideas the system outlined above will generate concerning so ordinary an object as a ballpoint pen.

1. *Viewing the subject as an isolated, static entity:* What features characterize it? The pen is a cylinder exactly five inches long. The upper two inches consist of a silverish metal, a little under one-half inch in diameter, and tapering slightly toward the top, which consists of a button that is depressed to retract or push out the ballpoint. Also on the metal part of the pen is a pocket clip, in the shape of an arrow, which is one and one-half inches long. The bottom three inches of the pen consist of a black plastic shaft, tipped with metal and tapering markedly from the middle of the pen to the tip. The top of the pen unscrews from the bottom, and inside is the ink cartridge, which could also be described in detail. (The features that characterize the pen—or anything else—can be described in detail or simply in general, depending on the writer's purpose. Since the point about describing the features of an object has been made, I will not go on with this description.)

2. *Viewing the subject as one among many of a class:* How does it differ from others of its class? Some ballpoints do not have retractable tips but rather have plastic caps that must be put on and removed. Most ballpoints tend to accumulate ink around the writing tip, so that periodically they leave a smear or blob of ink on the paper. The ballpoint being discussed here does not do that, perhaps because it is somewhat more expensive than others.

3. *Viewing the subject as part of a larger system:* How does it fit into the larger systems of which it is a part? If by larger system we mean "writing instruments," we can relate the ballpoint to the typewriter, chalk, fountain pens, and so on. However, we can also define larger system as "office supplies," "means of communication," "products that make money for the manufacturers," and so on.

4. *Viewing the subject as a process, rather than as a static entity:* How is it changing? In the case of the ballpoint, two questions immediately arise: How long does the ink supply last? How fast does the pen wear out?

5. *Viewing the subject as a closed system, rather than as an entity:* What are the parts, and how do they work together? We are now concerned with the way the ballpoint pen functions. Briefly, the plunger at the top of the pen forces the ballpoint out of the metal-reinforced tip. The point is an extremely small ball bearing at the end of a metal tube which is filled with ink about the consistency of printer's ink. As the ball moves over the paper, it turns; as it turns,

it picks up ink from the tube and deposits that ink on the paper, thus making the continuous trail demanded for writing.

This example illustrates that the procedure can be used to generate raw material for an essay on even so uninteresting a subject as a ballpoint pen. In fact, if you think about it, the materials in the example could, with some reworking, be turned into an essay.

Exercise

1. Your problem is to write an essay that will explain the functioning of one of your classes: how the class is managed, what attitudes the teacher and students have, what the goals of the class seem to be, and so on. In other words, you want to develop a complete report on the class. To discover ideas for that report, apply the five perspectives to the subject. You may want to do this in group discussion or alone.

2. This way of finding ideas is more useful than at first you might believe. To demonstrate its usefulness to yourself, you might go back and apply it to "Barbara Allan" (pages 68–69), "The Lottery" (pages 80–86), and the article on the United Nations (pages 74–78).

The Grid

Perhaps the most complicated discovery procedure that is widely used is a grid based on the tagmemic theory of language.[6] This procedure is based on two concepts, the first of which is a way of *knowing,* and the second of which is a way of *viewing.*

To *know* anything—a concrete object or an abstract concept— you must know these three things about it:

1. *Contrast: How it differs from everything else in its class.* If you cannot tell the difference between Fords, Chevrolets, and Plymouths, you cannot know for certain which kind of car you are looking at; if you do not know how democracy contrasts with other forms of govern-

---

[6] See Richard E. Young, Alton L. Becker, and Kenneth L. Pike, *Rhetoric: Discovery and Change* (New York: Harcourt Brace Jovanovich, 1970).

ment—socialism, communism, fascism—you do not understand democracy, even though you may have heard the term.

2. *Variation: How much it can change and still be itself.* At what point does a stool become a chair? When does an old piece of furniture become an antique? How much can a government change and still be a democracy?

3. *Distribution: Where it typically occurs in its class.* Among passenger cars, Pintos are sub-compacts, Aspens are compacts, Monte Carlos are full-sized autos, and so on. Each sort of car has a place in its whole system, and this place is its distribution. In judicial systems, the distributions include small claims courts, civil courts, criminal courts, courts of appeal. Again, knowing *distribution* is knowing where an item or class fits into the system of which it is a part.

Anything that you know can be *viewed* from three perspectives:

1. as a static, unchanging entity, as a *particle*. Physicists can "stop" the atom and view it as if it were not always changing, and describe its parts; linguists can "stop" the language and present a description of it as if it were not ever-changing. Anatomy views the human body as a particle (whereas physiology views it as a process).

2. as a process, a *wave*. Now we are interested in change, in process. We shift from the classification of the judicial system to a consideration of how it works; we are no longer interested in isolating and describing the parts of language, but inquire into how it works and how it is changing.

3. as a system of interrelated parts, as a *field*. Now we stand back and look at the whole system with an all-at-onceness. We get a bird's-eye view of it. From the standpoint of field, we are watching the Rose Bowl game from the Goodyear blimp, seeing all of the parts as they function together.

We have, then, six master questions that we can ask about anything:

Contrast

How does the item contrast with everything else in its class, thus enabling us to know it?

Variation

How much can the item change or be changed and still be itself?

Distribution

Where does the item typically appear in its class?

Features

What are the distinctive features of the item? (Some answers to this question will be the same as those to the question concerning contrast.)

Process

How does the item work? (How is it changing? What does it do? How does it do it?)

System

How do the parts of the item work together?

Exercise

Choose some item or process in your college that you believe needs to be improved (the cafeteria, registration procedures, scheduling of classes, etc.). Using the six master questions from tagmemics, assemble ideas for an essay on the subject. Remember that a good discovery procedure will generate

1. knowledge that you already have about the item;
2. questions that you can answer through reasoning or your own experience;
3. questions that you can answer through research.

While you will have some general ideas about your topic, the questions should (a) give you new insights and (b) open up possibilities for discovering further knowledge.

Suppose that we apply the ways of *knowing* (contrast, variation, distribution) to the ways of *viewing* (features, process, system). Then we will have a nine-item grid, like this:

	Contrast	*Variation*	*Distribution*
Features	1. How do the features contrast with those of other items in the same class?	4. How much can the features change and yet have the item remain the same?	7. What are the features' relations to the whole class?
Process	2. How does the process contrast with the processes of other systems?	5. How much can the process change without changing the item?	8. How does the process relate to the whole class?
System	3. How does the system contrast with other systems?	6. How much can the system change before the item becomes something else?	9. How does the system function within the larger system of which it is a part?

Exercise: Practice Using the Grid

Your problem is to do an analysis of a McDonald's fast-food outlet. Your purpose is to explain why this outlet is so efficient and successful. Here are some tips:

1. As the class, choose restaurants in general.
2. If one of the nine questions does not seem to produce any ideas, go on to another. You can jump around, skipping a question and then returning to it later. The only "rule" for a discovery procedure is that it must produce results. If it does not, then it is useless, regardless of how interesting it may appear.
3. Don't argue about the procedure itself. For example, if in response to question 2, one of your classmates comes up with an idea that you think fits question 5, pay no attention to the discrepancy; your purpose is to generate ideas, not to worry about where they belong in some system of classification.
4. Some of the questions may seem to overlap others. Don't worry about that. The point is this: each of the questions will give you a slightly different view of your subject.

Review and Discussion

1. Choose a down-to-earth topic—paper clips, toenails, light bulbs, typewriter paper, or something equally simple and common—and brainstorm it. For ten or fifteen minutes, write down every idea concerning it that pops into your head.

One way to do this is the following: Cut notebook or typing paper into slips, and enter each idea on a separate slip. After you have completed your short period of brainstorming, you can see if any pattern has emerged in your ideas. Arrange the slips so that related ideas are in the same pile.

Now choose the five most original ideas of those you generated. Compare your original ideas with those of the other members of your class, and be prepared to discuss this question: What makes original ideas original?

2. Now apply the first variation on brainstorming (pages 59–63) to the same item.

Did you get better results than with brainstorming? If you believe that you did, explain why.

3. Apply the second variation on brainstorming (pages 63–65) to the item. Results? Explain.

4. Apply the checklist for new ideas (pages 65–66) to another item. Be prepared to discuss how this discovery procedure compares with brainstorming and its variations. Is it more or less successful for you? Why?

5. Define a real problem you are facing (for example, lack of money, deciding on a major, getting along with a friend or relative, overcoming a sense of guilt about something you have done). Use brainstorming and its two variations and the checklist for new ideas to see if you can discover some reasonable solutions. In a brief, informal paper, explain the nature of the problem, and outline the possible solution or solutions that you have discovered.

6. Your problem is to give as complete an explanation as possible of "In Praise of BIC Pens," by David Hilton. Use *who-what-where-when-why-how* (pages 66–69) and then the Pentad (pages 69–86) to gain ideas that will help you explain the meaning of the poem to your classmates.

In Praise of BIC Pens

David Hilton

Others always skip over the word
That will bring the belligerents of the world
To the negotiating table, if only

I can get it written, or will
Teach thin kids in Woetown, West Virginia,
To rebound tough and read Ted Roethke—

I'm writing along in a conspiracy
Of birds and sun and pom-pom girls
Lines to cheer old ladies with shopping bags

Waiting by their busstops at 5PM
Or lines to get the 12-year-olds off cigarettes
Or save the suicides in gay-bar mensrooms

Or save the fat man from his refrigerator
Or the brilliant boy from color TV
Or the RA private from re-upping for six

Or the whole Midwest from wanting to conquer Asia and the Moon
Or the current president from his place in history—
Oh, if only I can get it written

No one will burn kittens or slap little boys or make little girls cry
Or cower at cancer or coronaries or plain palsied old age
Or get goofy from radiation in his cornflake milk—

If only I can get it written. But always
When I get close to the word and the crowd begins to roar
The common pen skips. Leaves the page blank—

But you, BIC pen, at nineteen cents, could trace truce terms on tank treads,
Could ratify in the most flourishing script
The amnesty of love for our most dreaded enemies:

The ugly, the poor, the stupid, the sexually screwed-up—
Etching their releases across the slippery communiqués of generals and governors,
For Behold you can write upon butter, Yea inscribe even through slime!

But at nineteen cents no one pays attention
To the deadwood you shatter or the manifestoes you slice in the ice—
For who would believe the Truth at *that* price.

7. Use the ideas that you have discovered to write an explanation of the poem. In this paper, you will attempt to give full answers to two questions: (1) What exactly does the poem mean? (2) How do I know what it means?

Developing Ideas:
The Paragraph

As marks of punctuation signal the structure of the sentences in a piece of writing, so paragraphing signals the structure of the whole subject—grouping the ideas in the way intended by the writer. The way in which paragraphing helps one read an extended piece of writing is illustrated in the exercise on pages 104–09.

THE REALITY OF THE PARAGRAPH

It is very difficult to define "sentence," and yet all of us can recognize sentences; that is to say, we know what a sentence is even though we cannot propose an adequate definition.

in fact I can easily demonstrate to you that you can recognize sentences this paragraph should give you such a demonstration put an X or a check mark before each word that begins a sentence now compare your sentencing with your classmates' almost certainly everyone is in agreement about the sentences in this paragraph

The last paragraph demonstrated that the sentence has what might be called "psychological reality"; a sentence cannot be just any string of words but must have certain characteristics, the nature of which we recognize since we can mark off sentence boundaries. (Again, we may not be able to explain the features that make a string of words a sentence, but we must recognize those features since, even in unpunctuated passages, we can agree pretty much on where the sentences begin and end.)

For experienced readers and writers, the paragraph has just such reality also. Take a well-structured expository essay, and reprint it so that all paragraph indentations are removed, and then submit the essay to a group of readers, asking them to indicate the points at which they believe paragraphs should begin. This experiment has been tried again and again, and the results are uniform: experienced readers overwhelmingly agree on the paragraphing, with only a small number of disputed or ambiguous cases.

Exercise

This exercise should demonstrate two points: the paragraph is "psychologically" real, and paragraphing is important for readers.

The following brief essay is printed first without paragraphs and then reprinted twice, each time with different paragraphing.

1. By making check marks in your book, indicate how you think the essay should be paragraphed.
2. Discuss the paragraphing in the second and third versions of the essay. Which is more effective? Why? Does the paragraphing in either of the versions create confusion and make reading more difficult? Explain.

And Now, the Ultramarathon . . .

Mark N. Grant

Just as the edge of the universe is beyond comprehension, so the distance humans can run seems to have no limits. Mere jogging has given way to the glamorous marathon, which may soon be outmoded by something even more exotic—the ultramarathon, of which Bruce Maxwell and Ken Crutchlow are exemplars. The ultramarathon, an ordeal fit for masochists and other pioneers in pain, is any race longer than the marathon's 26 miles, 385 yards. Its varieties thus far include 50 kilometers (31 miles), 50 miles, the double marathon, 100 kilometers (62 miles), 100 miles, the 24-hour race, and whatever else its slightly mad enthusiasts think of next. These races make Frank Shorter seem appropriately surnamed. The 24-hour record, for instance, is 160 miles. England's Ron Bentley set it in 1973, when he was 43 years old. (Bentley has also done 400 laps on a quarter–mile track in 12½ hours, but that's an hour slower than the world record for 100 miles.) If this seems outlandish, consider that several *thousand* runners routinely finish the Comrades' Double Marathon in South Africa every year. In addition to public ultraraces, such as the 52½-miler from London to Brighton, many ultrarunners pursue even longer solo jaunts. Siegfried Bauer ran the length of New Zealand—1,321 miles—in 18 days, 12 hours. Tom McGrath ran from New York to San Francisco in exactly 53 days, averaging 57 miles per day. A Canadian is now training to run the length of the Alaskan pipeline. And Patty Wilson jogged from her home in La Palma, California to Portland, Oregon—1,310 miles—in 41 days. She was then 15 years old. Ultras are not unique to our epoch. In the 1880s there was a craze for six-day races in which the runners covered 100 miles a day, largely through walking (some of the runners suffered mental derangements from sleep deprivation). The Tarahumara Indians of Mexico's Chihuahua province are known to run 50 to 100 miles in village games. But today's ultramarathoner is unlikely to get much attention or competition. World-class marathoners like Shorter and Bill Rodgers shun ultras. If it takes one month to recover from a marathon, it may take two months after a 50-miler. Running ultras would ruin their training season and prevent them from competing in the shorter races they prefer. On the other hand, some runners seem to have unlimited stamina—among them Park Barner, a 33-year-old computer operator in Harrisburg, Pennsylvania. He once ran a marathon *and* a 50-mile race in the same weekend. Barner talks of such feats as his recent traversal of 187 miles in 36 hours (including a four-hour catnap) with an aw-shucks, nothing-to-it bravado. "I started jogging at 24, and the fifth time out I did 18 miles. I've read that everybody's born with the ability to run a 2:40 marathon. In winter I can go 50 miles without a drink of water." Barner trains by running four miles to work, four miles during his lunch hour, then four miles home again. But the marathon, he says, is actually too fast a race for him. "It cuts up my legs." With near-comic understatement he adds, "I don't go overboard for this running." The secret is pace: the average Boston Marathon pace is seven and a half minutes a mile, the average ultra pace is eight. "If you go two minutes a mile slower than your racing pace, you can run practically indefinitely," asserts Dr. George Sheehan, the medical guru of modern running. "The ultra is an ordinary event for the human body." Most ultrarunners train 75 to 100 miles or more a week, and if it takes one and a half years for a novice to get in shape for a marathon, he may need four years for an ultra. Fritz Mueller, 41, a Manhattan chemist who started jogging in 1972, finished his first 50-miler in 1977. "It's really not as bad as it's made out to be. In a way it's less painful than a shorter race, because you don't run as fast." What happens to a long-distance runner's body? Even in cool weather, for example, a normal marathon runner's core body temperature can rise to 104 degrees or more. But with proper water replacement, there's a minimal danger. Biochemical data on ultrarunners suggest that this rule holds true for them as well. And what of the "wall," that much-discussed shorting-out of the body at approximately 20 miles, when a runner's normal glycogen reserves are exhausted? According to Tom Osler, a 37-year-old ultrarunner from Glassboro, New Jersey, "It's like a car running out of gas. You just keep refilling the tank as you run by drinking liquids high in sugar." Also, extreme distances allow enough time for the body to gear up its slow process of converting stored fat into energy—if the runner can hold out mentally. But the question left dangling is: Why attempt an ultra? Tom Osler, who's run over 50 marathons, ultimately found them boring. "After a while, they're not so exciting. You've had the good days and the bad days. With the ultra, the pacing problems are far more difficult. Walking becomes a part of it. It has incredible new dimensions. The longer races involve unknowns." Finally, the ultraquestion: Do ultrarunners ever tire of ultras? Says Ted Corbitt, who at 53 set the American record for the 24-hour run: "Psychologically, it becomes easier. After the first time, it's never as hard again. Some days it's enjoyable. But it never becomes completely easy, and the joy never lasts. So you keep on trying to find the perfect balance between pain and pleasure."

And Now, the Ultramarathon . . .

Mark N. Grant

Just as the edge of the universe is beyond comprehension, so the distance humans can run seems to have no limits. Mere jogging has given way to the glamorous marathon, which may soon be outmoded by something even more exotic—the ultramarathon, of which Bruce Maxwell and Ken Crutchlow are exemplars. The ultramarathon, an ordeal fit for masochists and other pioneers in pain, is any race longer than the marathon's 26 miles, 385 yards. Its varieties thus far include 50 kilometers (31 miles), 50 miles, the double marathon, 100 kilometers (62 miles), 100 miles, the 24-hour race, and whatever else its slightly mad enthusiasts think of next.

These races make Frank Shorter seem appropriately surnamed. The 24-hour record, for instance, is 160 miles. England's Ron Bentley set it in 1973, when he was 43 years old. (Bentley has also done 400 laps on a quarter-mile track in 12½ hours, but that's an hour slower than the world record for 100 miles.) If this seems outlandish, consider that several *thousand* runners routinely finish the Comrades' Double Marathon in South Africa every year. In addition to public ultraraces, such as the 52½-miler from London to Brighton, many ultrarunners pursue even longer solo jaunts. Siegfried Bauer ran the length of New Zealand—1,321 miles—in 18 days, 12 hours. Tom McGrath ran from New York to San Francisco in exactly 53 days, averaging 57 miles per day. A Canadian is now training to run the length of the Alaskan pipeline. And Patty Wilson jogged from her home in La Palma, California to Portland, Oregon—1,310 miles—in 41 days. She was then 15 years old.

Ultras are not unique to our epoch. In the 1880s there was a craze for six-day races in which the runners covered 100 miles a day, largely through walking (some of the runners suffered mental derangements from sleep deprivation). The Tarahumara Indians of Mexico's Chihuahua province are known to run 50 to 100 miles in village games.

But today's ultramarathoner is unlikely to get much attention or competition. World-class marathoners like Shorter and Bill Rodgers shun ultras. If it takes one month to recover from a marathon, it may take two months after a 50-miler. Running ultras would ruin their training season and prevent them from competing in the shorter races they prefer.

On the other hand, some runners seem to have unlimited stamina— among them Park Barner, a 33-year-old computer operator in Harrisburg, Pennsylvania. He once ran a marathon *and* a 50-mile race in the same weekend. Barner talks of such feats as his recent traversal of 187 miles in 36 hours (including a four-hour catnap) with an aw-shucks, nothing-to-it bravado. "I started jogging at 24, and the fifth time out I did 18 miles. I've read that everybody's born with the ability to run a 2:40 marathon. In winter I can go 50 miles without a drink of water." Barner trains by running four miles to work, four miles during his lunch hour, then four miles home again. But the marathon, he says, is actually too fast a race for him. "It cuts up my legs." With near-comic understatement he adds, "I don't go overboard for this running."

The secret is pace: the average Boston Marathon pace is seven and a half minutes a mile, the average ultra pace is eight. "If you go two minutes a mile slower than your racing pace, you can run practically indefinitely," asserts Dr. George Sheehan, the medical guru of modern running. "The ultra is an ordinary event for the human body." Most ultrarunners train 75 to 100 miles or more a week, and if it takes one and a half years for a novice to get in shape for a marathon, he may need four years for an ultra. Fritz Mueller, 41, a Manhattan chemist who started jogging in 1972, finished his first 50-miler in 1977. "It's really not as bad as it's made out to be. In a way it's less painful than a shorter race, because you don't run as fast."

What happens to a long-distance runner's body? Even in cool weather, for example, a normal marathon runner's core body temperature can rise to 104 degrees or more. But with proper water replacement, there's a minimal danger. Biochemical data on ultrarunners suggest that this rule holds true for them as well. And what of the "wall," that much-discussed shorting-out of the body at approximately 20 miles, when a runner's normal glycogen reserves are exhausted? According to Tom Osler, a 37-year-old ultrarunner from Glassboro, New Jersey, "It's like a car running out of gas. You just keep refilling the tank as you run by drinking liquids high in sugar." Also, extreme distances allow enough time for the body to gear up its slow process of converting stored fat into energy—if the runner can hold out mentally.

But the question left dangling is: Why attempt an ultra? Tom Osler, who's run over 50 marathons, ultimately found them boring. "After a while, they're not so exciting. You've had the good days and the bad days. With the ultra, the pacing problems are far more difficult. Walking becomes a part of it. It has incredible new dimensions. The longer races involve unknowns."

Finally, the ultraquestion: Do ultrarunners ever tire of ultras? Says Ted Corbitt, who at 53 set the American record for the 24-hour run: "Psychologically, it becomes easier. After the first time, it's never as hard again. Some days it's enjoyable. But it never becomes completely easy, and the joy never lasts. So you keep on trying to find the perfect balance between pain and pleasure."

And Now, the Ultramarathon . . .

Mark N. Grant

Just as the edge of the universe is beyond comprehension, so the distance humans can run seems to have no limits. Mere jogging has given way to the glamorous marathon, which may soon be outmoded by something even more exotic—the ultramarathon, of which Bruce Maxwell and Ken Crutchlow are exemplars. The ultramarathon, an ordeal fit for masochists and other pioneers in pain, is any race longer than the marathon's 26 miles, 385 yards.

Its varieties thus far include 50 kilometers (31 miles), 50 miles, the double marathon, 100 kilometers (62 miles), 100 miles, the 24-hour race, and whatever else its slightly mad enthusiasts think of next. These races make Frank Shorter seem appropriately surnamed. The 24-hour record, for instance, is 160 miles. England's Ron Bentley set it in 1973, when he was 43 years old. (Bentley has also done 400 laps on a quarter-mile track in 12½ hours, but that's an hour slower than the world record for 100 miles.)

If this seems outlandish, consider that several *thousand* runners routinely finish the Comrades' Double Marathon in South Africa every year. In addition to public ultraraces, such as the 52½-miler from London to Brighton, many ultrarunners pursue even longer solo jaunts. Siegfried Bauer ran the length of New Zealand—1,321 miles—in 18 days, 12 hours. Tom McGrath ran from New York to San Francisco in exactly 53 days, averaging 57 miles per day. A Canadian is now training to run the length of the Alaskan pipeline. And Patty Wilson jogged from her home in La Palma, California to Portland, Oregon—1,310 miles—in 41 days. She was then 15 years old. Ultras are not unique to our epoch.

In the 1880s there was a craze for six-day races in which the runners covered 100 miles a day, largely through walking (some of the runners suffered mental derangements from sleep deprivation). The Tarahumara Indians of Mexico's Chihuahua province are known to run 50 to 100 miles in village games. But today's ultramarathoner is unlikely to get much attention or competition. World-class marathoners like Shorter and Bill Rodgers shun ultras. If it takes one month to recover from a marathon, it may take two months after a 50-miler. Running ultras would ruin their training season and prevent them from competing in the shorter races they prefer. On the other hand, some runners seem to have unlimited stamina—among them Park Barner, a 33-year-old computer operator in Harrisburg, Pennsylvania.

He once ran a marathon *and* a 50-mile race in the same weekend. Barner talks of such feats as his recent traversal of 187 miles in 36 hours (including a four-hour catnap) with an aw-shucks, nothing-to-it bravado. "I started jogging at 24, and the fifth time out I did 18 miles. I've read that everybody's born with the ability to run a 2:40 marathon. In winter I can go 50 miles without a drink of water." Barner trains by running four miles to work, four miles during his lunch hour, then four miles home again. But the marathon, he says, is actually too fast a race for him. "It cuts up my legs." With near-comic understatement he adds, "I don't go overboard for this running." The secret is pace: the average Boston Marathon pace is seven and a half minutes a mile, the average ultra pace is eight. "If you go two minutes a mile slower than your racing pace, you can run practically indefinitely," asserts Dr. George Sheehan, the medical guru of modern running. "The ultra is an ordinary event for the human body."

Most ultrarunners train 75 to 100 miles or more a week, and if it takes one and a half years for a novice to get in shape for a marathon, he may need four years for an ultra.

Fritz Mueller, 41, a Manhattan chemist who started jogging in 1972, finished his first 50-miler in 1977.

"It's really not as bad as it's made out to be. In a way it's less painful than a shorter race, because you don't run as fast."

What happens to a long-distance runner's body?

Even in cool weather, for example, a normal marathon runner's core body temperature can rise to 104 degrees or more. But with proper water replacement, there's a minimal danger. Biochemical data on ultrarunners suggest that this rule holds true for them as well. And what of the "wall," that much-discussed shorting-out of the body at approximately 20 miles, when a runner's normal glycogen reserves are exhausted? According to Tom Osler, a 37-year-old ultrarunner from Glassboro, New Jersey, "It's like a car running out of gas. You just keep refilling the tank as you run by drinking liquids high in sugar." Also, extreme distances allow enough time for the body to gear up its slow process of converting stored fat into energy—if the runner can hold out mentally. But the question left dangling is: Why attempt an ultra? Tom Osler, who's run over 50 marathons, ultimately found them boring. "After a while, they're not so exciting. You've had the good days and the bad days. With the ultra, the pacing problems are far more difficult. Walking becomes a part of it. It has incredible new dimensions. The longer races involve un-knowns." Finally, the ultraquestion: Do ultrarunners ever tire of ultras?

Says Ted Corbitt, who at 53 set the American record for the 24-hour run: "Psychologically, it becomes easier. After the first time, it's never as hard again. Some days it's enjoyable. But it never becomes completely easy, and the joy never lasts. So you keep on trying to find the perfect balance between pain and pleasure."

The paragraph like the sentence, then, is a *real* structure. Just as punctuation or its lack does not change the basic nature of the sentence, so the indentation that you employ does not change the basic nature of the paragraph—and this is an important enough point to be underscored and illustrated.

We can identify the sentences in the following passage.

a. Rain was gently falling dripping off the eaves and the leaves it was fresh fresh and cool we enjoyed it after the heat of the August day

   1. Rain was gently falling, dripping off the eaves and the leaves.
   2. It was fresh, fresh and cool.
   3. We enjoyed it after the heat of the August day.

If we have good reason, we can violate the rules of edited standard English and punctuate this passage in a variety of ways (the purpose being, of course, to create a variety of effects):

b. The rain was gently falling. Dripping off the eaves and the leaves. It was fresh. Fresh and cool. We enjoyed it after the heat of the August day.

c. The rain was gently falling, dripping off the eaves—and the leaves. It was fresh, fresh and cool. We enjoyed it. After the heat of the August day.

Versions *b* and *c* may or may not be effective, depending upon the writer's *purpose* and *audience,* but the point is this: even though we violate the rules of punctuation for some reason, we do not change the nature of the sentence; "beneath" the surface of the different punctuations, we can find the sentences, as we can also in an unpunctuated passage. One might say that there are *real* sentences and a variety of *pseudo*-sentences created by punctuation.

This is exactly the case with paragraphs. We can break "real" paragraphs up into pseudo-paragraphs for many reasons, including *emphasis:*

> d. There is little to say about choosing a theme or topic from a group that are assigned. You have some latitude, but not very much, and you must work as best you can within the limits of the assignment. It is important to remember, though, that an essay results from the writer's encounter with the subject; if the subject does not come to you, you must bring yourself to the subject. Therefore, you ask yourself, "What do I know about this subject? What can I find out about it? How do I feel about it?" And so on. More about this later.

> e. There is little to say about choosing a theme or topic from a group that are assigned. You have some latitude, but not very much, and you must work as best you can within the limits of the assignment.
>
> It is important to remember, though, that an essay results from the writer's encounter with the subject; if the subject does not come to you, you must bring yourself to the subject.
>
> Therefore, you ask yourself, "What do I know about this subject? What can I find out about it? How do I feel about it?" And so on.
>
> More about this later.

In example *e,* the original paragraph *d* has been broken up into four shorter paragraphs. These choices of indentation have placed emphasis upon the second shorter paragraph ("It is important to remember. . . .") by isolating it and thus making it stand out. The final indentation ("More about this later") signals a transition to another subject.

Neither one is "better" or "worse" out of context, but one would probably be more effective than the other for some *purposes* with some *audiences.*

To end this section, a couple of brief comments. Throughout this section I have repeatedly mentioned *purpose* and *audience* and shall continue to do so throughout the book. In the exercise on pages 104–09, the second version of the essay on the ultramarathon represents the original paragraphing.

PARAGRAPH COHERENCE

The following group of sentences does not seem like a paragraph:

> The albacore are beginning to run. In Montana, it often snows in August. Freud created a revolution in the way we view the human mind. Grammar seems to be a dull subject.

But the next example, though it is extremely strange, does seem a bit more like a real paragraph (a paragraph written by a mad person, perhaps):

> The albacore are beginning to run. However, in Montana it often snows in August. That is why Freud created a revolution in the way we view the human mind. Therefore, grammar seems to be a dull subject.

In the second example, words and phrases such as *however, that is why,* and *therefore* make us feel that the writer of the paragraph was trying to make us see connections even though we remain puzzled.

In fact, *transitional* words and phrases (such as *however, thus, moreover, on the other hand, therefore,* and others) help create paragraph coherence. And so do *pointing words* such as *this* and *that, here* and *there, these* and *those,* and others.

> The members of the class seemed puzzled and frustrated. *Therefore,* the teacher stopped the lecture and asked if there were any questions. *This* brief pause was enough to allow everyone to become oriented so that the explanation could continue.

> In order to make a fortune, one might plan a spectacular robbery or perhaps blackmail a millionaire. *On the other hand,* some bright people have made great wealth with simple inventions. *For example,* Robert Abplanalp became a multimillionaire with his invention of the aerosol valve. *That* is the device which enables one to spray the contents from a can of deodorant or paint.

> Wine consumed in moderate quantities can enhance the quality of one's life. *In the first place,* a fine wine always makes dining more

pleasurable. *In the second place,* a glass of wine acts as a safe and effective tranquilizer. *These,* among others, are the reasons for wine's popularity.

Another reason for coherence is that paragraphs contain strings of words that relate to one another—which is only a way of saying that paragraphs deal with a limited number of subjects.

In the following paragraph from *The Bern Book,* by Vincent O. Carter, "chains" of words and phrases refer to the same subjects. Those in rectangles refer to *the United States of America,* and those in ovals refer to the *citizens* of the United States.

The United States of America may be described, among other things, as a land of great dynamic tensions. It is a land in which practically all of its citizens are emigrants. Most of the people who emigrated to America went as nobodies and their subsequent history, and therefore the history of America, is the history of their attempts to become somebodies. As to what ideas and culture those criminals, prostitutes, fortune-hunters, speculators, religiously oppressed and land-hungry folk possessed, they brought with them from England and France and Germany and Russia and Spain and Armenia and Ireland and Italy and anywhere else in the world one would wish to name. Are you surprised? Are you astonished to discover that they are your relations, only a few generations removed from the old country? You need not be surprised: grandchildren, look at grandparents! All of those European nobodies trying hard to become somebodies in a land that belonged to the Indian and the Eskimo— that's America!

So transitional words—like *however, therefore, thus,* and *then*—are part of the glue that keeps paragraphs together, and chains of words that refer to the same things are another part.

To get a sense of how transitional words and chains of words function to bring about paragraph coherence, let's look at one more interesting paragraph. In this paragraph, *transitional* words (such as *however, but,* and *thus*) are underlined; *adverbs* that give the reader the necessary time orientation are in rectangles; and words and phrases relating to *plows* and *plowing* are in ovals.

Until recently, agriculture has been the chief occupation even in "advanced" societies; hence, any change in methods of tillage has much importance. Early plows, drawn by two oxen, did not normally turn the sod but merely scratched it. Thus, cross-plowing was needed and fields tended to be squarish. In the fairly light soils and semi-arid climates of the Near East and Mediterranean, this worked well. But such a plow was inappropriate to the wet climate and often sticky soils of northern Europe. By the latter part of the seventh century after Christ, however, following obscure beginnings, certain northern peasants were using an entirely new kind of plow, equipped with a vertical knife to cut the line of the furrow, a horizontal share to slice under the sod, and a moldboard to turn it over. The friction of this plow with the soil was so great that it normally required not two but eight oxen. It attacked the land with such violence that cross-plowing was not needed, and fields tended to be shaped in long strips.

—Lynn White, Jr., "The Historical Roots
of Our Ecological Crisis"

Paragraphs hang together, then, because the words in them form chains of meaning, as in the series of words referring to plows and plowing; because time and space relationships are made clear ("Until recently," "By the latter part of the seventh century after Christ," and so on); and because transitional words establish logical relationships.

However, there is no particular reason for you to explain all of these technicalities. *The ability to write coherent paragraphs does not depend on the ability to explain why paragraphs are coherent.* Anyone who can write coherent paragraphs *knows* what makes for coherence, even though he or she cannot explain that knowledge, just as anyone who writes sentences knows what a sentence is even though no one can give a really adequate definition of "sentence."

In summary, you can create coherent paragraphs if (1) you do not shift subjects, that is, if you establish clear-cut chains of related words in your paragraphs and (2) if you give the reader the necessary relationships by the appropriate use of transitions (*however, moreover, thus,* etc.), adverbs (*now, then, here, there, last year, at present,* etc.), and pointing words (*this, that, such, these, those,* etc.).

Paragraphs in an Essay

The following exercise has several purposes. In the first place, the essay you will read, think about, analyze, and discuss is a good piece of writing that will, I believe, interest you. In the second place, the essay is about keeping a journal (which the author calls a "notebook"), and, as you have discovered, *The Contemporary Writer* urges all writers to maintain journals. And third, you will discover that you know a great deal that you did not think you knew; the questions concerning the essay will help you discover some important ideas about coherence and also about the nature of paragraphs.

When you have finished reading the essay, begin to ask yourself these questions:

1. Why did the author choose these particular spots for paragraph indentations? What purposes does the paragraphing serve?
2. What ties the paragraphs together? Words or phrases? Related subjects? Other devices? (For example, the first sentence of paragraph 11 is "And so we do." How does that sentence help tie paragraph 11 to paragraph 10?)
3. What makes for the coherence within the paragraphs? Chains of words? Adverbs? Transitional words and phrases?

In short, do as thorough a job as you can of analyzing the coherence of the essay—but don't, if you can help it, let the analysis interfere with your enjoyment of this lovely piece of writing.

On Keeping a Notebook

Joan Didion

1   " 'That woman Estelle,' " the note reads, " 'is partly the reason why George Sharp and I are separated today.' *Dirty crepe-de-Chine wrapper, hotel bar, Wilmington RR, 9:45 a.m. August Monday morning."*

2   Since the note is in my notebook, it presumably has some meaning to me. I study it for a long while. At first I have only the most general notion of what I was doing on an August Monday morning in the bar of the hotel across from the Pennsylvania Railroad station in Wilmington, Delaware (waiting for a train? missing one? 1960? 1961? why Wilmington?), but I do remember being

ON KEEPING A NOTEBOOK   Joan Didion, *Slouching Toward Bethlehem* (New York: Delta-Dell, 1969), pp. 131–41. Copyright © 1966 by Joan Didion. Reprinted by permission of Farrar, Straus and Giroux, Inc.

there. The woman in the dirty crepe-de-Chine wrapper had come down from her room for a beer, and the bartender had heard before the reason why George Sharp and she were separated today. "Sure," he said, and went on mopping the floor. "You told me." At the other end of the bar is a girl. She is talking, pointedly, not to the man beside her but to a cat lying in the triangle of sunlight cast through the open door. She is wearing a plaid silk dress from Peck & Peck, and the hem is coming down.

3   Here is what it is: the girl has been on the Eastern Shore, and now she is going back to the city, leaving the man beside her, and all she can see ahead are the viscous summer sidewalks and the 3 a.m. long-distance calls that will make her lie awake and then sleep drugged through all the steaming mornings left in August (1960? 1961?). Because she must go directly from the train to lunch in New York, she wishes that she had a safety pin for the hem of the plaid silk dress, and she also wishes that she could forget about the hem and the lunch and stay in the cool bar that smells of disinfectant and malt and make friends with the woman in the crepe-de-Chine wrapper. She is afflicted by a little self-pity, and she wants to compare Estelles. That is what that was all about.

4   Why did I write it down? In order to remember, of course, but exactly what was it I wanted to remember? How much of it actually happened? Did any of it? Why do I keep a notebook at all? It is easy to deceive oneself on all those scores. The impulse to write things down is a peculiarly compulsive one, inexplicable to those who do not share it, useful only accidentally, only secondarily, in the way that any compulsion tries to justify itself. I suppose that it begins or does not begin in the cradle. Although I have felt compelled to write things down since I was five years old, I doubt that my daughter ever will, for she is a singularly blessed and accepting child, delighted with life exactly as life presents itself to her, unafraid to go to sleep and unafraid to wake up. Keepers of private notebooks are a different breed altogether, lonely and resistant rearrangers of things, anxious malcontents, children afflicted apparently at birth with some presentiment of loss.

5   My first notebook was a Big Five tablet, given to me by my mother with the sensible suggestion that I stop whining and learn to amuse myself by writing down my thoughts. She returned the tablet to me a few years ago; the first entry is an account of a woman who believed herself to be freezing to death in the Arctic night, only to find, when day broke, that she had stumbled onto the Sahara Desert, where she would die of the heat before lunch. I have no idea what turn of a five-year-old's mind could have prompted so insistently "ironic" and exotic a story, but it does reveal a certain predilection for the extreme which has dogged me into adult life; perhaps if I were analytically inclined I would find it a truer story than any I might have told about Donald Johnson's birthday party or the day my cousin Brenda put Kitty Litter in the aquarium.

6   So the point of my keeping a notebook has never been, nor is it now, to have an accurate factual record of what I have been doing or thinking. That would be a different impulse entirely, an instinct for reality which I sometimes envy but do not possess. At no point have I ever been able successfully to keep a diary; my approach to daily life ranges from the grossly negligent to the merely absent, and on those few occasions when I have tried dutifully to record a day's events, boredom has so overcome me that the results are mys-

terious at best. What is this business about "shopping, typing piece, dinner with E, depressed"? Shopping for what? Typing what piece? Who is E? Was this "E" depressed, or was I depressed? Who cares?

7   In fact I have abandoned altogether that kind of pointless entry; instead I tell what some would call lies. "That's simply not true," the members of my family frequently tell me when they come up against my memory of a shared event. "The party was *not* for you, the spider was *not* a black widow, *it wasn't that way at all.*" Very likely they are right, for not only have I always had trouble distinguishing between what happened and what merely might have happened, but I remain unconvinced that the distinction, for my purposes, matters. The cracked crab that I recall having for lunch the day my father came home from Detroit in 1945 must certainly be embroidery, worked into the day's pattern to lend verisimilitude; I was ten years old and would not now remember the cracked crab. The day's events did not turn on cracked crab. And yet it is precisely that fictitious crab that makes me see the afternoon all over again, a home movie run all too often, the father bearing gifts, the child weeping, an exercise in family love and guilt. Or that is what it was to me. Similarly, perhaps it never did snow that August in Vermont; perhaps there never were flurries in the night wind, and maybe no one else felt the ground hardening and summer already dead even as we pretended to bask in it, but that was how it felt to me, and it might as well have snowed, could have snowed, did snow.

8   *How it felt to me:* that is getting closer to the truth about a notebook. I sometimes delude myself about why I keep a notebook, imagine that some thrifty virtue derives from preserving everything observed. See enough and write it down, I tell myself, and then some morning when the world seems drained of wonder, some day when I am only going through the motions of doing what I am supposed to do, which is write—on that bankrupt morning I will simply open my notebook and there it will all be, a forgotten account with accumulated interest, paid passage back to the world out there: dialogue overheard in hotels and elevators and at the hat-check counter in Pavillon (one middle-aged man shows his hat check to another and says, "That's my old football number"); impressions of Bettina Aptheker and Benjamin Sonnenberg and Teddy ("Mr. Acapulco") Stauffer; careful *aperçus* about tennis bums and failed fashion models and Greek shipping heiresses, one of whom taught me a significant lesson (a lesson I could have learned from F. Scott Fitzgerald, but perhaps we all must meet the very rich for ourselves) by asking, when I arrived to interview her in her orchid-filled sitting room on the second day of a paralyzing New York blizzard, whether it was snowing outside.

9   I imagine, in other words, that the notebook is about other people. But of course it is not. I have no real business with what one stranger said to another at the hat-check counter in Pavillon; in fact I suspect that the line "That's my old football number" touched not my own imagination at all, but merely some memory of something once read, probably "The Eighty-Yard Run." Nor is my concern with a woman in a dirty crepe-de-Chine wrapper in a Wilmington bar. My stake is always, of course, in the unmentioned girl in the plaid silk dress. *Remember what it was to be me:* that is always the point.

10   It is a difficult point to admit. We are brought up in the ethic that others, any others, all others, are by definition more interesting than ourselves; taught to be diffident, just this side of self-effacing. ("You're the least impor-

tant person in the room and don't forget it," Jessica Mitford's governess would hiss in her ear on the advent of any social occasion; I copied that into my notebook because it is only recently that I have been able to enter a room without hearing some such phrase in my inner ear.) Only the very young and the very old may recount their dreams at breakfast, dwell upon self, interrupt with memories of beach picnics and favorite Liberty lawn dresses and the rainbow trout in a creek near Colorado Springs. The rest of us are expected, rightly, to affect absorption in other people's favorite dresses, other people's trout.

11   And so we do. But our notebooks give us away, for however dutifully we record what we see around us, the common denominator of all we see is always, transparently, shamelessly, the implacable "I." We are not talking here about the kind of notebook that is patently for public consumption, a structural conceit for binding together a series of graceful *pensées;* we are talking about something private, about bits of the mind's string too short to use, an indiscriminate and erratic assemblage with meaning only for its maker.

12   And sometimes even the maker has difficulty with the meaning. There does not seem to be, for example, any point in my knowing for the rest of my life that, during 1964, 720 tons of soot fell on every square mile of New York City, yet there it is in my notebook, labeled "FACT." Nor do I really need to remember that Ambrose Bierce liked to spell Leland Stanford's name "£eland $tanford" or that "smart women almost always wear black in Cuba," a fashion hint without much potential for practical application. And does not the relevance of these notes seem marginal at best?:

> In the basement museum of the Inyo County Courthouse in Independence, California, sign pinned to a mandarin coat: "This MANDARIN COAT was often worn by Mrs. Minnie S. Brooks when giving lectures on her TEAPOT COLLECTION."

> Redhead getting out of car in front of Beverly Wilshire Hotel, chinchilla stole, Vuitton bags with tags reading:

MRS LOU FOX

HOTEL SAHARA

VEGAS

13   Well, perhaps not entirely marginal. As a matter of fact, Mrs. Minnie S. Brooks and her MANDARIN COAT pull me back into my own childhood, for although I never knew Mrs. Brooks and did not visit Inyo County until I was thirty, I grew up in just such a world, in houses cluttered with Indian relics and bits of gold ore and ambergris and the souvenirs my Aunt Mercy Farnsworth brought back from the Orient. It is a long way from that world to Mrs. Lou Fox's world, where we all live now, and is it not just as well to remember that? Might not Mrs. Minnie S. Brooks help me to remember what I am? Might not Mrs. Lou Fox help me to remember what I am not?

14   But sometimes the point is harder to discern. What exactly did I have in mind when I noted down that it cost the father of someone I know $650 a month to light the place on the Hudson in which he lived before the Crash? What use was I planning to make of this line by Jimmy Hoffa: "I may have my faults, but being wrong ain't one of them"? And although I think it interesting

to know where the girls who travel with the Syndicate have their hair done when they find themselves on the West Coast, will I ever make suitable use of it? Might I not be better off just passing it on to John O'Hara? What is a recipe for sauerkraut doing in my notebook? What kind of magpie keeps this notebook? *"He was born the night the Titanic went down."* That seems a nice enough line, and I even recall who said it, but is it not really a better line in life than it could ever be in fiction?

15   But of course that is exactly it: not that I should ever use the line, but that I should remember the woman who said it and the afternoon I heard it. We were on her terrace by the sea, and we were finishing the wine left from lunch, trying to get what sun there was, a California winter sun. The woman whose husband was born the night the *Titanic* went down wanted to rent her house, wanted to go back to her children in Paris. I remember wishing that I could afford the house, which cost $1,000 a month. "Someday you will," she said lazily. "Someday it all comes." There in the sun on her terrace it seemed easy to believe in someday, but later I had a low-grade afternoon hangover and ran over a black snake on the way to the supermarket and was flooded with inexplicable fear when I heard the checkout clerk explaining to the man ahead of me why she was finally divorcing her husband. "He left me no choice," she said over and over as she punched the register. "He has a little seven-month-old baby by her, he left me no choice." I would like to believe that my dread then was for the human condition, but of course it was for me, because I wanted a baby and did not then have one and because I wanted to own the house that cost $1,000 a month to rent and because I had a hang-over.

16   It all comes back. Perhaps it is difficult to see the value in having one's self back in that kind of mood, but I do see it; I think we are well advised to keep on nodding terms with the people we used to be, whether we find them attractive company or not. Otherwise they turn up unannounced and surprise us, come hammering on the mind's door at 4 a.m. of a bad night and demand to know who deserted them, who betrayed them, who is going to make amends. We forget all too soon the things we thought we could never forget. We forget the loves and the betrayals alike, forget what we whispered and what we screamed, forget who we were. I have already lost touch with a couple of people I used to be; one of them, a seventeen-year-old, presents little threat, although it would be of some interest to me to know again what it feels like to sit on a river levee drinking vodka-and-orange-juice and listening to Les Paul and Mary Ford and their echoes sing "How High the Moon" on the car radio. (You see I still have the scenes, but I no longer perceive myself among those present, no longer could even improvise the dialogue.) The other one, a twenty-three-year-old, bothers me more. She was always a good deal of trouble, and I suspect she will reappear when I least want to see her, skirts too long, shy to the point of aggravation, always the injured party, full of recriminations and little hurts and stories I do not want to hear again, at once saddening me and angering me with her vulnerability and ignorance, an apparition all the more insistent for being so long banished.

17   It is a good idea, then, to keep in touch, and I suppose that keeping in touch is what notebooks are all about. And we are all on our own when it comes to keeping those lines open to ourselves: your notebook will never help me, nor mine you. *"So what's new in the whiskey business?"* What could that possibly mean to you? To me it means a blonde in a Pucci bathing

suit sitting with a couple of fat men by the pool at the Beverly Hills Hotel. Another man approaches, and they all regard one another in silence for a while. "So what's new in the whiskey business?" one of the fat men finally says by way of welcome, and the blonde stands up, arches one foot and dips it in the pool, looking all the while at the cabaña where Baby Pignatari is talking on the telephone. That is all there is to that, except that several years later I saw the blonde coming out of Saks Fifth Avenue in New York with her California complexion and a voluminous mink coat. In the harsh wind that day she looked old and irrevocably tired to me, and even the skins in the mink coat were not worked the way they were doing them that year, not the way she would have wanted them done, and there is the point of the story. For a while after that I did not like to look in the mirror, and my eyes would skim the newspapers and pick out only the deaths, the cancer victims, the premature coronaries, the suicides, and I stopped riding the Lexington Avenue IRT because I noticed for the first time that all the strangers I had seen for years—the man with the seeing-eye dog, the spinster who read the classified pages every day, the fat girl who always got off with me at Grand Central—looked older than they once had.

18   It all comes back. Even that recipe for sauerkraut: even that brings it back. I was on Fire Island when I first made that sauerkraut, and it was raining, and we drank a lot of bourbon and ate the sauerkraut and went to bed at ten, and I listened to the rain and the Atlantic and felt safe. I made the sauerkraut again last night and it did not make me feel any safer, but that is, as they say, another story.

FORMULA PARAGRAPHS

It would be difficult if not impossible to give specific instructions for writing most of the paragraphs that we have read so far. But there are some kinds of useful paragraphs that are not so difficult to explain, and for which one can give specific instructions. These are certainly not the *only* kinds of paragraphs that you will need or want to write, but they are commonly used by all writers, and they have this advantage: *anyone can produce them by following a clearly stated set of rules.* Thus, one might call them "formula" paragraphs.

These paragraphs have the following parts: (1) a *topic;* (2) a *restriction* of that topic or sometimes more than one restriction; (3) one or more *illustrations.* We will call this the *TRI* paragraph. The topic is a general statement at the beginning; the restriction is a clarification or qualification; and the illustration is an example or instance.

> *Topic*   Like almost every professional football player, I'm simply not a one-dimensional figure.

Restriction   I'm a businessman much of the time.

Illustration   I own part of the American Archery Company in Wisconsin and part of the Packer Diving Company in Louisiana.

Illustration   I'm the host of a syndicated TV show once a week during the football season, and I'm involved in half a dozen advertising ventures.

Illustration   I follow the stock market.

Illustration   I keep looking for new opportunities for investments.

—Jerry Kramer, *Instant Replay*

In the example paragraph, Jerry Kramer makes a general statement with his topic. He then qualifies and explains the topic with his restriction. Finally, he gives four illustrations.

The instructions for writing such a TRI paragraph are obvious:

1. Provide a topic.
2. Restrict (qualify, explain) it one or more times.
3. Illustrate it one or more times by giving *specific examples.*

Here is another, somewhat more complex, example of the basic TRI pattern. (Notice that the author has added a *summary* or *conclusion* to the basic pattern.)

Topic   Every generation makes mistakes, always has and always will.

Restriction   We have made our share.

Restriction   But my generation has made America the most affluent country on earth.

Illustration   It has tackled, head-on, a racial problem which no nation on earth in the history of mankind has dared to do.

Illustration   It has publicly declared war on poverty

Illustration   and it has gone to the moon;

Illustration   it has desegregated schools and abolished polio;

Illustration   it has presided over what is probably the greatest social and economic revolution in man's history.

Summary   It has begun these things, not finished them. It has declared itself, and committed itself, and taxed itself,

INSTANT REPLAY   From *Instant Replay* by Jerry Kramer. Copyright © 1968 by Jerry Kramer and Dick Schaap. Reprinted by arrangement with The New American Library, Inc., New York, New York.

and damn near run itself into the ground in the cause of social justice and reform.

—K. Ross Toole, "I Am Tired of the Tyranny of Spoiled Brats," Billings, Montana, *Gazette*

Paragraph Practice

1. Choose one of the following *topics,* and by supplying one *restriction* and three *illustrations,* develop a TRI paragraph.

    a. Most people are guided by the principle of self-interest, looking out for themselves before they think of others.
    b. In theory, at least, classrooms should be democratic.
    c. Television programs often appeal to our lurid interest in violence.
    d. Team sports develop the character of the players.
    e. Arguments concerning capital punishment are often based on emotion, not reason.

2. Choose another one of the above topics. Develop it with two restrictions and one or more illustrations. Supply a summary or conclusion.

3. Write your own topic. Restrict it with a sentence that begins with *but* or *however.* Illustrate it one or more times. For example:

Topic	The formula paragraph is easy to write.
Restriction	*However,* in the real world of writing, not all paragraphs are of this kind, though many are.
Illustration	Some paragraphs are examples in and of themselves.
Illustration	Others serve as transitions and are very brief.
Illustration	As a glance at any essay will reveal, most paragraphs do not contain illustrations.

4. Write your own topic. Restrict it with a sentence that begins with *but* or *however.* Illustrate it one or more times. Finally, provide a summary sentence or conclusion. For example:

Topic	In most cases, correct punctuation and spelling are not essential to meaning.
Restriction	*But* there are excellent reasons for spelling and punctuating correctly in much of your writing.
Illustration	Most readers will simply expect you to follow the "rules" and will be offended if you do not.
Illustration	Even though readers can gain the meaning of error-riddled texts, these errors call attention to themselves and therefore make reading for meaning more difficult.

Summary   In general, a writer who violates the obvious norms of edited standard English runs the risk of losing effectiveness with readers.

Variations on Formula Paragraphs

We have seen that some paragraphs have the parts topic, restriction(s), illustration(s): TRI. Writers can use these "building blocks" in a great variety of ways. For example, some paragraphs consist merely of a topic and a restriction or two:

Topic   Most people who are considered mentally sick (especially those confined involuntarily) are defined by their relatives, friends, employers, or perhaps the police—*not* by themselves.

Restriction   These people have upset the social order—by disregarding the conventions of polite society or by violating laws—so we label them "mentally ill" and punish them by commitment to a mental institution.

—Thomas S. Szasz, "What Psychiatry Can and Cannot Do," *Harper's Magazine*

Topic   Obedience is as basic an element in the structure of social life as one can point to.

Restriction   Some system of authority is a requirement of all communal living, and it is only the person dwelling in isolation who is not forced to respond, with defiance or submission, to the commands of others.

Restriction   For many people, obedience is a deeply ingrained behavior tendency, indeed a potent impulse overriding training in ethics, sympathy, and moral conduct.

—Stanley Milgram, "The Perils of Obedience"

Other paragraphs consist of a topic and illustrations, with no restriction:

Topic   The reasons for depression are not so interesting as the way one handles it, simply to stay alive.

| Illustration | This morning I woke at four and lay awake for an hour or so in a bad state. It is raining again. I got up finally and went about the daily chores, waiting for the sense of doom to lift—and what did it was watering the house plants. Suddenly joy came back because I was fulfilling a simple need, a living one. |
| Illustration | Dusting never has this effect (and that may be why I am such a poor housekeeper!), but feeding the cats when they are hungry, giving Punch clean water, makes me suddenly feel calm and happy. |

—May Sarton, *Journal of Solitude*

In this paragraph, May Sarton tells us that the ways of handling depression are interesting, and then she illustrates two of those ways: watering her plants and feeding her cats.

Indeed, we can do all sorts of things with the Topic-Restriction-Illustration building blocks.

Notice how we can rearrange the paragraph by Jerry Kramer on pages 119–20, thereby achieving different emphasis but still having a coherent paragraph:

Illustration	I own part of the American Archery Company in Wisconsin and part of the Packer Diving Company in Louisiana.
Illustration	I'm the host of a syndicated TV show once a week during football season,
Illustration	and I'm involved in half a dozen advertising ventures.
Illustration	I follow the stock market.
Illustration	I keep looking for new opportunities for investments.
Topic	Like almost every professional football player, I'm simply not a one-dimensional figure.
Restriction	I'm a businessman much of the time.

It would appear, then, that our handy and simple TRI formula has a great deal of versatility: (1) we can create paragraphs that contain only TR; (2) we can also create paragraphs that contain only TI; (3) we can rearrange the parts in many ways. What started out as a series of rules that appeared restrictive has become a versatile guide to the creation of paragraphs.

Varying the Formula

1. Write a paragraph containing a topic, a restriction, and two illustrations: TRII. Next, *making whatever adjustments are necessary for coherence,* rearrange the TRII form so that the paragraph is IITR.

2. Write a paragraph containing a topic and two restrictions.

3. Write a paragraph containing a topic and two illustrations. Making adjustments necessary for coherence, change it to the form IIT.

4. Write a paragraph containing a topic, two restrictions, and one illustration: TRRI. Making adjustments necessary for coherence, change it to the form ITRR.

5. Explain why you would be unlikely to write a paragraph containing two topics.

6. If you are using a collection of essays in your class (a "reader"), look through it to find paragraphs that use the TRI formula and its variations.

7. Below are three formula paragraphs. Use these for the body of an essay, for which you supply a *beginning* and a *concluding* paragraph. In addition to writing an introductory paragraph that will explain what is to come and a final paragraph that draws a conclusion, identify the TRI pattern in the formula paragraphs.

> Because of its wide range of subjects, *Esquire* is currently one of the most interesting quality magazines published in America. Its articles range from the serious to the frivolous. The September 26, 1978 issue contains a penetrating article on General Alexander Haig, who at that time was the supreme commander of NATO forces. In the same issue is an article titled "Speedboats Now! Faster, Sexier."

> The *Atlantic,* one of America's oldest continuously published magazines, tends to be more dignified and restrained than *Esquire.* "The New York Scene" is a typical article. Another is "The Nonviolent War Against Nuclear Power."

> *Quest,* a new magazine, seems to be attempting to combine the dignity of the *Atlantic* with the wide range of interests characteristic of *Esquire.* However, since *Quest* is published by a religious foundation, it probably avoids some topics. Also, the tone of the magazine is always definitely upbeat. A typical article is "Samaritan for Eagles," which a blurb in the table of contents describes this way: "Phil Shultz is a retired surgeon who loves birds of prey, especially those gunned down by willful hunters. How he heals the victims and helps them fly again."

Some Other Forms

It can be useful to look at some other obvious paragraph forms.

The following paragraph is built on an interesting plan. The author states a topic, he gives an illustration supporting that generalization, and then he restates the topic.

a.

Topic	America is by far the most criminal nation in the world.
Illustration	On a per capita basis, Americans commit about twice as many assaults as Frenchmen, triple the number of rapes as Italians, and five times as many murders as Englishmen.
Restatement	From the price manipulations of Westinghouse-General Electric and the mass violence of Los Angeles down to the subway muggings and the petty thievery of juvenile gangs, it is apparent, in James Truslow Adams' words, that "lawlessness has been and is one of the most distinctive American traits."

—William M. McCord, "We Ask the Wrong
Questions About Crime"

The following two paragraphs are interesting, both in their structure and in their subject matter. Look closely at how they work.

I

b.

Example 1	Once another woman and I were talking about male resistance to Woman's Liberation, and she said that she didn't understand why men never worry about women taking their jobs away but worry only about the possibility that women may stop making love to them and bearing their children.
Example 2	And once I was arguing with a man I know about Woman's Liberation, and he said he wished he had a motorcycle gang with which to invade a Woman's Liberation meeting and rape everybody in it.
Conclusion based on examples	There are times when I understand the reason for men's feelings.
Explanation of conclusion	I have noticed that beyond the feminists' talk about the myth of the vaginal orgasm lies a radical resentment of their position in

WE ASK THE WRONG QUESTIONS ABOUT CRIME   William M. McCord, *New York Times Magazine,* 21 Nov. 1965, p. 27. Copyright © 1966/65 by The New York Times Company. Reprinted by permission.

the sexual act. And I have noticed that when I feel most militantly feminist I am hardly at all interested in sex.

II

Actual topic sentence for both paragraphs   Almost one could generalize from that: the feminist impulse is anti-sexual.

Restriction of the topic   The very notion of women gathering in groups is somehow anti-sexual, anti-male, just as the purposely all-male group is anti-female.

Extended illustration   There is often a sense of genuine cultural rebellion in the atmosphere of a Woman's Liberation meeting. Women sit with their legs apart, carelessly dressed, barely made-up, exhibiting their feelings or the holes at the knees of their jeans with an unprovocative candor which is hardly seen at all in the outside world. Of course, they are demonstrating by their postures that they are in effect off duty, absolved from the compulsion to make themselves attractive, and yet, as the world measures these things, such demonstrations could in themselves be seen as evidence of neurosis: we have all been brought up to believe that a woman who was "whole" would appear feminine even on the barricades.

—Sally Kempton, "Cutting Loose"

The second paragraph above is an example of a common and useful pattern: topic, one or more restrictions, and one or more illustrations.

Another common pattern is question-answer.

c.   Psychotic experience goes beyond the horizons of our common, that is, our communal, sense.

Question   What region of experience does this lead to?

Answers   It entails a loss of the usual foundations of the "sense" of the world that we share with one another. Old purposes no longer seem viable; old meanings are senseless; the distinctions between imagination, dream, external perceptions often seem no longer to apply in the same old way. External events may seem magically conjured up. Dreams may seem to be direct communications from others; imagination may seem to be objective reality.

—R. D. Laing, *The Politics of Experience*

Here is another example of the question-answer pattern:

d. Did Babe Ruth think up and execute that wonderful, simple visit to a sick child? Or was it cooked up by his wise, hard-boiled syndicate manager or some smart newspaperman scenting a heart story that would thrill the country? I don't know. I never really wanted to know, but I remember that at the time I had my suspicions. There were too many reporters and photographers present.

—Paul Gallico, *Farewell to Sport*

Paragraph Practice

Choosing your own subjects, use example paragraphs *a*, *b*, *c*, and *d* above as models for writing four paragraphs of your own. (In the case of example *b*, you will be writing two closely related paragraphs.)

FUNCTIONS OF PARAGRAPHS

Any piece of writing that contains more than two paragraphs has a beginning paragraph, a concluding paragraph, and body paragraphs. The paragraphs that we have dealt with so far have been "body" paragraphs, the kinds of paragraphs that develop ideas within essays. And there is yet another kind: *transitional* paragraphs, which help us get from one paragraph to another, to see the connection between the two.

The following brief essay illustrates the function of the four kinds of paragraphs.

Beginning   In this age of electronic marvels—of computers and calculators, tape recorders, television—we often forget that the book is an extremely efficient piece of technology. The glamour of the new hardware, the

FAREWELL TO SPORT   Paul Gallico (New York: Alfred A. Knopf, 1937). Copyright © 1937, 1938, and renewed in 1966 by Paul Gallico. Reprinted by permission of Alfred A. Knopf, Inc.

speed with which the machines function, the hint of futurism about them—these make books seem like quaint relics for some people.

Transition   And yet, the book has enormous advantages over all other information systems.

Body   Have you ever tried to glance quickly through the information on a computer screen, getting an almost instantaneous sense of the contents? As a matter of fact, the book allows just such sampling and riffling, for the main difference between a book and electronic devices is that the contents of a book exists in space and is stationary, whereas the contents of electronic devices exist in time and are ephemeral. You can even turn the corner of a page down to help find your place, and you can make marginal notes and underline.

Body   The book is completely portable. It needs no hookups, power sources, or phone lines. You can carry it with you wherever you go, as is the case with other print media such as newspapers and magazines. If you want to make computer data portable in this way, you get a printout, which is nothing more than a kind of "book."

Transition   The book probably has less whimsical importance than has so far been indicated in this discussion.

Body   It is just possible that the book enables humans to think in ways and with power that would be inconceivable in nonliterate electronic societies. We know, for instance, that literacy develops the logical, sequential powers of the brain's left hemisphere. The transfer of information from the printed page must be neurologically different from the transfer of information from a television screen; hence, we can safely speculate that total reliance on television for information would have a significant influence on thought processes. Furthermore, the book allows readers to get at information in "chunks" of varying sizes, and this is an important fact. For example, in reading a book on a subject that I am interested in and familiar with, I might race through one chapter, spend considerable time on a short section that contains information which is new to me, ponder an ambiguous sentence, and so on. In other words, I can choose my own reading speed and strategies.

Conclusion   It is unlikely that present or future electronic marvels will do away with the book. This means that the old literacy is here to stay—the old literacy and the joy that it brings to readers.

Notice in particular how the transitional paragraphs work. The first gets the reader into the subject; the second signals a change in tone and purpose.

What kinds of beginnings do professional authors use? And how do they conclude their writings?

The First Paragraph

Here are some typical kinds of opening paragraphs that you can adapt for your own writing.

A Summary Paragraph

American colleges and universities are wondering whether they are entering an era of basic change in the relations between students and their professors. The rules of student life are probably going to be liberalized; militant undergraduates, viewing themselves not without reason as an "exploited class," will ask for more than an advisory role in the formation of courses and curriculums. A new mode of student self-government, which extends both the duties and the rights of self-discipline, is long overdue. At the same time there is a growing concern that the demands for students' "rights" may take on the character of ideological pressures on the university and pose a threat to its fundamental work as the bearer and transmitter of the heritage of science and learning. An "ideological university" has ceased to be a community of free-minded scholars.

—Lewis S. Feuer, "The Risk Is Juvenocracy"

This opening paragraph is a summary of the essay that follows. In fact, one could make a pretty good outline of the entire essay just by looking at the ideas in the opening paragraph. If you can write such a paragraph *before* you produce the rest of the first draft, then you will have made a great leap forward in your writing task, for it is clear that you have the body of your essay firmly in mind, and the remainder of your job is to deal with each of the ideas fully enough to satisfy the reader. Of course, we can't say whether this author wrote his opening paragraph before or after he had completed the rest of his essay.

An Unexpected Twist

The wife of a new neighbor from up on the corner came down and walked up to my wife and started acting nice, which must have exhausted her.

—Jimmy Breslin, *The World of Jimmy Breslin*

This short first paragraph does not indicate what is to come in the essay, but it is vivid and arresting; it catches the reader's interest with its unexpected twist.

A Question

Why were so few voices raised in the ancient world in protest against the ruthlessness of man? Why are human beings so obsequious, ready to kill and ready to die at the call of kings and chieftains?

—Abraham J. Heschel, *The Prophets*

An essay can begin with a general question that the body of the essay answers.

"Once Upon a Time"

There was once a town in the heart of America where all life seemed in harmony with its surroundings. The town lay in the midst of a checkerboard of prosperous farms, with fields of grain and hillsides of orchards where, in spring, white clouds of bloom drifted above the green fields. In autumn, oak and maple and birch set up a blaze of color that flamed and flickered across a backdrop of pines. Then foxes barked in the hills and deer silently crossed the fields, half hidden in the mists of the fall mornings.

—Rachel Carson, *Silent Spring*

This descriptive-narrative paragraph is a variation of the "once-upon-a-time" beginning.

A Statement of Purpose

You know you have to read "between the lines" to get the most out of anything. I want to persuade you to do something equally important in the course of your reading. I want to persuade you to "write between the lines." Unless you do, you are not likely to do the most efficient kind of reading.

—Mortimer J. Adler, "How to Mark a Book,"
Saturday Review of Literature

This is a clear, blunt statement of purpose, and it was a very effective way to start this particular essay.

An Analogy

Drawing a daily comic strip is not unlike having an English theme hanging over your head every day for the rest of your life. I was never very good at writing those English themes in high school, and I usually put them off until the last minute. The only thing that saves me in trying to keep up with a comic strip schedule is the fact that it is quite a bit more enjoyable.

—Charles M. Schulz, "But a Comic Strip Has
to Grow," *Saturday Review*

The analogy points up the main problem that a comic strip artist faces and thus indicates the direction that the essay will take.

An Anecdote

Recently I have had occasion to live again near my old college campus. I went into a hole-in-the-wall bakery where the proprietor recognized me after ten years. "You haven't changed a bit, son," he said, "but can you still digest my pumpernickel? The stomach gets older, no? Maybe you want something softer now—a nice little loaf I got here."

—Herbert Gold, *The Age of Happy Problems*

You can start an essay with an anecdote from personal experience—one that is relevant to the topic of the essay.

Using Ingenuity

The point about opening paragraphs is simple: there is no reason for every essay to begin with a simple announcement of the subject ("In the following paragraphs I intend to discuss . . ."), even though that bare, direct kind of beginning is just right for some pieces. The first paragraph you use in your final draft may be the last one that you write, but whenever you compose it, you should think of your purpose and your audience. Do you want to amuse, inform, or convince? Do you want your *tone* to be serious? Ironic? Informal? Chatty?

Exercise

If you are using a collection of essays in your class, go through them to discover the kinds of openings the authors use. If any of the beginnings interest you particularly, be prepared to explain why. (If your class does not use a "reader," you can probably borrow one from a friend or find one in the library.)

Transitional Paragraphs

Transitional paragraphs are bridges that get readers from one idea to the next; they show connections and establish relationships. In the following example, notice how the short middle paragraph allows us to go easily from the ideas of the first to the ideas of the third.

But nothing in that end of town was as good as the dumpground that scattered along a little runoff coulee dipping down toward the river from the south bench. Through a historical process that went back, probably, to the roots of community sanitation and distaste for eyesores, but that in law dated from the Unincorporated Towns Ordinance of the territorial government, passed in 1888, the dump was one of the very first community enterprises, almost our town's first institution.

More than that, it contained relics of every individual who had ever lived there, and of every phase of the town's history.

The bedsprings on which the town's first child was begotten might be there; the skeleton of a boy's pet colt; two or three volumes of Shakespeare bought in haste and error from a peddler, later loaned in carelessness, soaked with water and chemicals in a house fire, and finally thrown out to flap their stained eloquence in the prairie wind.

—Wallace Stegner, *Wolf Willow*

WOLF WILLOW   Wallace Stegner (New York: Viking Press, 1962). Copyright © 1955, 1957, 1958, 1959, 1962 by Wallace Stegner. Reprinted by permission of Brant and Brant Literary Agents, Inc.

Transitional paragraphs can be very simple:

In Wonderland, Alice can shrink magically in an instant. Magic, though, can't shrivel prices.

Except perhaps the magic of technology.

A set of computations that cost $1.26 on an IBM computer in 1952 costs only 7/10ths of a cent today. That's because IBM scientists and engineers have put their imagination and intelligence to work to create and improve information technology.

—IBM advertisement, *Newsweek*

As a matter of fact, however, most transitions between paragraphs are words or phrases in the first sentence of the paragraph to be related to the one before it.

The best way to learn about transitions, though, is to see them in action, so read the following essay, and pay attention to all of the words and phrases in italics, for they are *transitions*.

The Eureka Phenomenon

Isaac Asimov

In the old days, when I was writing a great deal of fiction, there would come, once in a while, moments when I was stymied. Suddenly, I would find I had written myself into a hole and could see no way out. To take care of that, I developed a technique which invariably worked.

It was simply this—I went to the movies. Not just any movie. I had to pick a movie which was loaded with action but which made no demands on the intellect. As I watched, I did my best to avoid any conscious thinking concerning my problem, and when I came out of the movie I knew exactly what I would have to do to put the story back on the track.

It never failed.

In fact, when I was working on my doctoral dissertation, too many years ago, I suddenly came across a flaw in my logic that I had not noticed before and that knocked out everything I had done. In utter panic, I made my way to a Bob Hope movie—and came out with the necessary change in point of view.

It is my belief, *you see,* that thinking is a double phenomenon like breathing.

You can control breathing by deliberate voluntary action: you can breathe deeply and quickly, or you can hold your breath altogether, regardless of the body's needs at the time. This, however,

THE EUREKA PHENOMENON   Isaac Asimov, *The Left Hand of the Electron* (New York: Mercury Press-Doubleday, 1971). Reprinted by permission of Doubleday & Company, Inc.

doesn't work well for very long. Your chest muscles grow tired, your body clamors for more oxygen, or less, and you relax. The automatic involuntary control of breathing takes over, adjusts it to the body's needs and unless you have some respiratory disorder, you can forget about the whole thing.

Well, you can think by deliberate voluntary action, too, and I don't think it is much more efficient on the whole than voluntary breath control is. You can deliberately force your mind through channels of deductions and associations in search of a solution to some problem and before long you have dug mental furrows for yourself and find yourself circling round and round the same limited pathways. If those pathways yield no solution, no amount of further conscious thought will help.

On the other hand, if you let go, then the thinking process comes under automatic involuntary control and is more apt to take new pathways and make erratic associations you would not think of consciously. The solution will then come while you think you are not thinking.

The trouble is, *though,* that conscious thought involves no muscular action and so there is no sensation of physical weariness that would force you to quit. What's more, the panic of necessity tends to force you to go on uselessly, with each added bit of useless effort adding to the panic in a vicious cycle.

It is my feeling that it helps to relax, deliberately, by subjecting your mind to material complicated enough to occupy the voluntary faculty of thought, but superficial enough not to engage the deeper involuntary one. In my case, it is an action movie; in your case, it might be something else.

I suspect it is the involuntary faculty of thought that gives rise to what we call "a flash of intuition," something that I imagine must be merely the result of unnoticed thinking.

Perhaps the most famous flash of intuition in the history of science took place in the city of Syracuse in third-century B.C. Sicily. Bear with me and I will tell you the story—

About 250 B.C., the city of Syracuse was experiencing a kind of Golden Age. It was under the protection of the rising power of Rome, but it retained a king of its own and considerable self-government; it was prosperous; and it had a flourishing intellectual life.

The king was Hieron II, and he had commissioned a new golden crown from a goldsmith, to whom he had given an ingot of gold as raw material. Hieron, being a practical man, had carefully weighed the ingot and then weighed the crown he received back. The two weights were precisely equal. Good deal!

But then he sat and thought for a while. Suppose the goldsmith had subtracted a little bit of the gold, not too much, and had substituted an equal weight of the considerably less valuable copper. The resulting alloy would still have the appearance of pure gold, but the goldsmith would be plus a quantity of gold over and above his fee. He would be buying gold with copper, so to speak, and Hieron would be neatly cheated.

Hieron didn't like the thought of being cheated any more than you or I would, but he didn't know how to find out for sure if he had been. He could scarcely punish the goldsmith on mere suspicion. What to do?

Fortunately, Hieron had an advantage few rulers in the history of the world could boast. He had a relative of considerable talent. The relative was named Archimedes and he probably had the greatest intellect the world was to see prior to the birth of Newton.

Archimedes was called in and was posed the problem. He had to determine whether the crown Hieron showed him was pure gold, or was gold to which a small but significant quantity of copper had been added.

If we were to reconstruct Archimedes' reasoning, it might go as follows. Gold was the densest known substance (at that time). Its density in modern terms is 19.3 grams per cubic centimeter. This means that a given weight of gold takes up less volume than the same weight of anything else! In fact, a given weight of pure gold takes up less volume than the same weight of any kind of impure gold.

The density of copper is 8.92 grams per cubic centimeter, just about half that of gold. If we consider 100 grams of pure gold, for instance, it is easy to calculate it to have a volume of 5.18 cubic centimeters. But suppose that 100 grams of what looked like pure gold was really only 90 grams of gold and 10 grams of copper. The 90 grams of gold would have a volume of 4.66 cubic centimeters, while the 10 grams of copper would have a volume of 1.12 cubic centimeters; for a total value of 5.78 cubic centimeters.

The difference between 5.18 cubic centimeters and 5.78 cubic centimeters is quite a noticeable one, and would instantly tell if the crown were of pure gold, or if it contained 10 per cent copper (with the missing 10 per cent of gold tucked neatly in the goldsmith's strongbox).

All one had to do, *then,* was measure the volume of the crown and compare it with the volume of the same weight of pure gold.

The mathematics of the time made it easy to measure the volume of many simple shapes: a cube, a sphere, a cone, a cylinder, any flattened object of simple regular shape and known thickness, and so on.

We can imagine Archimedes saying, "All that is necessary, sire, is to pound that crown flat, shape it into a square of uniform thickness, and then I can have the answer for you in a moment."

Whereupon Hieron must certainly have snatched the crown away and said, "No such thing. I can do that much without you; I've studied the principles of mathematics, too. This crown is a highly satisfactory work of art and I won't have it damaged. Just calculate its volume without in any way altering it."

But Greek mathematics had no way of determining the volume of anything with a shape as irregular as the crown, since integral calculus had not yet been invented (and wouldn't be for two thousand years, almost). Archimedes would have had to say, "There is no known way, sire, to carry through a non-destructive determination of volume."

"Then think of one," said Hieron testily.

And Archimedes must have set about thinking of one, and gotten nowhere. Nobody knows how long he thought, or how hard, or what hypotheses he considered and discarded, or any of the details.

What we do know is that, worn out with thinking, Archimedes decided to visit the public baths and relax. I think we are quite safe in saying that Archimedes had no intention of taking his problem to the baths with him. It would be ridiculous to imagine he would, for the public baths of a Greek metropolis weren't intended for that sort of thing.

The Greek baths were a place for relaxation. Half the social aristocracy of the town would be there and there was a great deal more to do than wash. One steamed one's self, got a massage, exercised, and engaged in general socializing. We can be sure that Archimedes intended to forget the stupid crown for a while.

One can envisage him engaging in light talk, discussing the latest news from Alexandria and Carthage, the latest scandals in town, the latest funny jokes at the expense of the country-squire Romans—and then he lowered himself into a nice hot bath which some bumbling attendant had filled too full.

The water in the bath slopped over as Archimedes got in. Did Archimedes notice that at once, or did he sigh, sink back, and paddle his feet awhile before noting the water-slop. I guess the latter. But, whether soon or late, he noticed, and that one fact, added to all the chains of reasoning his brain had been working on during the period of relaxation when it was unhampered by the comparative stupidities (even in Archimedes) of voluntary thought, gave Archimedes his answer in one blinding flash of insight.

Jumping out of the bath, he proceeded to run home at top speed through the streets of Syracuse. He did not bother to put on his clothes. The thought of Archimedes running naked through Syracuse has titillated dozens of generations of youngsters who have heard this story, but I must explain that the ancient Greeks were quite lighthearted in their attitude toward nudity. They thought no more of seeing a naked man on the streets of Syracuse, than we would on the Broadway stage.

And as he ran, Archimedes shouted over and over, "I've got it! I've got it!" Of course, knowing no English, he was compelled to shout it in Greek, so it came out, "Eureka! Eureka!"

Archimedes' solution was so simple that anyone could understand it—once Archimedes explained it.

If an object that is not affected by water in any way, is immersed in water, it is bound to displace an amount of water equal to its own volume, since two objects cannot occupy the same space at the same time.

Suppose, *then,* you had a vessel large enough to hold the crown and suppose it had a small overflow spout set into the middle of its side. And suppose further that the vessel was filled with water exactly to the spout, so that if the water level were raised a bit higher, however slightly, some would overflow.

Next, suppose that you carefully lower the crown into the water. The water level would rise by an amount equal to the volume of the crown, and that volume of water would pour out the overflow and be caught in a small vessel. Next, a lump of gold, known to be pure and exactly equal in weight to the crown, is also immersed in the water and again the level rises and the overflow is caught in a second vessel.

If the crown were pure gold, the overflow would be exactly the same in each case, and the volume of water caught in the two small vessels would be equal. If, however, the crown were of alloy, it would produce a larger overflow than the pure gold would and this would be easily noticeable.

What's more, the crown would in no way be harmed, defaced, or even as much as scratched. More important, Archimedes had discovered the "principle of buoyancy."

And was the crown pure gold? I've heard that it turned out to be alloy and that the goldsmith was executed, but I wouldn't swear to it.

How often does this "Eureka phenomenon" happen? How often is there this flash of deep insight during a moment of relaxation, this triumphant cry of "I've got it! I've got it!" which must surely be a moment of the purest ecstasy this sorry world can afford?

I wish there were some way we could tell. I suspect that in the history of science it happens often; I suspect that very few significant discoveries are made by the pure technique of voluntary thought; I suspect that voluntary thought may possibly prepare the ground (if even that), but that the final touch, the real inspiration, comes when thinking is under involuntary control.

But the world is in a conspiracy to hide the fact. Scientists are wedded to reason, to the meticulous working out of consequences from assumptions to the careful organization of experiments designed to check those consequences. If a certain line of experiments ends nowhere, it is omitted from the final report. If an inspired guess turns out to be correct, it is not reported as an inspired guess. Instead, a solid line of voluntary thought is invented after the fact to lead up to the thought, and that is what is inserted in the final report.

The result is that anyone reading scientific papers would swear that nothing took place but voluntary thought maintaining a steady clumping stride from origin to destination, and that just can't be true.

It's such a shame. Not only does it deprive science of much of its glamour (how much of the dramatic story in Watson's *Double Helix* do you suppose got into the final reports announcing the great discovery of the structure of DNA?[1]), but it hands over the important process of "insight," "inspiration," "revelation" to the mystic.

The scientist actually becomes ashamed of having what we might call a revelation, as though to have one is to betray reason—when actually what we call revelation in a man who has devoted his life to reasoned thought, is after all merely reasoned thought that is not under voluntary control.

Only once in a while in modern times do we ever get a glimpse into the workings of involuntary reasoning, and when we do, it is always fascinating. Consider, for instance, the case of Friedrich August Kekule von Stradonitz.

In Kekule's time, a century and a quarter ago, a subject of great interest to chemists was the structure of organic molecules (those associated with living tissue). Inorganic molecules were generally simple in the sense that they were made up of few atoms. Water molecules, for instance, are made up of two atoms of hydrogen and one of oxygen (H_2O). Molecules of ordinary salt are made up of one atom of sodium and one of chlorine ($NaCl$), and so on.

Organic molecules, *on the other hand,* often contained a large number of atoms. Ethyl alcohol molecules have two carbon atoms, six hydrogen atoms, and an oxygen atom (C_2H_6O); the molecule of ordinary cane sugar is $C_{12}H_{22}O_{11}$, and other molecules are even more complex.

Then, too, it is sufficient, in the case of inorganic molecules generally, merely to know the kinds and numbers of atoms in the molecule; in organic molecules, more is necessary. Thus, dimethyl ether has the formula C_2H_6O, just as ethyl alcohol does, and yet the two are quite different in properties. Apparently, the atoms are arranged differently within the molecules—but how to determine the arrangements?

In 1852, an English chemist, Edward Frankland, had noticed that the atoms of a particular element tended to combine with a fixed number of other atoms. This combining number was called "valence." Kekule in 1858 reduced this notion to a system. The carbon atom, he decided (on the basis of plenty of chemical evidence) had a valence of four; the hydrogen atom, a valence of one; and the oxygen atom, a valence of two (and so on).

Why not represent the atoms as their symbols plus a number of attached dashes, that number being equal to the valence. Such atoms could then be put together as though they were so many Tinker Toy units and "structural formulas" could be built up.

It was possible to reason that the structural formula

---

[1] I'll tell you, in case you're curious. None! [Asimov's note].

of ethyl alcohol was

$$
\begin{array}{ccc}
\text{H} & \text{H} & \\
| & | & \\
\text{H}-\text{C}-\text{C}-\text{O}-\text{H} & & \\
| & | & \\
\text{H} & \text{H} &
\end{array}
$$

while that of dimethyl

ether was

$$
\begin{array}{ccc}
\text{H} & & \text{H} \\
| & & | \\
\text{H}-\text{C}-\text{O}-\text{C}-\text{H} \\
| & & | \\
\text{H} & & \text{H}
\end{array}
$$

In each case, there were two carbon atoms, each with four dashes attached; six hydrogen atoms, each with one dash attached; and an oxygen atom with two dashes attached. The molecules were built up of the same components, but in different arrangements.

Kekule's theory worked beautifully. It has been immensely deepened and elaborated since his day, but you can still find structures very much like Kekule's Tinker Toy formulas in any modern chemical textbook. They represent oversimplifications of the true situation, but they remain extremely useful in practice even so.

The Kekule structures were applied to many organic molecules in the years after 1858 and the similarities and contrasts in the structures neatly matched similarities and contrasts in properties. The key to the rationalization of organic chemistry had, it seemed, been found.

Yet there was one disturbing fact. The well-known chemical benzene wouldn't fit. It was known to have a molecule made up of equal numbers of carbon and hydrogen atoms. Its molecular weight was known to be 78 and a single carbon-hydrogen combination had a weight of 13. Therefore, the benzene molecule had to contain six carbon-hydrogen combinations and its formula had to be C_6H_6.

But that meant trouble. By the Kekule formulas, the hydrocarbons (molecules made up of carbon and hydrogen atoms only) could easily be envisioned as chains of carbon atoms with hydrogen atoms attached. If all the valences of the carbon atoms were filled with hydrogen atoms, as in "hexane," whose molecule looks like this—

$$
\begin{array}{ccccccc}
\text{H} & \text{H} & \text{H} & \text{H} & \text{H} & \text{H} \\
| & | & | & | & | & | \\
\text{H}-\text{C}-\text{C}-\text{C}-\text{C}-\text{C}-\text{C}-\text{H} \\
| & | & | & | & | & | \\
\text{H} & \text{H} & \text{H} & \text{H} & \text{H} & \text{H}
\end{array}
$$

the compound is said to be saturated. Such saturated hydrocarbons were found to have very little tendency to react with other substances.

If some of the valences were not filled, unused bonds were added to those connecting the carbon atoms. Double bonds were formed as in "hexene"—

$$H-\underset{\overset{|}{H}}{\overset{\overset{|}{H}}{C}}-\underset{\overset{|}{H}}{\overset{\overset{|}{H}}{C}}-\overset{\overset{|}{H}}{C}=\overset{\overset{|}{H}}{C}-\underset{\overset{|}{H}}{\overset{\overset{|}{H}}{C}}-\underset{\overset{|}{H}}{\overset{\overset{|}{H}}{C}}-H$$

Hexene is unsaturated, for that double bond has a tendency to open up and add other atoms. Hexene is chemically active.

When six carbons are present in a molecule, it takes fourteen hydrogen atoms to occupy all the valence bonds and make it inert—as in hexane. In hexene, on the other hand, there are only twelve hydrogens. If there were still fewer hydrogen atoms, there would be more than one double bond; there might even be triple bonds, and the compound would be still more active than hexene.

Yet benzene, which is C_6H_6 and has eight fewer hydrogen atoms than hexane, is less active than hexene, which has only two fewer hydrogen atoms than hexane. In fact, benzene is even less active than hexane itself. The six hydrogen atoms in the benzene molecule seem to satisfy the six carbon atoms to a greater extent than do the fourteen hydrogen atoms in hexane.

For heaven's sake, why?

This might seem unimportant. The Kekule formulas were so beautifully suitable in the case of so many compounds that one might simply dismiss benzene as an exception to the general rule.

Science, *however,* is not English grammar. You can't just categorize something as an exception. If the exception doesn't fit into the general system, then the general system must be wrong.

Or, take the more positive approach. An exception can often be made to fit into a general system, provided the general system is broadened. Such broadening generally represents a great advance and for this reason, exceptions ought to be paid great attention.

For some seven years, Kekule faced the problem of benzene and tried to puzzle out how a chain of six carbon atoms could be completely satisfied with as few as six hydrogen atoms in benzene and yet be left unsatisfied with twelve hydrogen atoms in hexene.

Nothing came to him!

And then one day in 1865 (he tells the story himself) he was in Ghent, Belgium, and in order to get to some destination, he boarded a public bus. He was tired and, undoubtedly, the droning beat of the horses' hooves on the cobblestones, lulled him. He fell into a comatose half-sleep.

In that sleep, he seemed to see a vision of atoms attaching themselves to each other in chains that moved about. (Why not? It was the sort of thing that constantly occupied his waking thoughts.) But then one chain twisted in such a way that head and tail joined, forming a ring—and Kekule woke with a start.

To himself, he must surely have shouted "Eureka," for indeed he had it. The six carbon atoms of benzene formed a ring and not a chain, so that the structural formula looked like this:

$$
\begin{array}{c}
\text{H} \\
| \\
\text{C} \\
\text{H—C} \qquad \text{C—H} \\
\text{H—C} \qquad \text{C—H} \\
\text{C} \\
| \\
\text{H}
\end{array}
$$

To be sure, there were still three double bonds, so you might think the molecule had to be very active—but now there was a difference. Atoms in a ring might be expected to have different properties from those in a chain and double bonds in one case might not have the properties of those in the other. At least, chemists could work on that assumption and see if it involved them in contradictions.

It didn't. The assumption worked excellently well. It turned out that organic molecules could be divided into two groups: aromatic and aliphatic. The former had the benzene ring (or certain other similar rings) as part of the structure and the latter did not. Allowing for different properties within each group, the Kekule structures worked very well.

For nearly seventy years, Kekule's vision held good in the hard field of actual chemical techniques, guiding the chemist through the jungle of reactions that led to the synthesis of more and more molecules. Then, in 1932, Linus Pauling applied quantum mechanics to chemical structure with sufficient subtlety to explain just why the benzene ring was so special and what had proven correct in practice proved correct in theory as well.

Other cases? Certainly.

In 1764, the Scottish engineer James Watt was working as an instrument maker for the University of Glasgow. The university gave him a model of a Newcomen steam engine, which didn't work well, and asked him to fix it. Watt fixed it without trouble, but even when it worked perfectly, it didn't work well. It was far too inefficient and consumed incredible quantities of fuel. Was there a way to improve that?

Thought didn't help; but a peaceful, relaxed walk on a Sunday afternoon did. Watt returned with the key notion in mind of using two separate chambers, one for steam only and one for cold water only, so that the same chamber did not have to be constantly cooled and reheated to the infinite waste of fuel.

The Irish mathematician William Rowan Hamilton worked up a theory of "quaternions" in 1843 but couldn't complete that theory until he grasped the fact that there were conditions under which $p \times q$ was not equal to $q \times p$. The necessary thought came to him in a flash one time when he was walking to town with his wife.

The German physiologist Otto Loewi was working on the mechanism of nerve action, in particular, on the chemicals produced by nerve endings. He awoke at 3 A.M. one night in 1921 with a perfectly clear notion of the type of experiment he would have to run to settle a key point that was puzzling him. He wrote it down and went back to sleep. When he woke in the morning, he found he couldn't remember what his inspiration had been. He remembered he had written it down, but he couldn't read his writing.

The next night, he woke again at 3 A.M. with the clear thought once more in mind. This time, he didn't fool around. He got up, dressed himself, went straight to the laboratory and began work. By 5 A.M. he had proved his point and the consequences of his findings became important enough in later years so that in 1936 he received a share in the Nobel prize in medicine and physiology.

How very often this sort of thing must happen, and what a shame that scientists are so devoted to their belief in conscious thought that they so consistently obscure the actual methods by which they obtain their results.

Conclusions

Conclusions bring a piece of writing to an end. They should not introduce new topics that leave the reader hanging. The following is the last paragraph of an essay on how off-road vehicles are ruining the desert, but notice that it does not really conclude, for it introduces a whole new line of thought about which the reader will be curious.

The California desert is part of one of the largest relatively unbroken stretches of wild land left in the United States. Now it is threatened by off-road vehicles and could be ruined. More interesting than the desert, however, is the damage that small motorized vehicles are doing to mountain forests and even the arctic tundra.

The writer has introduced a subject "more interesting" than the one covered in the essay, namely, damage to forests and the arctic tundra. The reader has every right to expect that these subjects should be developed.

The actual ending of the essay does not introduce new subject matter, and thus it really concludes.

> The California desert is part of one of the largest relatively unbroken stretches of wild land left in the United States outside Alaska. Now it is threatened and could become the genuine wasteland we once thought deserts to be. The smoke tree and the desert tortoise, the ironwood and Gambel's quail, the intaglios and the petroglyphs are disappearing. It is not yet too late, but the desert is a fragile place and cannot survive forever strip-mining by our adult playthings.
>
> —David Sheridan, "Dirt Motorbikes and Dune Buggies Threaten Deserts," *Smithsonian*

Conclusions now and then provide a summary of the piece that they end, but if an essay is relatively brief, the reader does not really need a summary.

It is very difficult to talk about conclusions out of context. A good piece of advice is this: watch the conclusions of the essays and other materials that you read. By doing this, you can learn a great deal about how to end your own writings.

DEVELOPMENT

Here is a simple and important point about paragraphs: if they are not used just to show transitions or to isolate ideas for emphasis, *they need to be developed*. So far, you have seen that paragraphs can be developed with restrictions and illustrations, and you have read a discussion of the functions of paragraphs. On pages 201–12 of Chapter 6, "Writing to Inform: Exposition," you will find a useful and thorough discussion of methods of development, illustrating how writers use comparison and contrast, classification, definition, data, and other techniques to make the main ideas of their paragraphs specific.

Often you need only sense detail, or imagery, to develop your paragraphs. For example, James Thurber *might* have written

> The room was big, and from its windows I could see the yard.

In fact, the room and the yard were important for his story "Remembrance of Things Past," and here is what he wrote about them:

> The room was long and high and musty, with a big, soft bed, and windows that looked out on the courtyard of the place. It was like a courtyard, anyway, in form and in feeling. It should have held old wagon wheels and busy men in leather aprons, but the activity I remember was that of several black-and-white kittens stalking each other in a circular bed of red geraniums, which, of course, is not like a courtyard, but nevertheless I remember the place in front of the house as being like a courtyard. A courtyard, let us say, with black-and-white kittens stalking each other in a circular bed of red geraniums.
>
> —James Thurber, *Let Your Mind Alone*

This paragraph is packed with sense details: the room *smells* musty; the bed *feels* soft; we *see* the black-and-white kittens and the red geraniums.

And notice how specific and detailed the following paragraph from "Holiday Memory," by Dylan Thomas is. (The bank holiday is celebrated in Great Britain in mid-August.)

> August Bank Holiday—a tune on an ice-cream cornet. A slap of sea and a tickle of sand. A fanfare of sunshades opening. A wince and whinny of bathers dancing into deceptive water. A tuck of dresses. A rolling of trousers. A compromise of paddlers. A sunburn of girls and a lark of boys. A silent hullabaloo of balloons.

This paragraph does not even contain sentences, just a series of images expressed in phrases.

Exercise

1. By supplying one vivid *image,* develop a paragraph on one of the following topics:

   a. Registration at my college is chaos.
   b. Scenes of nature can be awesome.
   c. The game was a battle to the death.
   d. Christmas morning was a blur of sounds, tastes, and colors.
   e. It sometimes takes courage to try new foods.

   If none of these topics appeals to you, invent your own. Here is an example:

Doing exercises for composition is excruciating. The student sits at his desk, his brow wrinkled, his muscles tense, his mind as blank as the page before him. His pen hovers above the sheet, trembling, but does not make contact. Minutes elapse, dripping away one by one, like intravenous fluid from a bottle suspended above a patient. The glare of the lamp makes a circle of brightness in the icy darkness of the room as the hopeful learner waits for inspiration to strike.

FINALLY

In conclusion, I would like to say that. . . .

No! That sort of trite statement will never serve to end this chapter—or anything else. A conclusion such as the one that I just started is enough to make any reader yawn, and who wants the last response of the reader to be a yawn (or a groan)? Instead, I'll end this chapter by purposely making it seem incomplete, by injecting, right here at the end, a note of inconclusiveness, thus:

This chapter has covered much territory, but has left some territory uncovered, for the subject of paragraphs is a very big one. Do you have any questions concerning paragraphs that the chapter has aroused but not answered?

Beyond the Paragraph

DISCOURSE BLOCKS

Not all discourse—written or spoken—is planned, but when language use is planned, the result is a series of what might be called "blocks" or "chunks." The first block, as we saw in the first chapter of this book (pages 8–11), is the *sentence;* the next higher level of structure is the *paragraph;* often, groups of paragraphs make up a *section.* (Glance at the essay "Zen: Technology and the Split Brain," which appears on pages 151–61, and you will see that it is made up of nine sections.)

Each "block" in a piece of writing—sentence, paragraph, section—contributes to the coherence and meaningfulness of the whole piece. (Books are divided into chapters, and chapters are often divided into subsections. In drama, the sections and subsections are acts and scenes.)

In this chapter, we will talk about the organization and coherence of discourse blocks.

THE WRITING TOPIC

If you have no material, you can't organize it, and if you have no purpose behind the material, you won't know how to organize it. For this reason, we will begin with a discussion of *subject* and *topic.* The subject of a piece of writing is the broad area with which

147

the writing deals: sports (or baseball), politics (or the upcoming elections), literature (or a novel by Thomas Hardy), for example. The *topic* is the point that the writer wants to make about that subject:

> Teaching young baseball players how to pitch
>
> Why everyone should support Phoghorn in the upcoming elections
>
> The idea of fate in Thomas Hardy's *Jude the Obscure*

The subject is what you write about; the topic is the point you want to make about your subject.

Sometimes this topic is relatively clear-cut and can be stated in a sentence:

> 1. The kinds of outlines are informal and formal; formal outlines consist of either phrases or sentences.

This clear-cut announcement of a topic leads the reader to expect a discussion of the three kinds of outlines.

> 2. Because she advocates a balanced municipal budget, a clampdown on pet owners who let their animals run free, and prosecution of drivers of noisy vehicles, you should support Norma Mandic for the city council.

In the essay based on this topic, one would expect to find explanation and support of the three claims made about candidate Mandic.

> 3. Carefully administered tests lead to the conclusion that consumers cannot tell the difference between Phizzy Cola and Eleven Down Cola.

Naturally, we want the details and an explanation of how the tests were conducted.

> 4. In the opinion of many historians, Harry S. Truman was one of the greatest of American presidents.

What are those opinions? Who holds them? Does the writer agree with them?

At times, however, the topic cannot be so easily stated (nor is it really necessary to confine the statement of a topic always to one sentence). Thomas Hoover, author of the essay on pages 151–61, needed the following sentences to explain his topic adequately:

. . . *the computer may actually be changing the way we use our minds.* By providing an artificial "intelligence" that amplifies the brain's capacity for logical thought, these machines may be nudging us toward an increasing reliance on "computerthink," a rigid, mechanical thought process devoid of intuition and creativity. We may be in danger of becoming no better thinkers than our machines.

Whether or not a topic is stated, *most* essays have a relatively clear-cut topic, for if they did not, readers would see no direction or purpose in the writing and, therefore, would become frustrated.

In theory, topics are arrived at by a simple process. One has a *subject.* Then one narrows that subject to manageable scope. Finally, one takes an attitude or viewpoint toward the subject, providing a slant or purpose. We can view the process like this:

1. *Subject*   The brain
   Narrowing The different functions of the two halves of the brain
   Topic   Our reliance on computers may be emphasizing the functions of one half of the brain to the detriment of the other half.

2. *Subject*   Food
   Narrowing Hamburgers
   Topic   Hamburgers in all of their varieties are really the great American food.

3. *Subject*   Education
   Narrowing My first year in college
   Topic   The major problem of my first year in college is learning to learn on my own, independently, without constant supervision.

4. *Subject*   Literature
   Narrowing My feelings about poetry
   Topic   Because it has no practical value, because I find it difficult to read, and because it was forced on me all through high school, I have a decided aversion to poetry.

5. *Subject*   Automobiles
   Narrowing The most practical family car
   Topic   The most practical family car is the Ford Fairmont or its Mercury version, the Zephyr.

Finding a Topic

1. Narrow the following subjects; then write a topic (sentence or sentences) that gives a viewpoint and purpose to the subject. In each case, you should be willing to write an essay based on the topic that you formulate.

> a. school   b. sports   c. politics   d. food   e. personal relationships   f. a phobia (an irrational fear, such as *agoraphobia,* or the fear of open places)   g. honesty   h. a hobby   i. art, music, or literature   j. the weather

2. Now that you have formulated several topics, you might want to use one for an essay. If you decide to write an essay based on the topic, remember to use the techniques for discovering subject matter that you practiced in Chapter 3 and the techniques for paragraph development that you learned in Chapter 4.

Discovered Topics

All that has been said about topics appears simple enough—an easy set of rules that anyone can apply. Actual writing, however, is often more complex than simple rules might imply. Interestingly enough, we often do not know what we want to say until we have begun to say it; we begin to develop a viewpoint and purpose as we explore the subject through writing. Sometimes we have a general interest in a subject, but don't really understand why. ("I've always been interested in astronomy. I read about it constantly, even though I'm not an astronomer. Just what is my reason for this interest?") Sometimes a subject troubles us—is problematic—for reasons that we don't fully understand. ("In most religious traditions, the principle of unselfishness, of loving one's neighbor, of self-sacrifice, is important. When I do something for someone else, am I motivated primarily by the pleasure that I receive from the act? Does this mean that I am selfish? Are human beings basically and inevitably selfish?") And sometimes we want to explore an idea just for the sake of exploring it. ("I wonder how much I really know about my own personality? How much could I learn through self-exploration?")

After having used techniques for exploring ideas and problems (see Chapter 3), the writer might still not understand the subject completely and *might begin to write about those ideas or problems in his or her journal,* the ideal discovery tool. On the other hand, the writer might simply begin to put a paper together, realizing that the act of composing—of getting ideas down in words—often brings about an understanding of what the topic actually is. The topic is discovered in the act of composing.

An Example Essay

The following essay will serve as the example for several points that will be made later in the chapter. Therefore, you should read the piece with some care.

Zen: Technology and the Split Brain

Thomas Hoover

I.

1. *In a story told not long ago in a galaxy not far away, a young space pilot named Luke Skywalker guides a high technology fighter plane on a last chance mission to destroy the forces of evil. He must thread his rocket through a nearly invisible opening, while speeding at full power. A targeting computer, which updates the ship's firing controls on a microsecond basis, is Luke's only hope.*
2. *Suddenly, at the crucial moment, he hears a voice from the past saying, "Use the* force, *Luke. The* force *is an energy field created by all living things. Trust your feelings, not the computer." Coming up hard on the target he hesitates, switches off the electronics and—when it feels right—squeezes the trigger.*
3. *Below him the enemy explodes in a blinding nova, like a thousand suns . . .*
4. That cliché-packed episode was, of course, from last year's movie blockbuster, *Star Wars,* acclaimed by many as the ultimate technology film. What did you feel when Luke switched off the computer and flew by intuition? A surge of pride—or perhaps relief—when he actually out-gunned the machine? Then you got the message: "Don't worry about all those intellectually threatening computers; a human being still can outperform a machine any day of the week." It's a reassuring tune—whistled in the dark.
5. In the real world, a computer's superior ability for split-second analysis is fact rather than futuristic fantasy. But the threat is not that the machine will outsmart us; it's that *the computer may actually be changing the way we use our own minds.* By providing an artificial

ZEN: TECHNOLOGY AND THE SPLIT BRAIN   Thomas Hoover, *Omni,* October 1978, pp. 123–28. Reprinted by permission of Thomas Hoover.

"intelligence" that amplifies the brain's capacity for logical thought, these machines may be nudging us toward an increasing reliance on "computerthink," a rigid, mechanical thought process devoid of intuition and creativity. We may be in danger of becoming no better thinkers than our machines.

II.   Two Sides of the Mind

1. Perhaps the easiest way to understand this development is to recall some findings about the brain itself. In the late 1960s, an experimental treatment for patients suffering from severe *grand mal* epilepsy was conceived by neurosurgeon Joseph Bogen and psychologist Roger Sperry. They decided to try the radical step of severing the bundle of nerves connecting the two halves of the brain. The two scientists suspected that this connector, called the *corpus callosum,* was leaking electrical malfunctions in one half of the brain to the other. They hoped a radical separation would isolate the source, diminishing its impact. To their delight the operations succeeded admirably in reducing both the occurrence and extent of seizures.

2. Afterwards, Sperry subjected his patients to some standard tests of identification and verbal response. To his amazement he discovered that the hemispheres of our brain are specialized, with each side handling different cognitive functions, and when they are separated they seem to act as *two* independent, autonomous types of consciousness. For example, language ability in many people seems to reside in the left side of the brain, so that it was possible for a patient from a split-brain operation to hold an unseen object in the hand controlled by the right-brain (this being the left hand, since we're cross-wired) and be unable to name the object. However, when the right hemisphere was shown a picture of an object, such as a spoon, the subject could use his left hand to pick that object from an unseen assortment of items. *But the spoon could not be named.* In this experiment, with apologies to an ancient Taoist/Zen adage, "The hemisphere that speaks does not know; the hemisphere that knows does not speak."

3. The discovery that many people have verbal ability concentrated in the left side of their brain led experimenters to wonder exactly what the right side was thinking while the left was talking. Ever since the Greeks, who used the same term—*logos*—for both "word" and "reason," we in the West have assumed that language and higher intelligence are synonymous. But further research found a number of differences in function. For example, the left hemisphere reads music from notes on a page, but the right remembers the music we hear; the left handles math, the right perceives poetry. Thus the brain seems divided by type of intellect. The language-using left side of the brain is process oriented and works through things sequentially (just like a computer), while the mute right hemisphere concerns itself with patterns, spatial relationships, concepts.

4.   Sperry's finding that half our brain contains knowledge we can't verbalize sounds curiously like an insight spelled out over 2000 years ago by one of the Chinese forerunners of Zen, a Taoist named Chuang Tzu. This philosopher quoted a story told by a wheelmaker that could have come from a 1970s paper on split-brain research.

5.   *When I am carving a wheel, if my stroke is too slow, then it bites deep but is not steady; if my stroke is too fast, then it is steady, but does not go deep. The right pace, neither slow nor fast, cannot get into the hand unless it comes from the heart. It is a thing that cannot be put into words; there is an art in it that I cannot explain to my son. That is why it is impossible for me to let him take over my work, and here I am at the age of seventy, still making wheels. In my opinion it must have been the same with the men of old. All that was worth handing on died with them; the rest, they put into their books.*

6.   The wheelmaker recognized that there was a nonverbal, intuitive kind of knowledge that had nothing to do with linear, structured analysis. There are some things that have to be worked out one step at a time (quick, divide 18 into 100!) and there are things you have to feel (at what point do you downshift your sports car for a curve?).

7.   Sperry's experiments have been well popularized by Robert Ornstein of the Langley Porter Neuropsychiatric Institute in San Francisco, who has gone on to test the brain hemisphere activity of normal people as they carry out various tasks, with findings that generally support Sperry's split-brain theory. Thus modern brain research has finally verified a quality of the mind we've suspected for a long time. Look around and you find examples of the two ways of thought everywhere: objective/subjective, law/art, rational/mystical, yin/yang, digital/analog, sequential/holistic.

III.   Science and Intuition

1.   How important is our power of nonanalytical thought to the practice of science? It's the most important thing we have, declares the Princeton physicist historian Thomas Kuhn who argues that major breakthroughs occur only after scientists finally concede that certain physical phenomena cannot be explained by extending the logic of old theories. Consider the belief that the sun and planets move around the earth, which reigned prior to 1500. This idea served nicely for a number of centuries, but then became too cumbersome to describe the motions of heavenly bodies. So the Polish astronomer Copernicus invented a new reality that was based on a totally different "paradigm" or model—that the earth and planets move around the sun.

2.   When the paradigm being dissected by the logical, scientific method finally fails to explain observations, the creative portion of our intelligence must jump outside this failed "reality." Which is not to say that a new paradigm is any more true than the older idea; it

merely explains observations a bit better for the time being. As did the ancient Zen teachers, Kuhn concludes that the real truth of our universe may be unknowable. But the important thing here is that the new reality doesn't come about by approaching a problem rationally, since rationality only can operate within the old rules. As does a computer, the human mind in its logical mode must follow the rules of logic. To go outside them would be "irrational."

3. There are many cases of scientists producing major breakthroughs by exploiting their mind's capacity for nonrational creativity. For example, the German chemist Kekulé in 1865 solved the mystery of benzene's molecular structure in a dream. (Most organic molecules are connected strings of carbon atoms; the benzene molecule is a hexagonal ring.) According to the traditional account, Kekulé nodded off one afternoon and dreamed of a snake writhing uncontrollably. It suddenly seized its own tail and slowly began to rotate, in a stable condition. When the scientist awoke, he knew he'd found the answer. Thus the cornerstone of organic chemistry came out of a dream, not a "logical" scientific experiment in the laboratory.

4. Similarly, the man who verified the existence of cosmic rays, Robert Millikan, in a burst of insight, conceived an experiment that first measured the charge of the electron while riding on a train. There even is a story, considered apocryphal by some, that Nobel-prize physicist Donald Glaser (now at the University of California Berkeley) envisioned the bubble chamber, a critical invention in sub-atomic particle research, while meditating on the beads forming in his beer glass at an Ann Arbor, Michigan, saloon.

5. Albert Einstein, whose atomic-age "reality" that mass is convertible to energy replaced the earlier Newtonian cornerstone that mass is always conserved, was another nonverbal thinker. "The real thing is intuition," he said. "A thought comes, and I may try to express it in words afterwards." But perhaps the best-known example of nonanalytical creativity was Leonardo da Vinci, whose notebooks are crammed with mechanical technology centuries ahead of his time. His *circa* 1490 drawings include a spring-driven car, a spinning wheel, even a rudimentary helicopter. Yet it was all apparently done visually, intuitively.

IV.   Zen and Creativity

1. The powers of intuition are nothing new to the thinkers of the Far East (the *force* in *Star Wars* is no more than a Broadway version of the 3000-year-old Chinese *tao,* that indescribable unity of all things). In fact, intuition was viewed in the Far East as the *only* adequate means of understanding the natural world. Many of the "realities" that arose from this non-logical intelligence were extremely perceptive, preceding similar realizations in the West by centuries.

2.   But how can intuition be more correct than hard scientific data? It turns out that facts alone are only one part of scientific truth. As we learned from Copernicus, science also is ideas. Arthur Koestler comments in *The Sleepwalkers:* "Insofar as factual knowledge is concerned, Copernicus was no better off, and in some respects worse off, than the Greek astronomers of Alexandria who lived at the time of Jesus Christ. . . . They had more precise instruments for observing stars than Copernicus had. Copernicus himself hardly bothered with star gazing: he relied on the observations of Hipparchus and Ptolemy (who) had the same observational data, the same instruments, the same know-how in geometry, as he did."

3.   An Eastern paradigm derived from intuitive wisdom that turned out to be more correct than the longstanding position of Western philosophy is dramatized by Werner Heisenberg's 1920's Uncertainty Principle. This landmark rethinking of physics in effect states that both the position and movement of a subatomic particle cannot be known simultaneously since one is affected by the act of measuring the other. In short, object and observer interact; they are not separate. Although they never put it in mathematical terms (as did Heisenberg), the intuitive thinkers of China asserted for centuries that independence of object and observer is a questionable concept, that we are at all time participants in the world around us. Detached, objective observation is consequently absurd.

4.   It cannot be entirely coincidence that many of the major scientists who ushered in the atomic age viewed Eastern philosophy as a system of thought more congenial to the new order. Physicist Neils Bohr declared that for a parallel to atomic theory it was necessary to turn "to those kinds of epistemological problems which thinkers like the Buddha and Lao Tzu (the father of Taoism) have already confronted."

V.   The Rise of "Computerthink"

1. The computer does many things for us. It provides the high-speed trajectory computations that allow us to land on the moon. It operates a telephone system that some have estimated might otherwise require the services of almost a quarter of the U.S. population. It is, in fact, well on the way to becoming an alternative kind of "intelligence." The next two generations, riding on the miniaturization made possible by the silicon chip, will most likely bring this instrument within striking range of many logical functions of the human brain, among them language. It already can organize and process sequential information much faster than we can. Teach a computer the rules of logic, and it will out-analyze you every time; from calculus to tic-tac-toe. Even now the Cyber 176 computer is providing a serious challenge to human superiority in that ultimate logical pastime, the game of chess. *Those who believe that the capacity for*

logical decisions is all that separates man from inanimate matter had best start preparing to go down with the chip.

2.   One might suspect that this reproduction of left-brain (or logical) intelligence by a machine would make us want to use our *own* minds in a different mode, one that the machine can't replicate. However, just the opposite seems to be happening. We have become increasingly disposed to attack problems the logical, numerical, "computerthink" way since it's easier to give the work to a brute-force machine than to try to find an elegant solution. Worse still, the powerful logic now at our disposal tempts us to approach design problems in a way congenial to the computer rather than to our own instincts. For example, we now prefer to break a problem down into small parts and then handle the parts separately, rather than view it as a whole. If each element is "logical," then it frequently occurs to no one that the whole entity may make no sense.

3.   The decline of nonverbal thought in technology was recently noted in the journal *Science* by University of Delaware professor of history and technology Eugene Ferguson, who related a disturbing fact: Current engineering graduates seem to have less and less capacity for visual, conceptual thought. One example Ferguson gave was the decline in students' ability to draw (remember Leonardo), which is so precipitous that "when the National Park Service's Historic American Engineering Record wishes to make drawings of machines and isometric views of industrial processes as part of its historical record of American engineering, the only students who have the requisite skills attend architectural schools." Drawing is a right-brain phenomenon; but as a result of the curricular emphasis on numerical analysis and computers as the basis of modern engineering design, we only are learning to do things the noncreative, left-brain way.

4.   What Ferguson is describing is the impending triumph of "computerthink." In the long run, concludes Ferguson, "engineers in charge of projects will lose their flexibility of approach to solving problems as they adhere to the doctrine that every problem must be treated as an exercise in numerical systems analysis." These same designers, he notes, will be "unaware that their nonverbal imagination and sense of fitness have been atrophied by an intellectually impoverished engineering approach."

5.   There are, of course, many scientists and scholars who do not accept this grim outlook. Buckminster Fuller, for example, views technology as a solution, not a problem, and Robert Pirsig, in *Zen and the Art of Motorcycle Maintenance,* advocates what he calls "spiritual rationality," a right-brain stroking of technology, in which we sort of meditate on its hard-edged metallic precision as a new form of aesthetics.

6.   But there also are many who sense in technology a threat to our own human superiority. It is understandably distressing to have our analytical powers suddenly topped by a machine we can hold in our

hands. A recent *Time* article noted that, "Some manufacturers of computer games have discovered that people are disconcerted when the computer responds instantly after the human has made his move. So the computers have been programmed to wait a little while before making counter moves, as if scratching their heads in contemplation."

7.   Indeed, many of us now tend to delude ourselves about the impact of technology. A study of attitudes toward computers not too long ago revealed that all persons questioned, regardless of their station, predicted that thinking machines would eventually replace all jobs below their own. Top to bottom, everyone asked believed his own job was the last one above the water line. The left brain is looking over its shoulder and seeing the computer gaining fast.

8.   But the real threat of the computer is not that it will outsmart us or replace our jobs. It is that we are relying more and more on this artificial "intelligence" rather than struggling to develop our own considerably more complex creativity.

VI.   Holistic Education

1.   A countermovement to the reign of sterile logic seems to be emerging, albeit confused and in disarray. Leslie Hart declares in *How the Brain Works,* "The great bulk of human brainpower suffers suppression and disparagement because of this witless, pompous, pretentious emphasis on largely nonproductive but respectable artificial modes of thought." Obviously we need to understand the potential of human intuition better if we are to reverse the trend.

2.   For example, how can this nonverbal, nonanalytical strength of the mind be communicated from one to another? The scientist R.G.H. Sui declared in *The Tao of Science* that, "One of the chief obstacles hindering its transmission is its indefinable character. Although real, it is as imprecise as an exhilarating spring day. It defies articulate description. It is not dispensed in measured doses. It is absorbed slowly and subconsciously into the moral fiber and intimate intuition of the person over a long period of time."

3.   There is, at the moment, much talk about holistic education, of developing "both sides of the brain." Recently author Paul Brandwein, director of research at Harcourt Brace Jovanovich, recommended, "First of all, teachers should recognize that all decisions need not be based on observable phenomena." He also suggested that the curriculum be liberalized and that students be taken to see things rather than just being told about them.

4.   Interesting, but it sounds a bit like intuitive intelligence is somehow less demanding than rational intelligence. The opposite is closer to the truth. It requires more discipline to be meaningfully creative than to work by rote. Right-brain (or creative) functions aren't less

demanding; they're just a bit bashful about making an appearance when the left-brain is awake and running the show. Consider how a logical chain of reasoning can so easily intimidate "better judgment," since intuition is hard to find and to defend. What is amazing about an intuitive thinker such as Albert Einstein (who, incidentally, didn't talk until he was three) is that he learned how to shut off and ignore the kind of thought that is merely internalized speech.

5.   Some interesting progress on the problem of suppressing left-brain functions and opening up spontaneous intelligence has recently been reported by a California art instructor, Dr. Betty Edwards, who discovered ways to enable students to see things without analysis. One technique is to force students to "scribble-draw," or draw so rapidly that there is no time to think about the process. Another approach is to make students focus on an object until they begin to see the space around it, rather than just the object itself. Still another method is to assign the drawing of a complex item such as the fine leaves on a tree, so that the attention can only be on the lines, not on an analysis of the object. The effect of all this is reported to be a release of the bashful right-brain.

6.   What seems not to be widely recognized is that *precisely* the same techniques were discovered around a thousand years ago by the Zen painters of China. Although they might study technique for decades, the actual process of painting was completely spontaneous. After meditating on a subject or a topic, until both it and the space it inhabited were a part of his intuition, a painter would then fling down the ink drawing seemingly by impulse, without recourse to reflecting or rationale. The act of stepping back to deliberate on a point was not in evidence. Meditation and the nonanalytical technique had the effect of releasing the intuitive powers of the mind while simultaneously circumventing the left brain.

VII.   Zen Education

1.   The Zen masters of the eighth century onward began what we today might call a research project to find ways to defeat the left-brain and thus expand the right-brain's potential. After many years they eventually settled on two basic techniques for stifling the dominance of the left hemisphere: 1) meditation, and 2) a structured form of mental harassment.

2.   Meditation, long the mainstay of Eastern practices, is now the subject of laboratory studies in the West. We have found that by sitting quietly in one place and suspending active thought processes, it is possible to significantly alter the measurable characteristics of the brain. But the objective of Zen meditation also was and is, among other things, to alter the way we relate to the world around us. Ideally, the sense of separation, the object-subject relationship to our en-

vironment that is so much a part of the analytical, rationalist tradition, gives way. Zen philosophy maintains that it is possible to "understand" our environment in a more meaningful way by seeing things without compartmentalization, analysis, or value judgments. To see a tree directly for itself rather than as an embodied scientific name is to participate in a kind of understanding that supersedes logic, analysis, or any of the other structured functions of the left brain. Meditation, in fact, apparently allows the mind to supersede these functions. It appears, however, to be more a passive than active approach to exploring the mind.

3.   As a result there were those who came to believe that the objectives of meditation could be realized by more dynamic means. After much trial and error Zen teachers developed a kind of deadly-serious zaniness, whose single-minded pursuit of the extrarational is reminiscent of our modern Theater of the Absurd. They developed a program of deliberate mental harassment designed to taunt the scholarly mind much the way the Marx brothers could taunt a straight-man. Take a typical Zen exchange and watch carefully as categories and logic are neatly exploded:

4.   *A monk once drew four lines in front of a famous Zen Master. The top line was long and the remaining three were short. The monk then demanded, "Besides saying that one line is long and the other three are short, what else could you say?" The Master drew one line on the ground and said, "This could be called either long or short. That is my answer."*

5.   Or take another example:

6.   *A new arrival said apologetically to the Master, "I have come here empty-handed!" "Lay it down then!" said the Master. "Since I have brought nothing with me, what can I lay down?" asked the visitor. "Then go on carrying it!" said the Master.*

7.   Given enough of this never-getting-a-straight-answer, the logical mind seems to burn out its circuits. The conundrum or *koan* method of Zen is to pose a question that at first *seems* as though it ought to have a logical answer (What is the sound of one hand clapping?) but which in fact does not. The logical left hemisphere is thus placed in the position of a computer called upon to produce the square root of a negative number. It just slugs away until it finally throws in the towel. Then, as the Zen teachers say, the chain of causation snaps (i.e., sequential reasoning breaks down), and the mind is ready to explore its capacity for intuitive holistic wisdom. Zen teachers merely demonstrate that the "left-brain" isn't so all-powerful after all.

8.   Out of this release of the latent capabilities of the right-brain there developed a novel culture, whose creations include arts that require complete spontaneity (impossible until the critical, nagging rational mind is discredited and silenced) and an aesthetic theory about materials and design that stressed the subtle manipulation of

perception (which forces the observer to become involved in the creative process and to experience the work intuitively).

VIII.   The Zen "Uncertainty Principle"

1.   It may turn out that the most important insight awaiting us in the realm of Eastern thought concerns right-brain intelligence itself. The question of how to reach this intelligence already seems destined to become the fashionable education issue of the 1980s, as even now we are struggling to try to understand—in rational terms—how the right brain works. But the Zen teachers, who have been working with this part of the brain for many centuries, would tell us that the rational part of the mind by definition can never understand the workings of the intuitive part.

2.   It is fundamental to Zen philosophy that self-conscious introspection is doomed to failure, since to understand your mind—using that very same mind—is like trying to grasp your own hand or see your own eye. And thinking about the intuitive mind logically is the one sure way never to understand its workings, since if you arrive at the understanding rationally or verbally, guarantees the understanding is wrong.

3.   As a ninth-century Zen master put it, "Zen formulates the study of intuitive wisdom only to receive and guide beginners. In reality this intuitive insight cannot be learned, for the study of it actually screens it from our understanding." This might be called the Zen "Uncertainty Principle," the proposition that attempting to understand the workings of one's own intuition through rational processes is futile. If this sounds "illogical," it should.

IX.   Summa Technologia

1.   The West's romance with rationalism now has evolved its final irony, the triumph of simplistic thought processes whereby we pay the machine our sincerest form of flattery—imitation. The longstanding belief that all problems can best be handled using logic and rationality—the more the better—has seduced us into easy dependence on synthetic machine logic. At the same time we have obligingly tailored our own thought process into the "computerthink" form, making it simplistic enough to be compatible with our machines. It seems almost a case of our being captivated by our own creation.

2.   Yet few among us would disagree that most really good ideas arise from intuition and only afterwards are they tested by our logic. This logical apparatus, far from giving us new ideas, can sometimes squelch an innovative concept prematurely by exercising too heavily its critical function. The Zen teachers, while believing that the intuitive process is itself beyond rational comprehension, also knew that the repressive tyranny of rationality could be suppressed via various physical and psychological disciplines. And they found some very

positive ways to explore, strengthen, and exploit this dormant creativity.

3.   If we in the West are to make this nonlinear creativity work for us, we too must restore the delicate relationship between rational and intuitive thought. We may find in the Eastern experience clues to the release of our own latent creativity. If we succeed in discovering the process whereby our nonverbal, nonrational mind can be turned on, we finally will be able to call on our own creativity—that fickle "muse" who now appears at her own convenience—when and where we wish. And with this may come a quantum jump in the mind's potential for ideas and insights. The computer can then be put firmly in its place, as a servant for all the left-brain chores we can unload, much the way that physical work is being relegated to machines. We, in turn, can then freely explore that extrarational realm called intuition, a potentially much higher intelligence with which we can create a new "reality."

SENSE AND NONSENSE ABOUT OUTLINING

Some writers prepare detailed outlines before they begin to write, but most don't. Most writers on occasion use some kind of brief outline or notes, but some don't. You just can't generalize. However, since outlines act both as guides and as stimulants to thought, they can be useful—if they don't become straightjackets!

To illustrate how they can be useful, we might discuss my planning of the first chapter of this book, "The Writing Process." I began with a fairly sketchy outline that looked something like this:

Introduction
    Purpose and nature of book
    Knowing about and knowing how

Territory to be covered
    Prewriting
        Finding a topic
        Discovering ideas
        Defining audience
        Defining constraints
    Writing
        Sentences
        Paragraphs
        Organization
    Rewriting
    Editing
The composing process

Now this was a *working outline,* intended merely to give some no-tion of where I was going—to keep me oriented during a rather lengthy job of composing.

As I typed the individual sections, I scribbled notes to myself on a sheet of paper. These scribblings were generated at the same time as the writing and helped me keep my direction. The result was a messy sheet that was useful to me, but would not be of much help to anyone else.

Formal outlines are generally written last, after the paper or book is completed. (The table of contents of this book is a formal outline.) They serve as guides for the reader and sometimes as checks for the writer since they can reveal structural flaws, illogical organization, and so on. (Some writers complete formal outlines before they begin to write; studies indicate, however, that most suc-cessful writers do not prepare detailed outlines before they start.)

Your Use of Outlines

Be prepared to discuss the following questions: When you compose, do you rely on a detailed outline? If so, what purpose does it serve? If not, how do you achieve your organization? Have any of your English teachers required that you make an outline before you write a theme? If so, what was the effect of this requirement on your writing?

Formal outlines can be made up exclusively of phrases or ex-clusively of sentences, but *phrases and sentences should never be mixed.*

A Formal Sentence Outline

The following is a sentence outline of "Zen: Technology and the Split Brain," on pages 151–61.

> I. The computer may be changing the way we use our minds.
>
>> A. In spite of "the force" of intuition and feeling that played such a large part in *Star Wars,* in the real world, the computer does analysis faster than the human brain.

B. The computer, though fast, is rigid, mechanical, and uncreative in its "thought."

II. The mind has two sides.

A. In an effort to treat severe epilepsy, Joseph Bogen, a neurosurgeon, cut the *corpus callosum* (the link between the two halves of the brain) of patients.

B. Roger Sperry, a psychologist, tested these patients to find what effect the operation had on their minds.

1. Sperry discovered that the left hemisphere controls language in many people and is process oriented.

2. The right hemisphere deals with patterns, spatial relationships, and concepts.

C. Robert Ornstein has verified and popularized Sperry's findings that there are two ways of thought.

III. Intuition (nonanalytical thought) is crucial to science.

A. As Thomas Kuhn points out, when a scientific model or paradigm fails to explain phenomena, the mind must make an "intuitive leap" to another paradigm or model.

B. There are countless examples of scientists who have made such leaps.

IV. Thousands of years ago, Far Eastern thinkers discussed and used the power of intuition as a means of understanding.

A. In the Far East, intuition was viewed as the only adequate means of understanding reality.

B. Since science proceeds on the basis of both facts and ideas, intuitive ideas are important to it.

1. For example, Copernicus made his breakthrough not because he had better instruments or newer data than those before him, but because he had an insight.

C. Heisenberg's uncertainty principle is in accord with the ancient Chinese doctrine that observer and object cannot be separated.

D. Many modern scientists view Eastern thought as necessary for understanding the natural world.

V. The development of computers seems to have made us rely more and more heavily on logical (left-brain) kinds of thought, to the exclusion of intuitive (right-brain) thought.

    A. Those who believe that logical, analytical thought is the only thing that makes human beings human should be prepared for the consequences as computers become more and more powerful.

    B. The efficiency of computers is compelling us to approach all problems in an analytical, left-brain fashion.

    C. Nonverbal thought is on the decline in technology, which, according to Eugene Ferguson, will bring about a loss of nonverbal imagination.

    D. Many scientists and scholars do not agree with this grim prediction.

        1. Buckminster Fuller looks to technology as the solution to human problems.

        2. Robert Pirsig argues for what he calls "spiritual rationality."

    E. A great number of people feel that computers pose a threat to human superiority.

VI. Holistic education—educating both halves of the brain—is a move to counter "computerthink."

    A. Since nonverbal, nonanalytical thought is difficult to communicate, holistic education is difficult.

    B. Some suggestions for educating the right hemisphere make it appear that intuitive thought is easy, but the opposite is the case.

        1. Since intuitive thought is hard to explain, a logical sequence of reasoning can overwhelm it.

        2. An intuitive thinker such as Einstein learns

to ignore thought that is merely internalized speech.

C. Betty Edwards, an art instructor, has developed techniques to release the right-brain's capabilities, her methods being very similar to those used by the Zen painters of China.

VII. Zen education is based on (1) meditation and (2) a structured form of mental harassment.

    A. Meditation is now the subject of laboratory tests in the West.

        1. Through meditation, it is possible to alter measurable characteristics of the brain.

        2. Zen philosophy contends that meditation allows one to overcome the observer-object split and thus gain a better understanding of reality.

    B. The Zen *koan* is a problem that does not admit a logical solution, thus forcing the thinker out of the left-brain mode.

VIII. The Zen "uncertainty principle" states that it is futile to attempt to understand intuition through logical means.

IX. Western rationalism has led us to imitate the computer, a machine.

    A. Paradoxically, almost everyone agrees that a good idea can come from intuition.

    B. Through Eastern philosophy we may find the way to develop our nonrational minds and thus achieve a higher intelligence.

The "rules" for the *sentence outline* are as follows:
(1) Do not use phrases. All headings must be complete sentences. The following is *incorrect* because the second head is a phrase, not a sentence:

1. The left hemisphere controls language and is process oriented.

2. Patterns, spatial relationships, and concepts in the right hemisphere.

(2) The usual numbering system for outlines is the following:

    I. [Roman numeral]
        A. [capital letter]
            1. [Arabic numeral]
                a. [lower case letter]
                b.
                c.
            2.
            3.
        B.
        C.
        D.
    II.
        A.
        B.

In other words, the sequence is Roman numeral (e.g., I, IX), capital letter (e.g., A, B, C), Arabic numeral (e.g., 4, 5), lower case letter (e.g., a, b), after which the sequence can be repeated if necessary. Note the system of indentation. Each level of subheading is placed the same distance from the margin. For example, all Roman numerals which indicate main topics are in line, as are all capital letters, and so on. Thus, the following outline is *incorrect:*

    I.
        A.
            B.
                1.
                    2.
        II.

The correct form is

    I.
        A.
        B.
            1.
            2.
    II.
        A.
        B.

(3) Since you cannot break something into one part, every head and subhead must have at least one equivalent. If there is a I at a given level, there must be at least a II; if there is an A, there must be at

least a B. For this reason, the following portion of an outline is *incorrect:*

> VII. Zen education is based on (1) meditation and (2) a structured form of mental harassment.
>> A. Meditation is now the subject of laboratory tests in the West.
>>> 1. Through meditation, it is possible to alter measurable characteristics of the brain.
>> B. The Zen *koan* is a problem that does not admit a logical solution, thus forcing the thinker out of the left-brain mode.
> VIII. The Zen "uncertainty principle" states that it is futile to attempt to understand intuition through logical means.

The entry VII-A-1 stands alone. It must be stated as part of VII-A, or VII-A-2 must be added, as is the case in the outline of the whole Zen essay.

(4) The exception to the principle stated in Rule 3 is the example, which may appear in isolation, with no coordinate subhead. Thus, the following is *correct:*

>> B. Since science proceeds on the basis of both facts and ideas, intuitive ideas are important to it.
>>> 1. For example, Copernicus made his breakthrough, not because he had better instruments or newer data than those before him, but because he had an insight.
>> C. Heisenberg's uncertainty principle is in accord. . . .

Exercise: Sentence Outlines

(1) Some of the following sections of outlines are incorrect. Find these, and explain the problems.

> (a) I. Domestic animals display a wide range of intelligence.
>> A. Horses are relatively stupid.
>> B. The intelligence of pigs.

II. Perhaps the most intelligent nonhuman mammals are dolphins.

(b)   a. Romance languages derive from Latin.

   I. The most widespread of the Romance group are French and Spanish.

   b. Dalmatian has the smallest number of speakers.

(c)   A. Many religions originated in America.

   1. An example is Mormonism.

   B. Americans are amazingly diverse in their religious beliefs.

   1. In the last decade or so, Oriental religions have been growing in the United States.

   a. The Hari Krishna movement appeals to young people.

   b. Many youths have also been attracted to Buddhism.

   2. The American fundamentalist sects are now in a period of growth.

(d)   I. There are many reasons for buying Le Car by Renault.

   A. Le Car looks like fun.

   II. Le Car drives like fun.

   A. Front-wheel drive.

   B. Four-wheel independent suspension.

   1. Rack and pinion steering.

(e)   I. Why America loves Scrabble.

   II. You can take a Scrabble game seriously.

   III. You can take it lightly.

   IV. You can play it any time or anywhere.

   V. Youngsters can have as much fun as adults.

   VI. Rules for playing Scrabble.

(2) Do a sentence outline of this chapter, up to the page you are now reading.

A Formal Topic Outline

Unlike the sentence outline, the topic outline is made up exclusively of *phrases;* there can be no sentences in a topic outline. Here is a topic outline of "Zen: Technology and the Split Brain":

I. The computer's influence on the mind
    A. Efficiency of the computer
    B. Rigid, mechanical nature of computer "thought"

II. Two sides of the brain
    A. Cutting the link between the two halves of the brain
    B. Studies of split-brain patients
        1. The nature of left hemisphere function
        2. The nature of right hemisphere function
    C. The two ways of thought

III. Science and intuition
    A. The intuitive leap
    B. Examples of scientists who have made the leap

IV. Zen and creativity
    A. Intuition as the means of understanding reality
    B. The importance of intuitive ideas for science
        1. The example of Copernicus
    C. Heisenberg's uncertainty principle
    D. Eastern thought and modern science

V. The rise of "computerthink"
    A. Computerthink and human thought
    B. The effect of the computer's efficiency on problem solving
    C. The decline of nonverbal thought
    D. Some dissenters
        1. Buckminster Fuller
        2. Robert Pirsig
    E. The computer's threat to human superiority

VI. Holistic education
    A. The difficulty of holistic education
    B. The difficulty of intuitive thinking
        1. The threat of logic
        2. Ignoring thought as internalized speech
    C. A technique for educating the right brain

VII. Zen education

    A. Meditation

        1. Alteration of measurable brain character-
istics

        2. Overcoming the observer-object split

    B. The Zen *koan*

VIII. The Zen "uncertainty principle"

IX. Summa technologia

    A. The usefulness of intuition

    B. The usefulness of Eastern philosophy

The following are "rules" governing the topic outline:

(1) The numbering system is the same as that for sentence
outlines.

(2) Do not mix sentences in with the phrases of the outline.

Because it contains a sentence, the following example is *incorrect:*

    A. Meditation

        1. Through meditation it is possible to alter measurable
characteristics of the brain.

        2. Overcoming the observer-object split

    B. The Zen *koan*

One note of caution: a *telegraphic sentence* (one with articles or
linking verbs left out) is not a phrase. The following are telegraphic
sentences:

Koan a problem [*The* koan *is* a problem.]
Zen education based on meditation and mental harassment
[Zen education *is* based on meditation and mental harass-
ment.]

The rest of the rules for topic outlines are just the same as
those for sentence outlines.

Exercise

On page 168, you were asked to do a sentence outline of the first part
of this chapter. Make that outline into a topic outline.

THE WHOLE ESSAY

Like most expository writing, "Zen: Technology and the Split Brain" is unified—which is to say that it has a clear-cut purpose from which it does not wander.

The general subject of the essay is Zen and technology, as the title implies. The topic, as we have seen, is stated in the first section: *"the computer may actually be changing the way we use our own minds.* By providing an artificial 'intelligence' that amplifies the brain's capacity for logical thought, these machines may be nudging us toward an increasing reliance on 'computerthink,' a rigid, mechanical thought process devoid of intuition and creativity."

A brief analysis will illustrate the unity of the essay. Each section contributes to the clarification and development of the topic:

Section I introduces the idea of intuition and feeling, characteristics of the right brain, but points out that computers are better than humans in rapid analysis, which is a left-brain function. The topic is then stated directly: the computer may be changing the ways in which we use our minds.

Section II, "Two Sides of the Mind," gives background on the nature of the brain and its functions and how these functions were discovered. This background is necessary if the reader is to understand what Hoover means by intuition, right-hemispheric thought, and so on.

Section III, "Science and Intuition," argues that intuition is necessary for science.

Section IV, "Zen and Creativity," argues that Zen philosophy and modern scientific method are not so far apart.

Section V, "The Rise of Computerthink," gives evidence that the computer is influencing thought more and more in the direction of analytical and logical modes, to the exclusion of the intuitive and nonanalytical.

Section VI, "Holistic Education," suggests that both sides of the brain can be educated.

Section VII, "Zen Education," explains how Zen goes about educating the right hemisphere.

Section VIII, "The Zen 'Uncertainty Principle,'" points out that logic is incapable of understanding intuition, a principle that could be the basis for a new attitude toward intelligence.

Section IX, "Summa Technologia," concludes that Western people must restore the balance between rational and intuitive thought.

Note that each section contributes to the topic and that no section diverts attention away.

Exercise

1. The brief analysis of "Zen: Technology and the Split Brain" was intended to show how each section contributes to the development of the topic. Excluding short transitional paragraphs, explain how each paragraph in a section contributes to the topic of that section.

For example, in Section I, the first three paragraphs use *Star Wars* as an example of the use of intuitive thought. The fourth paragraph analyzes the significance of the *Star Wars* example: the part of the movie discussed was intended to reassure human beings that, finally, they are superior to computers. But in the fifth paragraph, Hoover points out that computers are better than brains at split-second analysis, and this being the case, these machines may be influencing us to become more and more rational, rigid, and mechanical in our thought.

2. Can you explain how you know that each paragraph in a section relates to the one before it—except that the paragraphs follow one another on the page? For example, look at paragraph II.2. It begins with "Afterwards," which indicates a time sequence, and it contains the name "Sperry," which was important in II.1. Or look at paragraph IV.2, which begins with the transitional word *But*. (See Chapter 4, "Developing Ideas: The Paragraph," pp. 127–43.)

BEYOND THE ESSAY

When you begin your essay, you have an *intention* or *purpose:*

—to explore an idea or subject
> *Example:* a discussion of the pros and cons of atomic generation of electricity, without coming to a conclusion

—to explain an idea, process, or thing
> *Example:* an essay telling how to conduct a successful round-table discussion

—to demonstrate a conclusion scientifically, through the use of data
> *Example:* a research paper on the effects of noise pollution on human beings

—to construct imaginary or hypothetical worlds
> *Example:*   a narrative essay presenting a science-fiction view of the future

—to persuade
> *Example:*   an argument intended to convince the city council to construct a soccer field in the municipal park

When you have your purpose, you must develop or find ideas concerning it, and one way to do this is to use discovery procedures such as those demonstrated in Chapter 3. But these ideas must be expressed in structures, for they cannot simply float invisibly in the air; thus, it becomes necessary to put the ideas into meaningful forms: sentences, paragraphs, sections, essays.

Enter audience. The writer uses available forms to convey his or her intention to a reader or readers, and thus the readers control the form to some extent. In fact, successful writing is the result of the interaction among an *author's intention,* a *reader's expectations,* and *forms.*

However, another factor is perhaps more significant than these three: the *scene* in which the writing transaction takes place. For example, the very fact that you and your classmates share your composition class makes the *scene* meaningful to you, whereas an "outsider" might find it essentially meaningless. America in the 1980s is a large scene that influences everything you do, think, and feel. Scene is a series of concentric circles radiating outward from you in this time and at this place, progressively encompassing more and more of the physical, mental, and spiritual universe.

All of this can be expressed very neatly: any act of discourse (written or spoken) is the projection of an *intention* or *purpose* through *forms* or *structures* to an *audience* in a *scene.* The writer, then, must be concerned with the following questions:

What is my intention or purpose?
Who are my readers?
What forms are most appropriate?
What is the scene?

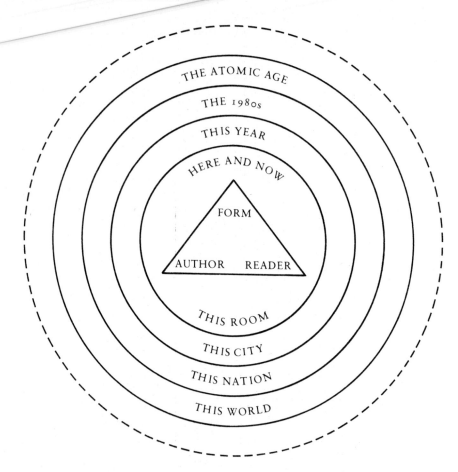

THE PROBLEM OF INTENTION

Suppose that the readers for an essay are a group of college students, and perhaps an instructor. The scene is a college composition class. Student Crumly turns in a flawless essay—well organized, mechanically perfect, fluently written. Suppose further that Crumly's purpose is to explain the problem of choosing dessert in the cafeteria.

From the point of view of the readers, the essay will probably not be successful, for the intention is trivial, not worth writing or reading about. If an intention is trivial or does not interest a given audience, then the writing will be unsuccessful, regardless of coherent organization, adequate development, mechanical accuracy, and clarity of style.

It is interesting, however, that an essay with a significant purpose can be about a trivial subject, such as choosing dessert. The purpose might be to

—reveal the writer's indecisive personality, which makes even the smallest decisions impossible;

—amuse the reader, by treating a trivial subject as if it were momentous;

—use such a brilliant style that readers will be interested in the complex sentence structure and original figures of speech.

The purpose might even be to offend the readers by insulting their intelligence, which is not a trivial purpose even though it might be misguided.

In fact, there are no trivial subjects, but there are trivial purposes, and no piece of writing that is trivial in purpose can be really successful.

The Writer's Intention

1. Listed below are some apparently trivial subjects. For each of these, state a writing purpose that is *not* trivial. For example:

a. The grade I got on my last theme
   Purpose: to show how this one grade thoroughly demoralized me, since to me it represented an accurate assessment of my potential in college

b. Picking apples
   Purpose: to write a personal essay on the annual ritual of picking apples with family and friends and to demonstrate that this yearly event symbolizes my relationship with those I am close to

c. Buying a new pair of shoes
   Purpose: to use all of my skills as a writer to demonstrate that elegant style, brilliant metaphors, humor, and irony can make the most mundane subject interesting

(1) shopping for groceries
(2) driving a car
(3) walking down the hall in a college building
(4) striking a match
(5) showering or bathing

(6) a birthday party
(7) a date
(8) a thoughtless act
(9) fingernails
(10) ordering from a menu in a restaurant

2. For each of these subjects, develop a topic that could serve as the controlling idea for an essay. Here is an example:

> *Subject:* shopping for groceries
> *Purpose:* to inform readers about the junk that the American food industry produces
> *Topic:* When one shops for groceries, a close look at container labels reveals that the American food industry is peddling an enormous amount of junk.

3. If you feel so inclined, write an essay based on one of your topics.

THE PROBLEM OF PROBLEMS

It is a truism, but, nonetheless, life is a series of problems: decisions that must be made, conundrums that must be unravelled, choices, difficult personal relationships, puzzles. This being the case—every day being a series of problems, one after the other—it is paradoxical that so few people think about the nature of problems.

In problem situations, things just don't "add up"; there is *dissonance*. Often we sense problems before we fully understand them, but if we are to find solutions, we must gain understanding.

For example, here is a real-world problem that many students face: choosing a major. There is often a clash among parents' expectations, career opportunities, and students' interests: Dad wants Junior to follow the family tradition and become an English teacher; the job market for English teachers is limited; and anyway, Junior wants to be a mechanical engineer. In order to understand the problem of choosing a major, the student must gain answers to a number of questions, such as:

1. What are the parents' motives? What are the student's? How might those motives be changed? (Do the motives relate to the parents' and student's backgrounds? How?)
2. What are the relationships of time and place to the problem? The economic scene? Social classes?
3. What about means for accomplishing goals? Finances? Intelligence? Availability of schools?
4. In detail, what is the exact nature of both the parents' and the student's motives?

You have probably discovered that behind these questions lie the five master questions that were discussed in Chapter 3, "Discovering Ideas" (pages 69–86).

Another series of questions might help the student understand this problem more fully:

1. Specifically, what are its features? What do the parents do or fail to do? The student himself?
2. How much change can the student reasonably expect in (a) his parents, (b) himself, and (c) the job situation?
3. How does this problem relate to others that the student confronts? Economic? Personal? Social?
4. What are the dynamics of the problem? What actually happens? In regard to the student himself? In regard to his parents?
5. What are the parts of the problem, and how do they seem to work together?

And you have probably recognized that this series of questions is based on the discovery procedures outlined on pages 93–99 of Chapter 3.

Every writing assignment is a problem. If you can define and understand the problem, you are well on your way to a successful piece of writing, and the discovery procedures that you learned in Chapter 3 will help you understand. Furthermore, problems are often the subjects of your writing—in your English class, to be sure, but also, and most particularly, in the real world.

Exploring Problems

How does the exploration of problems take place? Although everyone develops his or her own method, there are certain similarities among procedures, certain steps or facts in the process that seem to be common to a great many writers and thinkers. Understanding the process should be useful, and it is certainly interesting; therefore, let's take a look at what might happen when a person encounters a problem and goes about solving it.[1]

In the first place, you must have *a preliminary knowledge of the field.* If you know almost nothing about writing insurance policies or planning the defense in a football game, then you cannot be aware of problems in those fields, at least not in a way that is specific enough to be useful. To define your problem as the need for health insurance or a desire to beat the Oklahoma team will be of little use, for these are general goals; they are not penetrating

---

[1] This discussion is adapted from James L. Kinneavy, *A Theory of Discourse* (Englewood Cliffs, N.J.: Prentice-Hall, 1971).

enough to yield solutions, because in their very broadness they give you nothing to work with.

The next step is known as *cognitive dissonance,* the awareness of a difficulty. Cognitive dissonance reveals itself in wonder (Why should such and such be the case?); in instability (There is a contradiction here that I cannot resolve); in anomaly (On the basis of my current knowledge I cannot explain this phenomenon).

Next comes *focus.* The problem becomes clear. It can be exactly defined.

Fourth is *the search for a new model* that can be tested.

Fifth, *the new model is imposed on the field* to see if it eliminates the cognitive dissonance.

Finally, *a new hypothesis is formed;* a tentative explanation is offered. Here is a thumbnail example:

> Hanson's classic example of the whole exploration process vividly illustrates the use of the model. He uses Kepler's discovery of the elliptical orbit of Mars, for "Kepler typifies all reasoning in physical science" . . . [1. *Preliminary knowledge of field*] The dogma current from Aristotle to Galileo was that planetary orbits were necessarily circular. . . . He says, "Before Kepler, circular motion was to the concept of planet as 'tangibility' is to our concept of 'physical object' " . . . [2. *Cognitive dissonance*] But the circular model did not account for the anomalies in measurements of Mars's varied distances from the sun and of Mars's varied velocities at different points in its orbit. [3. *Focus of problem*] Even inaccuracies in measuring procedures should not have led to such notable departures from what the theory dictated. . . . [4. *Search for new model*] To explain these anomalies Kepler then repudiated the circular orbit model and cast about for another model. . . . He first tried an oval and then an ellipse as models, [5. *Imposition of new model*] settling eventually on the ellipse. . . . [6. *Hypothesis: tentative explanation*] The ellipse offered a plausible explanation of all the anomalies which had been bothering him and suggested other testable hypotheses. These he followed through and the results confirmed the validity of the new model. . . .[2]

This brief example is not meant to imply that problem solving takes place only in the exact sciences. Whenever a critic attempts to explain a poem, he or she goes through the same kind of procedure, and whenever you advance an opinion on any subject, you probably—consciously or not—go through at least some of these steps.

[2] Kinneavy, pp. 103–04.

An Exploratory Essay

Jill Aeschbacher, the author of the following essay, has probably not heard of the model for exploration that has just been outlined, but in exploring her problems as a writer, she intuitively followed the steps that we have been discussing. Stated as a question, her problem is this: "Why do I want to write, and why can't I now?"

It's Not Elves Exactly

Jill Aeschbacher

Something there is that doesn't love a wall,
That wants it down. I could say "Elves" to him,
But it's not elves exactly.
    —Robert Frost, "Mending Wall"

[The essay begins with an outline of the author's *preliminary knowledge of the field*—her almost unconscious drift toward a certain way of life.]

When I was a scrawny, copper-haired kid and someone asked me what I wanted to be when I grew up, I put my hand on my hip, imitating my mother's soup-stirring stance, and said, maintaining the imitation, that I wanted to be a mother because I liked children. Supposing that I didn't realize I was just a child myself, the interviewer would respond with odd warmth. It got to be a bore. Besides, when I was five, Elizabeth Taylor was much talked about around my house, and her life seemed far more glamorous than my mother's; so I started telling people I wanted to be an actress.

I kept that attitude toward self-creation until I was eleven. We were writing papers on our chosen professions, and apparently something about my diction impressed my fifth-grade teacher. He said, "You write very well; you should be a writer instead of an actress." I liked him and valued his opinion, so from then on, when people asked what I wanted to be when I grew up, I told them "a writer."

[Now comes a detailed exploration of the *cognitive dissonance*—the puzzlement, the irritation, the knowledge that the "model" doesn't "fit."]

Of course I had no idea what was involved in any of these careers, except that they seemed less boring than carrying mail and less demeaning than waiting on tables. But it didn't matter anyway, be-

IT'S NOT ELVES EXACTLY   Jill Aeschbacher, *College Composition and Communication,* 24 (1973), 204–46. Copyright © 1973 by the National Council of Teachers of English. Reprinted by permission of the publisher and the author.

cause I wasn't planning to grow up right away. It was all a matter of image; and I found in high school that I could impress boys whose vocabularies and cynicism were larger than mine, by telling them I would be "great and rich, like J. D. Salinger and John Updike." They thought I was charmingly naive for thinking it was that simple. But after all, this was America; you could be whatever you wanted.

Needless to say, I'm paying now for those green and essentialist attitudes with thousands of questions, rationalizations and other pains. Having begun writing on these tenuous grounds, I'm going to tell you some things I've been thinking about writing since I quit doing it. But because how I got started weighs heavily on how I got stalled, I think you should know more about that first.

I had early the notion that the writer wrote to give others pleasure, a noble occupation in my young estimation. That was my cheery social-working self coming out. And something else I think: my father kept my first story "Battle at Broken Branch Canyon" (age 10) his whole life. His pleasure over the story affected me considerably, even after I understood that the scaffold of his pleasure, like most fatherly love, was a little shaky. I wanted to say that Tough Bob kicked Mean Joe in the shin, but I figured "shin" was spelled like "chic." So Tough Bob ended up kicking Mean Joe in the chin. My father thought it was hilarious. I suppose now that his pleasure derived from my saying more about myself than I realized, something for which he had an obscure and personal appreciation; perhaps also he had just taught me the spelling of "chic."

Saying more than one realizes can be something of a risk. At any rate, writing to please others seems now both frivolous and vain. *Intellectually* speaking, of course. For I seldom wrote anything without anticipating the thrill of charming my friends and family. Unfortunately, they were usually impressed by what I thought were the wrong things, particularly if they thought they saw themselves, and no two of them reacted similarly. They were like too many birds for a hungry cat, and sent me scurrying in six directions at once. I wrote a story about kites to impress one friend with how precisely I saw the real world, and ended up charming another with my keen sense of fantasy. My readers were also, perhaps, too easily pleased. Like my father, they were pleased by the whole if one little word struck some odd and unintended chord.

Television, of course, can provide more people with more "pleasure" than any writer could hope to. And trying to make people love me for my writing proved to be a very risky and expensive enterprise. Thus my social and personal interests in writing for the pleasure of others disintegrated.

A second more recently developed notion, I had insisted that writings told great and important truths. By playing "the game" I became quite proficient at picking out these truths and explaining them in blue books. Standing in this reference frame, I made the not illogical leap from awareness that this proficiency won good grades from learned professors to the assumption that the writer wrote in order to give these truths. By the time I got through with them, the writers of "great books" had in their hearts the desire to save the world by preaching love, brotherhood and peace. That seemed like a *very* noble occupation, and I invested in the image of the profession the whole meaning of life. Since God and immortality were out, the telling of these important truths was the only meaning life could have. But I didn't know any important truths; I had to get some. So I set about speculating on the meanings of freedom, morality, femininity, art, relativity, love, peace, joy, time, beauty, progress, space, history, Americanism, reality, education, friendship, death, religion, and of course, truth itself. I took philosophy classes and philosophized. Needless to say, I was known among some people as a "weird chick." A friend of mine whom I hadn't seen for a time told me he was working on a story he planned to send to *Evergreen Review*. "Are you writing the truth?" I asked intensely. He said, "I don't know, what difference does that make?" I considered him immoral for some time after. I'm not suggesting that it makes no difference what a writer writes, only that waiting for truth to fall on my head was rather fruitless for me.

During this time, my stories were literally sets of class notes. One was anyway. It wasn't a bad set of class notes, but it wasn't a truthtelling story either. Another was a curious fugue about two kids searching for answers. The truth, skillessly told at the end, was, as I remember, that the teacher wasn't going to arrive. I didn't think that was a very important truth, and was disappointed again.

So when meaninglessness first presented itself to me as a notion, I thought it lovely and easy, and talked drolly about it in conversations over coffee. That nothing *meant* anything was always well understood by my favorite fictional characters, and they accepted it with a casualness I envied. Meursault knew it didn't make any difference what he did with his life.

Obviously, I had quite misunderstood Camus. So that, when meaninglessness forced itself upon my life, became more than just an idea, I had some trouble. It got its claws into me in these ways: the war and the bomb and the population explosion began preying on my mind; I graduated from college; my father finally drowned himself in alcohol; someone I'd long been in love with informed me of his love affair with another man; communication with my oldest friends wore thin; I approached (one Christmas vacation) a nervous breakdown over my own failures, which was prevented only by my mother's iron insistence that I keep busy helping her with trivial preparations, and concluded in my purchase of $27 worth of books. I'd had enough of the real world.

I had, however, to face the facts: the world would not be saved by important truths; no matter how well told they were, someone would have to come along tomorrow and tell them again in new words; and people simply weren't going to listen anyway. My life's ambition had lost its significance, for I had intended to create for myself and others the Meaning of Life. I didn't know that meaning is something one lives, not something one merely talks about.

Still, like W. D. Snodgrass, "I had not learned how often I can win, can love, can choose to die." This ignorance is certainly nothing to brag about, but there was a time when I didn't even realize I was making choices. Perhaps one must find his world vision *before* he can learn how often he can win, can love, but chooses death. Or perhaps, like form and meaning, they come together.

Fitzgerald and Hemingway taught me about a third reason a writer might have for writing. He might write down his life-difficulties in order to better understand them. I never did this consciously (as perhaps they did sometimes) because it seemed a little crazy to me. It's rather like talking to oneself. I also thought that this kind of writing usually failed to make very good reading. I found out how true that was: I had written a story called "Live People, Dead People, and Other People" about a young man who made lists. He was trying to create some order in his world. Unfortunately the story was pretty disorganized, as was my own mind at the time. It was I who was trying to create order, not my character. I wrote also a fictionalized set of letters which were an attempt to come to grips with what I've come to call "the mind-body problem" and learned that intellectualizing on paper was not the way to do that. Since then, I've been working in *other* ways toward ordering my world and maintaining a relationship between my mind and body.

Toward order, I started buying my cigarettes by the carton and putting things where I can find them; I try to be the one to put fresh towels in the bathroom because the other members of the family invariably hang up two blue-and-green-plaids and one pink-and-white, or vice-versa ("A towel is a towel, for chrissake!"); I sprayed the dead weeds in my room with clear plastic so they wouldn't disintegrate all over the floor (which didn't work); and I try to wash the car every other Saturday, even if it's going to rain, because order is one thing and logic is something else.

Toward a mind-body relationship, I stopped "thinking" about it and took up ice-skating.

[Now the problem starts to gain sharper *focus*.]

Since I never seriously thought a writer wrote for money and my other notions about writing to please others, build a new world, maintain sanity, and express love had crumbled, I found myself without a reason for doing it. But unfortunately, I have my brick wall, my ego-investment to contend with. I've given too much of my being over to the image of the profession, however vague and frightening that image has become. My brick wall has three dimensions; first, its width is the image I gave myself as "a writer"; second, it is long: my ego-oriented desire to express myself in words; and third, it is a tall fear of giving too much of myself. It keeps me from writing and from giving it up. What can I do about the wall, then? I can keep hitting my head against it. I can post sentries to guard it. I can dig under it, or bury it, or build another wall parallel to it. I can write my name on it or plant flowers on top. I could deny its existence; I could rent it for advertising space, or sell it to my neighbor at a profit. I could take it apart piece by piece, or desecrate it, or make a leap (of faith) over it. I can think about it; I could die for it. I can sit on it; I can write an article exposing it.

But worrying about it has proved almost valueless. On the other hand, I can't exactly ignore it. "Something there is that doesn't love a wall, that wants it down." What I have been doing then is teaching school and taking classes and (an alternative I didn't mention) waiting for the seasons to destroy the bricks and leave either rubble from which I can build a new self-conception or free passage to the pasture on the other side. Writers say, "If you don't have to write, don't do it." Obviously I don't have to; I've survived long periods without it. But something in me (it's not elves exactly) roots for the destruction of the wall to leave free passage to write again; I can't imagine why, since there's no "reason" for writing and I hardly remember the pleasure of doing it.

[The *search for a new model* begins.]

In studying my block, I've been forced to admit what it is not. I used to like to think that I could write if I only had more time. But I put that rationalization to the test last summer. I gave the summer to myself for writing, took few obligations and wasted my time wishing I were writing. Neither was "the man from Porlock" to blame, for I kept distractions at a distance (even emotionally) and insisted on being alone. I had no institutions to blame for making me into a research machine, a file clerk, or a hypocritical bureaucrat. My days were not unreasonably broken up by places to be and things to do, as they are at the other times of the year. I could order them as I wished; I could have been writing during any set of hours I chose. This home in suburbia has also taken the brunt of my blame at times. But last summer, it was, for hours on end, my place alone, a place I could have worked. It offers also, I've admitted, some protections I wouldn't have if I were on my own. Besides obvious financial worries I don't have, my friends visit me here almost seldom enough to suit me. That's right, I've even blamed my friends. But last summer I stayed away from them. I also avoided watching the news and thinking about the war.

Thus you see, there was nothing in the external world to keep me from writing. That was how I discovered that my brick wall exists inside me, well protected from the rages of time and the weather. I also learned how difficult it is to write out of boredom, not, I think, a worthless lesson.

These are hard things to admit, and existing consciously in bad faith is not painless. I promised myself that if I weren't writing at the end of the summer, I'd forget about it forever. I never did decide which took more courage, to give up the notion of writing, or stay (in conscious bad faith) with the absurd hope of someday doing it; but nevertheless, I couldn't give up.

That waiting has sometimes seemed dishonest to me, has forced me to consider its alternatives. With this severe freedom we all face of choosing what we want to do and making what we want to make of ourselves, it seems sometimes more honest to me to force myself to write, to do whatever I have to do to get it going. Would you believe I've considered arranging for my family to bribe me to write; but there's no predicting what that would cost me in the end. I've even considered becoming a speed freak, for writing, I know, comes easier on amphetamines.

But I suppose I am too much convinced that writing should come naturally or not at all, unless of course that is merely a convenient rationalization. At any rate, I have not been able to force myself to write.

Thus, aside from trying to remain emotionally alive, to give some orderly arrangement to the events of my life, and to sharpen my appreciation for the technical skills involved in putting words together, I have spent the wait thinking about the brick wall inside me. I'm not sure this does any good at all, but it hardly seems that better mental attitudes could hurt. This has meant generally that I have been working to change my attitudes toward writing (1) to destroy my image of myself as a writer; (2) to stop looking at it as an ego-investment; and (3) to establish enough security so that I don't have to fear giving myself away.

In trying not to think of myself as a writer, I've come to the rather obvious conclusion that writers are people who write. That excludes me. Joking about it has helped a little too, I think. "Oh no, I'm not a writer; I'm all talk." But I haven't thought it terribly funny.

I have an acquaintance who is very worried about passing his Ph.D. orals. He feels that if he fails, the whole effort of his life for the last twenty years will be discolored. I said to him, "I thought you were a writer." "Yes," he said, "what does that have to do with it?" "If you are a writer, failing your exams wouldn't mean anything but a six-month delay." "Oh!" he said, "I see what you mean. No, I'm a scholar; if I thought of myself as a writer, I'd be so tense I wouldn't be able to do it." I was amazed at his casual knowledge of the fact.

It's simple enough, I suppose, to think of myself as a student and a teacher.

It was viewing writing as an ego-investment, and my attempt to change that view that started me thinking in the first place about the reasons I'd had for writing. That they were all pretty flimsy has been, I think, a good thing to face, though of course I don't deny the value of books I like to read. Toward reducing my ego-orientation for writing, I've tried in other areas of my life to listen to my inner self and do pretty much what I feel like doing. I've tried to avoid world-building, and "accomplishing" things *merely* because I "should." I've also thought a bit about stories I might write about other people, since I wrote too directly about myself, and thereby increased my ego-investment in writing.

Of the changes I've been working to make in my attitude, developing an inner security has been most difficult. I've had some considerable paranoia to fight. My father's frustrated perfectionism, which I inherited, has also presented something of a battle. Admitting that I have no talent for cooking, for example, or for cool and sophisticated cocktail conversation, or for memorizing, admitting that I can't *be* everyone and be good at everything has been very difficult.

Seeking solutions in a conscious way, I have learned, wrinkles the brow. It is better to let the solutions find me. So, I don't know if changing my attitudes in these ways will allow me to write again, but if, when the bricks are down, they make of me a secure person who does what she likes doing, without attaching prefabricated labels to herself, that will be something.

[*The new model is imposed.*]

Recently, I've been filling up the wait with fun. (I can't think of a less irreverent way to say it.) Why nearly everything seems fun to me lately, I can't imagine, for my activities are not so different. I have admitted that I'm in love, but I'm almost certain that's not all there is to it. Anyway: fun. Teaching composition has become so enjoyable that it hardly matters what specifically happens during a class—when it ends, I can't keep the grin down. Though I still sometimes lose track of what I'm doing, taking classes has become, since graduate school, more fun; it seems less often absurd. I love to follow the train tracks under one billion stars to the brickyard, where brick walls are merely stacks of bricks, thick but very temporary. And I like to go dancing, though drinking with my friends is something I still do occasionally, mainly because (they seem to think) I "should." I've come to believe that hardly anything is worth doing if it isn't fun. If that is true, writing also should be fun, or skipped. Perhaps that's the only real reason people have for doing it: they think it's fun. But what does that mean?

If writing were merely fun as an activity, like swimming or skiing, there would be no need for others to read its results. But those activities too are more fun with other people. Part of the fun of writing, then, is sharing it with others (though one doesn't do it for the pleasure of others, any more than a skier skis for the pleasure of the people who wait in line at the lift and watch him). Like swimming, writing is more fun if you're good at it. So part of the fun is being good, and working continually to improve. Maybe also, the greatest swimmers feel within themselves the potential to be the BEST SWIM-MER. They have a confidence that comes from thinking they know more about swimming than anyone, or that they know some secret no one else knows, or that they are absolutely in tune with the life of the water. Maybe writers have that kind of confidence. If they do, when and how did they get it? They weren't born with it. Perhaps it started out as a kind of game. The better they got, the more fun the game was. When they recognized the need for a new world, maybe they felt within themselves the power to create it. But they must also have feared failure, and some probably experienced it. Still perhaps, the passion and the fun of the activity kept them going until they found the secret and the confidence.

Perhaps then, when they found the secret and the confidence, they knew that if their writing expressed or won love, or changed some small part of the world, or helped them understand themselves, or gave others pleasure, these were fortunate coincidences, but not their reasons or their motivations. Perhaps when they found the se-cret and the confidences their lives and their writing were passion-ately entwined, and that was their motivation. In fact, perhaps "reasons" for their writing were simply irrelevant, (their lives turned upside down) and they needed "reasons" for doing other things. But this is speculation.

In addition to the fact that there are some things about writing that can't be learned by thinking about it, waiting has made me aware of a curious paradox. Life seems very short to me. Discounting the possibility of auto accident, nuclear war and earthquake, I have at best three-quarters of my life left. What is three-quarters? Three-quarters of a quart of milk a shirtless boy in levis might come in from lawn mowing and drink in one gulp. People should do what they like with the last three-quarters of their lives, and waiting around has not been something I've really liked. It's a matter of making choices. The wait has chosen me; but when I'm done with waiting, if I can, I'll *choose* to write.

[*A new hypothesis is formed.*]

On the other hand, all that has kept me sane, if I am, in the hard moments of the wait is this:

There is here no measuring with time. No year matters and ten years are nothing. Being an artist means, not reckoning and counting, but ripening like the tree which does not force its sap but stands, confident in the storms of spring, without the fear that after them may come no summer. It does come, but only to the patient, who are there as though eternity lay before them, so unconcernedly still and wide. I learn it daily, learn it with pain to which I am grateful. Patience *is everything.*

—Rilke, *Letters to a Young Poet*

Defining a Problem

1. Choose a real-world problem that troubles you. It can be personal, local, international. Briefly state why the problem is really a problem.

Example

The area in which I live is increasingly subjected to senseless vandalism. The problem is to find the reasons for this mindless destruction of personal and public property. (It may well be that I cannot propose a reasonable solution, but I do want to know why the destruction goes on. The problem is really a problem for me because I don't understand—because the vandalism seems to be without any reasonable motive.)

2. Use the problem that you have defined as the basis for an essay.

A WRITER'S CHECKLIST

When you have finished a first or second draft of an essay—before you start to revise—you can ask yourself an important series of questions regarding your essay:

1. Concerning the *writer* (you): How do I "come across" in this piece? Do I sound ironic when I intend to be straightforward? Does it appear that I rave and rant when I should be calm and rational? In general, what writer's personality and tone of voice will the reader perceive? Are they appropriate? Is my purpose worth having, or will the reader feel that the essay is trivial?
2. Concerning *content:* Is the piece logical? Are the ideas adequately developed? Will the reader want more information? Is everything relevant to my purpose? Are there redundancies?
3. Concerning *form:* Is the organization logical? Are the paragraphs and sections coherent? Could a different organization be more effective?

4. Concerning *style:* Are my sentences clear and accurate? Is my prose choppy or long-winded? Are there any mechanical errors in the paper?
5. Concerning *audience:* All of the foregoing questions must be asked from the standpoint of what you intend to do in regard to your reader or readers.

Your answers to these questions should guide you in your revision.

REVISION

As we have seen, when you revise, you can

1. *delete* words, phrases, sentences, paragraphs, sections

> The ~~very rich~~ millionaire bought a new Rolls Royce.

2. *add . . .*

> The millionaire, *having made a killing on the stock market,* bought a new Rolls Royce.

3. *rearrange . . .*

> Having made a killing on the stock market, the millionaire bought a new Rolls Royce.

4. *substitute . . .*

> Having made a *considerable sum* in the stock market, the *tycoon* bought a new *limousine.*

Exercise

I'd pity James Bond if he ever messed with Hazel.

Hazel Jacobs is a twenty-six-year-old native New Yorker. She's about five feet six inches tall. She's bright. She's attractive. She's athletic. She's a marvelous dancer . . . at first blush a fun date. But have a few drinks with her, as I did the other week, and you'll meet the other side of Hazel—all business, devoid of humor, guarded, never relaxed, and whose only craving is success.

I asked Hazel, a karate teacher with a masters in phys. ed., whether she had ever had cause to use her skills to ward off some overzealous male. She had.

Hazel will start a personal bodyguard service for John C. Mandel Security Bureau Incorporated.

John Mandel rates the new service as an attractive venture on two counts, which should be operating in a few weeks: Would-be attackers would be least suspicious of women as protectors and female bodyguards should be especially appealing to women themselves.

Mandel expects to make piles of dough. His rates will be high.

"I was at a basketball game," she recalled, "and this fellow, about five feet eleven, grabbed my ass. I struck him in the solar plexus with a backhand thrust and sent him stumbling back several feet. When he recovered, he quickly walked away."

In conclusion, I would like to just merely say here at the end that some people will go to any lengths to defend a client.

—Adapted from "Only $100 for Eight Hours with Hazel"

Suppose that the author of this essay asked you for detailed comments regarding revisions that would improve the piece. What suggestions would you make?

> *Additions?* Since you do not know very much about the subject, you cannot tell exactly what to add, but you can indicate where you, as a reader, would like more information.
>
> *Deletions?* Cross out any unnecessary material.
>
> *Rearrangements?* Rearrange words, phrases, sentences, or paragraphs as you think necessary.
>
> *Substitutions?* Make substitutions that you think will improve the piece.

After you have completed your editorial work, compare the revisions that you suggest with the actual essay, which follows.

Only $100 for Eight Hours with Hazel— But Hands Off, She's a Killer

Dan Dorfman

Hazel Jacobs is a twenty-six-year-old native New Yorker who's about five feet six inches tall, bright, attractive, athletic, and a marvelous dancer . . . at first blush a fun date. But have a few drinks with her, as I did the other week, and you'll meet the other side of Hazel—all business, devoid of humor, guarded, never relaxed, and whose only craving is success. I wasn't about to complain, though, since Hazel has a skill that I surely wasn't interested in testing—the ability, as a top-flight black-belt karate expert, to maim or kill quickly. What makes it all very intriguing is that this ability—which she developed over the past eight years—will be the nucleus of an intriguing new business. In brief, a personal bodyguard service—for executives, dignitaries, and their wives and children—composed of attractive women highly skilled in the art of karate. And Hazel will head it all up as a division of John C. Mandel Security Bureau Incorporated, a leading New York-New Jersey security service with annual revenues of about $10 million.

John Mandel rates the new service—which should be operating in a few weeks—as an attractive venture on two counts: Would-be attackers would be least suspicious of women as protectors and female bodyguards should be especially appealing to women themselves. "It ought to be a million-dollar business in a year or two," says Mandel, who emphasizes that protection—and protection alone—will be the only service the women will provide. Rates will run a minimum $100 a day per karate expert for an eight-hour shift plus $10 for each additional hour.

I asked Hazel, a karate teacher with a masters in phys. ed. from Columbia University's Teachers College whether she ever had cause to use her skills to ward off some overzealous male. She had.

"I was at a basketball game," she recalled, "and this fellow, about five feet eleven, grabbed my ass. I struck him in the solar plexus with a backhand thrust and sent him stumbling back several feet. When he recovered, he quickly walked away. Maybe he realized that if he came back, I could have killed him. . . ."

Any limits in defending a client?

"If it came down to it, I'd kill," she responded. "And it wouldn't bother me in the least because I'd be doing my job. . . ."

I'd pity James Bond if he ever messed with Hazel.

Writing to Inform: Exposition

THE PURPOSES OF EXPOSITORY WRITING

Information

A GAIN and again, we have stressed that almost all writing is a transaction between a writer and a reader. Simple to understand, but sometimes difficult to apply, this is probably the most important concept in this or any other book about writing. To be informative, a piece of writing must give the reader information, and the two characteristics of information are that it has *surprise value* and *content*.

If I tell you that California is a state of the Union and that its westernmost extreme is on the Pacific Ocean, I have made a true statement, but I have probably not given you any information. Why? Because what I've said contains no surprises; you already know these facts about California. In other words, you can judge the information value of a sentence, a paragraph, an essay, or a book by how much you learn from it. Obviously a piece of writing that is highly informative for one reader or group of readers might not be so for another audience.

On the other hand, the following assertion is novel enough to surprise any reader: "The one who solved the problem of overpopulation was an earthworm with a ten-dollar calculator." It is uninformative because it lacks *content,* does not agree with the world as we know it. We might find the sentence whimsical, amus-

191

ing, poetic, zany, delightful—but not informative. If your interest were in solutions to the problem of overpopulation, you would pay no attention.

A piece of expository writing, then, will give information to the readers for whom it is intended.

Informative Writing

Read the following passage and answer the questions regarding it.

Biofeedback *sounds* so respectable. That Greek root "bio," as in biochemistry or biology, and "feedback" from the crisp, quantified world of engineering, from servomechanisms: "a method of controlling a system by reinserting into it the results of its past performance." Definition by Norbert Wiener. Your room thermostat turns the heat on when it senses that the room has gotten too cold. Biofeedback gives you a reading on something going on within your body, just as a thermometer does. But just knowing your temperature doesn't let you affect your temperature. Or does it?

Biofeedback machines monitor some function of the body and give you a continuous visual or aural report. And then—this is the part that got everybody so excited—you learn to change the signal, to alter the dynamics of that part of the body. But nobody knows how it's done. It seems to happen outside of the rational, language-using part of the mind. You can raise your arm if somebody tells you to raise your arm. But could you raise or lower your blood pressure, or your heartbeat, just by *thinking* about it? (Not *thinking*, precisely, because thinking implies the verbal and rational. Better say, putting your mind to it.) No Westerner believed it until recently; those functions belonged to the autonomic nervous system, over which we have no control. Or thought we had no control. The big outlines of the paradigm don't have to change, but they have to give in one sector.

The implications were terrific. If people could really control their own autonomic functions, they could bring down their blood pressure, relax, get to sleep, unlearn bad habits such as smoking and drinking, and do away with some of their daily drugs.

Unfortunately, biofeedback went through a fad stage where it was advertised as Electric Zen, where gushy reporters described it as the greatest advance since Copernicus. (The popular press was no more accurate on biofeedback than on drugs.) The Magic of Alpha.

—Adam Smith, *Powers of Mind*

1. If this selection was informative, explain why. What did you learn from it?

POWERS OF MIND   Adam Smith (New York: Random House, 1975). Copyright © 1975 by Adam Smith. Reprinted by permission of Random House, Inc.

2. For what readers would this selection be almost completely *un-informative*? Why?
3. Discuss the kinds of readers for whom Adam Smith apparently intended the piece. (What sorts of people would be interested in the subject and gain knowledge from the writing?)
4. Here is an interesting notion: a piece of writing cannot be completely informative, for in order to understand, you must interpret the new (i.e., information) in terms of the old (i.e., what you already know). For example, if you do not know what *puri* is, I can explain it to you by saying that it is like *tortillas* or *pita*, and if you know what they are, then you will also know what *puri* is. Explain how knowledge that you already had helped you understand the selection by Adam Smith.

A *truism* contains very little surprise value and hence almost no information. Here are some examples.

One must study in order to learn a difficult new subject.
A successful marriage involves give and take.
Children need nourishing food if they are to grow up strong and healthy.

Such statements make readers yawn.

The point is not that they are untrue, but simply that almost everyone agrees with them and has heard them (or variations on them) again and again.

An essay can be truistic—and will be so if the readers say to themselves, "I agree with the point, but why does it have to be developed again? I've heard all of this before."

Suppose, for instance, that an essay opened with the following sentence:

A mother is a guy's best friend.

Most readers would be definitely put off by the truism and might be reluctant to proceed into the body of the writing. If the whole piece is a series of truisms, readers become bored and annoyed.

In your own writing, you should avoid starting with the completely obvious, and on pages 129–32 are a variety of methods for gaining the reader's attention. Furthermore, the whole chapter on discovering ideas (pages 55–101) explains ways to get new perspectives and original ideas in regard to any subject.

Some Uses of Informative Writing

A brief glance at some examples of exposition makes one aware of its uses.

To Give Directions

To get from Huntington Beach to the University of Southern California, take the San Diego Freeway north to the interchange of the Harbor Freeway. Go north on the Harbor Freeway to the Exposition Boulevard exit. Go west on Exposition for approximately one-half block to Figueroa Street. The University of Southern California is located at the corner of Exposition and Figueroa.

To Give Instructions

To set the left margin on the Olivetti Praxis 48 typewriter, move the carriage as far as possible to the right. Depress the lever marked "EL MARG" and move the carriage either right or left to the desired space.

To Present Facts

limerick, type of humorous verse. It is always short, often nonsensical, and sometimes ribald. Of unknown origin, the limerick is popular rather than literary and has even been used in advertising. The rhyme scheme of most limericks is usually *aabba,* as in the following example:

> There was a young lady of Niger,
> Who smiled as she rode on a Tiger;
>   They returned from the ride
>   With the lady inside
> And a smile on the face of the tiger.

The most famous collection of limericks is Edward Lear's *Book of Nonsense* (1846). See Langford Reed, *The Complete Limerick Book* (1925); C. P. Aiken, *A Seizure of Limericks* (1964); V. B. Holland, *An Explosion of Limericks* (1967); W. S. Baring-Gould, *The Lure of the Limerick* (1967).

—*The New Columbia Encyclopedia*

To Explain Ideas and Opinions

Why Almost Everyone Is Wrong About Gold

Charles A. Cerami

Several thousand Americans bought English gold sovereigns for $11 or so in the early 1970s. They now find that each one is worth more than $100. Those who bought and saved the Austrian Corona coin, which has nearly a full ounce of gold, paid $50 or $60 for it at that time and now rejoice that the price is well above $300.

The emotions roused by this price movement are multi-faceted enough to mirror the whole economic trauma of the turbulent 1970s:

• Many who made these felicitous purchases feel a smug confidence in the contents of their safe-deposit boxes; but others wonder if it is time to take their gains and turn the coins back into paper dollars.

• The greater number of persons who never bought gold feel left out, and some lie awake nights trying to decide whether they should now start buying this apparently invincible metal.

• U.S. government officials try to ignore the fact that they sold off billions of dollars worth of their country's gold hoard at giveaway prices just before it soared in value.

• The "gold bugs," who always considered those government officials idiots deserving of impeachment, now declare that gold has proved itself the perfect risk-free investment, that it will shortly move on to $500, $600, and $1000 per ounce.

They are all wrong—the smug, the eager, the dejected, the anti-gold economists, and the fanatics who think that gold is a magic beanstalk which will grow to the sky.

In the short space of the last twenty years, gold has tried to re-teach man a lesson that he keeps refusing to absorb: Precious metal is the only real *money* in the world—the only steady standard of value—and being money, it cannot really be an investment at all. It cannot *for long* go up or down in true value. Distortions lasting weeks or a few months are possible. But over the years, it stands very nearly still while everything else around it bobs up and down. We will all be better investors and citizens when this "news" is more widely understood.

The gold bugs who elevate their admiration for gold to the status of a religion have won—but it is a Pyrrhic victory. They will find that while gold is every bit as special as they have claimed, it is not headed for greater heights. It is not headed anywhere. If its value appears to keep rising, that means only that paper money has fallen further—altering the numbers but not the relative values. The length of a yard-stick would not change if officials began to put more line markers on football fields. Neither does tampering with currencies and price tags alter the real value of gold. One ounce of it bought about fifteen barrels of oil years ago, and still does. This relationship could change if, for example, the total supply of oil should suddenly swell enormously; but even then, gold's value in relation to the sum total of all world goods would not—*could* not—change appreciably.

To see why this is so, consider what money really is. It is a store of value, of buying power. It has to be something imperishable, savable, easily transportable, plentiful enough to cover the needs of a growing population, but scarce enough to require quite a lot of effort to acquire. And it must be costly to produce. Otherwise, people would just make more of it and spoil its value.

There is nothing mystical that makes gold the ideal money; it is merely a matter of natural accident. Nothing else meets all the criteria quite so neatly. Silver has often served the purpose, but its supply is potentially too erratic to keep values steady. Diamonds are not as uniform, not as divisible into smaller units or usable for so many things. And as for paper "money," it is not money at all—only a warehouse receipt for the metal that a responsible government should keep in storage. Gold's one shortcoming is a scarcity that frustrates the desire of popularly elected governments to buy more favor from more voters. If they were to increase the amount of paper money that they print in a very orderly way—in line with the productivity of their economies—they could keep these paper receipts viable and respectable indefinitely. It has been done for long periods. (The British pound, and consequently Britain's government securities, were a steady store of value for most of the eighteenth and nineteenth centuries. There were lapses during wars and financial crises; each time the Bank of England resolutely went back to holding 100 percent coin or bullion against all notes it issued, making the banknotes "as good as gold.") But in the end, the desire of major governments to please too many people at once results in too much printing of "money." And then, as Voltaire said, "All paper money eventually returns to its intrinsic value—zero."

To Make Definitions

asthenic game plan
Asthenic describes a person suffering from fear, loss of general mental functions, and an inability to act decisively. *Game plan* is a much-loved phrase among big business types, probably because its sporty connotations disguise the often Machiavellian, often cruel practices it describes. The *asthenic game plan* is any method employed by a busi-

nessman to intimidate a subordinate (most common), a superior (least common), or a rival in line for the same job promotion.

—Joel Homer, "Big Business Talk"

Scrimmages in Exposition

After you have completed the following brief exercises, submit your writings to one or two of your classmates for comments. If your writings fail to accomplish the purpose for which you intended them, your readers will explain why this is so.

1. Write a set of directions that would enable a visitor to find the room on your campus in which your English class meets.
2. Choose a simple process—such as making a paper airplane—and write a set of instructions for that process.
3. Briefly explain one of your opinions on some subject.
4. Give a definition of a technical term with which you are familiar. The term can be related to a sport, a hobby, a field in which you are interested; it can even be a slang term.

Writing to Explain, Demonstrate, or Explore a Topic

Each of the following passages gives information, but with a different purpose.

Hold on. Don't step out the door. Not quite yet. It's best not to go into a jog with a cold body. Give it a warm-up. The process for beginning joggers should be gentle. Then, as the jogs grow in time and length, as the habit takes hold, the warm-up period will become more varied and complex.

For starters, do a little stretching. Roll your neck four or five times in small circles. That's to loosen the bunched-up muscles near the upper spine. Hunch and roll your shoulders, moving them back and forth three or four times to loosen chest and back muscles. Stick out your stomach, roll your hips, pull in your gut. Nothing too rambunctious. Just loosen your body. Place one foot out behind you, toe on the floor, heel raised, and rotate it clockwise. Repeat [the] proce-

BIG BUSINESS TALK   Joel Homer, *Atlantic*, Dec. 1979, p. 72. Copyright © 1979 by The Atlantic Monthly Company, Boston, Mass. Reprinted with permission.

dure with the other foot. Simple exercises, but they get the juices
flowing and the circulatory-muscular system activated.

—Jack Batten, *The Complete Jogger*

[The author of the following had received a letter from American Express, offering him flight insurance.]

In 1977, there were sixty-four fatalities on scheduled domestic
flights, 28,250 deaths in automobiles. You were thirty-three times
more likely to die driving a mile than flying a mile. In 1978, U.S.-
based air carriers made 4,995,000 scheduled flights here and abroad;
only four were what might be called "unsuccessful". . .

Three times as many people died in bathtubs in 1977 as on
scheduled domestic flights. Another seventy, according to the National Safety Council, drowned in "wells, cisterns, and cesspools."
According to one insurance agent, you are more likely to be *kid-
napped* than to be killed in a plane crash.

In fact, your chances of being killed on any given scheduled
flight are something less than one in a million.

If you are safer in the air than on the ground, as might be
argued, then it is hard to see why American Express considers it
"vital" that you obtain special coverage when you take to the safety
of the skies.

—Andrew Tobias, "American Express Flight Insurance," *Esquire*

The first passage is *explaining* something. The second is *demonstrating*.

In explanation, the writer's assumption is that the reader will
accept the information without questioning its validity. If I explain
to you how to get to my home, I do not expect you to question my
authority; it would be strange if you asked me, "But how do you
know?"

In the first selection, Mr. Batten is *explaining* how to warm up
before jogging. If he wanted to demonstrate that the procedures are
effective, he would need to present data based on a study of joggers
and perhaps would include the facts about the muscle system.

On the other hand, the second passage is attempting to *demonstrate* that flight insurance is not a good investment, and to do this,
the author presents data regarding the risks of flying as compared
with driving and other activities.

The difference between explanation and demonstration can be
boiled down this way. When you read an explanation and accept it,
your subconscious reaction is "All of this must be correct because
the author is an authority"; when you read demonstrative prose

and are convinced, your subconscious reaction is "All of this must be correct because the evidence is convincing." In explanation, the focus is on the authority of the writer; in demonstration, the focus is on the evidence.

Not all expository writing is as conclusive as explanation and demonstration. Writers often introduce and explore ideas that they do not fully understand, outlining the pros and cons of a subject without reaching a conclusion.

In the following passage of *exploratory* prose from *The Coming of Middle Age,* Dr. Arnold J. Mandell, a psychiatrist, reveals his feelings about his profession. Note the inconclusive ending: "Something has happened to the psychotherapy that I used to think was a good idea. Or has the something happened to me?"

Things became dada. Psychotherapy was the lifesaving argument of two immigrants who were on a boat that sank coming to America; gesticulating wildly kept them afloat while the waves swept them to shore. Psychotherapy was what a skinny, ugly call girl who earned three hundred a night taught me about the factors in her success: *griv* sense (the capacity to intuit the interpersonal and sexual style desired without being told—dominance, submission, activity, passivity) and never have an orgasm with a client (conducting the interaction properly distanced). Psychotherapy was the hairdresser who sells his client a new self that she can see in the mirror—the hypnosis lasting until the next comb-out. Psychotherapy was what the neighborhood bars and their tenders offer in a combination of chemotherapy and group process. What are we doing for our money, we, the full-time psychotherapists who don't give our patients an orgasm, hairdo, or drinks?

Do we create *more* trouble? The new breed of community psychiatrists have taken all the human dignity from the flophouse, the town greeter waving on the street corner, the village drunk, guttersnipe, bench polisher, and nut. We've swept away these valuable social institutions and in their place put diagnoses, a courtroom for commitment, the hospital ward, and an ever-more-bizarre group of psychotherapies.

Psychotherapy, like all art movements in their last days, has become degenerate. Or is it my problem with lost meaning? What was once a group of techniques for changing man's conscious experience has become a new set of shoulds, group invasions of the private soul, righteous ritual, personal charisma, fad, the rigidity of institutions, and the growing desperation of customers who were promised too much. The language and vision have invaded all of life: from a

THE COMING OF MIDDLE AGE   Arnold J. Mandell, M.D. (New York: Summit Books, 1977), pp. 113–15. Copyright © 1977 by Arnold J. Mandell, M.D. Reprinted by permission of Summit Books, a Simon & Schuster division of Gulf and Western Corporation.

French physician recommending a gentle delivery to avoid birth trauma (what?!) to the garbled psychoanalysis of a *New York Times* book review (". . . while avoiding the language, she has described beautifully the shock and emptiness of the discovery of her absent penis and her anger at her brother who . . .").

It sounds like a zoo. The hungry noises of a frenetic search for the release from bondage that will accompany the second coming of something, anything. The roars begin after smelling the newest meat in *Psychology Today:* primal screams; sensual groans of naked Esalen mud bathers; quiet chants of practitioners of Theravada, Mahayana, Tantra, and Zen; grunts from a forceful Rolfing; macho curses of a Synanon game; black marching boots moving to the rhythm of est; the righteous lecture of a strict vegetarian; the unhooked uh-huhs of today's burned-out psychoanalyst; bitter, funny stories of Alcoholics Anonymous; screams of triumph and despair during the weighing rituals of Take Off Pounds Sensibly; the bebop riffs, disjointed, in a group meeting of Schizophrenia Anonymous; and Pauling's ceaseless claims about a vitamin for every twisted thought.

I can't promise what I can't deliver. I tried for over fifteen thousand office hours. I'm not so sure now that it doesn't make as much trouble as it undoes. Something has happened to the psychotherapy that I used to think was a good idea. Or has the something happened to me?

In this selection, Dr. Mandell is, in effect, telling his readers, "Look, these ideas trouble me, but I have reached no firm conclusions. Let me explain the problem to you, but don't expect me to solve it."

Much of the writing in your journal should be exploratory, for, as you can see, through writing this kind of prose, you might well get a better handle on the problem areas of your life.

Exercise: Exploring

On pages 176–87 of this book is a discussion of the nature of problems. If you have not already done so, read that section. (If you have already read it, you may want to go back over it.)

In a brief piece of writing, explore a problem that troubles you. Your audience will be your teacher and classmates.

DEVELOPING EXPOSITORY WRITING

Chapter 4, "Developing Ideas: The Paragraph," discussed the need for supplying details concerning the main ideas of paragraphs. On pages 143–45, you saw the use of imagery as one method of developing details. Here we will examine additional organizational patterns and techniques of development common to exposition and other kinds of writing. The following are some of the ways in which writers make their ideas clear and convincing to readers.

Facts

Mere raw data—the facts of the case—can put life *and* vividness and meaning into a paragraph. For instance, the first paragraph of Mark Twain's *Life on the Mississippi* begins with these general statements:

> The Mississippi is well worth reading about. It is not a commonplace river, but on the contrary is in all ways remarkable.

Twain goes on to support his thesis by citing facts concerning the Mississippi:

> Considering the Missouri its main branch, it is the longest river in the world—four thousand three hundred miles. It seems safe to say that it is the crookedest river in the world, since in one part of its journey it uses up one thousand three hundred miles to cover the same ground that the crow could fly over in six hundred and seventy-five. It discharges three times as much water as the St. Lawrence, twenty-five times as much as the Rhine, and three hundred and thirty-eight times as much as the Thames. No other river has so vast a drainage basin; it draws its water-supply from twenty-eight states and territories; from Delaware on the Atlantic seaboard, and from all the country between that and Idaho on the Pacific slope—a spread of forty-five degrees of longitude. The Mississippi receives and carries to the Gulf water from fifty-four subordinate rivers that are navigable by steamboats, and from some hundreds that are navigable by flats and keels. The area of its drainage basin is as great as the combined areas of England, Wales, Scotland, Ireland, France, Spain, Portugal, Germany, Austria, Italy, and Turkey; and almost all this wide region is fertile; the Mississippi valley, proper, is exceptionally so.

Data, then, need not mean mere grubbiness. In *Life on the Mississippi*, Mark Twain talks about the Mississippi River as the mythic central artery of America and about the time he spent on it as the most glorious period of his life; the book is largely prose poetry. But the facts and nothing but the facts contribute to the overall impression that our most American of American authors achieves in his magnificent book.

One more paragraph from *Life on the Mississippi* illustrates how Mark Twain uses the facts to delineate a picture of the river at its full:

> From Cairo to Baton Rouge, when the river is over its banks, you have no particular trouble in the night; for the thousand-mile wall of dense forest that guards the two banks all the way is only gapped with a farm or wood-yard openings at intervals, and so you can't "get out of the river" much easier than you could get out of a fenced lane; but from Baton Rouge to New Orleans it is a different matter. The river is more than a mile wide, and very deep—as much as two hundred feet in places. Both banks, for a good deal over a hundred miles, are shorn of their timber and bordered by continuous sugar-plantations, with only here and there a scattering sapling or row of ornamental China trees. The timber is shorn off clear to the rear of the plantations, from two to four miles. When the first frost threatens to come, the planters snatch off their crops in a hurry. When they have finished grinding the cane, they form the refuse of the stalks (which they call *bagasse*) into great piles and set fire to them, though in other sugar countries the bagasse is used for fuel in the furnaces of the sugar mills. Now the piles of damp bagasse burn slowly, and smoke like Satan's own kitchen.

This paragraph is packed with details, giving the reader the sight and even the smell of the flooding Mississippi.

Analogy

Norman Mailer was exactly the right person to write the most complete journalistic report on the first flight to the moon. *Of a Fire on the Moon*, Mailer's account of the moon flight, is beyond doubt a classic in its own day, a consummately skillful interpretation of both the technical and mythic accomplishment of perching three men atop a giant firecracker (as Mailer termed the rocket) and propelling them out into space on a voyage that unbound humanity from earth. Below are two paragraphs from that book. In these paragraphs, Mailer uses analogy to explain the command module of Apollo 11 to the reader. *Analogy* is the process whereby the unfamiliar is made familiar through a description of the similarities between things or concepts that are in most respects dissimilar. It is a tremendously useful device for the writer. (See pages 34–35 and 36–37.)

> To speak of a self-contained universe when one is dealing with a vehicle which is self-sustaining for a short period is to trespass on the meaning. A man is a universe by that measure, indeed he is more self-contained in his ability to adapt and survive than the ship of Apollo 11. In fact the Command Module is more like the sort of universe complete in itself one glimpses in a flower cut for a vase. Such an ornament receives food, breathes, exudes, molts, can even preside over a fresh development like the opening of a bud, and presumably this cut flower is capable of sending and receiving messages from other flowers and plants (if such communication is one of the functions of a flower) but still! we know the flower will live only a few days. It is a self-contained universe whose continuation is sealed off from itself.
>
> The same was true of the Command Module. The men in it could live no longer than there were supplies of oxygen for them to breathe, and that was for two weeks. Nonetheless, Apollo 11 was more a cosmic expression than an ornament. Its vase was space, and through space it traveled, a ship, a species of man-made comet, a minuscule planet with an ability to steer. . . .

The comparison of the command module with a cut flower in a vase may at first seem outrageous, particularly when the comparison must be stretched to the breaking point by the assertion that flowers communicate, but in the second paragraph, Mailer redeems himself by saying, "Nonetheless, Apollo 11 was more a cosmic expression than an ornament." Finally, Mailer's outlandish comparison is more thought-provoking than, for instance, the following trite analogy:

> To summarize the role of estrogen in the pituitary control center in the brain, I should like to quote a simile I once heard at a popular medical lecture. The speaker compared the pituitary to an irascible man who controls his entire family with strict discipline. But if something goes wrong, he is likely to fly into a rage and smash up the whole house. Estrogen, on the other hand, is like a calm, tactful woman who smoothes his irascible temper and keeps him from going

OF A FIRE ON THE MOON Norman Mailer (Boston: Little, Brown, 1971). Copyright © 1969, 1970 by Norman Mailer. Reprinted by permission of Little, Brown and Co.

to extremes. As long as estrogen is on hand, the temperamental pituitary keeps calm order in the endocrine family. But when estrogen is absent the overwrought pituitary makes a shambles of the entire household of the body.

—Robert A. Wilson, M.D., *Feminine Forever*

Certainly this analogy—the pituitary as the irascible father, estrogen as the serene mother, the endocrine system as the family—is not terribly imaginative, and is it not just a bit too cute, too cloying? Notice also that we gain very little new understanding from the author's analogy between the endocrine system and a family. In fact, the analogy is as farfetched as Mailer's equation of the Apollo 11 command module with a cut flower—except that Mailer's analogy is richly evocative and provocative.

One more analogy, this one again from that glorious book, *Life on the Mississippi*.

But I am wandering from what I was intending to do; that is, make plainer than perhaps appears in the previous chapters some of the peculiar requirements of the science of piloting steamboats on the Mississippi. First of all, there is one faculty which a pilot must incessantly cultivate until he has brought it to absolute perfection. Nothing short of perfection will do. That faculty is memory. He cannot stop with merely thinking a thing is so and so; he must *know* it; for this is eminently one of the "exact" sciences. With what scorn a pilot was looked upon, in the old times, if he ever ventured to deal in that feeble phrase "I think," instead of the vigorous one, "I know!" One cannot easily realize what a tremendous thing it is to know every trivial detail of twelve hundred miles of river and know it with absolute exactness. If you will take the longest street in New York, and travel up and down it, conning its features patiently until you know every house and window and lamppost and big and little sign by heart, and know them so accurately that you can instantly name the one you are abreast of when you are set down at random in that street in the middle of an inky black night, you will then have a tolerable notion of the amount and exactness of a pilot's knowledge who carries the Mississippi River in his head. And then, if you will go on until you know every street-crossing, the character, size, and position of the crossing-stones, and the varying depth of mud in each of these numberless places, you will have some idea of what the pilot must know in order to keep a Mississippi steamer out of trouble. Next, if you will take half of the signs in that long street, and *change their places* once a month, and still manage to know their new positions accurately on dark nights, and keep up with these repeated changes without making any mistakes, you will understand what is required of a pilot's peerless memory by the fickle Mississippi.

Now that, it seems to me, is the perfect analogy, illuminating, imagistic in quality, completely worthy of the man who has been looked on as the father of American prose.

Definition

A definition does two things. First, it assigns a word to a class. For instance, an *oboe* (the word to be defined) is a *wind instrument* (the class to which it belongs). Second, the definition states the features of the word that make it differ from other members of the class. For example, the oboe is a double-reed instrument, it has a nasal tone, and its range is from B flat below middle C upward for three and one-half octaves.

In writing, key words sometimes need extended definition or explanation, and this definition makes up a paragraph, as in the following:

> What is "laid-back" anyway?
> The term originated in and derives its only precise meaning from the drug culture. If one was high enough frequently enough, chances are one was not going to be in a state of tension or acceleration or even in a straight-up position but, rather, laid-back. Taking on a broader meaning, it began to describe a mood of being easygoing and convincingly unconcerned with the power-money-fame-success game. The laid-back style crystalized in southern California in the early Seventies. It has since spread across the country and put many young men in a brand-new bind, contending as they must with the new duality problem—of success or personal freedom—while putting themselves through the necessary contortions to hide the old ambition on their sleeves.
>
> —Gail Sheehy, "The Laid-Back Philosophy"

Classification

When you classify, you group items into classes. For example, you might make the following classification of the books that you

THE LAID-BACK PHILOSOPHY   Gail Sheehy, *Esquire*, October, 1979. Reprinted by courtesy of *Esquire* magazine.

own: prose fiction, textbooks, reference books, and prose nonfiction books. The purpose of some paragraphs is to classify the aspects, phases, or parts of a subject. Such paragraphs often keep readers oriented with phrases like *on the one hand . . . on the other hand, in the first place . . . in the second place,* or merely enumerative words: *first . . . second . . . third.* In the following examples, these "orienters" are printed in *italics.*

> There are three kinds of book owners. *The first* has all the standard sets and best-sellers—unread, untouched. (This deluded individual owns woodpulp and ink, not books.) *The second* has a great many books—a few of them read through, most of them dipped into, but all of them as clean and shiny as the day they were bought. (This person would probably like to make books his own, but is restrained by a false respect for their physical appearance.) *The third* has a few books or many—every one of them dog-eared and dilapidated, shaken and loosened by continual use, marked and scribbled in from front to back. (This man owns books.)
>
> —Mortimer J. Adler, "How to Mark a Book,"
> *Saturday Review of Literature*

The next example is more complex, but it is still organized on the principle of classification, which is nothing more than a listing of parts or features.

> Motor racing is potentially the most exciting sport in the world. *For one thing,* it is the most personally valid form of competition, in this wheeled age. Few of us remember the last time we played football or can honestly identify with Sandy Koufax, but most of us drive. *For another,* racing, in its more rarefied forms, could be called a sport of superhumans: there are only twenty or so stock-car drivers who have any business pushing those two-ton 600-horsepower brutes to the fantastic speeds they attain, usually only inches from their neighbor or a guard rail; less than a dozen *grand prix* drivers of any real ability on the European circuit; a comparative handful of young men able to manage the big sports-racing cars being developed here in the United States; a tiny fraternity of Indianapolis drivers used to riding on the edge of oblivion.
>
> —Stephen Wilkinson, "Automobile Racing," *Holiday*

This paragraph is worth looking at a second time, for it makes use of those familiar building-blocks Topic-Restriction-Illustration that we studied in Chapter 4. Here's how.

> *Topic*   Motor racing is potentially the most exciting sport in the world.

Feature 1   *For one thing,* it is the most personally valid form of competition, in this wheeled age.

Restriction   Few of us remember the last time we played football or can honestly identify with Sandy Koufax, but most of us drive.

Feature 2   *For another,* racing, in its more rarefied forms, could be called a sport of superhumans:

Illustration   there are only twenty or so stock-car drivers who have any business pushing those two-ton, 600-horsepower brutes to the fantastic speeds they attain, usually only inches from their neighbor or a guard rail;

Illustration   less than a dozen *grand prix* drivers of any real ability on the European circuit;

Illustration   a comparative handful of young men able to manage the big sports-racing cars being developed here in the United States;

Illustration   a tiny fraternity of Indianapolis drivers used to riding on the edge of oblivion.

Comparison and Contrast

When we *compare* items, we point out and explain their similarities. When we *contrast* them, we focus on their differences. (Of course, contrast implies comparison. The difference between comparison and contrast is simply one of focus. No two things in the world are exactly alike; therefore, one can point out the differences, no matter how small.) Comparison and contrast are useful devices for paragraph development.

The following paragraph explains adult creativity by comparing it to and contrasting it with some of the qualities of children.

Many people have puzzled over the secret of creativity. I contend that it is no more than the extension into adult life of . . . childlike qualities. The child asks new questions; the adult answers old ones; the childlike adult finds answers to new questions. The child is inventive; the adult is productive; the childlike adult is inventively productive. The child explores his environment; the adult organizes it; the childlike adult organizes his explorations and, by bringing order to them, strengthens them. He creates.

—Desmond Morris, *The Human Zoo*

THE HUMAN ZOO   Desmond Morris (London: Jonathan Cape, n.d.). Reprinted by permission of Jonathan Cape Ltd.

In explaining how Jack Dempsey fought, the author of the following paragraph *contrasts* him with Gene Tunney:

> Perhaps the essential difference between two such champions as Dempsey and Tunney is best noticed when you listen to them discuss past contests. Dempsey will say: "When I *fought* Tommy Gibbons. . . ." Tunney will invariably say: "Ah—when I *boxed* Carpentier. . . ." Dempsey never boxed anybody, which is one reason why he was so worshiped and became such a glamorous figure. When the bell rang, he ran out and began to attack his opponent, and he never stopped attacking him, trying to batter him to the floor, until the bell ended the round.
>
> —Paul Gallico, *Farewell to Sport*

One more example, this one comparing the voyage of Columbus with our current ventures into space:

> When Columbus set sail into the Atlantic, he knew he was going to do something great, but he did not know what. This remark about Columbus is trite. It has been made a hundred times before by people discussing man's activities in space, yet it is the truest thing that can be said. In my personal view of the human situation, the exploration of space appears as the most hopeful feature of a dark landscape. Everything I say may well be as wrong and irrelevant as Columbus' reasons for sailing West. The important thing is that he did sail West and we do go into space. The true historical consequences of these events can only be known much later.
>
> —Freeman Dyson, "Human Consequences of the Exploration of Space"

Just for Fun

Many men are awed by the snow queen look—yards and yards of virginal white edged in lace or ruffles, with maybe a blue moire sash, the setting a canopy or elegant Empire bed covered with embroidered sheets, white satin coverlets and piles of pale silk pillows. The challenge of arousing and conquering icy, feminine, perfect *you* can become a fever to this kind of man. He will usually be an exceptionally ardent lover and buy you expensive trinkets.

—*The Sensuous Woman* by "J"

Exercise: Methods of Development

1. Write a paragraph that uses *facts* for development. For this exercise, choose your own subject. (See "Facts," pages 201–02.) To get the information for your subject, you might want to consult a reference source such as *The World Almanac*.

Example

Art is a big business. More and more, poeple are treating objects of art as vehicles for investment. Sotheby Parke Bernet, the international auction house, last summer announced sales of $112 million for its 1977–78 American season alone, an increase of $32 million over the previous year. In June, at the London auction of the estate of the German-born merchant Robert von Hirsch, two medieval enamels believed to have been made for Emperor Frederick Barbarossa were bought by a consortium of German museums for more than $2 million apiece. Great art—work generally acknowledged in this century to be first-rate—has for many years commanded enormous prices, but a new kind of market and buyer is emerging. The British Railway Workers Pension Fund successfully bid $1.5 million for a twelfth-century English gilt altar candlestick at the Hirsch sale. This was not an instance of a museum buying a work of great historical significance, or a private collector out to snare a jewel for his collection; this was a union pension fund making a fiduciary investment.

—Deborah Trustman, "The Art Market:
Investors Beware," *The Atlantic*

2. Write a paragraph based on *analogy*. (See "Analogy," pages 202–05.)

Example

In short, it was not difficult to visualize the tramps as pioneers. I reflected that if they were to find themselves in a singlehanded life-and-death struggle with nature, they would undoubtedly display persistence. For the pressure of responsibility and the heat of battle steel a character. The inadaptable would perish, and those who survived would be the equal of the successful pioneers.

—Eric Hoffer, *The Ordeal of Change*

3. Use *definition* to develop a paragraph. (See "Definition," page 205.)

Example

I have been using the term "information" as a synonym for the signals or messages that come to the brain from the outside world in the form of neural impulses from receptor organs such as the eyes or ears; these impulses are the brain's only points of contact with the outside world. The brain must use this information to answer cognitive questions, to reduce uncertainty. There is a useful technical definition of information that can be adopted from a field called "Information Theory" that is primarily concerned with the efficiency of communication systems. Information, in the technical sense, is defined as the reduction of uncertainty by the elimination of alternatives.

—Frank Smith, *Comprehension and Learning*

4. Use the principle of *classification* or enumeration to develop a paragraph. (See "Classification," pages 205–07.)

Example

Buck-passing is also reflected in the way that some travel companies handle their complaint correspondence. We have made an informal review of the ways complaints are answered:

A. The company does not respond at all.

B. The company blames the airline, the tour operator, the hotel, etc., and says that nothing can be done about the problem.

C. The company honestly tries to investigate your complaint and solve the problem.

D. The company sends you a form letter.

E. The company answers a *different* problem than the one you raised. (This mysterious ploy may work because most people do not write to the company again.)

—Hal Gieseking, *Consumer Handbook for Travelers*

5. Use *comparison* or *contrast* to develop a paragraph. (See "Comparison and Contrast," pages 207–08.)

Example

Nothing is more trendy than education. Yesterday's heresy is today's creed. Five years ago everyone was still calling for more "relevant" courses and dropping "obsolete" requirements. At that time those who saw a decline in academic standards were either afraid to say so or were not listened to when they talked. Now it is respectable to decry the decline, to advocate quality and getting back to basics.

—Alston Chase, "Skipping Through College"

6. Finally, you might like to try writing a put-on, such as the paragraph by "J" on pages 208–09. In your paragraph, try to capture the cynicism that characterizes the model.

CONSUMER HANDBOOK FOR TRAVELERS   Hal Gieseking. Taken from the Travel Advisor section, *Travel/Holiday* magazine, Floral Park, New York 11001.
SKIPPING THROUGH COLLEGE   Alston Chase, *Atlantic*, Sept. 1978, p. 35. Copyright © 1978 by The Atlantic Monthly Company, Boston, Mass. Reprinted with permission.

In Summary

You have surveyed and practiced several methods for developing ideas. The main point to be grasped right now is that the reader wants details.

The following paragraphs will give you a visual impression of how topics are developed on the basis of specific content.

> Paul and I fished a good many rivers, but when one of us referred to "the big river" the other knew that it was the Big Blackfoot.
>
> > It isn't the biggest river we fished, but it is the most powerful and, per pound, so are the fish.
> >
> > It runs straight and hard—on a map or from an airplane it is almost a straight line running due west from its headwaters at Rogers Pass on the Continental Divide to Bonner, Montana, where it empties into the South Fork of the Clark Fork of the Columbia.
> >
> > It runs hard all the way.
>
> —Norman Maclean, *A River Runs Through It and Other Stories*

> Learning to live and learning to use language are virtually synonymous.
>
> > We begin, almost as soon as we are born, to register and store, arrange and organise, impressions of what we encounter in our environment.
> >
> > > Language enters into this process as soon as the growing child becomes aware of it, so that we begin, early in life, to build up a map, or rather a catalogue of our experiences.
> > >
> > > When, in the course of our daily lives, we encounter something that is familiar, we draw upon our recollections of past experiences, our stored expressions, in order to handle the new experience.
>
> —Peter Doughty, John Pearce, and Geoffrey Thornton, *Exploring Language*

In the first paragraph, a series of details give us important information about the Big Blackfoot River. In the next paragraph,

A RIVER RUNS THROUGH IT AND OTHER STORIES   Norman Maclean (Chicago: University of Chicago Press, 1976). Reprinted from *A River Runs Through It and Other Stories* by Norman Maclean by permission of The University of Chicago Press. © 1976 by The University of Chicago.
EXPLORING LANGUAGE   Peter Doughty, John Pearce, and Geoffrey Thornton (London: Edward Arnold, 1972), p. 51. Reprinted by permission of the publisher.

each sentence becomes more specific, explaining the first and most general sentence.

Many paragraphs can be "diagrammed" in these ways.

THE WRITER'S CREDIBILITY

Since readers want information from the writer, they must have confidence in him or her, must feel that he or she knows the subject and is not withholding crucial information or lying.

To give the reader this confidence, the writer tries to establish his or her credibility in several ways. Perhaps the most obvious method of doing this is the writer's direct statement that he or she is an authority on the subject, that is, the writer presents his or her credentials. Another way to establish credibility is through the skillful use of words common to the subject and appropriate to the writer's audience, or, in the jargon of writing, through the skillful use of diction and tone. Yet another method, closely related to diction and tone, is the writer's adaptation of style or manner to an audience, that is, the writer adopts a rhetorical stance suitable to his or her readers.

Now, let us look a little more closely at each of these techniques.

Credentials

Writers often need to state their credentials in order to gain the reader's confidence, as does the author of an article on drug use:

> When we at Boston University's Mental Health Clinic were first confronted, five years ago, with the new drug scene we knew very little about it and all pharmacology books were of little help beyond the chemical analysis which they offered. Although we were well-trained psychiatrists, drugs other than for therapeutic purposes were not part of our training. Drugs for the most part had been a ghetto problem and thus neglected and the very hard-core users were being treated in isolated government hospitals, and the results were worse than a dismal failure. But we were trained in the psychoanalytic model so we knew that we could learn, that we could see with sufficient experience how and in what ways drugs affected personality, if at all.

> —Alan S. Katz, "The Use of Drugs in America: Toward a Better Understanding of Passivity"

In this passage, Dr. Katz indicates his connection with a major university, tells us that he is a psychiatrist, and outlines his experience with the subject, preparing the reader to accept the information and conclusions in the essay.

An extremely interesting freshman essay on computers begins like this:

> When I was a sophomore in high school, I became interested in computer science. Fortunately, my father, a computer specialist at McDonnell-Douglas, has a terminal in our home, and my math teacher was a genius at programming. Since I had access to a terminal, both at school and at home, and expert help in both places, I soon became "fluent" in two computer languages.
>
> During my senior year in high school, I helped my math teacher design a computerized record-keeping system for the school. Now all registration and class scheduling is done by the computer, saving the staff hundreds of hours and the students the frustration that usually goes along with registration.

Without some knowledge of the writer's background, his readers (classmates and teacher) might well have doubted his ability to discuss so complex a subject.

Project: A Search for Credentials

Look through five or six issues of magazines such as *Harper's*, the *Atlantic, Esquire, Saturday Review,* and *Scientific American.* What techniques are used to establish the authors' credentials, their credibility and authority in their subjects? Some of the techniques will undoubtedly be "internal," appearing as parts of the essays, but there are other ways in which journals "validate" their authors. What are some of these ways?

Tone and Diction

Tone is the attitude that the writer expresses toward his or her subject. The tone of an essay on, for instance, American funeral customs might be serious, ironic, comic, morbid, straightforward and factual, argumentative, melancholy, joyful. . . .

The main factor in tone is *diction,* the words that the writer chooses. (Diction is discussed on pages 399–410.) For one kind of writing, an author may choose one type of vocabulary, perhaps slang, and for another the same writer may choose an entirely different set of words. Sometimes, to get a special effect, a writer may mix the kinds of words he or she chooses, as Norman Mailer mixes formal and informal language in the following example:

> Another student came by, then another. One of them, slight, with a sharp face, wearing a sport shirt and dark glasses had the appearance of a Hollywood hustler, but that was misleading; he wore the dark glasses because his eyes were still weak from the Mace squirted in them by police at Oakland. This student had a Berkeley style which Mailer did not like altogether: it was cocky, knowledgeable, and quick to mock the generations over thirty. Predictably, this was about the first item on which the kid began to scold the multitude. "You want to come along with us," he told the Over-Thirties, "that's okay, that's your thing, but we've got our thing, and we're going to do it alone whether you come with us or not." Mailer always wanted to give a kick into the seat of all reflection when he was told he had his thing—one did not look forward to a revolution which would substitute "thing" for better words.
>
> —Norman Mailer, *The Armies of the Night*

Notice Mailer's use of such informal or slang words as "hustler" and "kid" alongside words like "appearance" (instead of *look*), "knowledgeable" (instead of *savvy*), or "predictably" (instead of the phrase *as you could've guessed*).

Even such small matters as contractions make a difference in tone, the contracted verbs being less formal:

> *It is* strange that the professor *had not* assigned any papers for three weeks.
> *It's* strange that the professor *hadn't* assigned any papers for three weeks.

Specialized jargon is another problem in diction. Often, vocabulary that is perfectly familiar to members of a profession or social group is unknown by outsiders. Thus, if you were an expert on foods of the world and were writing for other experts, the following would be quite acceptable:

> The dinner began with *billi bi,* followed by *maste khiar.* The main course was *moussaka à la grecque,* and for dessert our host served *riz à l'impératrice.*

However, you would need to "translate" if you were writing for non-experts:

> The dinner began with a rich seafood soup, followed by sliced cucumbers with yoghurt. The main course was an eggplant and lamb casserole, and for dessert our host served rice and cherry pudding.

Exercise

Using formal diction, write a paragraph concerning a serious subject, such as marriage or a religious custom. Then substitute informal diction or slang for words in the paragraph, thus creating a comic or ironic tone. (When you handle a serious subject informally or with slang, the result is often comic or ironic.) Here are two examples:

1. It is a custom in America to have a "viewing" of a body the evening before the funeral. After the corpse has been embalmed, the morticians apply cosmetics to make it appear lifelike. It is then dressed and placed in a coffin. The viewing takes place in what is often called a "slumber room," where friends and relatives come to pay their respects and to bid farewell to the loved one.

2. Americans have the custom of "viewing" stiffs before they're planted. The mortician stuffs the corpse and paints it up. It's dressed up in its best duds and stuck into a coffin, after which it's wheeled to what is called a "slumber room" so that friends and relatives can gawk at it.

For an example of a brilliant handling of tone, read the following:

The Kitchen Revolution

Verta Mae Smart-Grosvenor

there is confusion in the kitchen!
we've got to develop kitchen consciousness or we may very well see the end of kitchens as we now know them. kitchens are getting smaller. in some apts the closet is bigger than the kitchen. something that i saw the other day leads me to believe that there may well be a   5
subversive plot to take kitchens out of the home and put them in the street. i was sitting in the park knitting my old man a pair of socks

THE KITCHEN REVOLUTION   Verta Mae Smart-Grosvenor, in *The Black Woman*, ed. Toni Cade (New York: Signet Books, 1970), pp. 119–20. Copyright © 1970 by Verta Mae Smart-Grosvenor. Reprinted by permission of Verta Mae Smart-Grosvenor and Ron Hobbs.

for next winter when a tall well dressed man in his mid thirties sat
next to me.
i didnt pay him no mind until he went into his act.   10
he pulled his irish linen hankie from his lapel, spread it on his lap,
opened his attache case, took out a box, popped a pill, drank from
his thermos jug, and turned and offered the box to me. thank you no
said i. "i never eat with strangers."
that would have been all except that i am curious black and i looked   15
at the label on the box, then i screamed, the box said INSTANT
LUNCH PILL; (imitation ham and cheese on rye, with diet cola, and
apple pie flavor). i sat frozen while he did his next act. he folded his
hankie, put it back in his lapel, packed his thermos jug away, and
took out a piece of yellow plastic and blew into it, in less than 3 min- 20
utes it had turned into a yellow plastic castro convertible couch.
enough is enough i thought to myself. so i dropped the knitting and
ran like hell. last i saw of that dude he was stretched out on the couch
reading portnoys complaint.
the kitchens that are still left in the home are so instant they might as 25
well be out to lunch.
instant milk, instant coffee, instant tea, instant potatoes, instant old
fashioned oatmeal, everything is preprepared for the unprepared
women in the kitchen. the chicken is pre cut, the flour is pre measured, the rice is minute, the salt is pre seasoned, and the peas are pre   30
buttered. just goes to show you white folks will do anything for their
women. they had to invent instant food because the servant problem
got so bad that their women had to get in the kitchen herself with her
own two lily white hands. it is no accident that in the old old south
where they had slaves that they was eating fried chicken, coated with   35
batter, biscuits so light they could have flown across the mason dixon
line if they had wanted to. they was eating pound cake that had to be
beat 800 strokes. who do you think was doing this beating?
it sure wasnt missy. missy was beating the upstairs house nigger for
not bringing her mint julep quick enough. massa was out beating the   40
field niggers for not hoeing the cotton fast enough. meanwhile up in
the north country where they didnt have no slaves to speak of they
was eating baked beans and so called new england boiled dinner.

In this wonderful piece, there is a subtle shading of tone that is certainly as important as the overt content.

We know immediately that something is up, if for no other
reason than that the author uses no capitals, but up to line 4, she is
merely stating her thesis—literally, that kitchens are getting smaller
and less important. Beginning with line 4, the tone changes, and
soon we realize that we are dealing with some kind of satire, for we
don't believe that kitchens will literally be moved out of the home.

Enter the tall, well-dressed man who sits next to the author as she knits her "old man" a pair of socks. Lines 10 through 14 begin a funny, almost burlesque, sequence, which ends with the prim statement, "i never eat with strangers"—even though the man had apparently not eaten, but merely popped a pill. The comedy grows even more delightfully slapstick in the paragraph that runs from line 15 to line 21. The climax of the wild humor comes with the statement (lines 23–24), "last i saw of that dude he was stretched out on the couch reading portnoys complaint."

Up to this point, then, the tone of the passage is simply humorous, slapstick, and it contains no trace of bitterness or ill humor. But an almost violent change takes place from line 25 on, and the piece concludes as a vitriolic condemnation of white society, which was built on a foundation of black servitude.

The modulations of tone in this passage are quite remarkable, and the author's skill in conveying them constitutes the real strength of the message.

The writer has conveyed her opinions, to be sure, but she has given them the tonal quality that imbues them with *affective* significance. That is, she manages to tell us not only what she thinks but her emotional attitude toward what she thinks.

Rhetorical Stance

Closely related to tone is the concept of *rhetorical stance,* which is a fancy term for a simple idea.

Most language transactions are face-to-face: we can see the people we are talking to. In these situations, we all make subtle shifts in our way of talking, depending upon the audience, and it is these shifts—some of which are not so subtle—that make up our rhetorical stance in spoken discourse.

As an illustration, think of the many ways in which you adjust to different talk situations. When you're chatting with close friends on campus, you are probably quite at ease, your diction is likely to be slangy, and you probably use speech mannerisms that you would avoid in more formal situations—such as repeatedly interjecting *ya know.* When you talk with your professors about official business, undoubtedly you shift your diction and try to exclude slangy mannerisms. Probably even your posture is more formal; you don't slump and sprawl quite as much.

In short, when you talk, you adjust your rhetorical stance continually, using different techniques for different people in various situations.

In writing, tone is a part of rhetorical stance: seriousness, irony, humor, outrage, and so on. So is purpose: you can explain, explore, or demonstrate; you can attempt to *persuade* someone to take an action or make a decision. And, of course, you can try to rouse emotions with a poem or to amuse people with a fictional tale.

Exercise

Observe a friend or acquaintance in a conversation with another person. What can you discover about rhetorical stance? (Diction? Body language? Tone of voice? Distance between the two speakers?)

Orally or in writing, discuss what you discovered about rhetorical stance from your observations.

The Universal Audience

In some situations there are special conditions. For instance, when doctors talk to or write for other doctors, they can assume a shared body of knowledge that allows them to discuss their subjects in certain ways, as one specialist to another. Often this discussion involves the use of jargon, which would be almost meaningless to a person who has not had medical training. Or, to take another instance, think of a teacher speaking to a group of kindergarten children, a very special audience indeed. Here, ideas and words have to be handled with the utmost simplicity and care.

There are times, however, when a piece of writing seems to be aimed not at any particular individual or group, but at what might be called the *universal audience*.[1] This kind of audience is difficult to define, and writing for it involves some special problems that are well worth looking at. To begin with, let us examine the following paragraph by the French philosopher Jean-Paul Sartre.

Man is nothing else but what he makes of himself. Such is the first principle of existentialism. It is also what is called subjectivity, the name we are labeled with when charges are brought against us. But what do we mean by this, if not that man has a greater dignity than a stone or table? For we mean that man first exists, that is, that man

[1] Chaim Perelman and L. Olbrechts-Tyteca, *The New Rhetoric: A Treatise on Argumentation,* trans. John Wilkinson and Purcell Weaver (Notre Dame, Ind.: Univ. of Notre Dame Press, 1969), pp. 31–35.

first of all is the being who hurls himself toward a future and who is conscious of imagining himself as being in the future. Man is at the start of a plan which is aware of itself, rather than a patch of moss, a piece of garbage, or a cauliflower; nothing exists prior to this plan; there is nothing in heaven; man will be what he will have planned to be. Not what he will want to be. Because by the word "will" we generally mean a conscious decision, which is subsequent to what we have already made of ourselves. I may want to belong to a political party, write a book, get married; but all that is only a manifestation of an earlier, more spontaneous choice that is called "will." But if existence really does precede essence, man is responsible for what he is. Thus existentialism's first move is to make every man aware of what he is and to make the full responsibility of his existence rest on him. And when we say that a man is responsible for himself, we do not only mean that he is responsible for his own individuality, but that he is responsible for all men.

—Jean-Paul Sartre, *Existentialism*

This is not an easy paragraph, but neither does the reader need any specialized knowledge or vocabulary to understand it. In other words, you do not have to be a philosopher to grasp what Sartre is saying here. Well then, what sort of audience is he aiming at? Certainly not at kindergarten children and, as we have already observed, not specialists trained in philosophy. From the way language is used in this paragraph, we can assume that Sartre thought of something like this: "I am writing seriously for all intelligent, fairly well-educated people who might be interested in what I have to say." This provides us with at least a preliminary definition of the universal audience, which we can now say is composed of intelligent, educated people who might be interested in the subject that is written about.

But how does the writer conceive of such an audience? Here is the interesting—and useful—point to keep in mind: he or she must *imagine* it, for no group in actual existence will hold exactly the same views or have exactly the same background as the writer. He or she must say at every turn, "I am a reasonable person. Therefore, projecting my image, what can I expect other reasonable people, such as myself, to understand and agree with?" Which means that when writing for the universal audience, a person must at every point be his or her own reader.

When a piece is written for the universal audience, the writer must also think of *culture*. Though the writer can assume that the audience shares much of his or her culture, we all know that there will not be perfect agreement. For example, in the Mormon culture of central Utah, the drinking of coffee and tea is considered sinful (thought not heinously so). In writing for members of that culture, a writer could use coffee and tea drinking as examples of minor sin, but not in writing for the universal audience, unless he or she first explained the Mormon view.

Specialized Audiences

Many pieces of writing are intended for specialized audiences: a physicist writing in a technical journal that is read by other physicists; a college student writing to his or her parents; a committee drafting a report for the members of an organization.

When writing for a specialized readership, the author can make numerous assumptions that are not valid for the universal audience:

1. Readers will understand the technical vocabulary of a given field of study.
   A linguist writing for other linguists can assume that readers will know the meanings of such terms as *phoneme* and *modals*. In writing for the universal audience, the linguist would need to paraphrase or define: *phonemes* are the sounds that carry meaning in a language; *modals* are helping verbs such as *can, may,* and *must.*
2. Readers will share a common background in the subject.
   A historian writing for members of his or her profession would not explain the background and significance of the Treaty of Utrecht, but would probably do so in writing for the universal audience.
3. Readers will be interested in the subject.
   In writing for specialized audiences, an author can assume that readers are interested. For this reason, the beginnings of specialized pieces are often more direct and matter-of-fact than those intended for the universal audience.

Project: Recognizing the Audience

General circulation magazines are normally intended for universal audiences. Check a recent copy of *Harper's,* the *Atlantic, Saturday Review, Omni,* or the *Smithsonian* to determine how the writers handle

a. technical vocabulary,
b. background information,
c. beginnings.

After you have done this, go through a specialized journal in some field—science, the humanities, the arts, sports—and compare the handling of technical vocabulary, background information, and beginnings. Discuss your findings.

THE CONTENT OF EXPOSITORY WRITING

You can look at any piece of writing—say, a student theme—from various angles, but regardless of your point of view, you are still looking at the same thing, just as you can view an object from the top, bottom, or sides. So far, we have explored the reader's expectations of the writer and the writer's relationship to the reader. Now we can focus on the content of the writing, realizing that in doing so, we are discussing essentially the same concepts in a different way.

Sincerity, Adequacy, and Relevance

Readers come to a piece of expository writing with these expectations: that the writer is sincere, that the content is adequate, and that it is relevant.

First, unless they find good reason to believe otherwise, readers assume that the writer is sincere, that he or she is treating the subject in a straightforward manner. If readers suspect that the writer is not completely sincere, they may conclude that he or she is lying, but more probably will assume that the author is violating the *sincerity condition* for a reason. *Irony,* for example, often results from a violation of this condition, and irony is most simply defined as the failure of intention and statement to coincide. For example, in a *literal* statement, I may intend to inform you about the bad quality of food in the cafeteria, saying something like this:

The food in the cafeteria is tasteless, cold, and greasy.

If I use irony, my intention remains unchanged, but my statement will appear to say quite the opposite:

The food in the cafeteria is a gourmet's delight.

If you as a reader think that I could not possibly believe what I have said, you will assume that I am being ironic.

Perhaps the most famous piece of irony in all British and American literature is "A Modest Proposal," by Jonathan Swift. In this bitter essay, Swift "proposes" one solution to economic problems in eighteenth-century Ireland: using children for food, thus overcoming famine and decreasing the population. Taken literally, the essay is horrifying, but read as irony, it becomes a violent attack on the power structure that allows conditions of poverty and exploitation to prevail.

Second, readers assume that the writer will give them all the information they need to understand the subject, but no more than is necessary. If the writer does not follow this *adequacy condition,* readers will assume either (a) that he or she is inept or (b) that he or she is trying to achieve some effect of tone.

The following is an example of information that is withheld:

> A group of students are discussing popular entertainers, and one says, "As for Cher, she has beautiful fingernails."

The effect is, of course, once again ironic. The hearers assume that the speaker could give more information regarding the subject, but has chosen not to. In this case, the speaker implies, "There just isn't much good that can be said about Cher as a performer."

Giving more data than is necessary can also create a humorous tone:

> The woman that my father married and who gave birth to the eighteen-year-old who is now writing these lines taught me how to combine just the proper ingredients for the perfect chocolate mousse.

Said simply, this wordy statement comes out as, "My mother taught me how to make the perfect chocolate mousse."

Third, unless there is reason to believe otherwise, your reader will assume that all parts of your writing are relevant to the topic. In other words, you normally should make connections obvious, unless you have a reason for creating momentary confusion. For example, in the following paragraphs which begin a theme, the connection between the two sentences in the first paragraph is not obvious, but is clarified in the second:

> My favorite food is abalone. Therefore, when I visit relatives in Salt Lake City, I always go out to dinner.
> It is a strange fact, but true, that the best seafood restaurant in

the United States is not in San Francisco, Boston, or New York, but at the foot of the Rockies in the capital of Utah. And this restaurant, Bratten's, serves the most superb abalone I have found in all of my travels.

Studies in Irony and Relevance

1. Write a straightforward paragraph regarding some topic of common interest, such as registration procedures in your college or the rate of inflation. Then rewrite the paragraph so that it is ironic.

2. By withholding information, create an ironic paragraph about a television show or film.

3. Find examples of writings in which apparent irrelevance is used to capture reader interest.

The principles that can be derived from these exercises amount to some good advice for writers:

1. In regard to sincerity, ask yourself if your readers will believe that you are being straightforward with them. If you attempt irony you should first consider your purpose, subject matter, and readers.

2. As to adequacy, check to see that you have given all the information that is needed to understand what you have written. Make sure this information is neither irrelevant nor repetitious. In other words, considering your audience, what do you need to add or delete?

3. With regard to relevance, be certain that your readers can establish the connections which seem obvious to you, but might not to someone else.

Reliability and Reasonableness

Students of classical mythology would understand the following statement: "When the swan ravaged Leda, a civilization was doomed." Readers not familiar with classical myths would need an explanation such as the following:

According to myth, Zeus took the form of a swan and ravaged the mortal Leda. The issue of this rape was the extraordinarily beautiful

Helen. After Helen had married the Mycenaean prince Menelaus, she was abducted by Paris, the son of Priam, king of Troy. Menelaus gathered an army of rustic Greek warriors and laid siege to the much more civilized Troy, finally destroying this city-state.

As we have said repeatedly, content depends to a great extent on audience, but there are aspects of content that are more absolute and less influenced by the intended readers.

Content must be *reliable* and *reasonable*.

Reliability

Reliability depends on our sources. Much of what we know is firsthand, learned through experience, but other sources of knowledge are secondhand, gained from books, articles, conversations, newspapers, films, television, and so on. Obviously, some secondary sources are more reliable than others. For example:

> A friend of mine told me that there is a near miss between a commercial jet and a private light plane almost every week at John Wayne Airport.

> According to my neighbor, who is a shift supervisor in the control tower at John Wayne Airport, there is a near miss between a commercial jet and a private light plane almost every week at that airport.

The second example is more credible than the first because the source for the information is identified as a person who would be likely to know what he or she was talking about, an "expert witness."

In technical and scientific writing, reliability often depends on statistics and research design, factors that can be judged only by those who have special training. For our purposes, there are some common sense "rules" for judging the reliability of content in exposition.

1. *Are the sources timely?* A book about the effects of smoking on human health that was published in 1949 would not be judged reliable since the information in it would be out of date.

2. *Are the sources authoritative?* Some publications are more authoritative than others. *Scientific American*, for instance, is carefully edited, its authors are always experts in their fields, and articles submitted to it are judged in

advance by other experts; we can therefore have confidence in that magazine, whereas we would have less confidence in an article on the same subject that appeared in *Reader's Digest*.

3. *Is the source relevant to the subject?* For example, a professor of economics at a major university can be expected to have reliable opinions about the state of the economy, but his or her professional training in economics would not be relevant to child rearing. Well-known figures from the sports and entertainment worlds often endorse products, but movie stars and football heroes have no special expertness about the nutritive value of cereals or the effectiveness of deodorants.

4. *Is the source biased?* Advertisements are always biased in favor of the products they are selling. We can assume that a Marxist will be biased against the free enterprise system. A believer in genetic evolution will not have a disinterested attitude toward the account of divine creation in Genesis. (To some extent, bias is a given. It is impossible to approach any subject with a completely open mind, simply because we all have opinions and values—and must have them. Thus, we are speaking about matters of degree, not of absolutes. If the writer is frank about his or her own point of view, we can interpret the opinions and conclusions fairly.)

Therefore, *you should carefully scrutinize your sources to determine if they are reliable.* This could mean that you need to do some research. For example, if you are writing about extrasensory perception, you might want to check the authors of your sources to determine if they are recognized experts in their fields, or if you gain information from a conversation, you may want to ask how your informant knows what he or she is talking about.

The chapter on research writing (pages 373–97) deals with the problem of sources more extensively.

Determining Reliability

The following is information regarding a book on diet. On the basis of this information, discuss the reliability of the book as a source.

1. The cover of the book reads as follows:

   Dr. Frank's No-Aging Diet

   Eat & Grow Younger

   The first diet book based on the
   scientific breakthrough of our
   age. Every cell in your body can
   be young again.

   [by] Dr. Benjamin S. Frank with Philip Miele

2. The flyleaf of the book contains the following information about
   the authors:

   Dr. Benjamin S. Frank, now in private practice in New York
   City, is the author of *A New Approach to Degenerative Dis-
   ease and Aging* and *Nucleic Acid Therapy of Aging and
   Degenerative Disease.*

   Philip Miele, Professor of Communication Arts, New York
   Institute of Technology, is a longtime consultant in public
   relations.

3. The book was published by Dell Publishing Company in 1976.

4. The preface is by Sheldon S. Handler, Ph.D., who is identified as
   Chairman, Division of Basic Sciences, University of Baja California.

Reasonableness

Content must also be reasonable. At the very least, it must not
contain logical contradictions. (Informal logic is discussed at length
on pages 256–67). And it must not make preposterous claims.

A brief example. The claim that we must get the meaning of a
written sentence before we can pronounce it would seem preposterous to most people, for it is a common belief that sound conveys
meaning: that is, we see printed letters, translate them into their
sounds, and then get their meaning. My claim is that we see the
printed letters, get their meaning, and only then are able to pronounce them. Now this claim would not be preposterous to students of the psychology of reading. (In fact, it would be obvious.)
However, if I were writing for nonspecialists, I would need to back
the claim up.

There is much evidence in favor of the claim, but one example
will make it appear more reasonable. You cannot determine how to

pronounce the word *read* until you understand the sentence or phrase in which it appears. Thus:

I read a good book every day. [reed]
I read a good book yesterday. [red]

And I could go on to cite more evidence, but the point has been made: the writer must supply the audience with enough explanation and backing to make his or her point seem reasonable.

Fact and Opinion

The difference between a *fact* and an *opinion* is simply this: a statement that can be proven true or false is a fact; one that cannot is an opinion. Opinions can be more or less credible, more or less reasonable, but they cannot be true.

It is a fact that Springfield is the capital of Illinois. It is my opinion that Springfield is a charming town.

It is generally accepted as a fact that cigarette smoking often causes lung cancer. It is my opinion that cigarette smoking is stupid.

There is a twilight zone between fact and opinion in the case of statements that might be proven true or false through research or experimentation, but which are used to illustrate or clarify instead of to demonstrate factually or logically. We might call these "middle statements," lying somewhere in the region between fact and opinion. The following paragraph provides examples of both fact and opinion.

[1] In Baltimore, all-night walking tours have been arranged for insomniacs. [2] In Lee, Massachusetts, where a man named John Boyne had the wit to name his small motel The Morpheus Arms, would-be sleepers have to be turned away by the hundreds all summer long. [3] If we are not lying awake thinking about our own sleep, we are worrying that one of our children will wet the bed or walk in his sleep. [4] The babble about sleep ailments is all but deafening; specialists terrify us with the news that many people stop breathing the minute they go to sleep, or their hearts stop, or both. [5] Sleep clinics have become big business from coast to coast, and what it can cost you to have your insomnia studied will really wake you up.

—Ruth Mehrtens Galvin, "Probing the Mysteries of Sleep"

The first sentence is straight fact; you could go to Baltimore and check to see if walking tours have been arranged for insomniacs. The second sentence is a mixture of fact and opinion; Mr. Boyne undoubtedly did name his motel The Morpheus Arms, but it is the author's opinion that this was an intelligent move, and the inference that hundreds of customers came to the motel because of the name is a "middle statement" that might be proved a fact if one were interested in tracking down the customers to find why they chose the motel. The third sentence is a middle statement; we do not care how many people actually lie awake worrying about sleep, for it is possible that many do, and we are willing to grant the author her point. In the fourth sentence, the statement "The babble about sleep ailments is all but deafening" is strictly opinion, and specialists may indeed terrify some of us, but we have no impulse to check the factual accuracy of the statement. That sleep clinics have sprung up from coast to coast is a fact; that they have become big businesses depends on your opinion about what constitutes a big business.

The point is this: writers must not present opinions as facts, and they must support opinions with facts or reasons. We accept the middle statements because we feel that they are reasonable, that they might well be representing the world as it really is.

The Reasonable Demonstration

In the following paragraphs, the writer is presenting an argument to demonstrate how scientists determine cause and effect. The piece is not "factual," but it succeeds in making its point. Carefully read the selection, and then, in your own words, spell out the argument whereby the author explains how experimentation can establish a cause-effect relationship.

Imagine that a psychologist has devised a simple test, which a subject must either pass or fail, so that there can be no ambiguity in the results. The psychologist finds that some people pass and some fail, but he does not know what distinguishes the two groups other than their performance on the test itself. In other words, he cannot tell whether the test measures some real aptitude or attribute of the subjects or whether the results are haphazard.

It seems there is no general solution to this problem, but in a special case it might be solved. Suppose the test is administered not to a series of individuals but to a series of married couples and that a strong correlation is detected in their answers. The procedure might consist in separating the husbands from

THE QUANTUM THEORY AND REALITY   Bernard d' Espagnat, *Scientific American*, Nov. 1979, pp. 160 and 163. Copyright © 1979 by Scientific American, Inc. All rights reserved.

the wives before the test and then giving the test to each of them in isolation. When the results are analyzed, it is found again that part of the population has passed and part has failed, but in the case of each couple where the husband passed so did the wife; similarly, whenever the husband failed so did the wife.

If this correlation persists after many couples are tested, the psychologist is almost sure to conclude that the response of each subject is not determined randomly at the time of testing. On the contrary, the test must reveal some real property or attribute of the subjects. The property must already be present in the subjects before they are tested, and indeed before they are separated. Chance may have had some influence on the development of the property, since not all the couples possess it, but that influence must have been exerted at some time before the husbands and the wives were separated. It was only then, while the husbands and the wives were still united, that they could have acquired any traits that would induce them to respond consistently the same way. Thus the correlation is explained by attributing it to a common cause antecedent to the test.

One other explanation that must be excluded in deriving this conclusion is the possibility that husbands and wives could communicate with each other while they were taking the test. If some means of communication were available, there would be no need for any tested attribute to exist beforehand. Whichever spouse was given the test first could choose a response at random and send instructions to the other, thereby creating the observed correlation. In giving a psychological test it would not be hard to guard against subterfuge of this kind. In the extreme case the tests could be made so nearly simultaneous, or husbands and wives could be tested at sites so far apart, that a signal moving no faster than light could not arrive in time to be of any value.

Review

Carefully read (and enjoy) the following selection from *Word Play*, by Peter Farb, and then answer the questions regarding it.

Any transaction between two human beings—an exchange of words, silence, or a mutually intelligible gesture such as a wave of the hand—conforms to rules and conventions understood by all the members of that speech community. To have no firm rules at all is to have no language game at all. But to have the rules and to break them by lying or cheating confirms the very existence of such rules. The Marx Brothers were the masters of such an anarchic attack upon the rules of language, and most of the humor in their films is derived from their assault upon the conventions of their speech community.

Each brother inhabits a well-defined territory as a specialist in a different kind of language game. Groucho is the fast-talking sharpie, the dueler who employs the pointed wit of speech. Chico's habitat lies on the fringes of language. He is the speaker of a phony-Italian dialect who misconstrues both the meanings and the manners of the "foreign" American speech community in which he finds himself. Finally, the mute Harpo throws language back to the level of the beasts; instead of speech, he employs animal-like signaling systems, such as whistling or charades that substitute for words. Interacting with the verbal, dialectal, and animal systems of the three brothers is the imposing dowager Margaret Dumont, who steadfastly defends the narrowminded rules and conventions of the American speech community.

The methodology of the Marx Brothers is clearly displayed in their first film, *The Cocoanuts* (1929), which set the pattern for their future films. Groucho owns the incredibly mismanaged Hotel de Cocoanuts in Florida, and the opening scene shows him accosted by rebellious bellboys who clamor for their unpaid wages. Groucho listens to them in apparent incomprehension, as if they were complaining in some foreign tongue. Finally he appears to understand: "Oh, you want your *money?*" They affirm they indeed want to be paid their wages. Groucho replies, "So you want *my* money?"—a mere change of a pronoun plus a shift in the stressed word, which entirely alters the meaning. He continues: "Is that fair? Do I want *your* money? No, my friends, no. Money will never make you happy. And happy will never make you money." Groucho has switched "money" and "happy" as subjects and objects of the two sentences, thereby eliminating the dividing line between a noun and an adjective and making a logical shambles of the sentence.

Soon the bellboys' prospects are enhanced by the arrival of a telegram that makes a bizarre reservation for two floors and three ceilings. "Must be mice," concludes Groucho. Audiences usually are convulsed by this line because they intuitively sense that Groucho has performed linguistic sleight-of-hand, although they may not be certain exactly what it is. One cause for laughter is that space, such as "a room" or "floor space," and not boundaries is what is generally reserved in the English language (although it is just the opposite in the language of the Hopi Indians of Arizona, which has no word for "room" but does for "ceiling"). In English the reservation of two rooms implies the reservation also of three ceilings to enclose those two spaces. Once Groucho has committed himself to accepting the telegram on its literal terms, he must then explain what kind of guest would be interested in the three boundaries of the ceilings rather than in the two spaces for living. Unflagging logic leads him to the one inevitable conclusion—the guests must be mice.

Groucho, with practically every word, directs attention to how unreliable a vehicle language can be for communication. He fires off so many allusions and suggestions, tying them all together with such rapid shifts in usage or emphasis, that it is often difficult to determine exactly what causes the laughter. He misapplies clichés, thereby exposing them as the tricks of language they usually are. He uses strings of unlikely words to construct false analogies and false syllogisms, in that way showing how easy it is to bedevil the most innocent statements. When, later in the film, Margaret Dumont protests that Groucho is repeating what he already told her about Florida real estate, Groucho explains that he repeats himself because he left out a comma the last time. He thus doubly assaults the logic of language because the omission of a comma is irrelevant in speech and also because the omission is insufficient justification to repeat the entire sales pitch.

Enter the senders of the telegram, Chico and Harpo. Chico says, "We sent-a you telegram. We make reservash." Chico's use of "reservation" without the final syllable and his phony-Italian accent give warning of how freely he will play with the English language. His verbal play shows the improbability of words—in contrast to Groucho's puns, which cleverly enlist words to attack conventions. Chico does battle against the language of Shakespeare and Milton armed with only one weapon: unyielding literalness.

In a later scene, Chico demonstrates how formidable this weapon can be. Groucho attempts to employ him as a shill in a scheme to auction off worthless real estate:

> GROUCHO: If we're successful in disposing of these lots, I'll see that you get a nice commission.
> CHICO: How about some money?

"Commission" versus "money," both having approximately the same meaning in this context, dramatizes the historic conflict in English between the genteel and the plain vocabularies, between the Latinate upper-class speech and the Anglo-Saxon of the common people—the same sort of contrast as heard when a judge asks, "Did you apprehend the miscreant?" and the witness replies, "Yeah, I caught the chiseler!"

The brothers unite in their attacks upon cultural and linguistic decorum, as personified by the wealthy dowager Margaret Dumont. Through all of the confusion, she remains unruffled, protected by her faith that the rules and conventions will ultimately win out over anarchy. She innocently asks Chico when he sits down to perform at the piano, "What is the title of your first number?" Chico holds up one finger and replies, sticking to the point with relentless logic, "Number one!" A further example is the scene in which Groucho plays up to her with the object of financially rewarding matrimony:

> GROUCHO: Ah, if we could find a little bungalow. Eh? Of course I know we could find one, but maybe the people wouldn't get out. But if we could find a nice little empty bungalow just for me and you, where we could bill and cow—no—where we could bull and cow.

Groucho's mispronunciation of "coo" leads him, when he repeats the cliché in its second and even more distorted variation, to reduce the convention of romantic love to animal sex.

Scenes such as these, in film after film, show the Marx Brothers playing havoc with the conventions of the American speech community. They give the cliché, entrenched by generations of stubborn use, a new vitality. They impale words and ideas, then hold them aloft to show that they are stuffed with straw rather than sinew and muscle. The sound system of the English language meets its match in Chico's Italian-dialect distortions. Many of the conventional gestures and facial expressions that normally accompany speech or sometimes substitute for it become rude and barbaric. But the very recognition of distortion and lying and playing with language means that the brothers and their audience agree on one thing: Rules underlie the use of language in the American speech community. Since an anarchist can flourish only where institutions exist to be toppled, the anarchic Marx Brothers emphasize the presence of rules and conventions in language.

Nevertheless, the importance of rules has occasionally been exaggerated and the conventions too slavishly observed. In writing of Lemuel Gulliver's third voyage to the flying island of Laputa, Swift pokes fun at those people who believe an intimate connection exists between words and things. He describes a scheme to abolish words:

. . . . and this was urged as a great advantage in point of health as well as brevity. For it is plain that every word we speak is, in some degree, a diminution of our lungs by corrosion, and consequently contributes to the shortening of our lives. An expedient was therefore offered that since words are only names for things, it would be more convenient for all men to carry about them such things as were necessary to express a particular business they are to discourse on. . . . Many of the most learned and wise adhere to the new scheme of expressing themselves by things, which has only this inconvenience attending it, that if a man's business be very great, and of various kinds, he must be obliged, in proportion, to carry a greater bundle of things upon his back, unless he can afford one or two strong servants to attend him. I have often beheld two of these sages almost sinking under the weight of their packs, like peddlers among us; who, when they meet in the street, would lay down their loads, open their packs, hold conversation for an hour, and then put up their implements, help each other to resume their burdens, and take their leave.

Many people still take seriously what Swift ridiculed—but the only connection that exists between a word and the thing it stands for is whatever association the speech community has decided to make. The speech community arbitrarily arranges consonants and vowels to signify particular objects or ideas; the exact arrangement does not matter, so long as its association with its meaning is understood by all speakers and listeners.

In the speech situation of a busy luncheonette, a waitress might call out to a cook a rapid-fire series of orders:

Two burgers without . . . B.L.T. rye . . . ham and–white . . . barbeef fries . . . three green T.I. . . . boil five . . . a bowl

In this particular speech situation, abbreviated utterances are essential for the speedy transmission of messages. The waitress and the cook have arbitrarily agreed upon their own linguistic system which translates the above orders as:

"Two hamburgers without onions . . . bacon, lettuce, and tomato sandwich on rye bread . . . ham and egg sandwich on white bread . . . barbecued beef sandwich with french fried potatoes . . . three salads with Thousand Island dressing . . . an egg boiled for five minutes . . . one soup of the day"

The waitress and the cook have devised a system in which certain words arbitrarily signify certain things, such as *B.L.T.* for "bacon, lettuce, and tomato sandwich," a relationship that has little significance for someone who does not speak their particular jargon. To produce the jargon, the waitress and the cook have altered the traditional rule in the English speech community for ordering food—Quantity + Name + Describer (as in "two hamburgers without onions")—by eliminating at least one of the three terms. Sometimes Quantity is dropped, usually when the order refers to a single item (in *B.L.T. white* the Quantity *one* is understood). Sometimes the Describer noun is dropped, although the functor words like *and* or *without* may be preserved (as in *two burgers without*). This abbreviated communications system also involves the loss of segments of words (*ham* dropped from *hamburger*), the use of initials to stand for entire words (*B.L.T.* and *T.I.*), naming the preparation needed for an item rather than the item itself (*boil* instead of *egg*), and asking for the container rather than its contents (*a bowl* rather than *soup of the day*).

Free as the waitress and cook were to devise their own system, they could not be completely arbitrary. Unless they were willing to risk confusion during the noisy lunch-hour rush, they could not employ words difficult to tell apart, nor could they use a system in which *ham* was a shortened form for both "hamburger" and "ham sandwich." Conventional language systems similarly appear arbitrary, yet they offer the speaker a somewhat limited array of choices. The animal everyone in the English speech community knows by the arrangement of vowels and consonants that produces *horse* is known to be a *Pferd* in the German speech community, a *caballo* in the Spanish, a *farasi* in the Swahili, and an *uma* in the Japanese. Even though *horse* is an arbitrary English word for a certain kind of animal, speakers did not have complete free choice in creating it. They could not, for example, have called it a *bnug*, because such a combination of sounds does not exist in English, although it does in other languages. Nor would they arbitrarily have assigned the word *checken* to it, since that word is too close to the name of another animal (and in some English dialects both *chicken* and *checken* would be pronounced alike). For similar reasons, Spanish could not have designated the horse a *cdello*, which is an impossible sequence of sounds in that language, or a *cabello*, whose use had already been pre-empted to mean "hair."

The vocabulary of English encompasses several hundred thousand words—and every one of them was created out of only some three dozen sounds selected from the vast number that the human voice is capable of making. The sounds a particular language uses and the ways in which they are combined into words are significant to speakers of that language, but very likely they are not significant to speakers of other languages. For example, a speaker of English immediately detects a difference in the sounds of *law* and *raw* and would never confuse the two words. But a speaker of Japanese usually cannot detect any difference at all—not because his hearing differs from that of a speaker of English, but because his own language does not recognize a distinction between *l* and *r*. An English speaker, in turn, would fail to note distinctions that the Japanese find crucial in their language. Japanese speakers use different pronunciations for their words *to*, meaning "door," and *too*, meaning "ten"—both of which sounds are also words, of course with different meanings, that speakers of English pronounce in exactly the same way. Speakers of both Japanese and English have assented to the convention that certain arbitrary arrangements of sounds signify certain things. No special purpose, though, is served when English makes an arbitrary distinction between *l* and *r* but not between the Japanese *o* and *oo*—and no benefits accrue to the speakers of languages that make them or fail to make them. As Shakespeare observed long before the science of linguistics: "What's in a name? That which we call a rose by any other name would smell as sweet."

Another point should be apparent, yet a misconception exists to this day. No speech community gives birth to children with some special construction of the lips, tongue, nose, mouth, or larynx that enables them to speak the more "difficult" languages. An American child flawlessly utters the sounds of Japanese if he is reared in Japan or the clicks of the Bushman language if he is brought up in that speech community.

1. Write a brief summary of the piece.
2. What is the *tone* of the piece? (Serious? Playful? Pompous? Ironic? Other?) What features of the text lead you to this conclusion? (Vocabulary? Sentence structure? Intellectual level? Other?)

3. Is the content always adequate? Explain. If it is inadequate in places, explain.
4. Is all of the content relevant? Explain.
5. If the piece seems convincing to you, explain why. Is it always reasonable? Explain.
6. Characterize the sorts of readers that might find this writing interesting and informative.
7. Explain why you found the selection interesting or uninteresting.
8. Why does Farb use two extensive examples, that of the Marx Brothers and that of the waitress and the cook? What do you learn from these examples?

SUMMARY

We have seen that expository writing serves three general purposes: to explain, to demonstrate, and to explore. In explanation, the writer must be accepted as an authority on the subject, and the content must be adequate. In demonstration, the "burden of proof" is on the evidence and the logic of the piece. In exploration, the writer invites the reader to come along on a journey that probes difficult, undefined areas of thought and experience; whereas explanation and demonstration are conclusive, exploration by its very nature does not come to a final resolution.

The *writer* is presenting *content* to an *audience* of readers. One way of viewing this transaction is to say that the writer is looking outward toward the audience, and the readers are looking backward through the text at the writer. In other words, a communicative transaction is taking place.

Writing to Persuade

THE ELEMENTS OF PERSUASION

The Goal of Persuasion

As the last chapter explained, the goal of exposition is to inform, to give the reader information. The goals of persuasion are (a) to move people to some action or (b) to convince them to change an opinion.

Advertisements—the most common sort of persuasive writing—illustrate these two purposes.

The ad for Peugeot automobiles on page 236 first explains the advantages of these cars, but it concludes with a direct appeal for action: "For more information on buying, leasing, or overseas delivery see your Peugeot dealer. . . ."

The second advertisement (on page 237) makes no appeal for action, its purpose being to change or shape public opinion. "Energy for a strong America" proclaims Exxon, not "Buy Exxon gasoline." The ad is obviously intended to create a favorable image for the company.

Persuasion in Advertising

1. Regarding the Peugeot ad,
    a. What three reasons are given for preferring Peugeot to other diesels?

One of the world's leading diesel car makers now has a big following.

A lot of people are finally waking up to the advantages of diesel cars. Among them are the automakers — including Detroit — who are lining up to re-tool their gas cars into diesels.

Well, they're lining up behind Peugeot, because we don't have to re-tool anything. The Peugeot 504's diesel engine is one of very few automobile diesels in the world built from the ground up to be a diesel. And it reflects all the experience we've gained since we started production of automotive diesel engines fifty years ago.

Another reason is the way Peugeot combines comfort and handling. Both the 504 Diesel sedan and wagon have every bit of the luxurious feel and sure handling Peugeot is world famous for.

But the real reason people are turning to diesels in general and Peugeot in particular is economy. The Peugeot 504 Diesel has the best fuel economy of any compact, 34 mpg highway, 28 mpg city, 30 mpg combined.* And nationally, diesel fuel sells for about 10¢ a gallon less than unleaded regular.†

To all this, add the fact that you'll never again have to pay for a tune-up. Because the 504 Diesel has no points, choke, distributor, carburetor, condenser, coils, resistors or spark plugs.

So it's no wonder that a lot of people are getting interested in diesels. Or that a lot of them are coming to us.

Because if we were good enough to be a world leader when diesels weren't fashionable, we're certainly good enough to be a world leader when they are.

For more information on buying, leasing, or overseas delivery see your Peugeot dealer. Or call 800-243-6000 toll free (In Connecticut call 1-800-882-6500) Peugeot Motors of America, Incorporated, Lyndhurst, New Jersey 07071.

PEUGEOT
No one builds cars the way we build cars.

*1978 E.P.A. Estimates. Transmission M-4. Actual mileage depends on how and where you drive, car maintenance, optional equipment, and other variables. †Federal Energy Review, Nov. 1977 Local prices may vary.

236

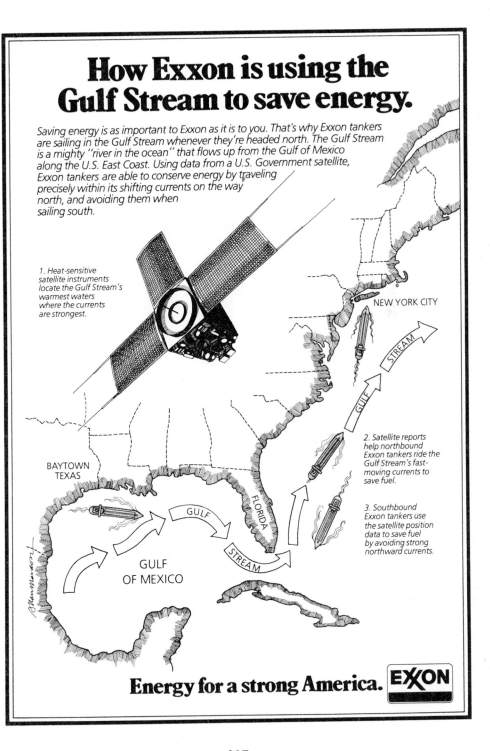

How Exxon is using the Gulf Stream to save energy.

Saving energy is as important to Exxon as it is to you. That's why Exxon tankers are sailing in the Gulf Stream whenever they're headed north. The Gulf Stream is a mighty "river in the ocean" that flows up from the Gulf of Mexico along the U.S. East Coast. Using data from a U.S. Government satellite, Exxon tankers are able to conserve energy by traveling precisely within its shifting currents on the way north, and avoiding them when sailing south.

1. Heat-sensitive satellite instruments locate the Gulf Stream's warmest waters where the currents are strongest.

NEW YORK CITY

2. Satellite reports help northbound Exxon tankers ride the Gulf Stream's fast-moving currents to save fuel.

3. Southbound Exxon tankers use the satellite position data to save fuel by avoiding strong northward currents.

BAYTOWN TEXAS

GULF

STREAM

FLORIDA

GULF OF MEXICO

Energy for a strong America. EXXON

237

   b. What reason is given for preferring diesel cars over those with gasoline engines?
   c. Do you find the slogan "No one builds cars the way we build cars" meaningful and convincing? If so, explain. If not, explain.
2. Do you find the Peugeot ad generally convincing or unconvincing? Explain.
3. In a few sentences—either written or oral—characterize the image of Exxon that is coveyed by the ad.
4. Point out some of the techniques used to create this image.
5. Do you feel that the Exxon ad is effective? Explain why or why not.
6. Why do you think Exxon spends large sums of money on advertising aimed at public opinion, not directly at sales?

In this chapter, we will not be primarily concerned with the sort of persuasion that one usually finds in ads, for there is another and more interesting kind: that in which a writer tries to gain agreement from his or her readers about important matters that go beyond self-interest. The goal in this kind of persuasion is to achieve "a meeting of minds."

Paradoxically, debate seldom involves this kind of persuasion, its goal being to advance the best argument and thus win. In the model arguments that we will discuss, both sides win, in that both sides learn, and the end result is mutual understanding, accommodation.

"You persuade a man only insofar as you can talk his language by speech, gesture, tonality, order, image, attitude, idea, identifying your ways with his," said Kenneth Burke. That is, you persuade a person only to the extent that you can understand the person sympathetically, only insofar as you can put yourself in his or her place.

Succinctly put, the goal of persuasion discussed in this chapter is to achieve cooperation, not conflict; understanding, not hostility.

The Persuader

On pages 212–21, we discussed *credibility*, the necessity that the readers be able to trust the writer and believe that he or she knows the subject. In persuasion, the problem of credibility is magnified, for you are asking the audience to make a change or even to take action; therefore, your readers must believe that you are honest or ethical and that you know what you are talking about.

If your audience knows you, knows that you are reliable and that you are an expert on your subject, then there is no problem of establishing credibility. But if your audience knows nothing about you, then your argument itself and the stance that you take toward your audience must establish your credibility.

The Substance of the Argument

The substance of your argument must not be based on a proposition that will gain immediate assent, but rather on one that is open to question. Furthermore, the proposition must be clearly definable; the vaguer the proposition, the less chance there is of persuasion. To state this point another way: *An arguable proposition has definition and uncertainty.*

The proposition "Some changes in government might be beneficial to the nation" lacks definition and therefore is not really arguable. What changes? Beneficial in what ways? This proposition is too unstable to serve as the base for the structure of an argument.

The proposition "Electing honest officials would improve government" is a truism; it does not contain the element of uncertainty. The response to this proposition is "So what else is new?" What we want is "Why do you say that?"

The proposition "Government financing of presidential election campaigns would make America a more democratic nation" is arguable. It has definition and can be questioned.

The substance itself will be the proof of your case—your attempt to convince an audience that they should agree with you. You will undoubtedly use logic, and it must not be fallacious; your analogies must hold, must not be false; your examples must be truly representative; your data must be accurate. All these matters will be discussed in this chapter.

Goals and Substance

1. Read the following paragraph; then, from your own experience, cite examples of the kinds of discord that the author outlines:

We seek universal communication, but we know that discourse will not yet free us from discord. Customarily, two contrary arguments cannot exist in the same space at the same time. Typically, one will subside. Sometimes, both will persist, and he who holds both will be rendered inactive for his inability to choose and act. Less commonly, both will persist, and he who holds both will remain active, but at the cost of cynicism or sadness engendered by his pursuit of one option in the presence of an attractive or virtuous opposite. Less commonly still, both will persist, and he who holds both may yet act, marveling at the copiousness of creation.

——Jim W. Corder, *Uses of Rhetoric*

2. Classical rhetoricians said that the arguer must demonstrate three characteristics in order to be convincing: good sense, good will, and good moral character. These characteristics might be called universals, for an audience will not be persuaded if it feels that the arguer is stupid, malicious, or immoral. Politicians use various means of establishing their apparent good sense, good will, and good moral character. Find examples of such attempts, bring them to class, and discuss whether or not they are successful, giving reasons for your judgment.

3. Some of the following propositions appear not to be arguable; they are either too ill-defined or they lack uncertainty. Which of the propositions do you think are arguable? Which are unarguable? Explain.

a. Development of the neutron bomb involves significant moral issues.

b. Revision of the general education requirements would benefit most students in this university.

c. Since early predictions about election results probably influence votes, there should be no projection of winners until after the polls have closed.

d. Every driver should know the "basics" about how a car works.

e. Since the ability to write well is not essential in every profession, the university should exempt certain majors—dental hygienists, computer technologists, and musicians—from the composition requirement.

f. Most Americans watch too much television.

g. If teachers received better training, public education in America would improve.

h. Since ignorance is bliss, it is folly to be wise.

i. The best government is the least government.

j. In order to conserve energy and reduce pollution, the federal government should impose a substantial horsepower tax on automobiles—the more the horsepower, the higher the tax.

k. Drivers should not be forced by law to wear seat belts.

l. The prices of many commodities are too high.

m. The incidence of lung cancer would decline if no one smoked cigarettes.

n. The United States should not increase its nuclear capability beyond the present level.

o. Both Russia and Iran produce caviar.

ARGUMENTATION

The Grounds for Argument

If two points of view are completely opposed, then there is no starting point for persuasion. For example, if Smith, a fundamentalist, is a confirmed believer in the literal creation story in the Bible and Jones, an evolutionist, is equally convinced of the theory of biological evolution, it is unlikely that either will be able to persuade the other, and the result of an attempt to do so could well be confrontation and "warfare," not persuasion. (For an example of such a confrontation, you might like to read about the Scopes "monkey trial.")

However, most points of view are not completely opposed to one another. For example, the firm believer in biological evolution might also believe in a guiding intelligence or in God. In this case, the fundamentalist and the evolutionist would share a belief: that there is a divine reason for creation, whether that creation came about in an instant, a week, or throughout millions of years. This shared belief could well be the grounds for argument—that is, the starting place for a piece of oral or written persuasion.

The principle, then, is that persuasion *must* begin on a point about which both writer and audience agree; if such a point cannot be found, then persuasion cannot be accomplished.

Alpha might be violently opposed to socialized medicine, and Beta might be as ardently in favor of it. Beta's argument to convince Alpha might begin something like this:

> A major national goal should be to provide good medical care for all Americans, regardless of their economic status or the region in which they live. About this, everyone can agree. Problems arise, however, when we begin to seek out means for accomplishing the goal. In the following essay, I intend to explain one way the health-care dilemma might be solved.

With this beginning, Beta has identified herself with Alpha; she does not make him an antagonist.

If Beta had begun her essay like this, she would have created an antagonist:

> Socialized medicine is the only answer to the health care dilemma in America. The free enterprise system has proven its inability to provide decent medicine for all Americans, regardless of economic status or the region in which they live.

Exercise

Choose a current issue—local or national—on which there is a sharp division of opinion and on which you hold a firm view.

Write an opening paragraph for an essay that attempts to persuade its readers. In this paragraph, outline a facet of the issue on which your opponents can agree with you.

Tone in Persuasion

In the discussion of *tone* on pages 213–17, we found that it is the way in which the writer expresses his or her *attitude* toward the subject matter and audience. A *diatribe*—heated language, ranting and raving—is seldom persuasive (in spite of examples to the contrary, such as Hitler's speeches), for real persuasion results when persuader and audience achieve that mystic union known as "a meeting of minds," which seldom results from browbeating.

It is a grave mistake to assume that the power of facts or logic or both inevitably results in persuasion. Both facts and logic indicate that smoking is harmful, but, nonetheless, millions of people puff away. The concerned and subtle remonstrances of a family member could well be more effective in persuading one to stop smoking than mountains of data and chains of logic.

Your attitude, revealed by your tone, is a crucial factor in persuasion, and attitude is not conveyed by the facts and nothing but the facts, nor by impeccable logic.

This is not to say that all successful arguments are reliable or ethical. All of us know enough about the world to realize that persuasion is often based on pretense and cheating. Again, this is not the kind of persuasion we are concerned with in this chapter—except that we want to learn to guard against it.

In argumentation, we "woo" the audience (to use Kenneth Burke's term), first by identifying with it—talking its language—and second by making certain that the substance of the argument is as reliable as possible.

Exercise

Write a one-paragraph argument for or against requiring all college students to take a course in freshman English, striving as you write to be objective and neutral in tone. Then rewrite the paragraph three times, so that it is, first, humorous; second, bitter; third, raving and ranting.

A Model for Persuasion

As we saw earlier, one does not argue about certain topics. For example, it would make no sense for me to use the techniques of persuasion to convince you that I weigh 165 pounds, for if you did not believe my statement that I do, you would simply ask me to step on a scale. It would be madness to argue about the size of the room that you are currently in, for a tape measure could immediately dispel all questions. We said that arguable topics have definition and uncertainty, and now we must add that *they cannot be resolved strictly by empirical means* (facts, figures, experiments). At the present time, we can be quite certain about the distance from the earth to the moon, for we have measured it, but we can never be absolutely certain about whether or not we should have spent billions of dollars on the moon missions. We can only be more or less convinced, depending on the arguments pro or con that are advanced.

Persuasion will always involve arguments that do contain, that might contain, or that imply words like *should, must, good, bad, better, best, moral, immoral, democratic, tyrannical,* and so on. In other words, persuasion always involves value judgments. When you persuade someone, you are making a *claim* that such and such *should* be the case.

Data, Link, Claim

In its most rudimentary form, an argument contains three elements: (1) the *claim,* (2) *data* or *evidence* in support of the claim, and (3) the *link*—sometimes called the *warrant*—between the data or evidence and the claim.[1]

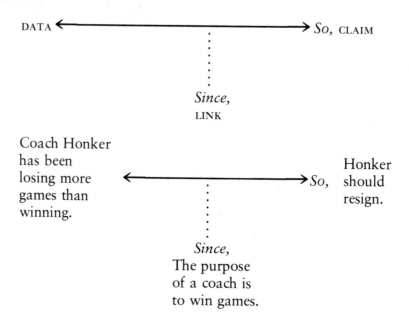

In many arguments, the link (warrant or since-element) is not expressed, but the audience must perceive it in order to understand the argument. Thus, the argument above can be expressed without the link:

Coach Honker has been losing more games than winning, so he should resign.

Exercise

1. Write (or roughly outline) a simple data/evidence-link-claim argument.

2. Find an example of such an argument, and bring it to class for discussion. (The editorial section of your newspaper is a good place to look.)

---

[1]The model for argumentation presented in this section is adapted from the work of Stephen Toulmin. See his *The Uses of Argument* (Cambridge: Cambridge University Press, 1969).

Support for the Link

The Coach Honker argument is simple enough:

Data/ *Evidence:*	This season, Honker lost more games than he's won.
Link:	The purpose of a coach is to win games.
Claim:	Honker should resign.

In the argument, however, the link is vulnerable to attack, as in the following counter-argument:

Data/ *Evidence:*	The great coaches of history—Knute Rockne, Ara Parseghian—are remembered because of the effect they had on players, not especially because their teams won. On the other hand, Woody Hayes will be remembered for his unsportsmanlike conduct.
Link:	(*Since*) We value character more than winning.
Claim:	(*So*) The main purpose of a coach should be to build character by teaching sportsmanship and fair play.

In abbreviated, diagrammatic form:

EVIDENCE
The great coaches
are remembered
because of the
effect they had
on players.

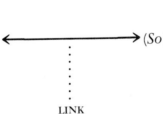

CLAIM
The main purpose
of a coach should be
(*So*) to build character by
teaching sportsman-
ship and fair play.

LINK
(*Since*) We value char-
acter more than winning.

This argument against the link in the Honker argument forces the author of the Honker argument to provide *backing* for the link. The author must provide reasons for us to believe that the purpose of the coach is to win games, which he might do in this way:

> The purpose of a coach is to win games, just as the purpose of the physician is to heal. We remember the great coaches of history as good people with high ethical standards, as people who had great in-

fluence on the character of their players, but if they had not been winning coaches, they would have failed in their primary responsibility
and thus would not have been remembered or respected enough to influence very many players. No matter how fine a man or woman a
physician is, if he or she is not a successful healer, that physician is
not worthy of our respect. Those who are not successful at their
chosen profession—be it medicine or coaching—should, as a matter
of principle, leave it.

Exercise

What sort of *backing* would be needed to strengthen the *links* in the
following arguments?

EVIDENCE	LINK (*Since*)	CLAIM (*So*)
1. Dilligan has served on the city council.	The most experienced candidate is usually the best candidate.	You should vote for Dilligan.
2. The U.S. is the only industrialized nation that retains capital punishment.	In the context of the modern world, capital punishment is cruel and unusual.	Capital punishment should be abolished in the United States.
3. More and more businesses and charitable organizations are doing telephone solicitation.	A telephone in the home is intended for maintaining social contacts.	Telephone solicitation violates the individual's right to privacy and should be outlawed.
4. Since 1913, the United States has had an income tax.	The income tax confiscates private property, which is unconstitutional.	The income tax violates the U.S. Constitution.
5. The courts are giving accused felons too much protection, as in the case where an illegally obtained confession cannot be used as evidence.	The security of its citizens against criminals is the responsibility of government.	The right to protection against crime must take precedence over an accused person's right to due process between the time of arrest and the time of arraignment.

Reservation and Qualification

Two more elements of argumentation are important: *reserva-tion* and *qualification*. The reservation applies to the link, and the qualification applies to the claim. Returning to the Honker argument, we can see that the author might want to state a reservation about his or her link:

> *Evidence:* This season, Honker has lost more games than he's won: five to one.
>
> *Link:* The purpose of a coach is to win games,
>
> RESERVATION: *unless the players are interested only in killing time and getting some exercise.*
>
> *Backing:* We might remember the great coaches of history because of their qualities as human beings, but if they had not been winners, they wouldn't have had the chance to display that fine character.
>
> *Claim:* Honker should resign.

Then, the author might want to *qualify* the claim:

> *Claim:* Honker should resign,
>
> QUALIFICATION: *unless he wins the rest of the games this season.*

The argument that has been used for an example is, of course, simplified and inadequately developed with detail, but the purpose has been to show, in a bare-bones way, how a persuasive essay can be constructed. The following diagram is extremely useful, for it sums up what we have seen about the model for persuasion:[2]

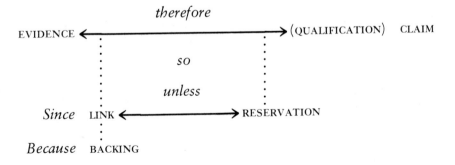

All of this may sound highly theoretical, but it is extremely practical for writers; after all, the model provides a guide to *prewriting* the persuasive essay. One must

1. have a reasonable claim;
2. assemble the evidence to support the claim;
3. make sure that there is a real link between the evidence and the claim;
4. discover any valid reservations to the link;
5. develop adequate backing for the link;
6. qualify the claim if necessary.

Review

1. Here is an actual argument (paraphrased) upon which an essay written by a college freshman was based. Explain why the argument succeeds or fails.

Evidence: California has now legalized some nude beaches. Pornography shops are legal in many cities in the state. Partially clad or nude dancers entertain in some cabarets.

Link: A decline in morals will bring about a general decline in the quality of life, affecting even the economy of the state.

Backing: It has often been said by historians that the downfall of the Roman Empire was brought about by the moral decay of its citizenry.

Claim: If the laws are not changed so that nude beaches, pornography shops, and lewd entertainment are abolished, the state of California will decay, as did the Roman Empire.

2. Use the model of persuasion as a prewriting device for an essay. After writing down a claim that you believe in and would be willing to argue, ask yourself the following questions and make notes about possible answers:

a. What is my evidence?
b. What is the defensible, logical link between my evidence and my claim?
c. What backing do I need for my link?
d. What reservations do I have concerning my link?
e. What qualifications should I make regarding my claim?

Remember that you can use discovery procedures (which were presented in Chapter 3) to develop answers to these questions.

3. Read the following argument, and discuss the questions concerning it.

Consciousness Not Necessary for Learning

Julian Jaynes

. . . A third important misconception of consciousness is that it is the basis for learning. Particularly for the long and illustrious series of Associationist psychologists through the eighteenth and nineteenth centuries, learning was a matter of ideas in consciousness being grouped by similarity, contiguity, or occasionally some other relationship. Nor did it matter whether we were speaking of a man or an animal; all learning was "profiting from experience" or ideas coming together in consciousness—as I said in the Introduction. And so contemporary common knowledge, without realizing quite why, has culturally inherited the notion that consciousness is necessary for learning.

The matter is somewhat complex. It is also unfortunately disfigured in psychology by a sometimes forbidding jargon, which is really an overgeneralization of the spinal-reflex terminology of the nineteenth century. But, for our purposes, we may consider the laboratory study of learning to have been of three central kinds, the learning of signals, skills, and solutions. Let us take up each in turn, asking the question, is consciousness necessary?

Signal learning (or classical or Pavlovian conditioning) is the simplest example. If a light signal immediately followed by a puff of air through a rubber tube is directed at a person's eye about ten times, the eyelid, which previously blinked only to the puff of air, will begin to blink to the light signal alone, and this becomes more and more frequent as trials proceed.[9] Subjects who have undergone this well-known procedure of signal learning report that it has no conscious component whatever. Indeed, consciousness, in this example the intrusion of voluntary eye blinks to try to assist the signal learning, blocks it from occurring.

In more everyday situations, the same simple associative learning can be shown to go on without any consciousness that it has occurred. If a distinct kind of music is played while you are eating a particularly delicious lunch, the next time you hear the music you will like its sounds slightly more and even have a little more saliva in your mouth. The music has become a signal for pleasure which mixes with your judgment. And the same is true for paintings.[10] Subjects who have gone through this kind of test in the laboratory, when asked why they liked the music or paintings better after lunch, could not

[9] G. A. Kimble, "Conditioning as a function of the time between conditioned and unconditioned stimuli," *Journal of Experimental Psychology,* 1947, 37:1–15.
[10] These studies are those of Gregory Razran and are discussed on page 232 of his *Mind in Evolution* (Boston: Houghton Mifflin, 1971). They are discussed critically in relation to the whole problem of unintentional learning by T. A. Ryan, *Intentional Behavior* (New York: Ronald Press, 1970), pp. 235–236.

say. They were not conscious they had learned anything. But the really interesting thing here is that if you know about the phenomenon beforehand and are conscious of the contingency between food and the music or painting, the learning does not occur. Again, consciousness actually *reduces* our learning abilities of this type, let alone not being necessary for them.

As we saw earlier in the performance of skills, so in the learning of skills, consciousness is indeed like a helpless spectator, having little to do. A simple experiment will demonstrate this fact. Take a coin in each hand and toss them both, crossing them in the air in such a way that each coin is caught by the opposite hand. This you can learn in a dozen trials. As you do, ask, are you conscious of everything you do? Is consciousness necessary at all? I think you will find that learning is much better described as being 'organic' rather than conscious. Consciousness takes you into the task, giving you the goal to be reached. But from then on, apart perhaps from fleeting neurotic concerns about your abilities at such tasks, it is as if the learning is done for you. Yet the nineteenth century, taking consciousness to be the whole architect of behavior, would have tried to explain such a task as consciously recognizing the good and bad motions, and by free choice repeating the former and dropping out the latter!

The learning of complex skills is no different in this respect. Typewriting has been extensively studied, it generally being agreed in the words of one experimenter "that all adaptations and short cuts in methods were unconsciously made, that is, fallen into by the learners quite unintentionally. The learners suddenly noticed that they were doing certain parts of the work in a new and better way."[11]

In the coin-tossing experiment, you may have even discovered that consciousness if present impeded your learning. This is a very common finding in the learning of skills, just as we saw it was in their performance. Let the learning go on without your being too conscious of it, and it is all done more smoothly and efficiently. Sometimes too much so, for, in complex skills like typing, one may learn to consistently type 'hte' for 'the'. The remedy is to reverse the process by consciously practicing the mistake 'hte', whereupon contrary to the usual idea of 'practice makes perfect', the mistake drops away—a phenomenon called negative practice.

In the common motor skills studied in the laboratory as well, such as complex pursuit-rotor systems or mirror-tracing, the subjects who are asked to be very conscious of their movements do worse.[12] And athletic trainers whom I have interviewed are unwittingly following such laboratory-proven principles when they urge their trainees not to think so much about what they are doing. The Zen exercise of learning archery is extremely explicit on this, advising the archer not to think of himself as drawing the bow and releasing the arrow, but releasing himself from the consciousness of what he is doing by letting the bow stretch itself and the arrow release itself from the fingers at the proper time.

---

[11] W. F. Book, *The Psychology of Skill* (New York: Gregg, 1925).

[12] H. L. Waskom, "An experimental analysis of incentive and forced application and their effect upon learning," *Journal of Psychology*, 1936, 2:393–408.

Solution learning (or instrumental learning or operant conditioning) is a more complex case. Usually when one is acquiring some solution to a problem or some path to a goal, consciousness plays a very considerable role in setting up the problem in a certain way. But consciousness is not necessary. Instances can be shown in which a person has no consciousness whatever of either the goal he is seeking or the solution he is finding to achieve that goal.

Another simple experiment can demonstrate this. Ask someone to sit opposite you and to say words, as many words as he can think of, pausing two or three seconds after each of them for you to write them down. If after every plural noun (or adjective, or abstract word, or whatever you choose) you say "good" or "right" as you write it down, or simply "mmm-hmm" or smile, or repeat the plural word pleasantly, the frequency of plural nouns (or whatever) will increase significantly as he goes on saying words. The important thing here is that the subject is not aware that he is learning anything at all.[13] He is not conscious that he is trying to find a way to make you increase your encouraging remarks, or even of his solution to that problem. Every day, in all our conversations, we are constantly training and being trained by each other in this manner, and yet we are never conscious of it.

Such unconscious learning is not confined to verbal behavior. Members of a psychology class were asked to compliment any girl at the college wearing red. Within a week the cafeteria was a blaze of red (and friendliness), and none of the girls was aware of being influenced. Another class, a week after being told about unconscious learning and training, tried it on the professor. Every time he moved toward the right side of the lecture hall, they paid rapt attention and roared at his jokes. It is reported that they were almost able to train him right out the door, he remaining unaware of anything unusual.[14]

The critical problem with most of these studies is that if the subject decided beforehand to look for such contingencies, he would of course be conscious of what he was learning to do. One way to get around this is to use a behavioral response which is imperceptible to the subject. And this has been done, using a very small muscle in the thumb whose movements are imperceptible to us and can only be detected by an electrical recording apparatus. The subjects were told that the experiments were concerned with the effect of intermittent unpleasant noise combined with music upon muscle tension. Four electrodes were placed on their bodies, the only real one being the one over the small thumb muscle, the other three being dummy electrodes. The apparatus was so arranged that whenever the imperceptible thumb-muscle twitch was electrically detected, the unpleasant noise was stopped for 15 seconds if

[13] J. Greenspoon, "The reinforcing effect of two spoken sounds on the frequency of two responses," *American Journal of Psychology*, 1955, 68:409–416. But there is considerable controversy here, particularly in the order and wording of postexperimental questions. There may even be a kind of tacit contract between subject and experimenter. See Robert Rosenthal, *Experimenter Effects in Behavioral Research* (New York: Appleton-Century-Crofts, 1966). In this controversy, I presently agree with Postman that the learning occurs *before* the subject becomes conscious of the reinforcement contingency, and indeed that consciousness would not occur unless this had been so. L. Postman and L. Sassenrath, "The automatic action of verbal rewards and punishment," *Journal of General Psychology*, 1961, 65:109–136.

[14] W. Lambert Gardiner, *Psychology: A Story of a Search* (Belmont, California: Brooks/Cole, 1970), p. 76.

it was already sounding, or delayed for 15 seconds if was not turned on at the time of the twitch. In all subjects, the imperceptible thumb twitch that turned off the distressing noise increased in rate without the subjects' being the slightest bit conscious that they were learning to turn off the unpleasant noise.[15]

Thus, consciousness is not a necessary part of the learning process, and this is true whether it be the learning of signals, skills, or solutions. There is, of course, much more to say on this fascinating subject, for the whole thrust of contemporary research in behavior modification is along these lines. But, for the present, we have simply established that the older doctrine that conscious experience is the substrate of all learning is clearly and absolutely false. At this point, we can at least conclude that it is possible—possible I say—to conceive of human beings who are not conscious and yet can learn and solve problems.

[15] R. F. Hefferline, B. Keenan, R. A. Harford, "Escape and avoidance conditioning in human subjects without their observation of the response," *Science*, 1959, 130:1338–1339. Another study which shows unconscious solution learning very clearly is that of J. D. Keehn: "Experimental studies of the unconscious: operant conditioning of unconscious eye blinking," *Behavior Research and Therapy*, 1967, 5:95–102.

   a. Either in your own words or in the author's, state the *claim* of the argument.
   b. The *link* is not stated directly in the argument. In your own words, state the link.
   c. In which paragraphs does one find *evidence* for the claim?
   d. Are there *reservations* to the link? If so, what are they?
   e. Does the link have *backing*? If so, what?
   f. Does the claim have qualifications? If so, what?
   g. What function do the first two paragraphs serve?

LOGIC

At the very least, an argument for or against a position must be consistent. Consistency is a *negative* virtue because no one would praise an argument for possessing it, whereas any reasonable audience would condemn inconsistency. For example, if I argue that all people are created equal, and therefore each is entitled to human dignity, no one will exclaim, "What a consistent argument!" However, if I argue that all people are created equal, but nonetheless some should be deprived of dignity, my audience will be puzzled by my inconsistency.

Formal Truth and Material Truth

Another way of stating that an argument must be consistent is to say that it must be *formally* true. Formal truth concerns the relationship *if-then necessarily*. *If* you believe such and such, *then necessarily* you must conclude this and that. Or *if* such is the case, *then necessarily* this must follow.

> *If* the moon is made of green cheese, *then necessarily* modern studies of it are misguided.

Material truth concerns the content of statements. Since we have overwhelming evidence that the moon is not made of green cheese, we can say that the argument above is materially untrue even though it is formally true.

The following brief argument is formally true in that the statements follow from one another:

> The horoscope is infallible, based as it is on the exact science of astrology. Your horoscope for today reads thus: "You are in the mood to make radical changes, but it is better to count your blessings instead." I know that you are planning to transfer to another college immediately, but since your horoscope advises against radical changes, you should count your present blessings and wait until a more favorable time to make changes.

If the person to whom the argument is addressed believes that astrology is an exact science and hence that the horoscope is infallible, the argument will probably be convincing. However, another person—an astronomer, for instance—might question the material truth of the statement that astrology is an exact science.

Logic is the branch of philosophy that studies the consistency of arguments. We will not, however, go into the details of that subject, for one does not need to be a logician in order to construct formally true arguments, nor does one need a course in logic to recognize inconsistency. But it will be worthwhile to look briefly at one form of logical argumentation, the syllogism, as in the following:

> If a professor is immoral, he or she should be discharged.
> Professor X is immoral.
> Therefore, Professor X should be discharged.

No one would question the formal truth of this argument, but in order for it to be persuasive, you as the arguer must accomplish a number of things. First, you must define satisfactorily what you mean by "immorality" and convince the audience to adhere to this definition. Next you must argue that morality is necessary for a professor. Then you must establish to the audience's satisfaction that Professor X is indeed immoral. If you do all this, the audience is then likely to conclude that Professor X should be fired. The formal truth of the argument is self-evident. On the basis of how you fill out that formal structure, the audience may conclude that the argument is also materially true.

Deduction and Induction

Traditionally, arguments are classified as deductive or inductive. A deductive argument moves from a general statement to a conclusion, and an inductive argument first states particulars and then reaches a conclusion on the basis of them. The deductive argument is best illustrated by the syllogism:

> All human beings are mortal. [major premise]
> Jones is a human being. [minor premise]
> Therefore, Jones is mortal. [conclusion]

If the premises are consistent, then the conclusion is inevitable.
An example of induction is the following:

> Apple A is green, feels hard, tastes sour.
> Apple B is green, feels hard, tastes sour.
> Apple C is green, feels hard, tastes sour.
> Apple D is green, and it feels hard; therefore, it will taste sour (that is, we conclude that hard, green apples are sour).

Now then, if you will take a close look at these two simple examples, you will come to the conclusion, I think, that even though they are radically different in organization, they are very similar in methodology. The experimenter in the second example was probably trying to establish a premise; otherwise, he or she would not have tested the apples.

It has often been said that the scientific method is inductive, but it is inconceivable that scientists would work with a set of data unless they felt that the data would establish some general principle (a hypothesis or theory) that they had already formulated on the basis of past knowledge or intuition. In other words, before scientists begin their work, they have a premise that they hope to prove or disprove. Scientists do not examine randomly selected sets of data in the hopes that they will accidentally come up with a universal principle.

Whether one is working deductively or inductively, there must be a thesis or premise.

Deductive and Inductive Organization

Even though deduction and induction are basically similar kinds of thought processes, they represent radically different forms of organization. Here is the argument regarding Professor X that was presented on page 253:

> If a professor is immoral, he or she should be discharged.
> Professor X is immoral.
> Therefore, Professor X should be discharged.

An essay on this topic that moved deductively would look something like this in outline:

Thesis: If a professor is immoral, he or she should be discharged.

   I. Definition of professorial morality
      A. Professional honesty
      B. Fairness
      C. Sobriety
      D. Chastity

  II. Relationship of morality to professsorial duties
      A. Need for integrity of scholarship
      B. Need for fairness
      C. Necessity of setting a good personal example for students

 III. Professor X's conduct
      A. Professional dishonesty
      B. Unfairness
      C. Drunkenness
      D. Promiscuity

 IV. Conclusion

That same topic handled inductively might look something like this:

   I.   Ideal professorial conduct [established inductively, on the basis of examples]
        A. Professor Y's conduct
        B. Professor Z's conduct
        C. Professor W's conduct
  II.   Professor X's conduct
 III.   Relationship of morality to professorial duties
  IV.   Conclusion [including statement of thesis and recommendations]

The concepts "induction" and "deduction" have a great deal of meaning in regard to organization.

Induction and Deduction

Write a letter to the president of your college, persuading him or her to support some action or policy that will improve the quality of student life. Organize the argument *deductively*.

In a second draft, use *inductive* organization.

Fallacies

Fallacies are two-edged swords: they are traps into which an unwary arguer can fall, and they are traps into which an immoral persuader can lure an audience. The fallacies that we will be dealing with here are usually called *informal*. Most of them will be familiar to you, for you have encountered them again and again in advertising (which is not to say that all advertisers are unreliable).

Most of the fallacies that will be discussed fall into the general category of *non sequitur*, a Latin term meaning "it does not follow." A non sequitur is an argument in which the conclusion does not follow from the premises.

Ad Hominem (Against the Man)

Suppose that the thesis of your argument is that the President should not have vetoed a certain bill; as your argument progresses, you shift from an attack on that particular action by the President to an attack on the President as a person. You have committed the *ad hominem* fallacy.

The ad hominem trick is particularly shoddy, for it confuses issues with those who advocate them, and, needless to say, perfectly valid issues can be supported by reprehensible people. Even Hitler supported some causes that most of us would agree with, such as full employment.

Here is an example of an ad hominem argument: "The city council should not have voted to spend a million and a half dollars on a new library when there are other, more urgent needs and a shortage of funds. One wonders how much in kickbacks the members of the council will get from the contractors who build the library."

Bandwagon

This common fallacy goes something like this: "Everyone else is doing it, so you should too." In southern California, for instance, the Ford Motor Company advertises over and over again that more people in the area drive Fords than any other make of car. The implication is that you should join the crowd and purchase a Ford, but, of course, that argument ignores (or evades) the issues of price, quality, gas mileage, service—the very issues that a car buyer should take into consideration.

In politics, the bandwagon effect is of great concern. Voting places in the East close three hours earlier than those in the West; thus, the TV networks can broadcast voting trends before many western voters have gone to the polls. Some think that these broadcasts may create a bandwagon effect, influencing western voters to follow the patterns set by the easterners.

Begging the Question

This is sometimes called arguing in a circle, and it involves using one's premises as conclusions. A simple example: I argue that students at Golden West College are exceptionally intelligent, and you ask me why I think so. I reply, "Because only intelligent students go to Golden West College." I have begged the question by restating my premise in different terms.

Composition

In this fallacy, one assumes that what is valid for each member of a class will be valid for the class as a whole. For instance: "The gross national product of Thailand must be greater than that of Tibet, because individual incomes are higher in Thailand than in Tibet." This argument overlooks the possibility that the population of Tibet is greater than that of Thailand, so Tibet's smaller individual incomes may contribute to a greater gross national product than Thailand's.

Division

This is the opposite of composition. It is the assumption that what holds for the group will also hold for each member. For example, more beer is consumed in West Germany, per capita, than in any other nation. Therefore, it is accurate to say that West Germans drink more beer than, say, Japanese, but it would be inaccurate to conclude on this basis that German X drinks more beer than Japanese Y, for X might be a teetotaler, whereas Y might guzzle the stuff continually. An amusing argument that involves the fallacy of division is this one: "Blacksmiths are vanishing. Uncle George is a blacksmith. Therefore, Uncle George is vanishing."

Equivocation

In equivocation, the sense of a key word is shifted, thus invalidating the argument. For instance: "The dictionary defines *republican* as 'one who favors a republic,' and *republic* is defined as 'a state in which the supreme power rests in the body of citizens entitled to vote.' Therefore, if you believe that the voters should control the government, vote Republican in the next election." The fallacy here lies in the shift of *republican* from its generic use, specifying one who favors a certain form of government, to its specific use as the designation for a political party.

Post Hoc, Ergo Propter Hoc

The Latin says: after this, therefore because of this. The *post hoc* fallacy consists in attributing a cause-and-effect relationship to what is merely a time relationship. For example: "After Murgatroyd was elected, property taxes decreased; therefore, Murgatroyd must have lowered property taxes." (Murgatroyd may well have done so, but the mere time relationship does not establish that fact.)

Reification

In this fallacy, an abstraction is treated as if it had concrete reality. Here is the Puritan Thomas Hooker (1586–1647) talking about sin: "We must see it clearly in its own Nature, its Native color and proper hue . . . ." We cannot, of course, "see" sin as a concrete object. In discussing such abstractions as democracy, many arguers reify, talking as if the concept itself were somehow physically embodied by the United States, or as if Russia embodied the concept "communism."

Testimonial

Sports figures endorse breakfast cereals, movie stars speak on behalf of presidential candidates, Arthur Godfrey and Art Linkletter give pitches for just about everything. These are testimonials—famous people giving their endorsements. But there is no reason why a sports figure should know more about the nutritive qualities of breakfast cereals than you or I do. Nor does the fact that Sammy Davis, Jr., is a great entertainer give him any particular authority to speak knowledgeably about politics. The testimonial is a mendacious use of well-known people to push products and ideas.

There are other kinds of fallacies, but the point has undoubtedly been made: bad thinking can lead one into bad arguments, and bad thinking can also set one up as a pigeon for immoral arguers. Who, after all, wants to be either a huckster or a pigeon?

Exercise

Read and enjoy the following essay. After you have done so, make an alphabetical list of the fallacies that are explained in it, define each fallacy, and invent an example of each.

Love Is a Fallacy

Max Shulman

Charles Lamb, as merry and enterprising a fellow as you will meet in a month of Sundays, unfettered the informal essay with his memorable *Old China* and *Dream Children*. There follows an informal essay that ventures even beyond Lamb's frontier. Indeed, "informal" may not be quite the right word to describe this essay; "limp" or "flaccid" or possibly "spongy" are perhaps more appropriate.

Vague though its category, it is without doubt an essay. It develops an argument; it cites instances; it reaches a conclusion. Could Carlyle do more? Could Ruskin?

LOVE IS A FALLACY Max Shulman, *The Many Loves of Dobie Gillis* (Garden City, N.Y.: Doubleday, 1953). Copyright © 1951 by Hearst Magazines, Inc., © renewed 1979 by Max Shulman. Reprinted by permission of Harold Matson Company, Inc.

Read, then, the following essay which undertakes to demonstrate that logic, far from being a dry, pedantic discipline, is a living, breathing thing, full of beauty, passion, and trauma.

—Author's Note

Cool was I and logical. Keen, calculating, perspicacious, acute and astute—I was all of these. My brain was as powerful as a dynamo, as precise as a chemist's scales, as penetrating as a scalpel. And—think of it!—I was only eighteen.

It is not often that one so young has such a giant intellect. Take, for example, Petey Burch, my roommate at the University of Minnesota. Same age, same background, but dumb as an ox. A nice enough fellow, you understand, but nothing upstairs. Emotional type. Unstable, Impressionable. Worst of all, a faddist. Fads, I submit, are the very negation of reason. To be swept up in every new craze that comes along, to surrender yourself to idiocy just because everybody else is doing it—this, to me, is the acme of mindlessness. Not, however, to Petey.

One afternoon I found Petey lying on his bed with an expression of such distress on his face that I immediately diagnosed appendicitis. "Don't move," I said. "Don't take a laxative. I'll get a doctor."

"Raccoon," he mumbled thickly.

"Raccoon?" I said, pausing in my flight.

"I want a raccoon coat," he wailed.

I perceived that this trouble was not physical, but mental. "Why do you want a raccoon coat?"

"I should have known it," he cried, pounding his temples. "I should have known they'd come back when the Charleston came back. Like a fool I spent all my money for textbooks, and now I can't get a raccoon coat."

"Can you mean," I said incredulously, "that people are actually wearing raccoon coats again?"

"All the Big Men on Campus are wearing them. Where've you been?"

"In the library," I said, naming a place not frequented by Big Men on Campus.

He leaped from the bed and paced the room. "I've got to have a raccoon coat," he said passionately. "I've got to!"

"Petey, why? Look at it rationally. Raccoon coats are unsanitary. They shed. They smell bad. They weigh too much. They're unsightly. They—"

"You don't understand." he interrupted impatiently. "It's the thing to do. Don't you want to be in the swim?"

"No," I said truthfully.

"Well, I do," he declared. "I'd give anything for a raccoon coat. Anything!"

My brain, that precision instrument, slipped into high gear. "Anything?" I asked, looking at him narrowly.

"Anything," he affirmed in ringing tones.

I stroked my chin thoughtfully. It so happened that I knew where to get my hands on a raccoon coat. My father had had one in his undergraduate days; it lay now in a trunk in the attic back home. It also happened that Petey had something I wanted. He didn't *have* it exactly, but at least he had first rights on it. I refer to this girl, Polly Espy.

I had long coveted Polly Espy. Let me emphasize that my desire for this young woman was not emotional in nature. She was, to be sure, a girl who excited the emotions, but I was not one to let my heart rule my head. I wanted Polly for a shrewdly calculated, entirely cerebral reason.

I was a freshman in law school. In a few years I would be out in practice. I was well aware of the importance of the right kind of wife in furthering a lawyer's career. The successful lawyers I had observed were, almost without exception, married to beautiful, gracious, intelligent women. With one omission, Polly fitted these specifications perfectly.

Beautiful she was. She was not yet of pin-up proportions, but I felt sure that time would supply the lack. She already had the makings.

Gracious she was. By gracious I mean full of graces. She had an erectness of carriage, an ease of bearing, a poise that clearly indicated the best of breeding. At table her manners were exquisite. I had seen her at the Kozy Kampus Korner eating the specialty of the house—a sandwich that contained scraps of pot roast, gravy, chopped nuts, and a dipper of sauerkraut—without even getting her fingers moist.

Intelligent she was not. In fact, she veered in the opposite direction. But I believed that under my guidance she would smarten up. At any rate, it was worth a try. It is, after all, easier to make a beautiful dumb girl smart than to make an ugly smart girl beautiful.

"Petey," I said, "are you in love with Polly Espy?"

"I think she's a keen kid," he replied, "but I don't know if you'd call it love. Why?"

"Do you," I asked, "have any kind of formal arrangement with her? I mean are you going steady or anything like that?"

"No. We see each other quite a bit, but we both have other dates. Why?"

"Is there," I asked, "any other man for whom she has a particular fondness?"

"Not that I know of. Why?"

I nodded with satisfaction. "In other words, if you were out of the picture, the field would be open. Is that right?"

"I guess so. What are you getting at?"

"Nothing, nothing," I said innocently, and took my suitcase out of the closet.

"Where are you going?" asked Petey.

"Home for the weekend." I threw a few things into the bag.

"Listen," he said, clutching my arm eagerly, "while you're home, you couldn't get some money from your old man, could you, and lend it to me so I can buy a raccoon coat?"

"I may do better than that," I said with a mysterious wink and closed my bag and left.

"Look," I said to Petey when I got back Monday morning. I threw open the suitcase and revealed the huge, hairy, gamy object that my father had worn in his Stutz Bearcat in 1925.

"Holy Toledo!" said Petey reverently. He plunged his hands into the raccoon coat and then his face. "Holy Toledo!" he repeated fifteen or twenty times.

"Would you like it?" I asked.

"Oh yes!" he cried, clutching the greasy pelt to him. Then a canny look came into his eyes. "What do you want for it?"

"Your girl," I said, mincing no words.

"Polly?" he said in a horrified whisper. "You want Polly?"

"That's right."

He flung the coat from him. "Never," he said stoutly.

I shrugged. "Okay. If you don't want to be in the swim, I guess it's your business."

I sat down in a chair and pretended to read a book, but out of the corner of my eye I kept watching Petey. He was a torn man. First he looked at the coat with the expression of a waif at a bakery window. Then he turned away and set his jaw resolutely. Then he looked back at the coat, with even more longing in his face. Then he turned away, but with not so much resolution this time. Back and forth his head swiveled, desire waxing, resolution waning. Finally he didn't turn away at all; he just stood and stared with mad lust at the coat.

"It isn't as though I was in love with Polly," he said thickly. "Or going steady or anything like that."

"That's right," I murmured.

"What's Polly to me, or me to Polly?"

"Not a thing," said I.

"It's just been a casual kick—just a few laughs, that's all."

"Try on the coat," said I.

He complied. The coat bunched high over his ears and dropped all the way down to his shoe tops. He looked like a mound of dead raccoons. "Fits fine," he said happily.

I rose from my chair. "Is it a deal?" I asked, extending my hand.

He swallowed. "It's a deal," he said, and shook my hand.

I had my first date with Polly the following evening. This was in the nature of a survey; I wanted to find out just how much work I had to do to get her mind up to the standard I required. I took her first to dinner. "Gee, that was a delish dinner," she said as we left the restaurant. Then I took her to a movie. "Gee, that was a marvy movie," she said as we left the theater. And then I took her home. "Gee, I had a sensaysh time," she said as she bade me good night.

I went back to my room with a heavy heart. I had gravely underestimated the size of my task. This girl's lack of information was terrifying. Nor would it be enough merely to supply her with information. First she had to be taught to *think*. This loomed as a project of no small dimension, and at first I was tempted to give her back to Petey. But then I got to thinking about her abundant physical charms and about the way she entered a room and the way she handled a knife and fork, and I decided to make an effort.

I went about it, as in all things, systematically. I gave her a course in logic. It happened that I, as a law student, was taking a course in logic myself, so I had all the facts at my finger tips. "Polly," I said to her when I picked her up on our next date, "tonight we are going over to the Knoll and talk."

"Oo, terrif," she replied. One thing I will say for this girl: you would go far to find another so agreeable.

We went to the Knoll, the campus trysting place, and we sat down under an old oak, and she looked at me expectantly. "What are we going to talk about?" she asked.

"Logic."

She thought this over for a minute and decided she liked it. "Magnif," she said.

"Logic," I said, clearing my throat, "is the science of thinking. Before we can think correctly, we must first learn to recognize the common fallacies of logic. These we will take up tonight."

"Wow-dow!" she cried, clapping her hands delightedly.

I winced, but went bravely on. "First let us examine the fallacy called Dicto Simpliciter."

"By all means," she urged, batting her lashes eagerly.

"Dicto Simpliciter means an argument based on an unqualified generalization. For example: Exercise is good. Therefore everybody should exercise."

"I agree," said Polly earnestly. "I mean exercise is wonderful. I mean it builds the body and everything."

"Polly," I said gently, "the argument is a fallacy. *Exercise is good* is an unqualified generalization. For instance, if you have heart disease, exercise is bad, not good. Many people are ordered by their doctors *not* to exercise. You must *qualify* the generalization. You must say exercise is *usually* good, or exercise is good for *most people*. Otherwise you have committed a Dicto Simpliciter. Do you see?"

"No," she confessed. "But this is marvy. Do more! Do more!"

"It will be better if you stop tugging at my sleeve," I told her, and when she desisted, I continued. "Next we take up a fallacy called Hasty Generalization. Listen carefully: You can't speak French. I can't speak French. Petey Burch can't speak French. I must therefore conclude that nobody at the University of Minnesota can speak French."

"Really?" said Polly, amazed. "Nobody?"

I hid my exasperation. "Polly, it's a fallacy. The generalization is reached too hastily. There are too few instances to support such a conclusion."

"Know any more fallacies?" she asked breathlessly. "This is more fun than dancing even."

I fought off a wave of despair. I was getting nowhere with this girl, absolutely nowhere. Still, I am nothing if not persistent. I continued, "Next comes Post Hoc. Listen to this: Let's not take Bill on our picnic. Every time we take him out with us, it rains."

"I know somebody just like that," she exclaimed. "A girl back home—Eula Becker, her name is. It never fails. Every single time we take her on a picnic—"

"Polly," I said sharply, "it's a fallacy. Eula Becker doesn't *cause* the rain. She has no connection with the rain. You are guilty of Post Hoc if you blame Eula Becker."

"I'll never do it again," she promised contritely. "Are you mad at me?"

I sighed deeply. "No, Polly, I'm not mad."

"Then tell me some more fallacies."

"All right. Let's try Contradictory Premises."

"Yes, let's," she chirped, blinking her eyes happily.

I frowned, but plunged ahead. "Here's an example of Contradictory Premises: If God can do anything, can He make a stone so heavy that He won't be able to lift it?"

"Of course," she replied promptly.

"But if He can do anything, He can lift the stone," I pointed out.

"Yeah," she said thoughtfully. "Well, then I guess He can't make the stone."

"But He can do anything," I reminded her.

She scratched her pretty, empty head. "I'm all confused," she admitted.

"Of course you are. Because when the premises of an argument contradict each other, there can be no argument. If there is an irresistible force, there can be no immovable object. If there is an immovable object, there can be no irresistible force. Get it?"

"Tell me more of this keen stuff," she said eagerly.

I consulted my watch. "I think we'd better call it a night. I'll take you home now, and you go over all the things you've learned. We'll have another session tomorrow night."

I deposited her at the girls' dormitory, where she assured me that she had had a perfectly terrif evening, and I went glumly home to my room. Petey lay snoring in his bed, the raccoon coat huddled like a great hairy beast at his feet. For a moment I considered waking him and telling him that he could have his girl back. It seemed clear that my project was doomed to failure. The girl simply had a logic-proof head.

But then I reconsidered. I had wasted one evening; I might as well waste another. Who knew? Maybe somewhere in the extinct crater of her mind, a few embers still smoldered. Maybe somehow I could fan them into flame. Admittedly, it was not a prospect fraught with hope, but I decided to give it one more try.

Seated under the oak the next evening I said, "Our first fallacy tonight is Ad Misericordiam."

She quivered with delight.

"Listen closely," I said. "A man applies for a job. When the boss asks him what his qualifications are, he replies that he has a wife and six children at home, the wife is a helpless cripple, the children have nothing to eat, no clothes to wear, no shoes on their feet, there are no beds in the house, no coal in the cellar, and winter is coming."

A tear rolled down each of Polly's pink cheeks. "Oh, this is awful, awful," she sobbed.

"Yes, it's awful," I agreed, "but it's no argument. The man never answered the boss's question about his qualifications. Instead he appealed to the boss's sympathy. He committed the fallacy of Ad Misericordiam. Do you understand?"

"Have you got a handkerchief?" she blubbered.

I handed her a handkerchief and tried to keep from screaming while she wiped her eyes. "Next," I said in a carefully controlled tone, "we will discuss False Analogy. Here is an example: Students should be allowed to look at their textbooks during examinations. After all, surgeons have X-rays to guide them during an operation, lawyers have briefs to guide them during a trial, carpenters have blueprints to guide them when they are building a house. Why, then, shouldn't students be allowed to look at their textbooks during an examination?"

"There now," she said enthusiastically, "is the most marvy idea I've heard in years."

"Polly," I said testily, "the argument is all wrong. Doctors, lawyers, and carpenters aren't taking a test to see how much they have learned, but students are. The situations are altogether different, and you can't make an analogy between them."

"I still think it's a good idea," said Polly.

"Nuts," I muttered. Doggedly I pressed on. "Next we'll try Hypothesis Contrary to Fact."

"Sounds yummy," was Polly's reaction.

"Listen: If Madame Curie had not happened to leave a photographic plate in a drawer with a chunk of pitchblende, the world today would not know about radium."

"True, true," said Polly, nodding her head. "Did you see the movie? Oh, it just knocked me out. That Walter Pidgeon is so dreamy. I mean he fractures me."

"If you can forget Mr. Pidgeon for a moment," I said coldly, "I would like to point out that the statement is a fallacy. Maybe Madame Curie would have discovered radium at some later date. Maybe somebody else would have discovered it. Maybe any number of things would have happened. You can't start with a hypothesis that is not true and then draw any supportable conclusions from it."

"They ought to put Walter Pidgeon in more pictures," said Polly. "I hardly ever see him any more."

One more chance, I decided. But just one more. There is a limit to what flesh and blood can bear. "The next fallacy is called Poisoning the Well."

"How cute," she gurgled.

"Two men are having a debate. The first one gets up and says, 'My opponent is a notorious liar. You can't believe a word that he is going to say.' . . . Now, Polly, think. Think hard. What's wrong?"

I watched her closely as she knit her creamy brow in concentration. Suddenly a glimmer of intelligence—the first I had seen—came into her eyes. "It's not fair," she said with indignation. "It's not a bit fair. What chance has the second man got if the first man calls him a liar before he even begins talking?"

"Right!" I cried exultantly. "One hundred per cent right. It's not fair. The first man has *poisoned the well* before anybody could drink from it. He has hamstrung his opponent before he could even start. . . . Polly, I'm proud of you."

"Pshaw," she murmured, blushing with pleasure.

"You see, my dear, these things aren't so hard. All you have to do is concentrate. Think—examine—evaluate. Come now, let's review everything we have learned."

"Fire away," she said with an airy wave of her hand.

Heartened by the knowledge that Polly was not altogether a cretin, I began a long, patient review of all I had told her. Over and over and over again I cited instances, pointed out flaws, kept hammering away without letup. It was like digging a tunnel. At first everything was work, sweat, and darkness. I had no idea when I would reach the light, or even *if* I would. But I persisted. I pounded and clawed and scraped, and finally I was rewarded. I saw a chink of light. And then the chink got bigger and the sun came pouring in and all was bright.

Five grueling nights this took, but it was worth it. I had made a logician out of Polly; I had taught her to think. My job was done. She was worthy of me at last. She was a fit wife for me, a proper hostess for my many mansions, a suitable mother for my well-heeled children.

It must not be thought that I was without love for this girl. Quite the contrary. Just as Pygmalion loved the perfect woman he had fashioned, so I loved mine. I determined to acquaint her with my feelings at our very next meeting.

The time had come to change our relationship from academic to romantic.

"Polly," I said when next we sat beneath our oak, "tonight we will not discuss fallacies."

"Aw, gee," she said, disappointed.

"My dear," I said, favoring her with a smile, "we have now spent five evenings together. We have gotten along splendidly. It is clear that we are well matched."

"Hasty Generalization," she repeated. "How can you say that we are well matched on the basis of only five dates?"

I chuckled with amusement. The dear child had learned her lessons well. "My dear," I said, patting her hand in a tolerant manner, "five dates is plenty. After all, you don't have to eat a whole cake to know that it's good."

"False Analogy," said Polly promptly. "I'm not a cake. I'm a girl." I chuckled with somewhat less amusement. The dear child had learned her lessons perhaps too well. I decided to change tactics. Obviously the best approach was a simple, strong, direct declaration of love. I paused for a moment while my massive brain chose the proper words. Then I began:

"Polly, I love you. You are the whole world to me, and the moon and the stars and the constellations of outer space. Please, my darling, say that you will go steady with me, for if you will not, life will be meaningless. I will languish. I will refuse my meals. I will wander the face of the earth, a shambling, hollow-eyed hulk."

There, I thought, folding my arms, that ought to do it.

"Ad Misericordiam," said Polly.

I ground my teeth. I was not Pygmalion; I was Frankenstein, and my monster had me by the throat. Frantically I fought back the tide of panic surging through me. At all costs I had to keep cool.

"Well, Polly," I said, forcing a smile, "you have certainly learned your fallacies."

"You're darn right," she said with a vigorous nod.

"And who taught them to you, Polly?"

"You did."

"That's right. So you do owe me something, don't you, my dear? If I hadn't come along you never would have learned about fallacies."

"Hypothesis Contrary to Fact," she said instantly.

I dashed perspiration from my brow. "Polly," I croaked, "you mustn't take all these things so literally. I mean this is just classroom stuff. You know that the things you learn in school don't have anything to do with life."

"Dicto Simpliciter," she said, wagging her finger at me playfully.

That did it. I leaped to my feet, bellowing like a bull. "Will you or will you not go steady with me?"

"I will not," she replied.

"Why not?" I demanded.

"Because this afternoon I promised Petey Burch I would go steady with him."

I reeled back, overcome with the infamy of it. After he promised, after he made a deal, after he shook my hand! "The rat!" I shrieked, kicking up great chunks of turf. "You can't go with him, Polly. He's a liar. He's a cheat. He's a rat."

"Poisoning the Well," said Polly, "and stop shouting. I think shouting must be a fallacy too."

With an immense effort of will, I modulated my voice. "All right," I said. "You're a logician. Let's look at this thing logically. How could you choose Petey Burch over me? Look at me—a brilliant student, a tremendous intellectual, a man with an assured future. Look at Petey—a knothead, a jitterbug, a guy who'll never know where his next meal is coming from. Can you give me one logical reason why you should go steady with Petey Burch?"

"I certainly can," declared Polly. "He's got a raccoon coat."

A STRUCTURE FOR THE PERSUASIVE ESSAY

In its classical form, the persuasive essay or oration has a six-part structure: (1) introduction, (2) explanation of the case under discussion, (3) outline of the argument, (4) proof, (5) refutation of counter-arguments, and (6) conclusion.

Now let's see how this squares with the model of persuasion that was explained on pages 243–52.

Introduction. This is a prelude to the argument, getting the audience's attention and establishing the character of the writer or speaker.

Explanation of the case under discussion. This section contains the *evidence* and a clear statement of the problem that the essay addresses. The explanation is background.

Outline of the argument. The persuasion model that we studied earlier did not have this feature. An essay or oration includes the outline to help the reader or listener see where the argument is going, to follow its details and relate them to the whole. The outline is much more useful in oral presentations than in written ones.

Proof. In this section, the *link* and its *backing* and *reservations* are developed.

Refutation. If there are likely to be significant counter-arguments against one's claim, this is the place to refute them.

Conclusion. The *claim* and its *qualifiers* are fully stated.

This traditional pattern of organization could be very useful to writers of persuasive essays.

A Persuasive Essay

After reading the following essay, answer these questions concerning it:

1. If the essay contains introduction, explanation of the case, outline

of the argument, proof, refutation, and conclusion, (a) tell which paragraphs constitute these sections, and (b) explain how the sections accomplish their purpose.

2. Referring to the model developed on pages 243–52, explain (a) evidence, (b) link, (c) reservations, (d) backing, (e) claim, (f) qualifications.

3. What devices does the author use to establish his (a) good sense
and authority or credibility, (b) good will, and (c) moral character?

The Injustice of Justice

Karl Menninger

Few words in our language arrest our attention as do "crime," "violence," "revenge," and "injustice."

We abhor crime; we adore justice; we boast that we live by the rule of
law. Violence and vengefulness we repudiate as unworthy of our civilization,
and we assume this sentiment to be unanimous among all human beings.

Yet crime continues to be a national disgrace and a world-wide problem.
It is threatening, alarming, wasteful, expensive, abundant, and apparently increasing! It seems to increase faster than the growth of population, faster than
the spread of civilization.

Included among the crimes that make up the total are those which *we*
commit, we noncriminals. These are not in the tabulations. They are not listed
in the statistics and are not described in the President's Crime Commission
studies. But *our* crimes help to make the recorded crimes possible, even necessary; and the worst of it is we do not even know we are guilty.

Perhaps our *worst* crime is our ignorance about crime; our easy satisfaction with headlines and the accounts of lurid cases; and our smug assumption
that it is all a matter of some tough "bad guys" whom the tough "good guys"
will soon capture. And even the assassination of one of our most beloved
Presidents has not really changed public thinking—or nonthinking—about
crime. The public still thinks of it as Lee Harvey Oswald's crime (with or
without accomplice). Respected and dignified authorities solemnly accumulate volumes of evidence to prove that he, and he alone, did this foul
deed. Our part in it is rarely, if ever, mentioned.

By our part, I mean the encouragement we give to criminal acts and criminal careers, including Oswald's, our neglect of preventive steps such as had
been recommended for Oswald long before he killed President Kennedy, and
our quickly subsiding hysterical reactions to sensational cases. I mean our
love of vindictive "justice," our generally smug detachment, and our prevail-
ing public apathy.

Only a few weeks before President Kennedy's death, another brave young
leader, who *also* had a young wife and children, was *also* shot from ambush
by a man who *also* used a telescope-sighted rifle. It was soon forgotten. How
many people today even remember the name of Medgar Evers?

And who even knows or remembers the names of any of the thousands of
other people in the United States who have been murdered, maimed, raped,

THE INJUSTICE OF JUSTICE   Karl Menninger, *The Crime of Punishment* (New York: The Viking
Press, 1968), pp. 3–15. Copyright © 1968 by Karl Menninger, M.D. Reprinted by permission of Viking Penguin Inc.

robbed, and beaten during every hour since? Who heeds the cries of alarm from scientific authorities, police authorities, governmental authorities, and even from the President? Commissions are appointed; books are written; research is approved. But the basic public attitude remains unchanged.

What is wrong with this picture?

Why don't we care? And if we *do* care, some of us, why not more intelligently and effectively?

The Scientific Position

I propose in this book to examine this strange paradox of social danger, social error, and social indifference. I shall do so from the standpoint of one whose life has been spent in scientific work.

Scientists are not illusion-proof. We are not always or altogether objective. We are not oracles. But we have been trained in a way of observing and interpreting things that has produced rich harvests for the civilized world. This is the systematic collection of certain facts, the orderly arrangement of those facts, and the drawing of tentative conclusions from them to be submitted to further investigation for proof or disproof. These conclusions often contradict and revise "commonsense" solutions which were the best we could do—until we learned better. People no longer have to rely upon common sense for traveling. The commonsense way is to walk, or to ride an animal. Science has discovered better ways by the use of *uncommon* sense. The commonsense time to go to bed is when it gets dark; the uncommon sense of artificial illumination has changed all that. Crime problems have been dealt with too long with only the aid of common sense. Catch criminals and lock them up; if they hit you, hit them back. This is common sense, but it does not work.

Now there *is* a science of criminology and there is a broader spectrum of social sciences. Psychiatry is only one of these. But sciences are all related, and social scientists all share a faith in the scientific method as contrasted to obsolete methods based on tradition, precedent, and common sense.

I am a psychiatrist. But do not think of me as one of those "alienists" called to the witness stand to prove some culprit "insane" and "irresponsible" and hence "not guilty." I abhor such performances worse than you, dear reader, possibly can.

Think of me as a doctor to whom people come to talk about their troubles, and talk very frankly. They may spend most of their time talking about the acts and attitudes of other people, people with whom they interact.

Think of me as a doctor who has worked for years with fellow scientists—physicians, neurologists, surgeons, psychiatrists, psychoanalysts, sociologists, anthropologists, psychiatric social workers, nurses, therapists—to try to alleviate painful situations. Our common objective has been to obtain a better understanding of why some people do certain things that hurt themselves or other people. We have tried to use this understanding to improve situations—sometimes by changing the particular subject of our study or getting him to change himself, and sometimes by trying to effect changes in his surroundings. Frequently, not always, we have been successful; the undesirable behavior ceased; the patient "got well," and he and his family and neighbors gave thanks. We rejoiced then, not merely in the pride of successful achievement and in human sympathy, but in the satisfaction of having our basic scientific working hypotheses confirmed as "true." This is the crowning reward of the scientist.

When, therefore, we turn our eyes or ears toward the great cry for help arising from the crime situation (better called the social safety problem), we tend to think in terms of the basic postulates and procedures that have guided us in responding to these other forms of human distress. But when we do, one great difficulty immediately arises:

Who is the patient we are to treat?

We should not jump to the assumption that the *criminal* is the obvious subject upon whom to concentrate our attention. For who *is* he? Do we mean, really, the *convicted* criminal? Knowing that most offenders are never convicted, do we perhaps mean to say the accused offender? But do we want to exclude the potential offender, whose crime might be or may have been prevented? And if we are seeking all the potential offenders, we surely must include ourselves.

Crime is *everybody's* temptation. It is easy to look with proud disdain upon "those people" who get caught—the stupid ones, the unlucky ones, the blatant ones. But who does not get nervous when a police car follows closely? We squirm over our income tax statements and make some "adjustments." We tell the customs officials that we have nothing to declare—well, practically nothing. Some of us who have never been convicted of any crime picked up over two billion dollars' worth of merchandise last year from the stores we patronize. Over a billion dollars was embezzled by employees last year. One hotel in New York lost over seventy-five thousand finger bowls, demitasse spoons, and other objects in its first ten months of operation. The Claims Bureau of the American Insurance Association estimates that seventy-five per cent of all claims are dishonest in some respect and the amount of overpayment more than $350,000,000 a year![1]

These facts disturb us, or should. They give us an uneasy feeling that we are all indicted. "Let him who is without sin cast the first stone."

But, we say, even if it be true that many of us *are* guilty of committing these petty crimes, they are at least petty crimes, they are at least "semi-respectable crimes." Everybody does it! What about those villains, thugs in the park, drug pushers, car thieves, rapists, killers? *We* do not do *those* terrible things. It is "those people" that the police are too easy with, *those* who prey upon society and do terrible, violent things. What with sentimentalists who give no thought to the plight of the victims, and psychiatrists who get criminals "off" by calling them "insane," and Supreme Court rulings that protect the "so-called rights" of villains who resist the police, is it any wonder crime is increasing in our country?

We cannot escape our responsibilities with vehement denials or with rhetoric and oratory, nor can we assume that offenders have no "rights." We *do* commit our crimes, too. Most crimes go undetected, including ours. And even those of us who have "forgotten" our offenses, hoping they will have been forgiven by God if not officially by man, will not deny the casual experience of criminal wishes or fantasies of criminal acts. "The moral man," said Freud, "is not he who is never tempted, but he who can resist his temptations."

[1] *Time*, September 9, 1966, pp. 26–27.

It was a brave and honest writer who, in reviewing the dreary Truman Capote record of one spectacular crime episode, began his article thus:

> When I was 14 I committed a series of crimes that were apparently motiveless. Technically, they were acts of vandalism. Once at night I climbed into an unlocked car, found some camera equipment and broke it. Four times, during broad daylight, I broke into homes, wandered around the emptiness, searched through desks and bureaus, made a few messes and left. Once I found a bottle of whiskey in a drawer and emptied it onto a bed. I did other things I can't bring myself to mention even now, after 20 years. I was seen twice, once only a few seconds after I had entered the house. The woman had not answered the door because she didn't feel like it, but right after I had expertly pried open a window and dropped to the hall floor, she came out and stared at me. I told her I had heard sounds and thought she might be in trouble. More talk, more lies, and I got away. I was not frightened for hours.
>
> This, of course, is the point of my confession: I was not scared. Normally I was a cowardly little boy and when I went out on these obviously sexual episodes, I felt nothing. I did not even feel like a master criminal. I did not attempt to justify myself to myself. I just did them. Something came over me, and out I would go. But this calmness was a form of emotion, it was an excitement beyond excitement, a feeling so powerful that it keyed all my reactions to their peak, gave me the ability to act, to escape when necessary, without panic or even fear.
>
> But my mind. Where was my mind? Lost, I think, in the aura of madness, returning only later, when I would enter a frenzied hangover of terror and guilt. Only then would I realize, with increasing panic, that only dumb luck kept me from being caught. But the next time the feeling would come over me I would forget the guilt and the terror and go out again. My criminal career lasted only a few weeks, and then went away.
>
> The point of all this belated confession is that I think it gives me a particular sense of empathy with the two men Capote writes about in *In Cold Blood*. When I put the book down all I could think was that a little more hate, an ounce less stability, and I might have been a murderer. That woman who caught me: mightn't I have decided it was too risky to let her live? What if she hadn't believed (or appeared to have believed) my story? At a moment like that, ethics or fear of any sort simply do not exist: the beast is in charge.[2]

This startling confession does not surprise any psychiatrist. We hear such recollections and "confessions" daily. Most people, however, do not report the derelictions of which they are consciously guilty. We repress the memory of them, if and as soon as possible. Then they never happened! " 'I *did* that,' says my memory. 'I *could not have done that*,' says my pride, and remains inexorable. Eventually—the memory yields."[3]

But I have no wish to make the reader feel uneasy or vaguely guilty about his past derelictions. We all do the best we can and, if we have made mistakes

---

[2] Carpenter, Don: Review of *In Cold Blood* by Truman Capote. *Ramparts*, April 1966, pp. 51–52.
[3] Nietzsche, F. W.: *Beyond Good and Evil*, Vol. 15 of *Complete Works of F. W. Nietzsche*, Helen Zimmern, tr. New York: Macmillan, 1910.

we deplore, we repent. We make such restitution or propitiation as we can. We will try to do better, but we must go on. But we should not displace our guilt feelings to official scapegoats in blind vindictiveness.

And there is one crime we all keep committing, over and over. I accuse the reader of this—and myself, too—and all the nonreaders. We commit the crime of damning some of our fellow citizens with the label "criminal." And having done this, we force them through an experience that is soul-searing and dehumanizing. In this way we exculpate ourselves from the guilt we feel and tell ourselves that we do it to "correct" the "criminal" and make us all safer from crime. We commit this crime every day that we retain our present stupid, futile, abominable practices against detected offenders.

Let us deal here with the unpleasant rhetorical ploy which some radio and television speakers have passed around for use in public attacks on the Supreme Court because of its recent definitions of the limitations of police authority.* "Doesn't anybody care about the victims?" cry some demagogues, with melodramatic flourishes. "Why should all this attention be given to the criminals and none to those they have beaten or robbed?"

This childish outcry has an appeal for the unthinking. Of course no victim should be neglected. But the *individual* victim has no more right to be protected than those of us *who may become victims*. We all want to be better protected. And we are not being protected by a system that attacks "criminals" as if they were the embodiment of all evil. That is what this book is about.

"The defendant has 'a constitution,' " says a sprightly lawyer and lecturer in an article for *Police* magazine.⁴ This constitution is "the one the nine men in Washington are always talking about." The author throughout his article refers to the Constitution of the United States as "the criminal's constitution" and implies that the person robbed or raped does not have this constitution. Why the victim of a crime would cease to be an American citizen is not made clear, but this young man is very angry because he feels that victims are not protected by the Constitution and implies that, therefore, offenders should not be protected by the Constitution either. He suggests that the victims "form some kind of a constitutional convention with delegates and platforms and banners and all that stuff and then they could draft some kind of a constitution for themselves."

This lawyer, no doubt, means well in this oration. He did not mean to sneer at the Constitution of his country. He really believes that the law is so occupied trying to do something fierce but legal to the offender that it neglects the person offended. In this, I think, he is right. The law neglects all of us. The more fiercely, the more ruthlessly, the more inhumanely the offender is

---

*"The Supreme Court's *Miranda* decision has dismayed some policemen, embittered some prosecutors, and baffled some judges. But United States television is taking it in stride. In Denver last week, a meeting of 500 district attorneys from across the country was visited by actor Ben Alexander, burly, laconic co-star with Jack Webb in the popular *Dragnet* series of the 1950s. Puffing his *Felony Squad* show, Alexander said: 'The Supreme Court says we can't interrogate crooks any more. So what choice do we have?' His answer: 'We shoot 'em. On our show the viewers will see the crime committed, so they know the guy's guilty. That way, nobody gets upset when we shoot him.' " (*Time*, August 26, 1966.)

⁴Shafer, William J., III: "How About a Constitution for the Victim?" *Police*, March–April 1967, pp. 82–84.

treated—however legally—the more certain we are to have *more* victims. *Of course* victims should not be forgotten in the hubbub of capturing and dealing with their victimizers, but neither should the next victim be forgotten—the one who is going to get hurt next so long as the vicious cycle of evil for evil and vengeance for vengeance perpetuates the revolving-door principle of penal justice.

"Justice"

We justify the perpetuation of this social anachronism by reference to the holy principle of justice. I am told that Justice Oliver Wendell Holmes was always outraged when a lawyer before the Supreme Court used the word "justice." He said it showed he was shirking his job. The problem in every case is what should be done in *this* situation. It does not advance a solution to use the word *justice*. It is a subjective emotional word. Every litigant thinks that justice demands a decision in his favor.

I propose to demonstrate the paradox that much of the laborious effort made in the noble name of justice results in its very opposite. The concept is so vague, so distorted in its applications, so hypocritical, and usually so irrelevant that it offers no help in the solution of the crime problem which it exists to combat but results in its exact opposite—injustice, injustice to everybody. Socrates defined justice as the awarding to each that which is due him. But Plato perceived the sophistry of this and admitted that justice basically means power, "the interest of the stronger," a clear note that has been repeated by Machiavelli, Hobbs, Spinoza, Marx, Kalsem, on down to Justice Holmes.*

Contrast the two ways in which the word is commonly used. On the one hand, we want to obtain justice for the unfairly treated; we render justice to an oppressed people, we deal justly with our neighbor. (Cf. Micah.) We think of justice in terms of fair dealing and the rescue of the exploited and we associate it with freedom and social progress and democracy.

On the other hand, when justice is "meted out," justice is "served," justice is "satisfied" or "paid." It is something terrible which somebody "sees to it" that somebody else gets; not something good, helpful, or valuable, but something that hurts. It is the whiplash of retribution about to descend on the naked back of transgressors. The end of justice is thus to give help to some, pain to others.

What is it that defeats and twists the idea of justice in its legal applications? Is it our trial court system? We would like to think of our courts as reflections of our civilization, bulwarks of public safety, tribunals for the insurance of fair and objective judgment. Should we revert to some earlier process of investigation of the alleged offender? Or is it that people confuse justice with the elimination of dangerousness from human misbehavior? Is protection from violence something obtained with the *aid* of justice or *in spite* of it?

A few years ago Dr. Frederick Hacker and Mrs. Menninger and I were in

---

*Historically, justice has been conceived of in the most diverse terms. *The Great Ideas: A Syntopicon of Great Books of the Western World,* Vol. I (Chicago: Encyclopedia Britannica, 1952) lists and discusses many of these, citing over a thousand supporting references. Some of these authorities all of us have read, some of them few of us. But any word that can elude precise usage by metamorphosis into scores of shades of meaning is apt to be more inspirational and rhetorical than scientifically useful (see especially pages 859–878).

a European city on tour. We had parked our car in front of our hotel for the night. As we came out in the morning after a pleasant night's rest, prepared to take our leave, the concierge came running toward us from the hotel. "Was there some mistake in the bill?" we inquired. Oh, no, everything was in order. But would we please go immediately to the police station?

"What for?" we asked indignantly. "What have we done?"

"Oh, nothing, nothing." The concierge was most apologetic. "Not at all. But there has been an attempted crime."

"By us?" we asked, in astonishment.

"No, no, no. But, please, the police will explain. Please go."

So to the police station we went. When we arrived, annoyed, mystified, and apprehensive, one clerk after another, in what seemed to be ascending echelons of authority, queried us. Where did we park our car last night? Had we missed anything? Had we seen the molesters?

"No, no," we all said.

"Was the car door pried open?"

Again, "No."

"Was anything taken?"

"No."

Where did we come from? Where were we going? Why were we there?

We explained in laborious French and Italian, and rose to take our leave. But no, we must remain.

"How long?"

"Perhaps for several days."

"But why? What for?"

"To testify at the trial!"

"What trial? Whose trial?"

Why, the trial of some prisoners now languishing in jail—"in vinculo." The officer illustrated this state of detention by clutching his own wrists with his opposing hands.

We began to be desperate. We said we knew no prisoner, we had seen no molester, we had suffered no damage, we had made no charge. So far as we knew, nothing had happened. Again we painfully "explained" and sought to leave.

Ah, but if the alert and clever police had not *seen* the marauder *about to open the Americans' car* and pounced upon him instantly, the Americans would have indeed suffered loss. But bravo! the *police!*

All right. Fine! Alert policemen, crime prevented. No crime. No trial. So, now, let's go!

Unfortunately not possible.

But why?

"Ah" (solemnly), "*Giustizia! Giustizia!*" (Justice! Justice!)

So for the sake of "justice" we must remain! And remain we did, continuing to argue and gesture. We looked angry and we looked sad. More police officials were called from upstairs offices. We identified ourselves again thoroughly and painstakingly. We laid before them our passports and identification. I certified that I was an American citizen, a physician, a psychiatrist, a member of the American Medical Association and of the American Psychiatric Association, the Masonic Lodge and the American Contract Bridge League. I even submitted a letter from my friend Commissioner Bennett of the United States Department of Justice.

None of this information seemed to have the slightest influence. *"Gius-tizia!"* they would murmur to one another and to us, shaking their heads significantly and remaining motionless. As good citizens surely we desired to see the law upheld. Would we have the prisoner languish in jail untried? Is it not the right of the accused to confront his accusers and to cross-examine? (But we had not accused.)

The abstract concept of justice never seemed to me so ridiculous. And I must confess that at the moment it was not the unjust plight of the prisoner that concerned me but the unjust plight of the innocent nonvictims!

Dr. Hacker suddenly recalled that he was carrying with him a large, bronze, deputy sheriff's badge from a southern California county where he was a consultant to the county court. With a magnificent flourish he tossed his badge, face up, upon the police desk and pointed.

The effect of this gesture was electric. The chief of police and his assistants leaped to their feet and saluted. The chief grasped both my friend's hands, then seized him and kissed him on both cheeks. All officers smiled broadly and bowed to each of us. With gestures of respect and friendliness they pointed to the door. As colleagues in the enforcement of the law we could be granted a special favor. Justice (!) had prevailed.

Of course this ludicrous incident does not do justice to justice. One might well ask what would have happened if we actually had lost some property. What would have happened if we had been less insistent, less self-assured, less prosperous than we seemed to these simple but officious men? It might have been we who invoked the principle of justice for a better disposition of the matter.

But the paradox is that we all extol justice as a principle when it is working against someone we do not like. Justice was not invented, as we think, to protect the weak but to protect the King's Peace; it was belatedly applied—in a measure—to the protection of (some of) the King's subjects.

Edmond Cahn made this brilliantly clear in various essays which he had intended to publish in a book entitled *The Meaning of Justice.* In it he intended to demonstrate that "Justice is not a collection of principles or criteria. . . . Justice is the active process of the preventing or repairing of injustice."

"Why is it," he asked, "that able minds of some two centuries have turned against the concept of justice and denigrated it? How account for the wide gap between justice according to the philosophers (a superfluous if not entirely irrelevant term) and justice according to the people (a vital necessity of their lives)? Surely the authors we have mentioned have not been callous to ideal values, nor have they been preaching the kind of academic cynicism that certain professors affect in every generation in order to impress unsophisticated students. If men of the caliber of Hume, Bentham, and Marx shock us by disparaging justice it is not because they are engaged in striking classroom poses. It is rather because the conceptions of justice which they find about them are genuinely inadequate."[5]

Unhappily, then, we must recognize that, in practice, justice does not mean fairness to all parties. To some people the law is an inexorable, inscrutable Sinai—the highest virtue is to submit unquestioningly. But to others, law

---

[5]Cahn, Lenore L., ed.: *Confronting Injustice: The Edmond Cahn Reader.* Boston: Little, Brown and Co., 1966, p. 385.

and the principle of justice should, as Cahn wrote, "embody the plasticity and reasonableness that Aristotle praised in his famous description of equity. He said: 'Equity bids us be merciful to the weakness of human nature; to think less about the laws than about the man who framed them, and less about what he said than about what he meant; not to consider the actions of the accused so much as his intentions, nor this or that detail so much as the whole story; to ask not what a man is now but what he has always or usually been. It bids us remember benefits rather than injuries, and benefits received rather than benefits conferred; to be patient when we are wronged; to settle a dispute by negotiation and not by force.' "[6]

[6]*Ibid.*, p. 239.

Writing about Literature

THE ACT OF READING

In one sense, reading the newspaper and a short story by Nathaniel Hawthorne are exactly the same. You "process" the page—employing your visual system and your mind—to gain meaning from print. Of course, it might be said that you read with your mind, not your eyes, since it is quite possible for you to see print clearly but not be able to gain the meaning, as, for instance, when you look at a page in a foreign language, and blind people read with their fingertips, not their eyes. Reading is, simply, the act of gaining meaning, not of seeing words and sentences and not of deriving sounds from those words and sentences. (One can learn to pronounce a foreign language without being able to understand the words that are pronounced.)

Reasons for Reading

But even though the *act* of reading—the interpretation of raw visual data by the mind—is essentially the same for all reading, purposes in reading vary widely. If you want to learn how to cultivate roses, you will most probably go to a reference source, such as the *Sunset Book of Gardening,* not to a poem about roses. On the other hand, millions of people do quite frequently read poems (about roses and other subjects). Their purpose in this kind of reading is radically different from their purpose in using a manual, a newspaper, or an encyclopedia.

The point, of course, is that we do not always read for information, to learn directly about the world "out there," but frequently take up a book—a novel, a collection of poems, an anthology of short stories—to gain the *experience* that this kind of reading affords.

It is fair to make a rough cut in the act of reading, dividing it into subcategories which we might call *informational* and *esthetic*. Baldly stated, we read either to gain information or to gain the experience that certain kinds of reading afford. In informational reading, purpose is firmly connected with results in the world "out there": we want to find out what's happening in the Middle East or what the current standings are among college football teams. When our purpose is esthetic, we want to immerse ourselves in the text, lose ourselves in the experience that the poem or story offers. And yet, when we read a novel, poem, story, or play, we gain an extremely complex sort of meaning.

In writing about literature, we can attempt to explain the nature of the experience or, on the other hand, we can try to explain the complex meaning of the work. In other words, we can write about our *response* to the work (what it means to *us*) or about the structure of the work itself and how that structure conveys meaning. The second kind of writing—that which explains how the story, poem, novel, or play "works"—is often called *explication*.

Below is a poem by James Dickey, followed by the poet's account of the "facts" of the events on which the poem is based. After you have carefully read the poem and Dickey's explanation of it, you should understand what the poem is "about."

The Performance

James Dickey

The last time I saw Donald Armstrong
He was staggering oddly off into the sun,
Going down, off the Philippine Islands.
I let my shovel fall, and put that hand
Above my eyes, and moved some way to one side
That his body might pass through the sun,

THE PERFORMANCE   James Dickey, *Poems 1957–1967* (Middletown, Conn.: Wesleyan University Press, 1967). Copyright © 1960, 1965 by James Dickey. Reprinted by permission of Wesleyan University Press.

And I saw how well he was not
Standing there on his hands,
On his spindle-shanked forearms balanced,
Unbalanced, with his big feet looming and waving
In the great, untrustworthy air
He flew in each night, when it darkened.

Dust fanned in scraped puffs from the earth
Between his arms, and blood turned his face inside out,
To demonstrate its suppleness
Of veins, as he perfected his role.
Next day, he toppled his head off
On an island beach to the south,

And the enemy's two-handed sword
Did not fall from anyone's hands
At that miraculous sight,
As the head rolled over upon
Its wide-eyed face, and fell
Into the inadequate grave

He had dug for himself, under pressure.
Yet I put my flat hand to my eyebrows
Months later, to see him again
In the sun, when I learned how he died,
And imagined him, there,
Come, judged, before his small captors,

Doing all his lean tricks to amaze them—
The back somersault, the kip-up—
And at last, the stand on his hands,
Perfect, with his feet together,
His head down, evenly breathing,
As the sun poured up from the sea

And the headsman broke down
In a blaze of tears, in that light
Of the thin, long human frame
Upside down in its own strange joy,
And, if some other one had not told him,
Would have cut off the feet

Instead of the head,
And if Armstrong had not presently risen
In kingly, round-shouldered attendance,
And then knelt down in himself
Beside his hacked, glittering grave, having done
All things in this life that he could.

Almost every word of "The Performance" is literally true, except that the interpretation of the facts is my own. It's a poem about a boy named Donald Armstrong, who came from somewhere in the West. He was in my squadron, the 418th Night Fighter Squadron, during the Second World War. He was probably my best friend in the squadron, a very lovable, ugly fellow. You need somebody like him in a combat situation, someone who sees the humorous side of everything and is happy-go-lucky and daring. He was an awfully good pilot, but he took a lot of unnecessary chances, and the older air crews in the squadron were a bit chary of him. He was always doing crazy things like going to sleep with the airplane on Automatic Pilot. He and his observer—the P61 had a two-man crew—sometimes would both go to sleep and just drone along coming back from convoy cover or wherever they'd been.

Most of our missions were to the north of the island we were on, Mindoro, the island immediately south of Luzon. But we also had missions to the south, to Panay. As nearly as I can remember, some Japanese held the island and were using Filipino labor to build an airstrip. Armstrong and his observer, Jim Lalley, went down to Panay in a P61 one evening on a strafing run. Apparently it was just at dusk, when it's hard to judge distances, and the plane hit the ground. It was damaged and began to come apart, so Armstrong made a crash landing. They were both hurt, according to the reports we got from the Filipino guerrillas, but they were alive. They were taken out of the aircraft by the Japanese, kept in an old schoolhouse, and beheaded the next day at dawn. We found out about this immediately from the guerrilla forces on Panay, but there was nothing we could have done about it.

Don Armstrong was always doing gymnastic tricks in the squadron area. He used to do flips and all kinds of such things, and would work on his handstands. He was a tall fellow, and because his center of gravity was high, it was hard for him to do handstands. I can remember him falling over on his head and back and getting up and trying again. For a long time I tried to write this poem, but the poems I wrote were all official tributes to my old buddy. They didn't have the distinctiveness that I thought the poem really ought to have. So I said to myself, "Goodness, Jim, what is the thing you remember *most* about Don? Do you remember how ugly he was, or how skinny he was, or something that he did?" There was a squadron movie area where we used to have movies when the Japanese weren't bombing us. Don and I saw a movie called *Laura* there, and he was wild about it. I remember sitting in the weeds watching that movie with him; so I put that into the poem, but it wasn't right. Then I remembered that he used to do all those flips and tricks in the squadron area. People would stand around watching him, but sometimes he'd just be out there by himself standing on his hands, or trying to. He never mastered it; I never saw him do a good handstand.

Finally I tried to bring together the unsuccessful handstand, the last trick he was trying to perfect, and the grotesque manner of his death, and I tried to describe the effect these would have on the beholders, the executioners, and on the poet who tells the poem. I thought, "Why not make it *really* crazy?" The poem isn't about the facts of Armstrong's death, because the narrator is trying to imagine them. I said to myself, "I'll bet that damned Armstrong would be crazy enough to throw off a dozen cartwheels before he got his head chopped off! And what would *that* do to the Japanese?"

Since you can make anything you like happen in a poem, I made it happen that way. I wrote the poem in a rather matter-of-fact way with no obvious rhetorical devices, like refrains. I did it straight because I didn't want to write amazingly about ordinary events, but matter-of-factly about extraordinary events. It seemed to be more effective that way, as well as much truer to the kind of experience that it might have been for the narrator. I suppose "The Performance" is the most anthologized of my poems. I've never taken an actual count, but I've come across it in more places than I have any other of my poems, maybe partly because it's been in circulation longer. I wrote it in the first part of 1958, also in an advertising office.

I'm always trying to synthesize, and I thought, "Boy, next week I'm going to try to get these two techniques together. (I had to drop poetry and do some radio commercials.) I'm going to use the crazy approach to subject matter I used in 'The Performance' and some other things, like refrains, and see what happens." As I said, experimentation is very, very important to me. That's what makes poetry so damned much fun! If you ask yourself the fundamental question, "What would happen if . . . ?" then the only one thing to do is to see what *would* happen if you did such-and-such a thing. That's always been very much a part of writing poetry for me, and that's the part I enjoy the most.[1]

Response

Informally, in your journal or in a formal essay, explain what "The Performance" means *to you.* In this writing, you will be focusing on your own experiences, interests, and values. To get under way, you might ask yourself the following questions, think about them, and record as many ideas as you can in the form of rough notes.

1. *You as reader.* Your interests? Fears? Attitudes toward war? Toward death? Your values (concerning life, bravery, etc.)? Your

[1] James Dickey, *Self-Interviews,* with Barbara and James Reiss (New York: Doubleday, 1970), pp. 92–95. Copyright © 1970 by James Dickey. Reprinted by permission of Doubleday & Company, Inc.

personality? Do you like poetry? (Explain.) What other questions can you think of?

2. *The events in the poem.* Have you had experiences that are in any way similar? (What about the death of a friend or a loved one?) How did you react to the mixture of comedy and tragedy in the poem? How do you feel about executions? What other questions can you think of?

3. *The characters.* Have you ever known anyone like Donald Armstrong? (How is that person like him?) Have you ever known people like the captors? (Explain.) What other questions can you think of?

4. *Time and place.* In what way is the setting of the poem like (or unlike) places you have known? What does the setting remind you of? Have you ever experienced a time of "war"? (In your imagination? In your family? In your neighborhood?) What does "wartime" mean to you? What other questions can you think of?

5. *The poem itself.* Did you enjoy the language? (Explain.) How about the images? What didn't you like about the poem? What other questions can you think of?

6. *Purposes.* Why did the events happen? Have you known of other events that happened for the same reasons? Have you been involved in such events? Were the events in the poem senseless? (Have you ever been the victim of senseless events?) What other questions can you think of?

Your notes regarding these questions should give you a basis for explaining your reaction to the poem.

Toward Explication

The following questions focus your attention more on the poem itself than on your reaction to it. By making notes of your answers to the questions, you can prepare to do an *explication,* an explanation of how the poem "works."

1. In both the poem and the explanation of how it came into being, the speaker is Dickey himself. (In some imaginative literature, the speaker, as we shall see, is a character invented by the author.) How does Dickey's attitude toward his subject in the poem differ from his attitude in the explanation?

2. If you want the "facts" about Donald Armstrong, Dickey's explanation is the best source. But what sort of *meaning* do you get from the poem that you can't get from the explanation?

3. The poem is more concrete, specific, visual than the explanation. What does this concreteness contribute to your reading of the poem?

4. Does it make any difference to your understanding of the poem that there was an actual Donald Armstrong? Explain.
5. In what ways does Dickey change the facts in the poem? Why does he do so?
6. What scenes and events does Dickey invent for the poem? Why does he do so?
7. Was your reading of the poem more intense than your reading of the explanation? If so, explain.
8. Explain what the following means in relation to the experience of reading: "The purpose of Dickey's explanation is to give information about the poem, but the purpose of the poem is to recreate an experience for the reader."
9. How do answers to the following questions help you explain the poem and your reaction to it?

> a. What happens in the poem?
> b. What sort of character is Donald Armstrong?
> c. By what means are the actions in the poem brought about?
> d. When and where do the actions take place?
> e. Why do the actions take place?

10. One of the main images in the poem is that of the sun. It appears in various guises throughout the poem (for example, it is suggested by its very absence in the last line of the second stanza, "He flew in each night, when it [the air, sky] darkened"). How does this image—and its varying appearance—help in understanding what Dickey is saying?

Response and Explication

With response, the focus is on the reader: his or her reaction to the work. With explication, the focus is on the poem or story: its plot, the nature of the characters, the setting, the reasons for the characters' doing what they do. Actually, response involves explication and vice versa. If I asked you to explain your response to "The Performance," and you said that you liked it because it is about the joys and frustrations of playing Frisbee, I would be puzzled, to say the least. I would ask you to show me *in the poem* where you found that subject matter, and you would need to explicate. On the other hand, if I gave you a thorough explication of the poem—plot, characters, structure, style—but nothing more, you would be justified in asking, "But did you like the poem, and if so, why? What did it mean *to you?*"

Exploring your response to a work of literature might be easier than doing an explication, for the simple reason that you don't need a special vocabulary to talk about the work; you know that it made sense and was satisfying, but can't explain why. The discussion that follows will teach you how to make such explanations.

ELEMENTS OF PROSE FICTION

The great storytellers throughout history have taken their places among the most highly honored of the world's heroes: Cervantes, Goethe, Dickens, Tolstoy, Twain, Hemingway. People have always thirsted for stories; their most basic response is the eager question "And then what?" What is so mysterious about our reaction to stories is that we know they are fictions, "untrue," and yet our thirst for this fictional experience drives us from story to story throughout our lives. (Almost without exception, even nonreaders hunger for stories, and to satisfy that hunger watch television or attend movies.) We feel that a person uninterested in stories is slightly less than human, lacking some spark of playfulness and imagination that makes a human being different from the less-than-human creatures that populate science fiction.

It makes no sense, of course, to talk about literature in a vacuum: we need a work to refer to. That work will be a classic American short story.

Young Goodman Brown

Nathaniel Hawthorne

Young Goodman Brown came forth at sunset into the street at Salem village; but put his head back, after crossing the threshold, to exchange a parting kiss with his young wife. And Faith, as the wife was aptly named, thrust her own pretty head into the street, letting the wind play with the pink ribbons of her cap while she called to Goodman Brown.

"Dearest heart," whispered she, softly and rather sadly, when her lips were close to his ear, "prithee put off your journey until sunrise and sleep in your own bed to-night. A lone woman is troubled
10 with such dreams and such thoughts that she's afeard of herself sometimes. Pray tarry with me this night, dear husband, of all nights in the year."

"My love and my Faith," replied young Goodman Brown, "of

all nights in the year, this one night must I tarry away from thee. My journey, as thou callest it, forth and back again, must needs be done 'twixt now and sunrise. What, my sweet, pretty wife, dost thou doubt me already, and we but three months married?"

"Then God bless you!" said Faith, with the pink ribbons; "and may you find all well when you come back."

20   "Amen!" cried Goodman Brown. "Say thy prayers, dear Faith, and go to bed at dusk, and no harm will come to thee."

So they parted; and the young man pursued his way until, being about to turn the corner by the meeting-house, he looked back and saw the head of Faith still peeping after him with a melancholy air, in spite of her pink ribbons.

"Poor little Faith!" thought he, for his heart smote him. "What a wretch am I to leave her on such an errand! She talks of dreams, too. Methought as she spoke there was trouble in her face, as if a dream had warned her what work is to be done to-night. But no, no;
30   'twould kill her to think it. Well, she's a blessed angel on earth; and after this one night I'll cling to her skirts and follow her to heaven."

With this excellent resolve for the future, Goodman Brown felt himself justified in making more haste on his present evil purpose. He had taken a dreary road, darkened by all the gloomiest trees of the forest, which barely stood aside to let the narrow path creep through, and closed immediately behind. It was all as lonely as could be; and there is this peculiarity in such a solitude, that the traveller knows not who may be concealed by the innumerable trunks and the thick boughs overhead; so that with lonely footsteps he may yet be passing
40   through an unseen multitude.

"There may be a devilish Indian behind every tree," said Goodman Brown to himself; and he glanced fearfully behind him as he added, "What if the devil himself should be at my very elbow!"

His head being turned back, he passed a crook of the road, and, looking forward again, beheld the figure of a man, in grave and decent attire, seated at the foot of an old tree. He arose at Goodman Brown's approach and walked onward side by side with him.

"You are late, Goodman Brown," said he. "The clock of the Old South was striking as I came through Boston, and that is full fifteen
50   minutes agone."

"Faith kept me back a while," replied the young man, with a tremor in his voice, caused by the sudden appearance of his companion, though not wholly unexpected.

It was now deep dusk in the forest, and deepest in that part of it where these two were journeying. As nearly as could be discerned, the second traveller was about fifty years old, apparently in the same rank of life as Goodman Brown, and bearing a considerable resemblance to him, though perhaps more in expression than features. Still they might have been taken for father and son. And yet, though the
60   elder person was as simply clad as the younger, and as simple in man-

ner too, he had an indescribable air of one who knew the world, and who would not have felt abashed at the governor's dinner table or in King William's court, were it possible that his affairs should call him thither. But the only thing about him that could be fixed upon as re- markable was his staff, which bore the likeness of a great black snake, so curiously wrought that it might almost be seen to twist and wriggle itself like a living serpent. This, of course, must have been an ocular deception, assisted by the uncertain light.

70   "Come, Goodman Brown," cried his fellow-traveller, "this is a dull pace for the beginning of a journey. Take my staff, if you are so soon weary."

"Friend," said the other, exchanging his slow pace for a full stop, "having kept covenant by meeting thee here, it is my purpose now to return whence I came. I have scruples touching the matter thou wot'st of."

"Sayest thou so?" replied he of the serpent, smiling apart. "Let us walk on, nevertheless, reasoning as we go; and if I convince thee not thou shalt turn back. We are but a little way in the forest yet."

"Too far! too far!" exclaimed the goodman, unconsciously re- 80   suming his walk. "My father never went into the woods on such an errand, nor his father before him. We have been a race of honest men and good Christians since the days of the martyrs; and shall I be the first of the name of Brown that ever took this path and kept"—

"Such company, thou wouldst say," observed the elder person, interpreting his pause. "Well said, Goodman Brown! I have been as well acquainted with your family as with ever a one among the Puri- tans; and that's no trifle to say. I helped your grandfather, the con- stable, when he lashed the Quaker woman so smartly through the streets of Salem; and it was I that brought your father a pitchpine 90   knot, kindled at my own hearth, to set fire to an Indian village, in King Philip's war. They were my good friends, both; and many a pleasant walk have we had along this path, and returned merrily after midnight. I would fain be friends with you for their sake."

"If it be as thou sayest," replied Goodman Brown, "I marvel they never spoke of these matters; or, verily, I marvel not, seeing that the least rumor of the sort would have driven them from New Eng- land. We are a people of prayer, and good works to boot, and abide no such wickedness."

"Wickedness or not," said the traveller with the twisted staff, "I 100   have a very general acquaintance here in New England. The deacons of many a church have drunk the communion wine with me; the selectmen of divers towns make me their chairman; and a majority of the Great and General Court are firm supporters of my interest. The governor and I, too—But these are state secrets."

"Can this be so?" cried Goodman Brown, with a stare of amaze- ment at his undisturbed companion. "Howbeit, I have nothing to do with the governor and council; they have their own ways, and are no rule for a simple husbandman like me. But, were I to go on with thee, how should I meet the eye of that good old man, our minister, at Salem village? Oh, his voice would make me tremble both Sabbath day and lecture day."

Thus far the elder traveller had listened with due gravity; but now burst into a fit of irrepressible mirth, shaking himself so violently that his snake-like staff actually seemed to wriggle in sympathy.

"Ha! ha! ha!" shouted he again and again; then composing himself, "Well, go on, Goodman Brown, go on; but, prithee, don't kill me with laughing."

"Well, then, to end the matter at once," said Goodman Brown, considerably nettled, "there is my wife, Faith. It would break her dear little heart; and I'd rather break my own."

"Nay, if that be the case," answered the other, "e'en go thy ways, Goodman Brown. I would not for twenty old women like the one hobbling before us that Faith should come to any harm."

As he spoke he pointed his staff at a female figure on the path, in whom Goodman Brown recognized a very pious and exemplary dame, who had taught him his catechism in youth, and was still his moral and spiritual adviser, jointly with the minister and Deacon Gookin.

"A marvel, truly, that Goody Cloyse should be so far in the wilderness at nightfall," said he. "But with your leave, friend, I shall take a cut through the woods until we have left this Christian woman behind. Being a stranger to you, she might ask whom I was consorting with and whither I was going."

"Be it so," said his fellow-traveller. "Betake you to the woods, and let me keep the path."

Accordingly the young man turned aside, but took care to watch his companion, who advanced softly along the road until he had come within a staff's length of the old dame. She, meanwhile, was making the best of her way, with singular speed for so aged a woman, and mumbling some indistinct words—a prayer, doubtless— as she went. The traveller put forth his staff and touched her withered neck with what seemed the serpent's tail.

"The devil!" screamed the pious old lady.

"Then Goody Cloyse knows her old friend?" observed the traveller, confronting her and leaning on his writhing stick.

"Ah, forsooth, and is it your worship indeed?" cried the good dame. "Yea, truly is it, and in the very image of my old gossip, Goodman Brown, the grandfather of the silly fellow that now is. But— would your worship believe it?—my broomstick hath strangely disappeared, stolen, as I suspect, by that unhanged witch, Goody Cory, and that, too, when I was all anointed with juice of smallage, and cinquefoil, and wolf's bane"—

"Mingled with fine wheat and the fat of a new-born babe," said the shape of old Goodman Brown.

"Ah, your worship knows the recipe," cried the old lady, cack-
ling aloud. "So, as I was saying, being all ready for the meeting, and
no horse to ride on, I made up my mind to foot it; for they tell me
there is a nice young man to be taken into communion to-night. But
now your good worship will lend me your arm, and we shall be there
160 in a twinkling."

"That can hardly be," answered her friend. "I may not spare you
my arm, Goody Cloyse; but here is my staff, if you will."

So saying, he threw it down at her feet, where, perhaps, it assumed life, being one of the rods which its owner had formerly lent to
the Egyptian magi. Of this fact, however, Goodman Brown could not
take cognizance. He had cast up his eyes in astonishment, and, looking down again, beheld neither Goody Cloyse nor the serpentine
staff, but his fellow-traveller alone, who waited for him as calmly as
if nothing had happened.

170 "That old woman taught me my catechism," said the young
man; and there was a world of meaning in this simple comment.

They continued to walk onward, while the elder traveller ex-
horted his companion to make good speed and persevere in the path,
discoursing so aptly that his arguments seemed rather to spring up in
the bosom of his auditor than to be suggested by himself. As they
went, he plucked a branch of maple to serve for a walking stick, and
began to strip it of the twigs and little boughs, which were wet with
evening dew. The moment his fingers touched them they became
strangely withered and dried up as with a week's sunshine. Thus the
180 pair proceeded, at a good free pace, until suddenly, in a gloomy
hollow of the road, Goodman Brown sat himself down on the stump
of a tree and refused to go any farther.

"Friend," said he, stubbornly, "my mind is made up. Not another step will I budge on this errand. What if a wretched old woman
do choose to go to the devil when I thought she was going to heaven:
is that any reason why I should quit my dear Faith and go after her?"

"You will think better of this by and by," said his acquaintance,
composedly. "Sit here and rest yourself a while; and when you feel
like moving again, there is my staff to help you along."

190 Without more words, he threw his companion the maple stick,
and was as speedily out of sight as if he had vanished into the deepen-
ing gloom. The young man sat a few moments by the roadside, ap-
plauding himself greatly, and thinking with how clear a conscience he
should meet the minister in his morning walk, nor shrink from the
eye of good old Deacon Gookin. And what calm sleep would be his
that very night, which was to have been spent so wickedly, but so
purely and sweetly now, in the arms of Faith! Amidst these pleasant
and praiseworthy meditations, Goodman Brown heard the tramp of
horses along the road, and deemed it advisable to conceal himself
200 within the verge of the forest, conscious of the guilty purpose that
had brought him thither, though now so happily turned from it.

On came the hoof tramps and the voices of the riders, two grave old voices, conversing soberly as they drew near. These mingled sounds appeared to pass along the road, within a few yards of the young man's hiding-place; but, owing doubtless to the depth of the gloom at that particular spot, neither the travellers nor their steeds were visible. Though their figures brushed the small boughs by the wayside, it could not be seen that they intercepted, even for a moment, the faint gleam from the strip of bright sky athwart which they

210   must have passed. Goodman Brown alternately crouched and stood on tiptoe, pulling aside the branches and thrusting forth his head as far as he durst without discerning so much as a shadow. It vexed him the more, because he could have sworn, were such a thing possible, that he recognized the voices of the minister and Deacon Gookin, jogging along quietly, as they were wont to do, when bound to some ordination or ecclesiastical council. While yet within hearing, one of the riders stopped to pluck a switch.

"Of the two, reverend sir," said the voice like the deacon's, "I had rather miss an ordination dinner than to-night's meeting. They

220   tell me that some of our community are to be here from Falmouth and beyond, and others from Connecticut and Rhode Island, besides several of Indian powwows, who, after their fashion, know almost as much deviltry as the best of us. Moreover, there is a goodly young woman to be taken into communion."

"Mighty well, Deacon Gookin!" replied the solemn old tones of the minister. "Spur up, or we shall be late. Nothing can be done you know until I get on the ground."

The hoofs clattered again; and the voices, talking so strangely in the empty air, passed on through the forest, where no church had

230   ever been gathered or solitary Christian prayed. Whither, then, could these holy men be journeying so deep into the heathen wilderness? Young Goodman Brown caught hold of a tree for support, being ready to sink down on the ground, faint and overburdened with the heavy sickness of his heart. He looked up to the sky, doubting whether there really was a heaven above him. Yet there was the blue arch, and the stars brightening in it.

"With heaven above and Faith below, I will yet stand firm against the devil!" cried Goodman Brown.

While he still gazed upward into the deep arch of the firmament

240   and had lifted his hands to pray, a cloud, though no wind was stirring, hurried across the zenith and hid the brightening stars. The blue sky was still visible, except directly overhead, where this black mass of cloud was sweeping swiftly northward. Aloft in the air, as if from the depths of the cloud, came a confused and doubtful sound of voices. Once the listener fancied that he could distinguish the accents of towns-people of his own, men, and women, both pious and ungodly, many of whom he had met at the communion table, and had seen others rioting at the tavern. The next moment, so indistinct

were the sounds, he doubted whether he had heard aught but the
250 murmur of the old forest, whispering without a wind. Then came a
stronger swell of those familiar tones, heard daily in the sunshine at
Salem village, but never until now from a cloud of night. There was
one voice of a young woman, uttering lamentations, yet with an uncertain sorrow, and entreating for some favor, which, perhaps, it
would grieve her to obtain; and all the unseen multitude, both saints
and sinners, seemed to encourage her onward.

"Faith!" shouted Goodman Brown, in a voice of agony and desperation; and the echoes of the forest mocked him, crying, "Faith!
Faith!" as if bewildered wretches were seeking her all through the
260 wilderness.

The cry of grief, rage, and terror was yet piercing the night,
when the unhappy husband held his breath for a response. There was
a scream, drowned immediately in a louder murmur of voices, fading
into far-off laughter, as the dark cloud swept away, leaving the clear
and silent sky above Goodman Brown. But something fluttered lightly
down through the air and caught on the branch of a tree. The young
man seized it, and beheld a pink ribbon.

"My Faith is gone!" cried he, after one stupefied moment.
"There is no good on earth; and sin is but a name. Come, devil; for
270 to thee is this world given."

And, maddened with despair, so that he laughed loud and long,
did Goodman Brown grasp his staff and set forth again, at such a rate
that he seemed to fly along the forest path rather than to walk or run.
The road grew wilder and drearier and more faintly traced, and vanished at length, leaving him in the heart of the dark wilderness, still
rushing onward with the instinct that guides mortal man to evil. The
whole forest was peopled with frightful sounds—the creaking of the
trees, the howling of wild beasts, and the yell of Indians; while sometimes the wind tolled like a distant church bell, and sometimes gave a
280 broad roar around the traveller, as if all Nature were laughing him to
scorn. But he was himself the chief horror of the scene, and shrank
not from its other horrors.

"Ha! ha! ha!" roared Goodman Brown when the wind laughed
at him. "Let us hear which will laugh loudest. Think not to frighten
me with your deviltry. Come witch, come wizard, come Indian pow-
wow, come devil himself, and here comes Goodman Brown. You may
as well fear him as he fear you."

In truth, all through the haunted forest there could be nothing
more frightful than the figure of Goodman Brown. On he flew among
290 the black pines, brandishing his staff with frenzied gestures, now giving vent to an inspiration of horrid blasphemy, and now shouting
forth such laughter as set all the echoes of the forest laughing like
demons around him. The fiend in his own shape is less hideous than
when he rages in the breast of man. Thus sped the demoniac on his
course, until, quivering among the trees, he saw a red light before
him, as when the felled trunks and branches of a clearing have been

set on fire, and throw up their lurid blaze against the sky, at the hour of midnight. He paused, in a lull of the tempest that had driven him onward, and heard the swell of what seemed a hymn, rolling
300 solemnly from a distance with the weight of many voices. He knew the tune; it was a familiar one in the choir of the village meeting-house. The verse died heavily away, and was lengthened by a chorus, not of human voices, but of all the sounds of the benighted wilderness pealing in awful harmony together. Goodman Brown cried out, and his cry was lost to his own ear by its unison with the cry of the desert.

In the interval of silence he stole forward until the light glared full upon his eyes. At one extremity of an open space, hemmed in by the dark wall of the forest, arose a rock, bearing some rude, natural
310 resemblance either to an altar or a pulpit, and surrounded by four blazing pines, their tops aflame, their stems untouched, like candles at an evening meeting. The mass of foliage that had overgrown the summit of the rock was all on fire, blazing high into the night and fitfully illuminating the whole field. Each pendant twig and leafy festoon was in a blaze. As the red light arose and fell, a numerous congregation alternately shone forth, then disappeared in shadow, and again grew, as it were, out of the darkness, peopling the heart of the solitary woods at once.

"A grave and dark-clad company," quoth Goodman Brown.

320 In truth they were such. Among them, quivering to and fro between gloom and splendor, appeared faces that would be seen next day at the council board of the province, and others which, Sabbath after Sabbath, looked devoutly heavenward, and benignantly over the crowded pews, from the holiest pulpits in the land. Some affirm that the lady of the governor was there. At least there were high dames well known to her, and wives of honored husbands, and widows, a great multitude, and ancient maidens, all of excellent repute, and fair young girls, who trembled lest their mothers should espy them. Either the sudden gleams of light flashing over the obscure field bedazzled
330 Goodman Brown, or he recognized a score of the church members of Salem village famous for their especial sanctity. Good old Deacon Gookin had arrived, and waited at the skirts of that venerable saint, his revered pastor. But, irreverently consorting with these grave, reputable, and pious people, these elders of the church, these chaste dames and dewy virgins, there were men of dissolute lives and women of spotted fame, wretches given over to all mean and filthy vice, and suspected even of horrid crimes. It was strange to see that the good shrank not from the wicked, nor were the sinners abashed by the saints. Scattered also among their pale-faced enemies were the Indian
340 priests, or powwows, who had often scared their native forest with more hideous incantations than any known to English witchcraft.

"But where is Faith?" thought Goodman Brown; and, as hope came into his heart, he trembled.

Another verse of the hymn arose, a slow and mournful strain, such as the pious love, but joined to words which expressed all that our nature can conceive of sin, and darkly hinted at far more. Unfathomable to mere mortals is the lore of fiends. Verse after verse was sung; and still the chorus of the desert swelled between like the deepest tone of a mighty organ; and with the final peal of that dreadful

350   anthem there came a sound, as if the roaring wind, the rushing streams, the howling beasts, and every other voice of the unconcerted wilderness were mingling and according with the voice of guilty man in homage to the prince of all. The four blazing pines threw up a loftier flame, and obscurely discovered shapes and visages of horror on the smoke wreaths above the impious assembly. At the same moment the fire on the rock shot redly forth and formed a glowing arch above its base, where now appeared a figure. With reverence be it spoken, the figure bore no slight similitude, both in garb and manner, to some grave divine of the New England churches.

360   "Bring forth the converts!" cried a voice that echoed through the field and rolled into the forest.

At the word, Goodman Brown stepped forth from the shadow of the trees and approached the congregation, with whom he felt a loathful brotherhood by the sympathy of all that was wicked in his heart. He could have well-nigh sworn that the shape of his own dead father beckoned him to advance, looking downward from a smoke wreath, while a woman, with dim features of despair, threw out her hand to warn him back. Was it his mother? But he had no power to retreat one step, nor to resist, even in thought, when the minister and

370   good old Deacon Gookin seized his arms and led him to the blazing rock. Thither came also the slender form of a veiled female, led between Goody Cloyse, that pious teacher of the catechism, and Martha Carrier, who had received the devil's promise to be queen of hell. A rampant hag was she. And there stood the proselytes beneath the canopy of fire.

"Welcome, my children," said the dark figure, "to the communion of your race. Ye have found thus young your nature and your destiny. My children, look behind you!"

They turned; and flashing forth, as it were, in a sheet of flame,

380   the fiend worshippers were seen; the smile of welcome gleamed darkly on every visage.

"There," resumed the sable form, "are all whom ye have reverenced from youth. Ye deemed them holier than yourselves, and shrank from your own sin, contrasting it with their lives of righteousness and prayerful aspirations heavenward. Yet here are they all in my worshipping assembly. This night it shall be granted you to know their secret deeds: how hoary-bearded elders of the church have whispered wanton words to the young maids of their households; how many a woman, eager for widows' weeds, has given her husband a

390   drink at bedtime and let him sleep his last sleep in her bosom; how beardless youths have made haste to inherit their fathers' wealth; and

how fair damsels—blush not, sweet ones—have dug little graves in
the garden, and bidden me, the sole guest to an infant's funeral. By
the sympathy of your human hearts for sin ye shall scent out all the
places—whether in church, bed-chamber, street, field, or forest—
where crime has been committed, and shall exult to behold the whole
earth one stain of guilt, one mighty blood spot. Far more than this. It
shall be yours to penetrate, in every bosom, the deep mystery of sin,
the fountain of all wicked arts, and which inexhaustibly supplies
400   more evil impulses than human power—than my power at its
utmost—can make manifest in deeds. And now, my children, look
upon each other."

They did so; and, by the blaze of the hell-kindled torches, the
wretched man beheld his Faith, and the wife her husband, trembling
before that unhallowed altar.

"Lo, there ye stand, my children," said the figure, in a deep and
solemn tone, almost sad with its despairing awfulness, as if his once
angelic nature could yet mourn for our miserable race. "Depending
upon one another's hearts, ye had still hoped that virtue were not all
410   a dream. Now are ye undeceived. Evil is the nature of mankind. Evil
must be your only happiness. Welcome again, my children, to the
communion of your race."

"Welcome," repeated the fiend worshippers, in one cry of despair and triumph.

And there they stood, the only pair, as it seemed, who were yet
hesitating on the verge of wickedness in this dark world. A basin was
hollowed, naturally, in the rock. Did it contain water, reddened by
the lurid light? or was it blood? or, perchance, a liquid flame? Herein
did the shape of evil dip his hand and prepare to lay the mark of bap-
420   tism upon their foreheads, that they might be partakers of the mystery of sin, more conscious of the secret guilt of others, both in deed
and thought, than they could now be of their own. The husband cast
one look at his pale wife, and Faith at him. What polluted wretches
would the next glance show them to each other, shuddering alike at
what they disclosed and what they saw!

"Faith! Faith!" cried the husband, "look up to heaven, and resist
the wicked one."

Whether Faith obeyed he knew not. Hardly had he spoken when
he found himself amid calm night and solitude, listening to a roar of
430   the wind which died heavily away through the forest. He staggered
against the rock, and felt it chill and damp; while a hanging twig,
that had been all on fire, besprinkled his cheek with the coldest dew.

The next morning young Goodman Brown came slowly into the
street of Salem village, staring around him like a bewildered man.
The good old minister was taking a walk along the graveyard to get
an appetite for breakfast and meditate his sermon, and bestowed a
blessing, as he passed, on Goodman Brown. He shrank from the venerable saint as if to avoid an anathema. Old Deacon Gookin was at

domestic worship, and the holy words of his prayer were heard
440   through the open window. "What God doth the wizard pray to?"
quoth Goodman Brown. Goody Cloyse, that excellent old Christian,
stood in the early sunshine at her own lattice, catechizing a little girl
who had brought her a pint of morning's milk. Goodman Brown
snatched away the child as from the grasp of the fiend himself. Turning the corner by the meeting-house, he spied the head of Faith, with
the pink ribbons, gazing anxiously forth, and bursting into such joy
at sight of him that she skipped along the street and almost kissed her
husband before the whole village. But Goodman Brown looked
sternly and sadly into her face, and passed on without a greeting.
450   Had Goodman Brown fallen asleep in the forest and only
dreamed a wild dream of a witch-meeting?

Be it so if you will; but, alas! it was a dream of evil omen for
young Goodman Brown. A stern, a sad, a darkly meditative, a distrustful, if not a desperate man did he become from the night of that
fearful dream. On the Sabbath day, when the congregation were singing a holy psalm, he could not listen because an anthem of sin rushed
loudly upon his ear and drowned all the blessed strain. When the
minister spoke from the pulpit with power and fervid eloquence, and,
with his hand on the open Bible, of the sacred truths of our religion,
460   and of saint-like lives and triumphant deaths, and of future bliss or
misery unutterable, then did Goodman Brown turn pale, dreading lest
the roof should thunder down upon the gray blasphemer and his
hearers. Often, waking suddenly at midnight, he shrank from the
bosom of Faith; and at morning or eventide, when the family knelt
down at prayer, he scowled and muttered to himself, and gazed
sternly at his wife, and turned away. And when he had lived long,
and was borne to his grave a hoary corpse, followed by Faith, an
aged woman, and children and grandchildren, a goodly procession,
besides neighbors not a few, they carved no hopeful verse upon his
470   tombstone, for his dying hour was gloom.

The Narrator

Who tells the story of "Young Goodman Brown"? The obvious, but misleading, answer would be, "Nathaniel Hawthorne."
Hawthorne *wrote* the tale, true enough, but we must separate the
author from the character that tells the story. This is a simple but
very important point. Nathaniel Hawthorne the author is not *omniscient;* that is, he cannot know everything—just as you could not
know of two actions that are going on in different parts of the
world at the same time, and just as you cannot know all of the
secrets of the human heart.

Narrators in fiction, however, can know anything that their authors want them to know. For example, in lines 32–33, the narrator says, "With this excellent resolve for the future, Goodman Brown felt himself justified in making more haste on his present evil purpose." So the narrator knows something that the mere observer could not possibly know, for the narrator can see into the character's mind.

First person narration. When a character *in* a story is also the narrator, we have first person narration. (The pronoun *I* is first person singular.)

Here is the first paragraph of Charles Dickens' *Great Expectations,* in which the main character tells his own story:

> My father's family name being Pirrip, and my Christian name Philip, my infant tongue could make of both names nothing longer or more explicit than Pip. So I called myself Pip, and came to be called Pip.

The first person narrator is limited; he cannot read minds or take a godlike view of all that happens everywhere. In first person narration, the story we read is "viewed" through the mind of the narrator.

Third person narration. The third person pronouns are *she, he, it,* and *they,* and we use them to report what others did. In making fictional "reports," the third person narrator can be either a camera, recording the sights and sounds within his or her range, or a godlike being who knows all and sees all—perceiving actions that take place simultaneously on opposite sides of the earth, knowing the innermost thoughts and feelings of the characters. On the other hand, the third person narrator can take a position between these extremes, knowing more than a mere mortal could, but not having a godlike omniscience. The narrator in "Young Goodman Brown" seems to occupy this middle position.

In *The Plumed Serpent,* by D. H. Lawrence, the narrator is omniscient:

> Cipriano sat motionless as a statue. But from his breast came that dark, surging passion of tenderness the Indians are capable of. Perhaps it would pass, leaving him indifferent and fatalistic again. But at any rate for the moment he sat in a dark, fiery cloud of passionate male tenderness. He looked at her soft, wet white hands over her face, and at the one big emerald on her finger, in a sort of wonder. The wonder, the mystery, the magic that used to flood over him as a boy and a youth, when he kneeled before the babyish figure of the Santa Maria de la Soledad, flooded him again. He was in the presence

of the goddess, white-handed, mysterious, gleaming with a moon-like power and the intense potency of grief.

Narrative point of view is one of the major factors in creating the magic of a story. When we hear someone tell a story, face to face, we can easily sense the personality and skill of the teller and understand how these factors permeate and shape the narrative. Though the personality of the teller is not so obvious in stories that we read, nonetheless there is a fictional person who does the telling and who shapes our attitudes and expectations. Sometimes this teller is a hazy, impersonal figure whom we don't get to know very well, as in the case of the narrator of "Young Goodman Brown." Sometimes the teller is vividly realized.

Point of View

1. Characterize the narrators as they appear in the following selections. Some questions you might ask yourself are these: (1) Who is the narrator? That is, what is the narrative point of view? Is it a first person or a third person narration? (2) What are the narrator's values and what is the tone of the narration? Cynical? Naive? Sincere? (3) What narrative devices are used to establish contact with the reader? For example, does the narrator address the reader directly? (4) What is the "voice" of the narrator? That of a child? A foreigner? An educated person? An imbecile?

a.   You don't know about me without you have read a book by the name of *The Adventures of Tom Sawyer;* but that ain't no matter. That book was made by Mr. Mark Twain, and he told the truth mainly. There was things which he stretched, but mainly he told the truth. That is nothing. I never seen anybody but lied one time or another, without it was Aunt Polly, or the Widow, or maybe Mary. Aunt Polly—Tom's Aunt Polly, she is—and Mary, and the Widow Douglas is all told about in that book, which is mostly a true book, with some stretchers, as I said before.

—Mark Twain, *The Adventures of Huckleberry Finn*

b.   Krebs went to the war from a Methodist college in Kansas. There is a picture which shows him among his fraternity brothers, all of them wearing exactly the same height and style collar. He enlisted in the Marines in 1917 and did not return to the United States until the second division returned from the Rhine in the summer of 1919.

There is a picture which shows him on the Rhine with two German girls and another corporal. Krebs and the corporal look too big for their uniforms. The German girls are not beautiful. The Rhine does not show in the picture.

—Ernest Hemingway, "Soldier's Home"

c.   To begin with I wish to disclaim the possession of those high gifts of imagination and expression which would have enabled my pen to create for the reader the personality of the man who called himself, after the Russian custom, Cyril son of Isidor—Kirylo Sidorovitch—Razumov.

If I have ever had these gifts in any sort of living form they have been smothered out of existence a long time ago under a wilderness of words. Words, as is well known, are the great foes of reality. I have been for many years a teacher of languages. It is an occupation which at length becomes fatal to whatever share of imagination, observation, and insight an ordinary person may be heir to. To a teacher of languages there comes a time when the world is but a place of many words and man appears a mere talking animal not much more wonderful than a parrot.

This being so, I could not have observed Mr. Razumov or guessed at his reality by the force of insight, much less have imagined him as he was. Even to invent the mere bald facts of his life would have been utterly beyond my powers. But I think that without this declaration the readers of these pages will be able to detect in the story the marks of documentary evidence. And that is perfectly correct. It is based on a document; all I have brought to it is my knowledge of the Russian language, which is sufficient for what is attempted here. The document, of course, is something in the nature of a journal, a diary, yet not exactly that in its actual form. For instance, most of it was not written up from day to day, though all the entries are dated. Some of these entries cover months of time and extend over dozens of pages. All the earlier part is a retrospect, in a narrative form, relating to an event which took place about a year before.

I must mention that I have lived for a long time in Geneva. A whole quarter of that town, on account of many Russians residing there, is called La Petite Russie—Little Russia. I had a rather extensive connexion in little Russia at that time. Yet I confess that I have no comprehension of the Russian character. The illogicality of their attitude, the arbitrariness of their conclusions, the frequency of the exceptional, should present no difficulty to a student of many grammars; but there must be something else in the way, some special human trait—one of those subtle differences that are beyond the ken of mere professors. What must remain striking to a teacher of languages is the Russians' extraordinary love of words. They gather them up; they cherish them, but they don't hoard them in their breasts; on the contrary, they are always ready to pour them out by the hour or by the night with an enthusiasm, a sweeping abundance, with such an aptness of application sometimes that, as in the case of very accomplished parrots, one can't defend oneself from the suspicion that they really understand what they say. There is a generosity in their ardour of speech which removes it as far as possible from common loquacity; and it is ever too disconnected to be classed as eloquence. . . . . But I must apologize for this digression.

—Joseph Conrad, *Under Western Eyes*

d.   Alice was beginning to get very tired of sitting by her sister on the bank, and of having nothing to do: once or twice she had peeped into the book her sister was reading, but it had no pictures or conversations in it, "and what is the use of a book," thought Alice, "without pictures or conversations?"

So she was considering in her own mind (as well as she could, for the hot

day made her feel very sleepy and stupid), whether the pleasure of making a
daisy-chain would be worth the trouble of getting up and picking the daisies,
when suddenly a White Rabbit with pink eyes ran close by her.

There was nothing so very remarkable in that; nor did Alice think it so
very much out of the way to hear the Rabbit say to itself ''Oh dear! Oh dear! I
shall be too late!'' (when she thought it over afterwards, it occurred to her that
she ought to have wondered at this, but at the time it all seemed quite
natural); but when the Rabbit actually *took a watch out of its waistcoat-pocket*,
and looked at it, Alice started to her feet, for it flashed across her mind that
she had never before seen a rabbit with either a waistcoat-pocket, or a watch
to take out of it, and, burning with curiosity, she ran across the field after it,
and was just in time to see it pop down a large rabbit-hole under the hedge.

—Lewis Carroll, *Alice's Adventures in Wonderland*

2. Answer and discuss the following questions about the narrator of
''Young Goodman Brown.''

    a. In lines 32–33 of the story, the narrative viewpoint changes.
Explain that change. What happens? (Compare lines 32–33 with
the first 31 lines.)

    b. Perhaps you feel that ''Young Goodman Brown'' is ambiguous.
Was the experience real, or was it a dream? Explain how the
narrative viewpoint helps create the ambiguity. (See, for instance, lines 64–68.)

    c. The narrator holds certain values. What are they? How do you
know? For instance, how do you know that the narrator is a
devout Christian? How do these values help shape the story?

    d. Characterize the ''voice'' of the narrator. What evidence do you
have for this characterization?

*Make notes of your answers to these questions, for you will have use for
your ideas later.*

The Theme

Most works of literature have a theme; they are "about" something. The plot of a story is what happens. The *theme* of a story is
the deeper meaning, the idea that underlies the narrative. The plot
of "Young Goodman Brown" concerns a young man's experience
with the Devil. The theme of the story concerns the loss of innocence; it might be stated like this: The loss of innocence through
the discovery of humanity's wickedness is one of the great tragedies
of life.

When you write about literature, you need an organizational pivot for your essay—a thesis that will allow you to begin, a point of departure, something to work *from*. The theme of the work that you are discussing can well serve as the basis for your essay. For example, if you can state the theme of a work of literature, then you can ask how that theme was developed, and your answer to that question will be your essay.

This is a simple but important point. Which of the following two statements would better serve to get an essay under way?

"Young Goodman Brown" is about a young man's visit to a witches' sabbath.
"Young Goodman Brown" is about the tragedy of the loss of innocence.

To demonstrate the first statement, about all one could do would be to retell the story. To discuss the second statement—which is the theme of the story—one would have to analyze and interpret the work. So the second statement will produce more subject matter than the first.

For example, here is one of Aesop's fables:

The Wolf and the Lamb

Once upon a time a Wolf was lapping at a spring on a hillside, when, looking up, what should he see but a Lamb just beginning to drink a little lower down. "There's my supper," thought he, "if only I can find some excuse to seize it." Then he called out to the Lamb, "How dare you muddle the water from which I am drinking?"

"Nay, master, nay," said Lambikin; "if the water be muddy up there, I cannot be the cause of it, for it runs down from you to me."

"Well, then," said the Wolf, "Why did you call me bad names this time last year?"

"That cannot be," said the Lamb; "I am only six months old."

"I don't care," snarled the Wolf; "if it was not you it was your father"; and with that he rushed upon the poor little Lamb and—*warra warra warra warra warra*—ate her all up. But before she died she gasped out:

"ANY EXCUSE WILL SERVE A TYRANT."

The fable ends with a moral, some lesson that should be learned from it: "Any excuse will serve a tyrant." This moral is very near to the theme, which might be stated thus: In tyranny there is no law except the whim of the tyrant.

Exercise

1. What are the themes of the following fables?

Androcles

A slave named Androcles once escaped from his master and fled to the forest. As he was wandering about there, he came upon a Lion lying down moaning and groaning. At first he turned to flee, but finding that the Lion did not pursue him, he turned back and went up to him. As he came near, the Lion put out his paw, which was all swollen and bleeding, and Androcles found that a huge thorn had got into it and was causing all the pain. He pulled out the thorn and bound up the paw of the Lion, who was soon able to rise and lick the hand of Androcles like a dog. Then the Lion took Androcles to his cave, and every day used to bring him meat from which to live. But shortly afterward, both Androcles and the Lion were captured, and the slave was sentenced to be thrown to the Lion, after the latter had been kept without food for several days. The Emperor and all his Court came to see the spectacle, and Androcles was led out into the middle of the arena. Soon the Lion was let loose from his den and rushed bounding and roaring toward his victim. But as soon as he came near to Androcles, he recognized his friend and fawned upon him and licked his hands like a friendly dog. The Emperor, surprised at this, summoned Androcles to him, who told him the whole story. Whereupon the slave was pardoned and was set free, and the Lion was let loose to his native forest.

Belling the Cat

Long ago, the mice had a general council to consider what measures they could take to outwit their common enemy, the Cat. Some said this, and some said that; but at last a young mouse got up and said he had a proposal to make which he thought would meet the case. "You will all agree," said he, "that our chief danger consists in the sly and treacherous manner in which the enemy approaches us. Now, if we could receive some signal of her approach, we could easily escape from her. I venture, therefore, to propose that a small bell be procured and attached by a ribbon round the neck of the Cat. By this means we should always know when she was about and could easily retire while she was in the neighborhood."

This proposal met with general applause, until an old mouse got up and said, "That is all very well, but who is to bell the Cat?" The mice looked at one another and nobody spoke. Then the old mouse said. . . .

2. What is the theme of the following tale from Native American lore?

Assemoka, the Singer of Sweet Songs

(From the Mississaugas Indian)

"Long, long ago two brothers lived together in an Indian village on the shore of a great lake. One was a hunter, swift of foot, strong of arm, and keen of eye. Whenever his arrow darted through the air, something fell dead, with the result that there was never any hunger nor cold in the tepee where he lived. The other brother, Assemoka, was a dreamer whose feet never pursued the fleeing deer, whose arm never hurled the deadly club nor let loose the whirring string of the bow. Instead of following the trail where the deer fled, he remained at home, doing all needful things and dreaming strange dreams which were full of high, sweet songs.

As time went by, this quiet dreamer grew discontented. "Alas," said he, "here I stay forever in one spot, dreaming dreams. In my dreams creatures sing. I must go far away into the world and find these singers and sing with them."

"Brother," said Assemoka the next morning, "I am going away on a long journey."

"Foolish fellow," said the brother. "You will be wiser if you stay right here where there is peace and plenty. You would not go far before something or other would lead you astray."

"I am going away just the same," said Assemoka.

"Very well," replied his brother. "When you need me, tell the wind and I shall come to you."

Assemoka had not traveled many miles before he came to two trees that bent over the lake. One tree had been blown down and lay heavily on the trunk of the other. When the wind blew, it rubbed back and forth and chanted a high, shrill song.

"I-iu, I-iu," it sang. "I-iu, I-iu!"

Assemoka listened as if he had fallen under a spell. "It is beautiful," he cried. "I want to be the tree that gives forth such sweet music."

"Oh, no, no," groaned the tree. "Don't say that. I am not happy at all. I am very sad indeed in spite of the shrill, clear song I sing."

Just then the wind blew and the tree began to sing, "I-iu" again in so shrill and clear a voice that Assemoka, in spite of the warning, shoved it aside and took its place, letting the fallen tree rest on his own bosom. Once again the wind blew strongly, but no sound came forth as the heavy trunk sawed back and forth across Assemoka's chest.

"Alas," he cried in his pain, "this song is not for me to sing. Only sorrow has come to me for trying to do another's work."

In his tepee the brother heard Assemoka's cry and came to him. "It is just as I told you," he said as he lifted off the fallen tree and cast it into the brush. "Now you must come back home with me."

"No, no," said Assemoka. "I must go on another journey. I have not seen the other singers in the world."

"Very well," agreed the brother. "If you need me, tell the wind and I shall come to you."

Before long Assemoka came to a swift stream in which a long stick, whose end was driven into the mud, was whirled round and round by the current. As it sped through the water, the stick sang a shrill, clear song. "I-iu!" it sang, "I-iu! I-iu!"

Assemoka stood and listened. "It is beautiful," he cried. "I have heard it in my dreams. I want to be that stick and sing its song there in the swift waters."

"Oh, no, no," begged the stick. "Do not wish that. Although I sing a shrill, clear song I am most unhappy. It is so lonesome here in the swift water. Nothing comes to visit me but the pale blue dragon fly."

"I like the song you sing," cried Assemoka. "I shall take your place." In a second he had plunged into the stream. Round and round he swung with a dull swish, swish, as the swift waters raced by.

"Alas," he cried, half smothered by the white foam, "where is the shrill, clear song of the stick? Can it be that once again I have learned that I cannot sing another's song?"

Assemoka's brother heard the high wail and came and stood on the bank. "Brother," said he, "it is just as I said. Now you see clearly that you must sing your own song. For every song there is a singer and for every singer a song. Come forth, now, and let us sit down here on the bank and take counsel together."

When the brother had drawn Assemoka from the water, the two sat in silence long hours. Below them stretched the reedy margin of the river. "Assemoka," said the brother at last, "listen to the music of the wind among the reeds. What the breath of the wind does, you can do also. It is true that you have a singing soul, but it is I who must give you the means to sing; thus must the mighty hunters and the strong of arm protect the dreamer and the singers of song."

As he spoke, the brother cut off a stout reed and fashioned it with his stone knife. Swiftly he fitted a mouthpiece and a tongue and gave it to Assemoka.

"Blow on it, my brother," said he. "In it is the song that you wish to sing, the song of your sweetest dream."

It was so. No sooner did the lips of Assemoka touch the slender reed than the air was full of song as if a thousand birds fluttered by on happy wings.

"Come now," said the brother, "let the birds sing in the wilderness, for that is their appointed place; but you must sing close to the ears of men in the lodges of the braves and around the camp fires where the old people and the children sit."

Structure

Theme emerges from the imaginative structure of a work of literature; it is seldom stated directly. The structure of any narrative consists of three elements: *plot* (the actions or events of the story), *characters*, and *scenes*. Our understanding of a work comes about when we discover how these elements of structure—as controlled by the narrator—relate to form a whole.

Plot

In its simplest form, a story is nothing more than a series of events: first this happened, then that, and then the other. But this sort of narrative seldom interests anyone except children, who seem insatiable in their curiosity about "What happened next?" "And then what?"—that's the most basic response to a story.

However, as one matures, another question becomes just as important as "Then what?": the question "Why?" A very simple story—"First the king died, and then the queen died"—can be given a very simple plot through the addition of *motivation*, the reason for the events: "First the king died, and then the queen died *of grief*." Now we know *why* the queen died.

Most often questions regarding motivation relate to character. However, natural disasters, fate, the will of the gods, or mere chance can provide motivation.

Exercise

Write a plot synopsis of "Young Goodman Brown." In this, you will outline the major episodes (events) in the story and explain *why* they come about.

Character

In the attempt to understand and explain the characters in a story, we can ask questions regarding:

actions:	What do the characters do? Do they have any typical or identifying actions? What parts do the characters play in the plot?
motivation:	Why do the characters do what they do?
appearance:	What does the character look and dress like?
manner of talking:	How does the character talk?
scene:	Does the character appear in or is the character associated with any particular scene?

One of the chief reasons for the effectiveness of literature is the people that we get to know through it. Ahab and Ishmael, Don Quixote, Becky Sharp, Emma Bovary, King Lear, Dorothea Brooke,

Walter Mitty—all of these characters have entered into the imaginative life of people who have read *Moby Dick, Dox Quixote, Vanity Fair, Madame Bovary, King Lear, Middlemarch,* and "The Secret Life of Walter Mitty."

Exercise

Make and *keep* notes regarding the characters in "Young Goodman Brown." Ask yourself about *actions, motivation, appearance, manner of talking,* and *scene.* Ask yourself, furthermore, if any of these factors influences others. For instance, when the scene changes in the story, does the manner of talking also change?

Scene

In fiction, scene is frequently very important, as it is in "Young Goodman Brown." The forest that Goodman Brown enters is literally a gloomy and dangerous place, but it is also symbolically the "forest of evil." (We will discuss symbols later.)

In real life, tragedy can take place on a sunny spring morning, with the birds chirping and cherry trees in bloom, but in fiction, scene is often symbolic: the place is matched to the action. (Think of the movies: very seldom do the scene and the action clash in emotional content.) Here are the first two paragraphs of *The Return of the Native,* by Thomas Hardy. On the basis of this description of the scene of the novel, one can predict the emotional tone of the book:

A Saturday afternoon in November was approaching the time of twilight, and the vast tract of unenclosed wild known as Egdon Heath embrowned itself moment by moment. Overhead the hollow stretch of whitish cloud shutting out the sky was a tent which had the whole earth for its floor.

The heaven being spread with this pallid screen and the earth with the darkest vegetation, their meeting-line at the horizon was clearly marked. In such contrast the heath wore the appearance of an instalment of night which had taken up its place before its astronomical hour was come: darkness had to a great extent arrived hereon, while day stood distinct in the sky. Looking upwards, a furze-cutter would have been inclined to continue work; looking down, he would have decided to finish his faggot and go home. The distant rims of the world and of the firmament seemed to be a division in time no less than a division in matter. The face of the heath by its mere complexion added half an hour to evening; it could in like manner retard the dawn, sadden noon, anticipate the frowning of storms scarcely generated, and intensify the opacity of a moonless midnight to a cause of shaking and dread.

Writing a Story

You might now want to try your hand at writing a story. If you can't think of anything to write about, try the following exercise, which should get you under way in the process of creating an imaginative universe. The exercise is based on this passage from *Ecclesiastes:*

> I returned, and saw under the sun, that the race is not to the swift, nor the battle to the strong, neither yet bread to the wise, nor yet riches to men of understanding, nor yet favour to men of skill; but time and chance happeneth to them all.

The theme of this passage will be your theme.

1. Choose an instance from your life that seems to illustrate the theme—an occasion when someone you considered undeserving gained success of some kind. The event should be one that had great meaning for you, that took on great importance in your own life, that caused you bitter disappointment. Briefly narrate that incident "like it was," making no attempt to tell anything but what actually happened as clearly as you can.
2. Choose a narrative viewpoint, and create a narrator for your story. For the purposes of this exercise, don't assume that you are the narrator. Imagine someone else who will tell the story. The speaker might be someone who was involved (excluding yourself) or an onlooker who knew what happened but didn't participate. It might be a good friend or a psychiatrist to whom you told the story. You might have a very wise or a very foolish speaker, and the speaker could be young or old, male or female. In two or three paragraphs, characterize this speaker. Who is he or she? What sort of person? Relationship to you? Remember that your speaker can be based on some actual person or can be completely imaginary.
3. You have already told your story as it happened. Now make any changes that you feel will make it more dramatic. You have no obligation to stick to the facts of the case; what you want is a plot that will best convey your theme. The result may be almost identical with the actual event or almost completely different. As

briefly as you can (without sacrificing pertinent details), write a plot outline. Remember that you can change the actual event as much as you like in order to construct a satisfactory plot.

4. Now sketch the characters who are to play roles in your story. Some of them may be flat, always reacting in exactly the same predictable way. You should be able to present each character in one paragraph. Concentrate on showing the reader those aspects of the character that will be useful to you in the story. For instance, one character may never say a word, but merely be a threatening presence in the story; in this case, we must know why he or she seems threatening. Another character may have a mannerism that is important. And so on.

5. Now sketch (in words) a scene in which your drama can take place. The scene should contribute to the total effect of your story.

6. You now have all the elements for a story. Write it.

Symbols

Both *signs* and *symbols* convey meanings, but they are different in their functions. Signs stand in lieu of their objects or referents. For example, a red light at an intersection can be either a sign or a symbol. If it causes pedestrians and drivers to stop, it is merely a sign. But if it triggers the idea of "danger" in the minds of drivers and pedestrians, it is a symbol.

As readers, we should realize that characters, actions, and scenes may be taken either literally or symbolically. Faith is literally Goodman Brown's wife, but she is symbolically the principle of faith. At the literal level, Goodman Brown's walk is merely a trip into a forest, but at the symbolic level, the journey is from innocence to the knowledge of human wickedness. And the forest is on the one hand just a forest, but on the other, it is the place deep in the human heart where wickedness lies.

Exercise

Find and explain other symbols in "Young Goodman Brown." In your opinion, which symbols are the most important? Explain.

Metaphors

On pages 425–30, you will find a complete discussion of metaphors, which are essentially comparisons. For example,

> Inside its cocoon of work or social obligation, the human spirit slumbers for the most part, registering the distinction between pleasure and pain, but not nearly as alert as we pretend.
>
> —E. M. Forster, *A Passage to India*

Forster compares the human spirit to a pupa in its cocoon, alive but inert, barely sensible of changes in the environment, but, nonetheless, having the potential to come forth as a butterfly.

Since all writers use metaphor, you must understand this figure of speech if you are to gain meaning from prose (fiction or nonfiction) and poetry. If you have trouble dealing with metaphor in your reading, turn now to pages 425–30 of this book.

Toward the Interpretive Essay

An essay that interprets a work of literature tells first what the work is about, that is, explains the theme. Second, the essay explains how the theme or meaning is developed. The body of an interpretive essay is an *explication* of a piece of literature.

At this point, you have gathered a large number of ideas concerning "Young Goodman Brown." Your notes concern *the narrator* (the teller of the tale), *the theme* (the meaning of the story or the ideas that it is about), *the structure* (including plot, characters, and scene), *symbols,* and *metaphors*. You should be ready to start putting together an interpretation.

A final series of questions will help you understand the story more fully.

1. How do you know the work is what it is? (If you say that the work is a story, then you should be able to "point to" the features that bring you to that conclusion.)
2. What is its meaning? Can you state its theme? How does it convey its meaning? Plot? Scene? Character? Symbols? Direct statements?
3. What is its structure? Does it have parts? What are they?
4. How is it different from other works of literature with which you are familiar? How much could it be changed and still be the same kind of thing?
5. How did you go about gaining your understanding of the work?

(Understanding of a complex work does not come in a flash but grows through analysis and thought.) How is your understanding of the work growing?

6. What are the various artistic devices in the different sections of the work?
7. How does the work relate to other kinds of statements concerning its theme? (Theological, sociological, biological, psychological, and philosophic statements concerning the loss of innocence would differ in significant ways from "Young Goodman Brown.")
8. How does the work fit into or square with your understanding of life? Does it contradict or reinforce your value system?

An Interpretation of "Young Goodman Brown"

Now that you have thought about and discussed "Young Goodman Brown," it might interest you to read what a professional critic and scholar has to say about the tale.

Ambiguity and Clarity in Hawthorne's "Young Goodman Brown"

Richard H. Fogle

"Young Goodman Brown" is generally felt to be one of Hawthorne's more difficult tales, from the ambiguity of the conclusions which may be drawn from it. Its hero, a naïve young man who accepts both society in general and his fellowmen as individuals at their own valuation, is in one terrible night presented with the vision of human Evil, and is ever afterwards "A stern, a sad, a darkly meditative, a distrustful, if not a desperate man . . . ," whose "dying hour was gloom." So far we are clear enough, but there are confusing factors. In the first place, are the events of the night merely subjective, a dream; or do they actually occur? Again, at the crucial point in his ordeal Goodman Brown summons the strength to cry to his wife Faith, "look up to heaven, and resist the evil one." It would appear from this that he has successfully resisted the supreme temptation—but evidently he is not therefore saved. Henceforth, "On the Sabbath day, when the congregation were singing a holy psalm, he could not listen because an anthem of sin rushed loudly upon his ear and drowned all the blessed strain." On the other hand, he is not wholly lost, for in the sequel he is only at intervals estranged from "the

AMBIGUITY AND CLARITY IN HAWTHORNE'S "YOUNG GOODMAN BROWN"   Richard H. Fogle, *New England Quarterly*, 18 (Dec. 1943), 448–65. Reprinted by permission of *New England Quarterly* and the author.

bosom of Faith." Has Hawthorne himself failed to control the implications of his allegory?

I should say rather that these ambiguities of meaning are intentional, an integral part of his purpose. Hawthorne wishes to propose, not flatly that man is primarily evil, but instead the gnawing doubt lest this should indeed be true. "Come, devil; for to thee is this world given," exclaims Goodman Brown at the height of his agony, but he finds strength to resist the devil, and in the ambiguous conclusion he does not entirely reject his former faith. His trial, then, comes not from the certainty but the dread of Evil. Hawthorne poses the dangerous question of the relations of Good and Evil in man, but withholds his answer. Nor does he permit himself to settle whether the events of the night of trial are real or the mere figment of a dream.

These ambiguities he conveys and fortifies by what Yvor Winters has called "the formula of alternative possibilities," [1] and F. O. Matthiessen "the device of multiple choice," [2] in which are suggested two or more interpretations of a single action or event. Perhaps the most striking instance of the use of this device in "Young Goodman Brown" is the final word on the reality of the hero's night experience:

Had Goodman Brown fallen asleep in the forest and only dreamed a wild dream of a witch-meeting?

Be it so if you will; [3] but alas! it was a dream of evil omen for young Goodman Brown.

This device of multiple choice, or ambiguity, is the very essence of Hawthorne's tale. Nowhere does he permit us a simple meaning, a merely single interpretation. At the outset, young Goodman Brown leaves the arms of his wife Faith and the safe limits of Salem town to keep a mysterious appointment in the forest. Soon he encounters his conductor, a man "in grave and decent attire," commonplace enough save for an indefinable air of acquaintanceship with the great world. ". . . the only thing about him that could be fixed upon as remarkable was his staff, which bore the likeness of a great black snake, so curiously wrought that it might almost be seen to twist and wriggle itself like a living serpent. *This, of course, must have been an ocular deception, assisted by the uncertain light.*" [4]

This man is, of course, the Devil, who seeks to lure the still-

---

[1] *Maule's Curse* (Norfolk, Connecticut, 1938), 18. Mr. Winters limits his discussion of the device to Hawthorne's novels.

[2] *American Renaissance* (New York, 1941), 276.

[3] These and all subsequent italics are mine.

[4] Hawthorne may have taken this suggestion from the serpent-staff of Mercury. He later uses it for lighter purposes on at least two occasions in *A Wonder Book*. Mercury's staff is described by Epimetheus as "like two serpents twisting around a stick, and . . . carved so naturally that I, at first, thought the serpents were alive" ("The Paradise of Children"). Again, in "The Miraculous Pitcher," "Two snakes, carved in the wood, were represented as twining themselves about the staff, and were so very skilfully executed that old Philemon (whose eyes, you know, were getting rather dim) almost thought them alive, and that he could see them wriggling and twisting."

reluctant goodman to a witch-meeting. In the process he progressively undermines the young man's faith in the institutions and the men whom he has heretofore revered. First Goody Cloyse, "a very pious and exemplary dame, who had taught him his catechism in youth, and was still his moral and spiritual adviser," is shown to have more than casual acquaintance with the Devil—to be, in fact, a witch. Goodman Brown is shaken, but still minded to turn back and save himself. He is then faced with a still harder test. Just as he is about to return home, filled with self-applause, he hears the tramp of horses along the road:

On came the hoof tramps and the voices of the riders, two grave old voices, conversing soberly as they drew near. These mingled sounds appeared to pass along the road, within a few yards of the young man's hiding-place; *but, owing doubtless to the depth of the gloom at that particular spot, neither the travellers nor their steeds were visible. Though their figures brushed the small boughs by the wayside, it could not be seen that they intercepted, even for a moment, the faint gleam from the strip of bright sky athwart which they must have passed.* It vexed him the more, because he could have sworn, *were such a thing possible,* that he recognized the voices of the minister and Deacon Gookin, jogging along quietly, as they were wont to do, when bound to some ordination or ecclesiastical council.

The conversation of the minister and the deacon makes it only too clear that they also are in league with the evil one. Yet Goodman Brown, although now even more deeply dismayed, still resolves to stand firm, heartened by the blue arch of the sky and the stars brightening in it.[5] At that moment a cloud, "though no wind was stirring," hides the stars, and he hears a confused babble of voices. *"Once the listener fancied that he could distinguish* the accents of townspeople of his own . . . The next moment, so indistinct were the sounds, *he doubted whether he had heard aught* but the murmur of the old forest, whispering without a wind." But to his horror he believes that he hears the voice of his wife Faith, uttering only weak and insincere objections as she is borne through the air to the witch-meeting.

Now comes a circumstance which at first sight would appear to break the chain of ambiguities, for his suspicions seem concretely verified. A pink ribbon, which he remembers having seen in his wife's hair, comes fluttering down into his grasp. This ribbon, an apparently solid object like the fatal handkerchief in *Othello,* seems out of keeping with the atmosphere of doubt which has enveloped the preceding incidents.[6] Two considerations, however, make it possible to defend

---

[5] Cf. Bosola to the Duchess at a comparably tragic moment in Webster's *Duchess of Malfi:* "Look you, the stars shine still."

[6] "As long as what Brown saw is left wholly in the realm of hallucination, Hawthorne's created illusion is compelling. . . . Only the literal insistence on that damaging pink ribbon obtrudes the labels of a confining allegory, and short-circuits the range of association." Matthiessen, *American Renaissance,* 284.

it. One is that if Goodman Brown is dreaming, the ribbon like the rest may be taken as part-and-parcel of his dream. It is to be noted that this pink ribbon appears in his wife's hair once more as she meets him at his return to Salem in the morning. The other is that for the moment the ribbon vanishes from the story, melting into its shadowy background. Its impact is merely temporary.

Be it as you will, as Hawthorne would say. At any rate the effect on Goodman Brown is instantaneous and devastating. Casting aside all further scruples, he rages through the wild forest to the meeting of witches, for the time at least fully accepting the domination of Evil. He soon comes upon a "numerous congregation," alternately shadowy and clear in the flickering red light of four blazing pines above a central rock.

Among them, *quivering to and fro between gloom and splendor,* appeared faces that would be seen next day at the council board of the province, and others which, Sabbath after Sabbath, looked devoutly heavenward, and benignantly over the crowded pews, from the holiest pulpits in the land. *Some affirm that* the lady of the governor was there. . . . *Either the sudden gleams of light flashing over the obscure field bedazzled Goodman Brown, or he recognized* a score of the church members of Salem village famous for their especial sanctity.

Before this company steps out a presiding figure who bears "With reverence be it spoken . . . *no slight similitude,* both in garb and manner, to some grave divine of the New England churches," and calls forth the "converts." At the word young Goodman Brown comes forward. *"He could have well-nigh sworn that* the shape of his own dead father beckoned him to advance, looking downward from a smoke wreath, while a woman, with dim features of despair, threw out her hand to warn him back. *Was it his mother?"* But he is quickly seized and led to the rock, along with a veiled woman whom he dimly discerns to be his wife Faith. The two are welcomed by the dark and ambiguous leader into the fraternity of Evil, and the final, irretrievable step is prepared.

A basin was hollowed, naturally, in the rock. *Did it contain water, reddened by the lurid light? or was it blood? or, perchance, a liquid flame?* Herein did the shape of evil dip his hand and prepare to lay the mark of baptism upon their foreheads, that they might be partakers of the mystery of sin, more conscious of the secret guilt of others, both in deed and thought, than they could now be of their own. The husband cast one look at his pale wife, and Faith at him. What polluted wretches would the next glance show them to each other, shuddering alike at what they disclosed and what they saw!

"Faith! Faith!" cried the husband, "look up to heaven, and resist the wicked one."

Whether Faith obeyed he knew not.

Hawthorne then concludes with the central ambiguity, which we have already noticed, whether the events of the night were actual or a dream? The uses of this device, if so it may be called, are multiple in consonance with its nature. Primarily it offers opportunity for freedom and richness of suggestion. By it Hawthorne is able to suggest something of the density and incalculability of life, the difficulties which clog the interpretation of even the simplest incidents, the impossibility of achieving a single and certain insight into the actions and motives of others. This ambiguity adds depth and tone to Hawthorne's thin and delicate fabric. It covers the bareness of allegory, imparting to its one-to-one equivalence of object and idea a wider range of allusiveness, a hint of rich meaning still untapped. By means of it the thesis of "Young Goodman Brown" is made to inhere firmly in the situation, whence the reader himself must extract it to interpret. Hawthorne the artist refuses to limit himself to a single and doctrinaire conclusion,[7] proceeding instead by indirection. Further, it permits him to make free with the two opposed worlds of actuality and of imagination without incongruity or the need to commit himself entirely to either; while avoiding a frontal attack upon the reader's feeling for everyday verisimilitude, it affords the author licence of fancy. It allows him to draw upon sources of legend and superstition which still strike a responsive chord in us, possessing something of the validity of universal symbols.[8] Hawthorne's own definition of Romance may very aptly be applied to his use of ambiguity: it gives him scope "so [to] manage his atmospherical medium as to bring out or mellow the lights and deepen and enrich the shadows of the picture."[9]

These scanty observations must suffice here for the general importance of Hawthorne's characteristic ambiguity. It remains to describe its immediate significance in "Young Goodman Brown." Above all, the separate instances of this "multiple choice device" organically cohere to reproduce in the reader's mind the feel of the central ambiguity of theme, the horror of the hero's doubt. Goodman Brown, a simple and pious nature, is wrecked as a result of the disappearance of the fixed poles of his belief. His orderly cosmos dissolves into chaos as church and state, the twin pillars of his society, are hinted to be rotten, with their foundations undermined.[10] The yearn-

[7] "For Hawthorne its value consisted in the variety of explanations to which it gave rise." *American Renaissance*, 277. The extent of my indebtedness to Mr. Matthiessen is only inadequately indicated in my documentation.

[8] "It is only by . . . symbols that have numberless meanings beside the one or two the writer lays an emphasis upon, or the half-score he knows of, that any highly subjective art can escape from the barrenness and shallowness of a too conscious arrangement, into the abundance and depth of nature. . . ." W. B. Yeats, "The Philosophy of Shelley's Poetry," *Ideas of Good and Evil* (London, 1914), 90. Thus Hawthorne by drawing upon Puritan superstition and demonology is able to add another dimension to his story.

[9] Preface, *The House of the Seven Gables*.

[10] Goodman Brown is disillusioned with the church in the persons of Goody Cloyse, the minister, and Deacon Gookin, and it will be recalled that the figure of Satan at the

ing for certainty is basic to his spirit—and he is left without the comfort even of a firm reliance in the Devil.[11] His better qualities avail him in his desperation little more than the inner evil which prompted him to court temptation, for they prevent him from seeking the only remaining refuge—the confraternity of Sin. Henceforth he is fated to a dubious battle with shadows, to struggle with limed feet toward a redemption which must forever elude him, since he has lost the vision of Good while rejecting the proffered opportunity to embrace Evil fully. Individual instances of ambiguity, then, merge and coalesce in the theme itself to produce an all-pervading atmosphere of uneasiness and anguished doubt.

Ambiguity alone, however, is not a satisfactory aesthetic principle. Flexibility, suggestiveness, allusiveness, variety—all these are without meaning if there is no pattern from which to vary, no center from which to flee outward. And, indeed, ambiguity of itself will not adequately account for the individual phenomenon of "Young Goodman Brown." The deliberate haziness and multiple implications of its meaning are counterbalanced by the firm clarity of its technique, in structure and in style.

This clarity is embodied in the lucid simplicity of the basic action; in the skilful foreshadowing by which the plot is bound together; in balance of episode and scene; in the continuous use of contrast; in the firmness and selectivity of Hawthorne's pictorial composition; in the carefully arranged climactic order of incident and tone; in the detachment and irony of Hawthorne's attitude; and finally in the purity, the grave formality, and the rhetorical balance of the style. His amalgamation of these elements achieves an effect of totality, of exquisite craftsmanship, of consummate artistic economy in fitting the means to the attempted ends.

The general framework of the story has a large simplicity. Goodman Brown leaves his wife Faith and the safe confines of Salem town at sunset, spends the night in the forest, and at dawn returns a changed man. Within this simple pattern plot and allegory unfold symmetrically and simultaneously. The movement of "Young Goodman Brown" is the single revolution of a wheel, which turns full-circle upon itself. As by this basic structure, the action is likewise given form by the device of foreshadowing, through which the entire development of the plot is already implicit in the opening paragraph. Thus Faith is troubled by her husband's expedition, and begs him to put it off till sunrise. "A lone woman is troubled with such dreams and such thoughts that she's afeard of herself sometimes," says she,

---

meeting "bore no slight similitude . . . to some grave divine of the New England churches." As to the secular power, the devil tells Brown that ". . . the selectmen of divers towns make me their chairman; and a majority of the Great and General Court are firm supporters of my interest. The governor and I, too—But these are state secrets."

[11] The story could conceivably be read as intellectual satire, showing the pitfalls that lie in wait for a too-shallow and unquestioning faith. Tone and emphasis clearly show, however, a more tragic intention.

hinting the ominous sequel of her own baptism in sin. " 'My love and my Faith,' replied young Goodman Brown, 'of all nights in the year, this one night must I tarry away from thee. My journey . . . forth and back again, must needs be done 'twixt now and sunrise.' " They part, but Brown looking back sees "the head of Faith still peeping after him with a melancholy air, in spite of her pink ribbons."

"Poor little Faith!" thought he, for his heart smote him. "What a wretch am I to leave her on such an errand! She talks of dreams, too. Methought as she spoke there was trouble in her face, as if a dream had warned her what work is to be done to-night. But no, no; 'twould kill her to think of it. Well, she's a blessed angel on earth; and after this one night I'll cling to her skirts and follow her to heaven."

This speech, it must be confessed, is in several respects clumsy, obvious, and melodramatic; [12] but beneath the surface lurks a deeper layer. The pervasive ambiguity of the story is foreshadowed in the subtle emphasizing of the dream-motif, which paves the way for the ultimate uncertainty whether the incidents of the night are dream or reality; and in his simple-minded aspiration to "cling to her skirts and follow her to heaven," Goodman Brown is laying an ironic foundation for his later horror of doubt. A broader irony is apparent, in the light of future events, in the general emphasis upon Faith's angelic goodness.

Hawthorne's seemingly casual references to Faith's pink ribbons, which are mentioned three times in the opening paragraphs, are likewise far from artless. These ribbons, as we have seen, are an important factor in the plot; and as an emblem of heavenly Faith their color gradually deepens into the liquid flame or blood of the baptism into sin. [13]

Another instance of Hawthorne's careful workmanship is his architectural balance of episodes or scenes. The encounter with Goody Cloyse, the female hypocrite and sinner, is set off against the conversation of the minister and Deacon Gookin immediately afterward. The exact correspondence of the two episodes is brought into high relief by two balancing speeches. Goody Cloyse has lost her broomstick, and must perforce walk to the witch-meeting—a sacrifice she is willing to make since "they tell me there is a nice young man to be

[12] It has the earmarks of the set dramatic soliloquy, serving in this case to provide both information about the plot and revelation of character. Mr. Matthiessen attributes Hawthorne's general use of theatrical devices to the influence of Scott, who leads in turn to Shakespeare. *American Renaissance*, 203.

[13] Further, in welcoming the two candidates to the communion of Evil, the Devil says, "By the sympathy of your human hearts for sin ye shall scent out all the places . . . where crime has been committed, and shall exult to behold the whole earth one stain of guilt, *one mighty blood spot*." For this discussion of the pink ribbons I am largely indebted to Leland Schubert, *Hawthorne, the Artist* (Chapel Hill, 1944), 79–80.

taken into communion to-night." A few minutes later Deacon Goo-kin, in high anticipation, remarks that "there is a goodly young woman to be taken into communion." A still more significant example of this balance is contained in the full swing of the wheel—in the departure at sunset and the return at sunrise. At the beginning of the story Brown takes leave of "Faith with the pink ribbons," turns the corner by the meeting-house and leaves the town; in the conclusion

. . . Young Goodman Brown came slowly into the street of Salem village, staring around him like a bewildered man. The good old minister was taking a walk along the graveyard to get an appetite for breakfast and meditate his sermon, and bestowed a blessing, as he passed, on Goodman Brown. He shrank from the venerable saint as if to avoid an anathema. Old Deacon Gookin was at domestic worship, and the holy words of his prayer were heard through the open window. "What God doth the wizard pray to?" quoth Goodman Brown. Goody Cloyse, that excellent old Christian, stood in the early sunshine at her own lattice, catechizing a little girl who had brought her a pint of morning's milk.[14] Goodman Brown snatched the child away as from the grasp of the fiend himself. Turning the corner by the meeting-house, he spied the head of Faith, with the pink ribbons, gazing anxiously forth, and bursting into such joy at the sight of him that she skipped along the street and almost kissed her husband before the whole village. But Goodman Brown looked sternly and sadly into her face, and passed on without a greeting.

The exact parallel between the earlier and the later situation serves to dramatize intensely the change which the real or fancied happenings of the night have brought about in Goodman Brown.[15]

Contrast, a form of balance, is still more prominent in "Young Goodman Brown" than the kind of analogy of scene and episode which I have mentioned. The broad antitheses of day against night, the town against the forest, which signify in general a sharp dualism of Good and Evil, are supplemented by a color-contrast of red-and-black at the witch-meeting, by the swift transition of the forest scene from leaping flame to damp and chill, and by the consistent cleavage between outward decorum and inner corruption in the characters.[16]

---

[14] This touch takes on an ironic and ominous significance if it is noticed that Goody Cloyse has that night been Faith's sponsor, along with the "rampant hag" Martha Carrier, at the baptism into sin by blood and flame.

[15] Here we may anticipate a little in order to point out the steady and premeditated irony arising from the locutions "good old minister," "venerable saint," and "excellent old Christian"; and the climactic effect produced by the balance and repetition of the encounters, which are duplicated in the sentence-structure and the repetition of "Goodman Brown."

[16] Epitomized by Brown's description of the assemblage at the meeting as "a grave and dark-clad company."

The symbols of Day and Night, of Town and Forest, are almost indistinguishable in meaning. Goodman Brown leaves the limits of Salem at dusk and reenters them at sunrise; the night he spends in the forest. Day and the Town are clearly emblematic of Good, of the seemly outward appearance of human convention and society. They stand for the safety of an unquestioning and unspeculative faith. Oddly enough, Goodman Brown in the daylight of the Salem streets is a young man too simple and straightforward to be interesting, and a little distasteful in his boundless reverence for such unspectacular worthies as the minister, the deacon, and Goody Cloyse. Night and the Forest are the domains of the Evil One, symbols of doubt and wandering, where the dark subterraneous forces of the human spirit riot unchecked.[17] By the dramatic necessities of the plot Brown is a larger figure in the Forest of Evil,[18] and as a chief actor at the witch-meeting, than within the safe bounds of the town.

The contrast of the red of fire and blood against the black of night and the forest at the witch-meeting has a different import. As the flames rise and fall, the faces of the worshippers of Evil are alternately seen in clear outline and deep shadow, and all the details of the scene are at one moment revealed, the next obscured. It seems, then, that the red is Sin or Evil, plain and unequivocal; the black is that doubt of the reality either of Evil or Good which tortures Goodman Brown and is the central ambiguity of Hawthorne's story.[19]

A further contrast follows in the swift transformation of scene when young Goodman Brown finds himself "amid calm night and solitude. . . . He staggered against the rock, and felt it chill and damp; while a hanging twig, that had been all on fire, besprinkled his cheek with the coldest dew."[20]

Most pervasive of the contrasts in "Young Goodman Brown" is the consistent discrepancy between appearance and reality,[21] which

[17] "The conception of the dark and evil-haunted wilderness came to him [Hawthorne] from the days of Cotton Mather who held that 'the New Englanders are a people of God settled in those which were once the devil's territories.' " Matthiessen, *American Renaissance*, 282–283. See also Matthiessen's remark of *The Scarlet Letter* that ". . . the forest itself, with its straggling path, images to Hester 'the moral wilderness in which she had so long been wandering'; and while describing it Hawthorne may have taken a glance back at Spenser's Wood of Errour." *American Renaissance*, 279–280. This reference to Spenser may as fitly be applied to the path of Young Goodman Brown, "darkened by all the gloomiest trees of the forest, which barely stood aside to let the narrow path creep through, and closed immediately behind."

[18] "But he was himself the chief horror of the scene, and shrank not from its other horrors."

[19] Hawthorne not infrequently uses color for symbol. See such familiar instances as *The Scarlet Letter* and "The Minister's Black Veil."

[20] See Schubert, *Hawthorne, the Artist*, 63. One would presume this device to be traditional in the story of the supernatural, where a return to actuality must eventually be made. An obvious example is the vanishing at cockcrow of the Ghost in *Hamlet*. See also the conclusion of Hawthorne's own "Ethan Brand."

[21] Evil must provisionally be taken for reality during the night in the forest, in spite of the ambiguity of the ending.

helps to produce its heavy atmosphere of doubt and shadow. The church is represented by the highly respectable figures of Goody Cloyse, the minister, and Deacon Gookin, who in the forest are witch and wizards. The devil appears to Brown in the guise of his grandfather, "in grave and decent attire." As the goodman approaches the meeting, his ears are greeted by "the swell of what seemed a hymn, rolling solemnly from a distance with the weight of many voices. He knew the tune; it was a familiar one in the choir of the village meeting-house." The Communion of Sin is, in fact, the faithful counterpart of a grave and pious ceremony at a Puritan meeting-house. "At one extremity of an open space, hemmed in by the dark wall of the forest, arose a rock, bearing some rude, natural resemblance either to an altar or a pulpit, and surrounded by four blazing pines, their tops aflame, their stems untouched, like candles at an evening meeting." The worshippers are "a numerous congregation," Satan resembles some grave divine, and the initiation into sin takes the form of a baptism.[22]

Along with this steady use of contrast at the Sabbath should be noticed its firmly composed pictorial quality. The rock, the center of the picture, is lighted by the blazing pines. The chief actors are as it were spotlighted in turn as they advance to the rock, while the congregation is generalized in the dimmer light at the outer edges. The whole composition is simple and definite, in contrast with the ambiguity occasioned by the rise and fall of the flame, in which the mass of the worshippers alternately shines forth and disappears in shadow.[23]

The clarity and simple structural solidity of "Young Goodman Brown" evinces itself in its tight dramatic framework. Within the basic form of the turning wheel it further divides into four separate scenes, the first and last of which, of course, are the balancing departure from and return to Salem. The night in the forest falls naturally into two parts: the temptation by the Devil and the witch-meeting. These two scenes, particularly the first, make full and careful use of the dramatic devices of suspense and climactic arrangement; and Hawthorne so manipulates his materials as to divide them as sharply as by a dropped curtain.

The temptation at first has the stylized and abstract delicacy of Restoration Comedy, or of the formalized seductions of Molière's *Don Juan*. The simple goodman, half-eager and half-reluctant, is

[22] The hint of the perverse desecration of the Black Mass adds powerfully here to the connotative scope of the allegory.

[23] The general effect is very like that of the famous Balinese Monkey Dance, which is performed at night, usually in a clearing of the forest, by the light of a single torch. The chief figures, the Monkey King and the King of the Demons, advance in turn to this central torch, while the chorus of dancers remains in the semi-obscurity of the background. This dancing is allegorical, the Monkeys, as helpers of the Balinese, representing Good against the Evil of the Demons.

wholly at the mercy of Satan, who leads him step by step to the inevitable end. The tone of the earlier part of this scene is lightly ironic: an irony reinforced by the inherent irony of the situation, which elicits a double meaning at every turn.

"Come, Goodman Brown," cried his fellow-traveller, "this is a dull pace for the beginning of a journey. Take my staff, if you are so soon weary."

"Friend," said the other, exchanging his slow pace for a full stop, "having kept convenant by meeting thee here, it is my purpose now to return whence I came. I have scruples touching the matter thou wot'st of."

"Sayest thou so?" replied he of the serpent, smiling apart. "Let us walk on, nevertheless, reasoning as we go; and if I convince thee not thou shalt turn back. We are but a little way in the forest yet."

Then begins a skilful and relentless attack upon all the values which Goodman Brown has lived by. His reverence for his Puritan ancestors, "a people of prayer, and good works to boot," is speedily turned against him as the Devil claims them for tried and dear companions. Next comes the episode of Goody Cloyse, who taught the young man his catechism. Brown is sorely cast down, but at length sturdily concludes: "What if a wretched old woman do choose to go to the devil when I thought she was going to heaven: is that any reason why I should quit my dear Faith and go after her?" But no sooner has he rallied from this blow than he is beset by another, still more shrewdly placed: he hears the voices of the minister and Deacon Gookin, and from their conversation gathers that they are bound for the meeting, and eagerly anticipating it. This is nearly final, but he still holds out. " 'With heaven above, and Faith below, I will yet stand firm against the devil!' cried Goodman Brown"; only to be utterly overthrown by the sound of his wife's voice in the air, and the crushing evidence of the fatal pink ribbon.

The style has gradually deepened and intensified along with the carefully graduated intensity of the action, and now Hawthorne calls upon all his resources to seize and represent the immense significance of the moment. Nature itself is made at once to sympathize with and to mock the anguished chaos of the young man's breast; in his rage he is both at one with and opposed to the forest and the wind.[24] The symphony of sound, which began with the confused babble of voices

---

[24]"The intensity of the situation is sustained by all the devices Hawthorne had learned from the seventeenth century, for just as the heavens groaned in Milton's fall of the angels, the winds are made to whisper sadly at the loss of this man's faith." Matthiessen, *American Renaissance,* 284. The winds, however, roar rather than "whisper sadly."

in the sky as Faith and her witch-attendants swept overhead, rises to a wild crescendo.[25]

And, maddened with despair, so that he laughed loud and long, did Goodman Brown grasp his staff and set forth again, at such a rate that he seemed to fly along the forest path rather than to walk or run. The road grew wilder and drearier and more faintly traced, and vanished at length, leaving him in the heart of the dark wilderness, still rushing onward with the instinct that guides mortal man to evil. The whole forest was peopled with frightful sounds—the creaking of the trees, the howling of wild beasts, and the yell of Indians; while sometimes the wind tolled like a distant church bell, and sometimes gave a broad roar around the traveller, as if all Nature were laughing him to scorn. But he was himself the chief horror of the scene, and shrank not from its other horrors.

After ascending to this climax, Hawthorne disengages himself and separates his scenes with the definiteness of the dropping of a curtain—by the simple expedient of shifting his view from the hero to his surroundings. Goodman Brown coming upon the witch-meeting is a mere onlooker until the moment comes for him to step forward for his baptism into sin. Up to that moment Satan usurps the stage. The eye is first directed to the central rock-altar, then to the four blazing pines which light it. Next there is the sense of a numerous assembly, vaguely seen in the fitful firelight. Finally the figure of Satan appears at the base of the rock, framed in an arch of flame. Only when he is summoned are we once more fully aware of Goodman Brown, as he stands at the altar by his wife Faith. Then, a moment later, comes the second crashing climax when Brown calls upon his wife to "look up to heaven, and resist the wicked one"—cut off abruptly by anticlimax as the meeting vanishes in a roaring wind, and Brown leaning against the rock finds it chill and damp to his touch.

The satisfaction one feels in the clean line of the structure of the story is enhanced by Hawthorne's steady detachment from his materials: an attitude which deepens the impression of classic balance, which in turn stands against the painful ambiguity of the theme. Even the full tone of the intensest scenes, as Goodman Brown rushing through the forest, is tempered by restraint. The participant is overweighted by the calm, impartial (though not unfeeling) spectator; Hawthorne does not permit himself to become identified with his hero. He displays young Goodman Brown not in and for himself, but

---

[25] Cf. Schubert's account of the sound-effects in "Young Goodman Brown," *Hawthorne, the Artist,* 114–117. Mr. Schubert distorts the effect and purpose of Hawthorne's use of sound in the story by comparing it to "the last movement of Beethoven's Ninth Symphony"—description of sound is not the sound itself—but his perception is extremely valuable.

always in relation to the whole situation and set of circumstances. This detachment of attitude is plainest in the almost continuous irony, unemphatic but nonetheless relentless: an irony organically related to the ever-present ambiguities of the situation, but most evident in sustained tone. Thus, after recording Goodman Brown's aspiration to "cling to Faith's skirts and follow her to heaven," the author adds with deadly calm, "With this excellent resolve for the future, Goodman Brown felt himself justified in making more haste on his present evil purpose."

This detachment is implicit in the quiet, the abstractness, and the exquisite gravity of Hawthorne's style, everywhere formal and exactly though subtly cadenced. It throws a light and idealizing veil over the action,[26] and as it were maintains an aesthetic distance from it, while hinting at the ugliness it mercifully covers. The difference between the saying and the thing said, at times provides dramatic tension and a kind of ironic fillip. Note, for example, the grave decorum and eighteenth-century stateliness, the perverted courtliness, of Satan's welcome to young Brown and Faith:

This night it shall be granted you to know their secret deeds: how hoary-bearded elders of the church have whispered wanton words to the young maids of their households; how many a woman, eager for widows' weeds, has given her husband a drink at bedtime and let him sleep his last sleep in her bosom; how beardless youths have made haste to inherit their fathers' wealth; and how fair damsels—blush not, sweet ones—have dug little graves in the garden, and bidden me, the sole guest, to an infant's funeral.

The steady procession of measured, ceremonious generalizations—"hoary-bearded elders," "wanton words," "beardless youths," and "fair damsels," is in radical contrast with the implication of the meaning; and the grisly archness of "blush not, sweet ones" is deeply suggestive in its incongruity.[27]

---

[26] Hawthorne's notion of the ideality which art should lend to nature is apparent in his comment in the introductory essay to *Mosses from an Old Manse* upon the reflection of a natural scene in water: "Each tree and rock, and every blade of grass, is distinctly imaged, and however unsightly in reality, assumes ideal beauty in the reflection." And a few pages later—"Of all this scene, the slumbering river has a dream picture in its bosom. Which, after all was the most real—the picture, or the original? the objects palpable to our grosser senses, or their apotheosis in the stream beneath? Surely the disembodied images stand in closer relation to the soul."

[27] I would not be understood to affirm that this adaptation of the eighteenth-century mock-heroic is the sole effect of Hawthorne's style in "Young Goodman Brown." The seventeenth century plays its part too. The agony of the goodman in the forest, and the sympathy of the elements, is Miltonic. And in this same scene of the witch-meeting Hawthorne twice touches upon Miltonic tenderness and sublimity: " 'Lo, there ye stand, my children,' said the figure, in a deep and solemn tone, almost sad with its despairing awfulness, as if his once angelic nature could yet mourn for our miserable race. . . . And there they stood, the only pair, as it seemed, who were yet hesitating on the verge of wickedness in this dark world."

In "Young Goodman Brown," then, Hawthorne has achieved that reconciliation of opposites which Coleridge deemed the highest art. The combination of clarity of technique, embodied in simplicity and balance of structure, in firm pictorial composition, in contrast and climactic arrangement, in irony and detachment, with ambiguity of meaning as signalized by the "device of multiple choice," in its interrelationships produces the story's characteristic effect. By means of these two elements Hawthorne reconciles oneness of action with multiplicity of suggestion, and enriches the bareness of systematic allegory. Contrarily, by them he holds in check the danger of lapsing into mere speculation without substance or form. The phantasmagoric light-and-shadow of the rising and falling fire, obscuring and softening the clear, hard outline of the witch-meeting, is an image which will stand for the essential effect of the story itself, compact of ambiguity and clarity harmoniously interfused.

WRITING ABOUT POETRY

Some poems are narrative, telling a story, as does "Barbara Allen," which appears in this book on pages 68–69. To interpret a narrative poem, you employ the same principles as those for a prose story. After all, a narrative poem is nothing but a story with the addition, often, of meter and rhyme (about which we will talk in a moment).

Lyric poetry, however, does not tell a story; it uses symbol, image, metaphor, and other figures of speech to convey a meaning and the emotional charge that is appropriate to that meaning.

Here, for example, is a well-known lyric poem:

The Lake Isle of Innisfree

William Butler Yeats

I will arise and go now, and go to Innisfree,
And a small cabin build there, of clay and wattles made;
Nine bean rows will I have there, a hive for the honey bee,
And live alone in the bee-loud glade.

And I shall have some peace there, for peace comes dropping slow,
Dropping from the veils of the morning to where the cricket sings;
There midnight's all a glimmer, and noon a purple glow,
And evening full of the linnet's wings.

I will arise and go now, for always night and day
I hear lake water lapping with low sounds by the shore;
While I stand on the roadway, or on the pavements grey,
I hear it in the deep heart's core.

In this poem, Innisfree stands for (symbolizes) the peace that can be found only away from the city, and the poet's theme is the longing to get away from the busyness of life and retire to a beautiful, peaceful, and remote spot. We find metaphor in the poem: "for peace comes dropping slow, / Dropping from the veils of the morning to where the cricket sings." And, of course, the poem is full of images.

The language of the poem has special features, such as *rhyme:* Innisfree-bee, made-glade, slow-glow, sings-wings, day-grey, shore-core.

To interpret a lyric poem, we must see how all of its features work together to create a meaning and an emotional response.

Literal Meaning

The first step in interpretation is to see if we can state the literal meaning of the poem in our own words. This kind of statement is known as a *paraphrase.* For example, here is one of the most popular poems in English, followed by a paraphrase:

To His Coy Mistress

Andrew Marvell

Had we but world enough, and time,
This coyness, lady, were no crime.
We could sit down and think which way
To walk, and pass our long love's day;
Thou by the Indian Ganges' side   5
Shouldst rubies find; I by the tide
Of Humber would complain. I would
Love you ten years before the Flood;
And you should, if you please, refuse

TO HIS COY MISTRESS   Mistress: not kept woman, but sweetheart or beloved.   2. coyness: shyness, modesty.   5. Ganges: a river in India, a distant and exotic place, at least from the standpoint of a seventeenth-century Englishman.   7. Humber: a humble English stream, on the banks of which stood Marvell's family home.   8. the Flood: the biblical deluge.

Till the conversion of the Jews.   10
My vegetable love should grow
Vaster than empires, and more slow.
An hundred years should go to praise
Thine eyes, and on thy forehead gaze;
Two hundred to adore each breast,   15
But thirty thousand to the rest;
An age at least to every part,
And the last age should show your heart.
For, lady, you deserve this state,
Nor would I love at lower rate.   20

But at my back I always hear
Time's wingèd chariot hurrying near;
And yonder all before us lie
Deserts of vast eternity.
Thy beauty shall no more be found,   25
Nor in thy marble vault shall sound
My echoing song; then worms shall try
That long preserved virginity,
And your quaint honor turn to dust,
And into ashes all my lust.   30
The grave's a fine and private place,
But none, I think, do there embrace.

Now therefore, while the youthful hue
Sits on thy skin like morning dew,
And while thy willing soul transpires   35
At every pore with instant fires,
Now let us sport us while we may;
And now, like am'rous birds of prey,
Rather at once our time devour,
Than languish in his slow-chapped power.   40
Let us roll all our strength, and all
Our sweetness, up into one ball;
And tear our pleasure with rough strife
Thorough the iron gates of life.
Thus, though we cannot make our sun   45
Stand still, yet we will make him run.

10. the conversion of the Jews: not supposed to occur until the Last Judgment.
26. they marble vault: your marble tomb. 29. quaint: possessing a strange, but
charming oddness. 40. slow-chapped: slow-jawed; we get the image of Time
slowly but systematically chewing up the poet and his mistress. 44. thorough:
simply a version of through.

The paraphrase might be:

> If we had enough time, lady, I wouldn't be in any hurry. We could plan, and think, and travel, and wait. I would love you for the whole age of the earth. I'd be willing to spend hundreds of years on preliminaries, such as praising your beauty. For you're such a wonderful person that you deserve all the honor and dignity that I could bestow upon you, and, furthermore, I'm not a piker; I'm willing to give you everything that is your due.
>
> However, I'm always aware of the brevity of life, and I know that before us lies the eternity of death. In the grave, we'll have no chance for love.
>
> Therefore, while we're young and passionate, let's make love. We can't stop time, but we can fill every moment that we have.

Now, then, if all that we wanted from a work of literature were its literal meaning, we would like the paraphrase just as well as we do the poem. Obviously, a work of literature gives us something more than bare meaning, something more than information or opinion.

Formal Structure

Works of literature have structure. For instance, plays are divided into acts, which break the movement into segments; novels are divided into chapters and sometimes sections; poems often have clearly defined, formal patterns of stanzas. There is no need for you to be able to name these patterns, but you should be aware of them, for at least some of the enjoyment of poetry comes from the skill with which the poet embodies ideas in strictly defined patterns. For instance, the *sonnet* follows a pattern of just fourteen lines of ten syllables each (with some little room for variation in the number of syllables). As an example, here is Shakespeare's Sonnet 129, about lust:

> Th' expense of spirit in a waste of shame
> Is lust in action; and, till action, lust
> Is perjured, murd'rous, bloody, full of blame,
> Savage, extreme, rude, cruel, not to trust;
> Enjoyed no sooner but despisèd straight;
> Past reason hunted, and no sooner had,
> Past reason hated as a swallowed bait
> On purpose laid to make the taker mad;
> Mad in pursuit, and in possession so;

Had, having, and in quest to have, extreme;
A bliss in proof, and proved, a very woe,
Before, a joy proposed; behind, a dream.
 All this the world well knows, yet none knows well
 To shun the heaven that leads men to this hell.

Readers take pleasure in the forms of poems; after all, it is an accomplishment to fit one's ideas and language into a form as strictly defined as a sonnet. When we read for information, we are normally unaware of form—unless the piece is disorganized or in some other way flawed or atypical—but the form of poems is one feature that contributes to our enjoyment of them.

Form

The following poem has an extremely intricate structure. After reading the poem, describe its form, *paying special attention to word repetitions.* In order to do this, you need no fancy terminology. Merely describe what you see on the page.

Here in Katmandu

Donald Justice

We have climbed the mountain,
There's nothing more to do.
It is terrible to come down
To the valley
Where, amidst many flowers,
One thinks of snow.

As, formerly, amidst snow,
Climbing the mountain,
One thought of flowers,
Tremulous, ruddy with dew,
In the valley,
One caught their scent coming down.

It is difficult to adjust, once down,
To the absence of snow.
Clear days, from the valley,
One looks up at the mountain.

HERE IN KATMANDU Donald Justice, *The Summer Anniversaries* (Middletown, Conn.: Wesleyan Univ. Press, 1956). Copyright © 1956 by Donald Justice. Reprinted by permission of Wesleyan University Press. "Here in Katmandu" first appeared in *Poetry.*

What else is there to do?
Prayerwheels, flowers!

Let the flowers
Fade, the prayerwheels run down.
What have these to do
With us who have stood atop the snow
Atop the mountain,
Flags seen from the valley?

It might be possible to live in the valley,
To bury oneself among flowers,
If one could forget the mountain,
How, setting out before dawn,
Blinded with snow,
One knew what to do.

Meanwhile it is not easy here in Katmandu,
Especially when to the valley
That wind which means snow
Elsewhere, but here means flowers,
Comes down,
As soon it must, from the mountain.

The Language of Poetry

The language of poetry often, but not always, contains features that are not found in prose—for instance, meter and rhyme.

As we have seen, rhyme is the sound-alike words that end lines of poetry (and that sometimes occur within lines):

> Above the pines the moon was slowly *drifting*,
>   The river sang *below;*
> The dim Sierras, far beyond, *uplifting*
>   Their minarets of *snow*.

> —Bret Harte

Thus: drifting-uplifting, below-snow.

Meter is the regular alternation of stressed and unstressed syllables in poetry, creating a definite rhythm.

Iambic meter consists of an unstressed and a stressed syllable.

> Had WE but WORLD eNOUGH and TIME,
> This COYness, LAdy, WERE no CRIME.

Trochaic meter consists of a stressed syllable followed by an unstressed syllable.

> DOUble, DOUble, TOIL and TROUble,
> FIre BURN and CAULdron BUBble.

Anapestic meter consists of two unstressed syllables followed by a stressed syllable.

> Like a CHILD from the WOMB, like a GHOST from the TOMB,
> I aRISE and unBUILD it aGAIN.

Another meter, not often used in English, is *dactylic:* a stressed syllable followed by two unstressed, as in the word MANikin.

Poetic language also tends to be more *connotative* than that of prose. (For a discussion of *connotation* and *denotation,* see pages 401–02.) Think, for instance, of the connotations that the word *love* takes on in "To His Coy Mistress." It means, first of all, a tender emotion, but it soon comes to mean "sexual union," as in "to make love." In short, the language of poetry is likely to have more shades of meaning than is the case in prose.

Most poetry is imagistic, it is metaphoric, and it is intense. For instance, here's an anonymous medieval lyric:

Western Wind

> Western wind, when wilt thou blow?
> The small rain down can rain.
> Christ, that my love were in my arms,
> And I in my bed again.

Now, I'm not at all sure what this simple little poem means. But it has strong images; that is, it gives me a visual experience: I see rain, and I see two lovers snuggled close in a warm bed. I interpret "western wind" as a metaphor for autumn, simply because I have at the back of my mind Shelley's "Ode to the West Wind," the first line of which is "O wild West Wind, thou breath of Autumn's being." So "western wind" is imagistic and metaphoric. What about its intensity? The intensity arises, I think, from these other two qualities.

Images are based on observation. As a rule, the closer the observation, the more vivid the image. In writing, this results in focusing on the particulars of an experience and representing that experience through the use of concrete words rather than abstract ones. Below are two very different poems that project striking visual experiences through vivid images.

The Red Wheelbarrow

William Carlos Williams

so much depends
upon

a red wheel
barrow

glazed with rain
water

beside the white
chickens

In a Station of the Metro

Ezra Pound

The apparition of these faces in the crowd;
Petals on a wet, black bough.

In Williams' poem, the image is clear and entirely descriptive; it fulfills his demand that a poem should possess "no ideas but in things." From these few lines we can easily visualize the red wheelbarrow, so important to a farmer, sitting under the rain in a farmyard. The poem by Ezra Pound is a little more complex. Here, the second line is a metaphor of the first and serves to convey, in Pound's words, "the precise instant when a thing outward and objective transforms itself, or darts into a thing inward and subjective." The "thing outward and objective," in this case, is the crowd in a subway station.

Above all other literary artists, poets don't *tell;* they *show,* through their use of images and metaphors. Here is one more example of how poets show.

The following is merely a statement. It tells:

THE RED WHEELBARROW   William Carlos Williams, *Collected Earlier Poems: Before Nineteen Forty* (New York: New Directions, 1951). Copyright © 1938 by New Directions Publishing Corporation. Reprinted by permission of New Directions.

Once I saw some beautiful daffodils. They still live in my memory. The beauty that we experience stays with us as an inner resource that we can call on for pleasure and solace.

Here is a familiar poem in which William Wordsworth *shows* us what that statement meant to him:

> I wandered lonely as a cloud
> That floats on high o'er vales and hills,
> When all at once I saw a crowd,
> A host, of golden daffodils;
> Beside the lake, beneath the trees,
> Fluttering and dancing in the breeze.
>
> Continuous as the stars that shine
> And twinkle on the milky way,
> They stretched in never-ending line
> Along the margin of a bay;
> Ten thousand saw I at a glance,
> Tossing their heads in sprightly dance.
>
> The waves beside them danced; but they
> Out-did the sparkling waves in glee:
> A poet could not but be gay,
> In such a jocund company:
> I gazed—and gazed—but little thought
> What wealth the show to me had brought:
>
> For oft, when on my couch I lie
> In vacant or in pensive mood,
> They flash upon that inward eye
> Which is the bliss of solitude;
> And then my heart with pleasure fills,
> And dances with the daffodils.

The poem is not really about the uses of beauty in life, but concerns an experience of beauty and conveys that experience to the reader. The poem is not a philosophical statement, but a small chunk of experience vividly conveyed.

One of the devices of writing poetry is to use the specific in order to evoke the general—which is what we've been saying all along. Notice how specific and imagistic proverbs are:

Don't count your chickens before they're hatched.

A bird in the hand is worth two in the bush.

That's water under the bridge.

The squeaking wheel gets the grease.

Birds of a feather flock together.

When in Rome, do as the Romans do.

Looking at the Language of Poetry

1. You have now become somewhat familiar with the way language is used in poetry. Study the five poems below and describe the use of rhyme, image, and metaphor. What patterns of language can you see in each of the poems? Read them aloud, to yourself or to a friend. What patterns of sound do you hear?

Richard Cory

Edwin Arlington Robinson

Whenever Richard Cory went down town,
We people on the pavement looked at him:
He was a gentleman from sole to crown,
Clean favored, and imperially slim.

And he was always quietly arrayed,
And he was always human when he talked;
But still he fluttered pulses when he said,
"Good-morning," and he glittered when he walked.

And he was rich—yes, richer than a king—
And admirably schooled in every grace:
In fine, we thought that he was everything
To make us wish that we were in his place.

So on we worked, and waited for the light,
And went without the meat, and cursed the bread;
And Richard Cory, one calm summer night,
Went home and put a bullet through his head.

Elegy

Chidiock Tichborne

My prime of youth is but a frost of cares,
My feast of joy is but a dish of pain,
My crop of corn is but a field of tares,

RICHARD CORY Edwin Arlington Robinson from *The Children of Night* (1897). Reprinted by permission of Charles Scribner's Sons.

And all my good is but vain hope of gain;
The day is past, and yet I saw no sun,
And now I live, and now my life is done.

My tale was heard and yet it was not told,
My fruit is fallen and yet my leaves are green,
My youth is spent and yet I am not old,
I saw the world and yet I was not seen;
My thread is cut and yet it is not spun,
And now I live, and now my life is done.

I sought my death and found it in my womb,
I looked for life and saw it was a shade,
I trod the earth and knew it was my tomb,
And now I die, and now I was but made;
My glass is full, and now my glass is run,
And now I live, and now my life is done.

The Tyger

William Blake

Tyger, Tyger, burning bright,
In the forests of the night:
What immortal hand or eye
Could frame thy fearful symmetry?

In what distant deeps or skies
Burnt the fire of thine eyes!
On what wings dare he aspire?
What the hand, dare seize the fire?

And what shoulder, and what art,
Could twist the sinews of thy heart?
And when thy heart began to beat,
What dread hand? and what dread feet?

What the hammer? what the chain,
In what furnace was thy brain?
What the anvil? what dread gasp,
Dare its deadly terrors clasp?

When the stars threw down their spears
And watered heaven with their tears:
Did he smile his work to see?
Did he who made the Lamb make thee?

Tyger, Tyger, burning bright,
In the forests of the night:
What immortal hand or eye
Dare frame thy fearful symmetry?

Dream Deferred

Langston Hughes

What happens to a dream deferred?

    Does it dry up
    like a raisin in the sun?
    Or fester like a sore—
    And then run?
    Does it stink like rotten meat?
    Or crust and sugar over—
    like a syrupy sweet?

    Maybe it just sags
    like a heavy load.

    Or does it explode?

The Rhodora

Ralph Waldo Emerson

In May, when sea-winds pierced our solitudes,
I found the fresh Rhodora in the woods,
Spreading its leafless blooms in a damp nook,
To please the desert and the sluggish brook.
The purple petals, fallen in the pool,
Made the black water with their beauty gay;
Here might the red-bird come his plumes to cool,
And court the flower that cheapens his array.
Rhodora! if the sages ask thee why
This charm is wasted on the earth and sky,
Tell them, dear, that if eyes were made for seeing,
Then Beauty is its own excuse for being;
Why thou wert there, O rival of the rose!
I never thought to ask, I never knew;
But, in my simple ignorance, suppose
The self-same Power that brought me there brought you.

2. Write a paper discussing the meaning of the poem below. What is your reaction to the poem? Do you think it is good? If so, why? Do you think it bad? Why? What is the quality of language in the poem? For example, what is the quality of the rhyme? Are the rhyming words unusual or obvious? What about the images? Can you visualize the garden mentioned in the poem? What are the connotations of the word "gloat"? Do they fit the poem? In other words, explain your reactions by responding to the poem in detail.

DREAM DEFERRED   Langston Hughes. Reprinted from *The Panther and The Lash: Poems of Our Times,* by Langston Hughes, by permission of Alfred A. Knopf, Inc.

A Garden of Love and Beauty

Silas Pennypacker

There's a garden, as named above,
A garden of beauty and love;
Gardeners, toiling all the year round,
Go there as if Paradise-bound!

Clime without frost to fear, all year
Plants from over the earth brought here;
Folks over so much beauty gloat;
In the warm breeze, butterflies float!

Many paths here for lovers' feet.
Loves here walk and loves here meet.
My feet come here as of duty
To spend the day with love and beauty.

SUMMARY AND SUGGESTIONS FOR WRITING

In this chapter, we could not discuss all of the possible kinds of writing about literature. It goes without saying, however, that understanding the work precedes any response or written commentary. For this reason the chapter has focused on the interpretive essay, which is an attempt to explain the complex meaning of a work of literature and to demonstrate how the author conveys that meaning through his or her work. Therefore, most of the chapter has dealt with technical matters, such as plot, character, form, metaphor, symbol, image, and so on.

But you should keep in mind the other kind of essay that was discussed at the beginning of this chapter—the kind in which you explain the relationship of a work—its plot, theme, characters—to your life.

Some other possibilities are

1. a comparison of one work with others like it, or a comparison of a novel with a dramatic version of the book, as in film or television;
2. a critique of the ethics or values that the work expresses;
3. an explanation of why you did or did not enjoy the work.

It is even possible that you would respond to a poem by writing a poem or to a story by writing a story.

Writing

Business Letters

Betty P. Pytlik, University of Southern California

WRITING business letters, like every writing task, involves a series of problems to be solved, and the best approach to solving them is common sense. Consider, for example, the purpose, the reader, and the tone of the following letter to an inspection supervisor at the Department of Motor Vehicles. The letter was prompted by the refusal of a Department of Motor Vehicles inspector to approve registration for on-the-road use of a student's 1937 Packard. Because the student was angered by the refusal, the inspector suggested the student write to the supervisor. Here is the student's letter.

Dear Mr. Harris:

On June 15, 1979, Inspector Grey declined to approve registration for on-the-road use of my 1937 Packard. When I pointed out that the car is a part of the American tradition, is constructed better than any newer models, and creates less pollution than a high compression engine does, he suggested that I explain his assessment to you and request a new inspection.

Inspector Grey cited three problems with the car: the Packard achieves a top speed of 55 miles per hour. Since that is the legal speed limit, I am puzzled by the requirement that it be capable of exceeding the speed limit. Second, the car does not have seal-beam headlights, although the Packard's lights do emit well above the standard candle power required for auto headlights. Could brightness tests be conducted? Third, the brakes are mechanical rather than hydraulic. Aren't hydraulic brakes more a matter of convenience than safety?

Because I have driven the car in city traffic and on freeways across the country without any mechanical problems, I believe you will find my request for a new inspection justifiable. May I bring my car to the Inspection Center for you to inspect it personally? Any weekday between nine and noon that is convenient for you would be fine.

The three least effective arguments—the car is a part of the American tradition, it is constructed better than today's cars, and it creates less pollution—are presented in the opening paragraph as an introduction and explanation of the student's request. The more convincing arguments for a new inspection—those about the maximum speed, headlights, and brakes—are couched in the form of questions.

Exercise

1. Discuss the words and phrases that help create the tone in the student's letter to the Department of Motor Vehicles supervisor.

2. Write a response to the following *Last Notice* letter. The purpose of your letter is to clear your account immediately, so you must provide all the information the reader needs in order to do that.

LAST NOTICE

You now have 48 hours to settle your winter-quarter fee bill. If there is some reason you cannot settle it, you must contact the Financial Audit Office, Stone Hall 121, *now*. If you are a CCC student, and wish to remain one, you must respond today.

Sincerely,

Marjorie Anton, Bursar
Financial Audit Office
Stone Hall 121
Phone 233-2369

3. The purpose of the following letter to the CCC bursar from a student is not clear. Analyze the letter by discussing the following questions:

    a. What does the student want the bursar to do?

    b. How can the writer's ideas be organized so that his or her purpose is clear?

    c. What comments should be omitted to make the tone less offensive and thus increase the chances that the bursar will consider the student's suggestions rather than discount the letter as coming from a crank?

Gentlemen:

I have just wasted an hour and a half of my time trying to pay my summer fee bill. All of the problems stem from the fact that my classes ended several weeks ago and my financial award letter arrived after those classes ended. Furthermore, I could not pay the bill on time because I was out of town on school business when my award letter came in. That problem, fortunately, has been straightened out.

Nevertheless, I feel it my duty to inform you of the inefficiency that pervades the entire bureaucratic structure of Financial Services, including Tuition Audit and the Department of Collections. Not one person seems to know what he is speaking about. Matters seem to get more confused instead of being resolved. Furthermore, students seem to suffer the consequences of the inefficiency of your personnel. I hope you will not take this letter personally. I am writing not only because I am angry, but also because I hope you can do something to make dealing with your office staff an easy task, instead of a painful one.

Sincerely,

TONE

Tone, as we have seen earlier, reflects the writer's attitude toward the reader. Because the tone you use in business communications is determined by your purpose in writing, it is essential to consider what the reader already knows and what he or she needs to learn in order for your letter to be effective.

So far, the comments on tone and consideration of the reader have been very general. However, there are specific ways to adapt your tone to the reader. The following suggestions assume that you know you must always consider two primary questions: (1) What do you want the reader to do (the purpose of the communication)? (2) What does the reader need to know in order to do it (the information you will include in the letter)? Tone, then, becomes important when you answer a third question: (3) What would encourage the reader to do what you want him or her to do?

Here are some suggestions to guide you in answering this last question:

1. Tell the reader only what he or she needs to know. Put negatively, that means don't waste the reader's time by saying something he or she already knows.

2. Emphasize the reader's interests, not yours or those of your company or organization. Put yourself in the reader's place; compose your letters with a "you" attitude. Notice how the first sen-

tence from a sales letter focuses on the benefits for a potential customer:

> As a Culver Community College student, you can open a Twain Bank and Trust Company checking account with no monthly service charge and no monthly minimum balance required.

3. Emphasize the positive, not the negative. Tell the reader what you can do, not what you can't do, as in the response of a student who has had no experience directly related to the job of collecting signatures for getting candidates on the ballot.

> I have helped my fraternity brothers raise money for scholarships and have assisted my neighborhood council in collecting money for block parties to send inner-city children to summer camp.

4. Be confident that your ideas will be accepted. If something is worth asking for, it is worth asking for with confidence. Similarly, if something is worth reporting, it is worth reporting with confidence. For example:

> Is there a convenient time during the week of October 10–17 that eleven of my Culver Community College classmates and I may visit your office so that we can learn how your computerized purchasing system operates?

5. Eliminate deadwood. It is a courtesy to your reader to save his or her time by presenting your message clearly and concisely. If you want information, ask for it. If you want to order something, get right to the order. Phrases like "I would like to know if . . ." and "I am interested in . . ." are time wasters. Use a direct approach, as in the following example.

> Does Apex make carbon ribbons for its portable typewriters?

6. Avoid criticizing the reader. Three points to remember when you are inclined to criticize a reader: (a) that the inconvenience you have suffered was not intentional, (b) that the reader of your letter probably was not responsible for your annoyance, and (c) that your chances of getting a favorable response are greater if you present your case concisely and objectively. The following sentences illustrate courtesy to the reader:

> The twelve looseleaf binders that I ordered on January 10 have still not arrived. Please let me know if they have been shipped.

7. Proofread your letters. While most of our errors in business letters are typographical ones, they are often seen as carelessness and must be eliminated if the reader is to respond favorably. Using the proofreader's technique of reading lines backwards may help you find typos. Because grammar, punctuation, and spelling errors are so various, and because each of us knows by now the kinds of errors he or she is apt to make, they won't be discussed here.

8. Follow the conventions in setting up your letters. The sample letters throughout this chapter illustrate a variety of acceptable formats for letters. A form that deviates from custom is distracting, that is, it draws the reader's attention away from what is said in the same way that typos and other errors do. Check the sample letters for the placement of the following required parts of a standard business letter: the return address and date; the inside address; the salutation; the body; the complimentary close; and the typed signature. On page 353, you can see an illustration of a subject line; on page 368, attachments; and on pages 343 and 349, enclosures.

Exercise

1. Collect business correspondence that you and your friends have received and evaluate the tone of several of the letters.

2. Reexamine the irate student's letter to the bursar (in the preceding exercise) in terms of the suggestions about tone.

3. Discuss the tone of the following refusal of an order. Be specific about what makes this letter a reader-oriented one.

> Your August 21 order for filing cabinets, office desks, and lamps indicates an optimistic outlook for Samson's Office Supplies. We are proud to have been part of your financial success for the past ten years.
>
> In July, 1970, when you made your first purchase from us, you agreed to a balance limit of $10,000. Since then, because of your company's rapid growth and your excellent credit record, the balance limit has risen until you now have a $25,000 balance limit.
>
> Because your recent order would exceed your limit by $5,000, may we send you one half of your order now and the other half soon, when your balance has reached $25,000? That way your credit rating remains excellent and you can continue to provide your customers with the superior office furniture they have come to expect from Samson's.
>
> Will you call us collect so that the furniture can be shipped soon?

JOB SEARCH LETTERS

Perhaps the most important letters you will write are those seeking employment. To apply for a job that has been advertised is easier than to apply for one that you are not sure exists. For one thing, when you apply for an advertised position, you often know the name of the person to whom you can write, and letters directed to individuals usually receive more attention than letters directed to "Gentlemen" or "To Whom It May Concern." Also, the job requirements are often stated in the advertisement so that you can match them with your qualifications for the position. However, applying for a position that has not been announced may offer you more advantages. For example, you will face less competition from students seeking summer employment if you apply for a job that has not been advertised. A second advantage is that you are forced to consider carefully how your skills, temperament, experience, and education relate specifically to the company and its needs. What kinds of positions might they have that you might fit? Third, if you have limited your job search to one area—your home town or your campus town, for example—you can blanket the town with applications, and thus increase your chances of getting summer or part-time employment. Fourth, when you do get an interview, you may find that other jobs than those you expected are available in the company, and that these tap your skills as well.

Because the unsolicited letter may produce more job choices for you, the rest of this section discusses that kind of letter. Moreover, when you have mastered the more difficult task of selling your qualifications for a position that has not been advertised, you can more easily write a solicited letter.

In addition to discussing how to compose an unsolicited letter seeking employment, this section will also deal with a request for a recommendation, a thank-you for an interview, and a resumé.

Letters of Application

Three considerations are important in writing letters for employment: your purpose in writing the letter, the employer's needs and expectations, the qualities you possess that can satisfy those needs. Each requires the application of common sense.

The purpose of the application letter is, of course, to persuade the employer that your qualifications match the requirements of the company or a specific position; the immediate goal is to get an interview with the employer so that you can elaborate on the qualifications you have mentioned in your letter.

What does the person reading your letter need to know in order to arrange an interview? First, he or she needs to know exactly what kind of position you are interested in. Second, do you want a part-time or full-time job? Do you want one for the summer only? Obviously, "summer employment" is not specific enough: the employer needs to know what date you will be available to begin work, what date you will have to leave the job, and what date or dates you will be available for an interview. Third, he or she must know your qualifications for the position you have identified. Finally, the reader of your letter must know the names of several respected people who can support your claims.

Clearly, those four reader-oriented considerations reflect common sense. Some additional common-sense procedures to follow when you are composing your letter of application are these:

1. Direct your letter to the person in the company who is responsible for arranging interviews, usually the personnel director, but not always. It is a simple matter to call the company to learn the name of this person; the call is worth your time and money because, as we have already seen, letters that are addressed to individuals usually receive more attention than those that aren't.

2. If you are not sure about the requirements of the job—those that you must match with your qualifications—check the want ads. The following ad, for example, provides you with information on which to base your application, even though you are not applying for the position advertised:

WANTED

Security Guard—full-time/part-time, evenings and nights; must be willing and able to prevent unlawful entry or intrusion, check employee and visitor identification, and apply for pistol license. Please write letter stating educational background and previous experience. XYZ Manufacturing Company, Inc., P.O. Box 543, Tucson.

3. Because the impression that your letter makes is the only basis the reader has for deciding whether to grant you an interview, the appearance of the letter and the care you take in editing and proofreading it are important factors. Typographical errors, for example, reflect a carelessness

that the reader may assume you have about all of your work.

This last instance of common sense leads to the third consideration in writing your letter. Your letter should convey to the reader those qualities you think he or she would want in an employee. Neatness and carefulness are, of course, among the chief requirements for any job. But intelligence and confidence are also generally required. These qualities will be strongly implied in your letter if you assume that you will get the job and if you relate some previous experience to the position you are interested in. Imagine that you are interested in a position as an office clerk in an insurance company. The following sentences indicate related previous experience and confidence in the writer's qualifications.

I worked as a stock clerk for Mr. John Ackerman of Home-Builders Emporium in the evenings and on weekends during my senior year in high school. He can tell you about my dependability and sense of responsibility. You will find his address and telephone number on the attached resumé.

Notice that the second of these sentences points to two other very important qualities that most employers demand of their employees: dependability and sense of responsibility.

On page 343 is a letter of application from a student who is applying for an unadvertised position as a security guard, although he has had no previous experience directly connected to the job. Note the information that reflects common-sense items mentioned above.

Now consider another unsolicited letter from a student who has had a different background from that of Robert Altman. Mary Hymes brings to her letter experience as a dietitian's aide for a hospital. The purpose of the letter is to persuade Mrs. Watkins, whose name Mary obtained by calling the hospital, that the skills she learned as dietitian's aide at Queensbury Hospital match the requirements for a position as a supervisor of aides at Hanover Convalescent Home. Mary believes her personal qualities justify Mrs. Watkins' considering her for this position. Her immediate goal is to obtain an interview so that she can discuss her qualifications further. See her letter on page 344.

In what ways does Mary demonstrate an awareness of her reader? First, she makes the purpose of the letter clear in the first paragraph. Second, she summarizes the skills she would bring to a supervisory position. The third paragraph achieves two things: it names references who can and will attest to Mary's strengths, and it

3271 Ash Drive
Evansville, Indiana 46015
March 2, 19--

Ms. Marsha Bennett
Personnel Director
Anderson Building Supplies
South Bend, Indiana 47901

Dear Ms. Bennett:

Please consider my qualifications for a position with Anderson Building Supplies as a full-time security guard from June 1 until September 4.

While I attended Henry Morrison High School, I played on both the football and baseball teams. Currently, as a freshman at Culver Community College, I am on the soccer and baseball intramural teams. Thus, I would be able to meet the physical requirements for a position as a security guard.

During my junior and senior years in high school, I worked as an usher at Grant's Movie Theatre on weekends. This position required the discreet and responsible exercise of authority. Mr. Harold Rusk, Manager of Grant's, can tell you about my performance in this position. You will find his address and telephone number on the enclosed resumé.

During Easter vacation, April 1 to 5, I will be in South Bend. May I call for an appointment within this period so that I can discuss the possibility of working for Anderson Building Supplies during the summer?

Sincerely,

Robert R. Altman

Resumé Enclosed

6610 Milford Street, Apt. 2B
Somerset, Pennsylvania 15501
April 1, 19--

Mrs. Alicia Watkins
Chief Dietitian
Hanover Convalescent Home
Somerset, Pennsylvania 15501

Dear Mrs. Watkins:

Will Hanover Convalescent Home need a supervisor of
dietitian's aides during the summer and on weekends and
evenings during the year? If so, please consider my qualifications.

During my senior year at Eddington High School, I worked
on the weekends and in the evenings as a dietitian's aide
at Queensbury Hospital. Last summer, before I entered
Culver Community College, I worked full-time in the same
position. My responsibilities were to check that all patients had correct menus, to write salt-free diets, to
prepare tube feedings and special cold foods like juice,
salads, and special requests, and to keep the menu file
up-to-date.

Mrs. Harriet Ohms, Head Dietitian at Queensbury Hospital, can tell you that I was quick to learn the procedures
and that I was willing to do more than my job required. For
example, I helped train new dietitian's aides and met
with aides during meals to discuss problems. Also, Mr.
Samuel Scott, Director of Personnel, will tell you that I
was always prompt and dependable, and that I adapted well
to the hospital's need for flexibility in scheduling
hours.

Could you arrange a time when I may come in to talk with
you about the possibility of supervising dietitian's
aides from June 1 through September 4 and part-time during the school year? I can be reached at 929-9113 any weekday from nine until noon.

Sincerely,

Mary Hymes

Resumé Enclosed

lists personal attributes that Mary knows from experience to be essential to a supervisory position. In addition to stating what actions Mary wants Mrs. Watkins to take, the last paragraph makes it easy for the reader to respond to Mary's request for an interview by establishing convenient times for Mrs. Watkins to call her and by giving her the phone number at which Mary can be reached.

Beginning writers of such letters sometimes include irrelevant information. Notice that Mary does *not* say that she is a botany major, a Methodist, and five feet six inches tall. Those facts will not help Mrs. Watkins make her decision about whether to interview Mary; thus, it makes no sense to include them in the letter. What else in the letter demonstrates Mary's common sense?

Now that you have a general notion of what is involved in composing your letter and recognize that you have skills other than those of Robert and Mary, consider how your skills, temperament, experience, and education relate to a temporary summer position you would like to have in your home town.

If you want a position that will combine past work experience with your career goals—say you have baby-sat since you were fourteen, have worked two summers in a city-sponsored recreation program, and are studying to be an elementary teacher—you can check the Yellow Pages for recreational programs, camps, nurseries, and so on. Even though you are applying for an unannounced position, you can get some ideas about jobs that fall within your area of interest by checking state employment offices, college placement offices, campus newspapers, and local newspapers.

Collecting the Material for the Application Letter

By way of summarizing what has been said about the job search process, here is a list of questions that will help you compose your letter of application. Answer each of the questions.

1. What kinds of temporary positions are you qualified for?
2. What are the skills required for those positions?
3. What kinds of skills do you have? Which skills match the skills required for the position in which you are interested?
4. What personality traits and habits—for example, the ability to get along with others, dependability—do you have that will match the needs of the position?
5. What courses or training have you had that would help you perform well on the job?
6. What work experience have you had that relates either directly or indirectly to the position you want?

7. Who can and will vouch for those qualifications you have listed?
8. When will you be available for interviews?
9. To whom should you write your letter of application?
10. When can you start working? When will you have to stop?

Now write a letter to an imagined employer. Take into consideration the following items.

1. What is the purpose of the letter? In the first paragraph be sure to state the specific position for which you are applying, when you want to begin, and what kind of employment you want, for example, evenings only, full-time for the summer.
2. How can you relate the skills, education, personality traits, and job experience that you listed above to the job requirements? Use one or two paragraphs to discuss the qualifications.
3. Who will recommend you? In one paragraph name one or two references who have agreed to provide evidence that your qualifications match the job requirements.
4. When would you like an interview? How can the reader contact you? In the final paragraph make it convenient for the reader to contact you.

Requests for Recommendations

Robert and Mary name people whom Ms. Bennett and Mrs. Watkins can contact to learn more about their respective qualifications. They know it makes no sense to name people who will perhaps give them bad recommendations, or even weak ones; they also know that no one can be certain about a supervisor's assessment of his or her work, so they ask their former supervisors for permission to use their names as references before they actually use them. Then, Mr. Rusk, Mrs. Ohms, and Mr. Scott have a chance to tell Robert or Mary if they don't feel confident about recommending them or if they don't believe Robert's or Mary's qualifications match the requirements of the jobs for which they are applying.

If you are more comfortable calling to ask permission to use names as references or if calling is more convenient, there is no harm in using that approach. But a letter is always appropriate. The purpose of the letter is to ask permission to use the reader's name. The reader needs to know the kind of job you are applying for and with whom. He also needs to know when he should expect to hear from the company in case he will not be available at the time of the request.

If your reference agrees to recommend you, one of three things may happen. The personnel director could simply call the reference you listed (thus, you must include the phone number of the reference on your resumé). Second, the company may write directly to the reference for information about your qualifications. Third, the company may ask you to have the reference send a recommendation. In the last case, you will need to provide the reference with a stamped envelope addressed to the personnel director. Here are examples of the last two cases:

Dear Mr. Rusk:

I am applying for a position as a security guard with Anderson Building Supplies in South Bend for the summer. May I please tell Ms. Bennett, the Personnel Director, that she may contact you within the next month to ask about my qualifications for that position?

Dear Mr. Rusk:

In March you wrote that Anderson Building Supplies could contact you to discuss my qualifications for a summer position as a security guard. Would you please write to Ms. Bennett, the Director of Personnel for Anderson's? She is especially interested in knowing how you assess my dependability and sense of responsibility. I have enclosed a stamped, addressed envelope for your convenience.

Exercise

Compose a request for permission to use the name of a former supervisor or an acquaintance who can vouch for your qualifications for the position for which you applied in your letter. Here are some questions that will help you compose the request:

1. What is your professional or personal relationship with the person you will ask for a recommendation?
2. What kind of support of your qualifications can the reader give?
3. When will the company contact the reference?

Writing Thank-you's for Interviews

Let us say that Ms. Bennett responded to Robert's letter by saying that there will be no security guard positions for the summer, but that Anderson's usually hires four or five college students for the summer to replace vacationing employees. She suggested that Robert call her when he is in South Bend at Easter so that she can arrange interviews with Mrs. Harvey, the sales manager, and Mr. Jackson, the purchasing agent. Robert does call her, and after he has been interviewed by Mrs. Harvey and Mr. Jackson, within a week he thanks Ms. Bennett. In addition to showing courtesy, a thank-you letter also reminds the reader that Robert has been there.

Dear Ms. Bennett:

Thank you for arranging the appointments with Mrs. Harvey and Mr. Jackson last week. I will call again in late May, as you suggested, to find out if you plan to hire students for the summer.

In the meantime, please thank Mrs. Harvey for her explanation of the summer openings and Mr. Jackson for the tour of the buildings.

There are several points to remember about a thank-you letter for an interview. First, if someone has been especially helpful to you, you should direct special thanks to him or her. Second, you need to confirm whatever instructions were given you regarding your next step, in this case, to call again in May.

Preparing a Resumé

The resumé that will accompany your letter has been mentioned several times. The purpose of the resumé, as you have already inferred, is to give the reader information about your work experiences, your skills, your personal qualities, and your education that will help him or her assess your potential as an employee. When you analyzed your qualifications by answering the questions on pages 345–46, you completed the most difficult task in writing a resumé. Now, the easiest steps remain. Consider the process Mary Hymes used in composing her resumés:

1. What is my job objective? A full-time summer job which I can continue on weekends and evenings during the school year.
2. To whom am I applying? Hanover Convalescent Home, Mrs. Watkins, Chief Dietitian.
3. What work experience have I had? Weekends and evenings as dietitian's aide at Queensbury Hospital; full-time last summer.
4. What skills did I acquire in this position? Checked menus, wrote salt-free diets, prepared tube feedings and cold foods, and kept menu file up-to-date.

5. What personality traits will help me do the job well? I'm quick to learn, I get along well with others, I'm prompt, dependable, flexible.

6. What education have I had to prepare me for this job? Nothing directly related.

7. Who can and will recommend me? Mrs. Harriet Ohms, Head Dietitian, Queensbury Hospital; Mr. Samuel Scott, Director of Personnel, Queensbury Hospital; Mr. Frank Sullivan, Guidance Counselor, Eddington High School; Mrs. Helen Burrows, English Instructor, Culver Community College.

8. How can Mrs. Watkins contact me? Call 929-9113 any weekday from 9 until noon.

9. What is the best order in which to present the information?

The importance of neatness and correctness cannot be stressed enough. A resumé, along with the application letter, is the first contact the reader will have with you. A second consideration is conciseness. Perhaps it would help you to think of the resumé as an ordered summary of all the information you presented in your letter. Then, your letter gives the reader more details about the qualifications you have listed on your resumé.

Once you have composed your resumé and set it up on the page in such a way as to make your qualifications and personal information clear and concise, you can use the resumé for all the companies to which you write. Simply have the resumé duplicated without the title, and, using the same typewriter you used to type the resumé, rewrite the title so that it mentions the name of each company you are sending it to.

On page 350 is a form of a resumé. You have probably seen other forms which are also acceptable. If you decide to use another format, the important thing is to be consistent in your use of headings. For example, if a major heading is typed in capital letters, then you must type all the other major headings in capital letters.

Exercise

1. After reviewing the questions on pages 345–46, prepare a resumé to accompany the letter to the employer that you wrote.

2. Examine the sample resumé on page 350, and then answer the following questions.

<u>MARY HYMES'S</u> QUALIFICATIONS FOR A POSITION AS
A SUPERVISOR OF DIETITIAN'S AIDES
AT HANOVER CONVALESCENT HOME

6610 Milford Street, Apt. 2B　　　　Born May 23, 1961
Somerset, Pennsylvania 15510　　　　Excellent Health
929-9113

Professional Experience

Dietitian's Aide. Queensbury Hospital. Weekends and evenings during school year, full-time during summer, September, 1978-August, 1979

Responsibilities: Checked patients' menus, wrote salt-free diets, prepared tube feedings and special cold foods, kept menu file up-to-date

Education

Attend Culver Community College, September, 1980-
Graduated from Eddington High School, Somerset, Pennsylvania, June, 1979

References

Mrs. Harriet Ohms
Head Dietitian
Queensbury Hospital
Somerset, Pennsylvania 15501
932-7751

Mr. Samuel Scott
Director of Personnel
Queensbury Hospital
Somerset, Pennsylvania 15501
932-7754

Mr. Frank Sullivan
Guidance Counselor
Eddington High School
Somerset, Pennsylvania 15501
933-8900

Mrs. Helen Burrows
English Instructor
Department of English
Culver Community College
Somerset, Pennsylvania 15501
955-6767

a. What are the principal elements in the resumé?
b. How are they organized? What comes first and what comes afterward? Why?
c. What has been omitted from the resumé? What has been included? What is the basis of selection?
d. What is the verbal style of the resumé? In contrast to the letter? In contrast to the other kinds of writing?

We mentioned earlier that there are various ways of organizing resumés. Now that you have answered the above questions, reorganize Mary Hymes's resumé. Remember that as with all other forms of business writing, the resumé will be read by someone who is very busy.

WRITING REQUESTS

The success of a *request for information,* a *request for an adjustment* (sometimes called a claim)—for example, a refund or an exchange of merchandise—and an *appeal to a reader to do something that he or she may not be inclined to do* depends on telling the reader what he or she needs to know in order to satisfy the request. In these three kinds of requests, *clarity* and *conciseness* are important.

Requesting Information

Requests for information should be clear, complete, and to the point. Imagine, for example, the task that faces the employee of the Environmental Protection Agency who must fill this request for information:

Please send me information about government regulation of industrial emissions.

Because the request lacks clarity, the EPA employee has two choices: Should he or she send packets of printed material, knowing that much of it will be irrelevant to the writer's needs? Or should the employee request that the writer be more specific about what is wanted? In both cases, time is wasted, and both the EPA employee and the writer are frustrated. If the writer had named the industry or industries he or she needed information about and explained the need for the EPA material, the reader could have satisfied the request quickly and efficiently. And a request that is clear and concise is a courteous one, for it makes the reader's job easier.

Subject lines, typed below or in place of the salutation, also make the reader's job easier. The following subject line not only directs the EPA employee to specific printed material but also makes the request more concise:

> SUBJECT   A Request for Information about Government Regulation of Emission Control in the Aluminum and Asbestos Industries

Even if you use a subject line, an inquiry should still begin with a clear announcement of the subject, perhaps in question form. The request or question should be phrased so that it elicits yes or no answers (if, of course, it is a yes or no answer that you need). Sometimes questions require elaboration, as the following one does:

> Where can I learn which aluminum and asbestos companies have consistently complied with government emission standards? The information will be part of a class report on pollution in the Southwest, so I am especially interested in companies in that region.

If you need the information you have requested by a specific date, it is courteous to let the reader know that. Indicating the date, plus adding a courteous comment, is an effective way to make a favorable impression on your reader.

The letter on the facing page illustrates the elements that make up an effective request for information: a subject line; a clear, concise announcement of the subject; a list of questions, with explanations if they will help the reader answer the questions adequately; a courteous, reader-oriented ending.

Exercise

As a class, you have decided to spend a weekend together at a mountain inn. There are several inns in your area that you are considering. Using a subject line and itemizing your questions, compose an inquiry about group rates, recreational facilities, check-in time, public transportation from the bus stop to the inn, and whatever additional information you need to have in order to decide which inn to go to. Consider first, however, what the reader needs to know in order to satisfy your request.

Requesting Adjustments

In your personal and academic lives you have probably had to explain to someone that a service you paid for was unsatisfactory or

202 Harrison Hall
7321 Hoover Avenue
Somerset, Pennsylvania 15501
April 2, 19—

Mr. Jack Holmes, Director
Financial Services Office
Stone Hall 402
Culver Community College
Somerset, Pennsylvania 15501

Dear Mr. Holmes:

SUBJECT: Inquiry about Work—Study Program

As a second—semester freshman at Culver Community College, am I eligible for the Work—Study Program? If so, may I please have an application and answers to the following questions:

1. What are the maximum hours I could work?
2. Is there summer work that would continue through the regular academic year?
3. Would I have a choice of work—study positions? Because I have spent two summers living in Korea, I would especially like to work with foreign students.
4. Would my pay be deducted from my tuition, or would I be paid directly?

I would appreciate having the application and the information in time to apply for summer work.

Sincerely,

John McDowell

that merchandise you had purchased was damaged or that the wrong item was shipped. Perhaps the Campus Parking Office issued you a nontransferable parking permit instead of the transferable one you requested; or you were overcharged for work on your car; or a shirt you ordered was the wrong size. To call a letter in which you request an adjustment a "complaint" letter—as many people still do—is to assign the wrong purpose to the letter. The purpose of such a letter is not to complain, but rather to ask the reader to remedy a situation which you believe merits correction. Moreover, businesses generally welcome adjustment letters because they offer these organizations feedback on their products and services. In short, requests for adjustments help control quality, so everyone benefits from them.

This positive view of requests for adjustments will help you remain objective when you write. It will also encourage you to provide all the information the reader needs in order to remedy the situation. Keep in mind that the purpose of your letter is not to relieve your frustration and anger but to get the problem solved.

When you request an adjustment, the specific action you want the reader to take determines the details of the letter. Therefore, before you begin to write, you must formulate your reason for writing. For example, do you want an item replaced? Your money refunded? A damaged article repaired free? Parts of an incomplete order shipped?

Here is an example of a request for an adjustment that makes clear what the writer wants the reader to do.

SUBJECT: Request for Shipment of Second Bookcase in May 12 Order

Thank you for your prompt shipment of my fiberboard bookcase. My check for $19.49 was for two bookcases, plus shipping charges, and only one bookcase was delivered on June 10. Please ship the second one immediately.

Some requested adjustments are not so simple for the company as this example, however. For instance, another unhappy customer who had purchased five bookcases wrote the following letter:

On May 12 I ordered five fiberboard bookcases, four for $8.98 each, and one for $12.98. My check for $53.90 included $5.00 for shipping. On June 10, only three bookcases were delivered. Although I am pleased with two of them, the $12.98 case had four one-eighth-inch-deep scratches on the top.

Because I have thirty unpacked boxes of books, I cannot wait for the replacement and the other bookcases to be shipped. Therefore, I have returned the damaged one and would appreciate a speedy refund so that I can buy cases at a nearby store. Please send your check for $30.94 representing $12.98 for the bookcase I have returned and $17.96 for the two bookcases you have not shipped.

As with the first letter, the action the writer wants the reader to take is clear: in this case, he or she wants a refund for the damaged bookcase and the two not shipped. This courteous letter gives the date of the order, the method and amount of the payment, the problem with the products, the justification for the request, and the exact amount of the expected refund with an explanation of the figure. Notice, too, that the writer blames no one for the inconvenience.

Exercise

You paid for a three-year subscription to a monthly magazine. When the first issue arrived, the address sticker showed that your subscription will expire in one year. Request that the circulation department correct the error.

Special Requests

A special request may require persuasion to get the reader to do something. Requests to contribute time or money, to complete a questionnaire, to speak to a special-interest group, are a few examples. Assume, for purposes of discussion, that you want a business person to hold practice interviews with your class in preparation for your summer job search. You know that to ask a business person to sacrifice a morning out of his or her busy schedule is an imposition. However, if you approach the letter-writing task with the attitude that the interviewer will benefit from the visit to your class, your special request can be effective. It is, first of all, good public relations for a company representative to perform a public service. Second, interviewing you and your classmates gives the representative a chance to assess the calibre of students who may be applying for part-time positions with the company. It also reveals what kinds of questions and job interests students have. Fi-

English Department
Elkton College
Henderson, Kentucky 42420
March 24, 19——

Ms. Ellen Walters
Personnel Director
Hudson Chemical Company
Henderson, Kentucky 42420

Dear Ms. Walters:

In April and May, approximately two thousand Henderson
area college students will be seeking summer employment.
Because Hudson Chemical Company is known to fill summer
positions by hiring students, many will be applying to
your company. To prepare for our summer job search, my
freshman English class is inviting several personnel directors from companies with policies similar to yours to
come to campus and conduct practice interviews. The interviews will give us experience with interview techniques and would give you a chance to learn what kinds of
skills and aptitudes Hudson's potential applicants have.

Can you interview three of us in front of our class on Monday, Wednesday, or Friday, April 21, 23, or 25? Our class
meets from 9:00 until 10:20 a.m. in 302 Stover Hall.

As soon as we hear from you, we will send you our application letters and resumés so that you can select the people
you want to interview. Our instructor, Professor Janet
Green, can be reached in her office from 9:00 until noon on
Tuesdays and Thursdays. Her number is 727-4556.

Respectfully,

John Hamilton
Coordinator of Student Interviews

nally, mock interviews give students practice for the real interview situations, and the interviews that the representative conducts will be all the more productive because he or she has participated in the mock interviews.

From this discussion we can see that there are basically two important prewriting considerations for a special request: deciding how the reader will benefit from satisfying your request, and approaching the request with confidence that the reader will do what you want. Both of these can be seen in the illustration of a special request on page 356. Notice, too, that the beginning of the letter captures the reader's attention. Next, the writer is persuasive by pointing out the benefits to the reader. Then, he includes details that the reader must know in order to satisfy the request. Finally, the writer makes it easy for the reader to respond to the request.

Exercise

1. Assume that you want to invite a staff member of your college administration office to speak to your class. Before you begin to write your request, discuss these questions:

    a. How would a visit to your class benefit the reader of your letter?
    b. How can you capture the reader's attention?
    c. What does the reader need to know in order to agree to your request?
    d. How can you make it easy for the reader to respond?

Now, write your request.

2. As an annual project, an organization to which you belong is collecting toys and money to buy toys to distribute to children in a nearby children's hospital. Write a special request to local businesses asking for their contributions.

ANSWERING REQUESTS

Responding to Requests for Information

Some replies to requests for information need only a preprinted postcard or form letter that either says that the material requested is on its way or answers questions which are frequently asked. In those instances when unusual questions are asked, however, a personalized business letter may be required, such as this response to the student's inquiry on page 358.

The Financial Services Office
CULVER COMMUNITY COLLEGE
Somerset, Pennsylvania 15501

April 15, 19——

Mr. John McDowell
202 Harrison Hall
7321 Hoover Avenue
Somerset, Pennsylvania 15501

Dear John:

As a second—semester freshman, you are eligible to apply for a position in the Work—Study Program at Culver Community College. The enclosed application and a financial statement from your parents or legal guardian must be submitted by May 10 in order for you to be considered for summer employment. As Item 21 on the application explains, to be eligible for summer employment, you must commit yourself to fall employment also.

After the Financial Services Office notifies you of your eligibility for work—study employment, you will find job lists posted in the Work—Study Center, Stone Hall 301. You then apply directly to the office or department that has announced a position you are interested in and for which you are qualified. Once you have accepted a position, you and your supervisor determine your weekly schedule. Although there is a maximum limit of forty hours a month and no minimum limit, Financial Services will specify the maximum number of hours you will be permitted to work. This decision is based on your course load and your financial needs.

Salaries for work—study positions range from $3.50 to $5.00 an hour, depending upon the position you apply for, and checks are issued directly to you every two weeks.

Since you are interested in working with foreign students, you may want to contact Dr. Jayne Hansen, Director of the English Language and Orientation Institute in Washington Hall, Room 2. Each semester ELOI employs twenty students to assist instructors in conversation classes and to supervise the audio—visual laboratory sections for foreign students.

We look forward to receiving your application and financial statement before May 10.

Sincerely,

Jack Holmes, Director

Application and Financial
Statement Enclosed

  Mr. Holmes's reply illustrates several elements that are characteristic of effective responses to inquiries. First, he opened his reply with the answer John was most interested in, the one John needed in order for the following answers to make sense. He did not waste John's time by beginning with an empty comment like "Thank you for your interest in CCC's Work-Study Program." Instead, Mr. Holmes showed his appreciation for John's interest by telling him what was most important immediately: "Yes, you are eligible." Second, he answered all of John's questions clearly, concisely, and thoroughly. If an answer had been omitted, John might have thought the writer intended to mislead him or had not read his inquiry carefully. Third, Mr. Holmes combined answers to John's questions. For example, the first paragraph answers John's first and third questions: "Am I eligible?" and "Is there summer employment?" Finally, the letter closes with clear instructions for John.

  Mr. Holmes's response was limited to answering questions in John's inquiry. There are occasions, however, when an inquiry offers a company an opportunity to sell its service or product. Besides answering the questions posed in the inquiry, the response then should include incentives for the reader to buy the product or use the service he or she has inquired about. The purpose of this kind of response is twofold: to answer the questions and to convince the reader to do business with the company.

  As an example, let us imagine that a student requested information about group rates for theater tickets. Although this request is not a ticket order, it has the potential of becoming an order if the response is effective. Therefore, the ticket manager must not only answer the questions, but also encourage the student to buy tickets. In the following reply to a request for information about twenty tickets for a Saturday matinee, the italicized parts do not answer questions asked in the inquiry: the information is included to encourage the reader to order tickets and to make ordering easy.

You and your nineteen classmates can purchase tickets at group rate for the June 7, 14, 21, and 28 matinees of "Annie," *which begin at 2:30*. Individual tickets for all seats are $7.50, and prices for groups larger than ten are $6.50 per individual. As students, you will also receive an additional $1.00 discount, provided you order the tickets two weeks in advance of the performance.

So that you can take advantage of the student group rates, an order form is enclosed, along with reviews and order forms for the July and August performances of Tom Stoppard's "Rosencrantz and Guildenstern Are Dead" and George Bernard Shaw's "Major Barbara."

We look forward to receiving your ticket order soon so that you and your class can enjoy a delightful production of "Annie" for only $5.50 a person.

Like Mr. Holmes's response to John McDowell's inquiry, the ticket manager's reply begins with an answer to the question the student was most interested in: "Yes, group rates are available." And the letter ends with a courteous comment that combines praise of the play and a reminder of the deadline for ordering discount tickets. In addition, the ticket manager also added information that will encourage the class to get tickets for "Annie" and perhaps for the Stoppard and Shaw plays.

Some correspondents think that providing information beyond the answers to questions asked in an inquiry is overly aggressive. On the contrary. It is a courteous touch, as in the case of the mention of the Stoppard and Shaw plays. If the class cannot make the "Annie" shows, they may want to see one of the other shows, especially after they have read the reviews. To guard against having your promotional information seem aggressive, add only that information which is directly related to the questions asked in the inquiry. Another guide to adding details is this: If you don't add it, will the reader need to write again? Will you save both yourself and the reader time by adding it?

Requests for information cannot always be satisfied. If the information is no longer available, rather than saying, "I'm sorry, we don't have that information," the writer of the response attempts to retain the reader's good will by offering alternatives. The guide for handling negative responses is this: Tell the reader what you *can* do, not what you *cannot* do.

While all letters require careful planning to be effective, planning is crucial in a negative letter. The purpose is to refuse the request and at the same time retain the good will of the reader. But the message doesn't say "No." Nor does it say "No. . . . How-

ever." Instead, it implies the "No" by emphasizing the reasons behind the "however," as the following example illustrates. In this
case, the person receiving the negative response had asked for free
road maps and lists of camping sites from an oil company.

MeCo
Public Relations Division
130278 Gateway Boulevard
Chicago, Illinois 60646

May 10, 19--

Ms. Sarah Smalley
9201 Quebec Street
Granston, Ohio 44057

Dear Ms. Smalley:

The road maps and lists of camping sites that MeCo customers have used for over twenty years to plan their trips
continue to make vacation planning more pleasant for hundreds of thousands of travelers.

In order to make the maps and lists available to as many
MeCo customers as possible—and as quickly as possible—
your local MeCo dealer now distributes them for fifty
cents each. Your Yellow Pages will tell you where you can
pick up the maps and lists so that you can plan your trips
with confidence and ease.

Sincerely,

Jason M. Smith, Director
Public Relations Division

Exercise

1. Compose a refusal of a request based on the following situation: A customer of long standing, the owner of a retail furniture store, has requested two hundred free copies of your annual catalogue of home furnishings to distribute to his customers. Your wholesale company has decided the service is too expensive to continue, but the catalogues are available for $2.50 if the retailer's customers would like to order them directly from your company. With your letter, include several dozen forms and six catalogues for the retailer's use in his showrooms.

2. Working in several groups, compose lists of four or five questions about a product or service that everyone in your class knows something about (or can make up details about). Exchange the lists with other groups and write responses. Consider the following questions before you begin composing the response:

a. What is the best order in which to answer the questions?
b. Do you have answers to *all* of the questions?
c. What additional information will you include?
d. What means of response will you include? A number to be called collect? An order form?
e. Can you combine some of the answers?

Responding to Requests for Adjustments

When customers ask for adjustments—refunds, exchanges, replacements, parts of incomplete orders shipped—many companies usually do exactly what the customer has requested. They think of the customer as a potential buyer and, therefore, will do what he or she asks in the hope of making future sales. Whatever loss they take, they make up in creating good will for the company. Effective favorable responses to a disappointed customer convince that customer that he or she comes first with the company.

Apologizing for the source of displeasure is not effective in convincing the customer that he or she comes first with the company. Thus, using words like "damaged," "broken," or "malfunction" defeat the purpose of the letter: to keep the customer. You can do this by promoting a service or product related to the one he or she has sought an adjustment for or by announcing a forthcoming sale, as is the method used in the following example. The four throw pillows Mrs. Jones charged to her account do not match the shades of brown in her living room, and thus she returned them to the store. The policy of the company is to accept all reasonable requests for adjustments.

> The four 18-inch by 24-inch throw pillows have arrived, and $29.95 has been credited to your account.
>
> Your announcement of Hancock's annual household furnishings sale is enclosed. The prices of three thousand cushions and other decorator items have been reduced twenty percent. Calling us collect at (800) 777-6263 or ordering with the form on page 3 can save you time and money on attractive May and June shower gifts.

It is relatively easy to write an adjustment letter when the company's policy is that "the customer is always right." However, many companies do not have such a policy. The alternative is to handle each adjustment request on its own merits.

Like the negative response to a request for information, a rejection of an adjustment request has a twofold purpose: to refuse the adjustment and yet hold the customer's positive attitude toward the company's product or service. Again, the strategy is to prepare the reader for the refusal by establishing the writer's reasonableness. An effective beginning avoids hints of either acceptance or rejection, and it avoids negative reminders of the reader's annoyance. Yet, the opening sentence or two that the writer is confident the reader will agree to must be related to the product or service for which the request was made. The second part of the letter gives a reason that should be so sound, so logical, that the implied refusal will be obvious to the reader, perhaps before he or she reads it. The next step is to offer an alternative to the requested adjustment. It is essential to make the alternative attractive and thereby retain the reader's favorable attitude. The final step is to make it easy for the reader to respond favorably to the counterproposal. This can be done with a specific suggestion about how to respond and a final reminder of the reader's positive attitude toward the product or service.

Emphasis on the benefits the reader will gain from the alternative is important. One of the most successful ways to emphasize these benefits is to make the reader see, hear, feel, or smell the product in his or her own environment. The first and last sentences of the following letter illustrate effective applications of this principle. The request for an adjustment was from a woman who had paid $175.00 for an Egyptian tray. After several unsuccessful attempts to hang it on her wall by using adhesive mounts, she wants to return the tray and get her money back.

EVERETT'S IMPORTS, LTD.
1202 Lincolnshire Boulevard
Des Moines, Iowa 50316

August 12, 19--

Mrs. Cherly Gibbs
7261 Granville Road
Harriston, Minnesota 55102

Dear Mrs. Gibbs:

You are certainly correct in expecting that the thirty-six-inch copper Egyptian tray which you purchased from Everett's on July 20 can be hung securely on the wall.

Your experience with adhesive mounts is a common one for owners of trays that weigh from eight to ten pounds. Adhesive mounts usually do not sustain that much weight for more than a week or so. That is why we recommend a three-quarter-inch metal loop be soldered to the back of the tray approximately three inches above the center.

Because you are pleased with the compliments your tray has received, may we arrange to have the soldering done for you by the company that has done our work for the past ten years? Their charge to retailers is $15.00, nearly $7.00 less than you would probably pay if you had the soldering done locally. Ten days after we receive the enclosed postcard indicating your decision, your copper tray can be securely hung again, and you will be receiving compliments on the unique tray.

Sincerely,

Marjorie Goode
Sales Manager

Exercise

1. A customer has requested that your leather goods store exchange a brown pigskin wallet for a black pigskin one or else give him a refund. Because the manufacturer of his wallet no longer produces the wallet in black pigskin, you send him a refund. However, you also send him advertisements for new designs in wallets that you will be receiving in a month. Suggest he apply the refund to one of the new designs. Send him an order form.

2. As the manager of an office furniture store, you must refuse a request for a refund on a four-drawer legal-size filing cabinet ($69.95). The buyer, Mr. Smith, was pleased with the cabinet, but it does not fit under the window of his den, the only space he has for it. Rather than refund his money, you suggest he take instead two two-drawer cabinets, which are on sale for $34.98 each. You will send the two for $5.00 shipping charges.

Before you begin composing the letter, consider the following:

   a. What do you both agree upon—something related to the filing cabinets that you can discuss in the opening paragraph to indicate you are reasonable?
   b. Why would it benefit the reader to accept your offer?
   c. How can you create a vivid picture of the two cabinets situated under the window in his den?
   d. How can you make it easy for him to respond?

WRITING MEMORANDUMS

Communication within an organization, such as between members of a university department or employees in different divisions of a company, is usually in the form of an interdepartmental or interoffice memorandum. Memo forms are generally available within the organization; however, there may be times when you will need to create your own form. In that case, you simply type MEMORANDUM at the top of the page; then, type the reader's name and position, your name and position, the date, and the subject of the memo, which tells the reader at a glance what the memo is about. Although placement of that information can take several forms, the following is the most commonly used one.

MEMORANDUM

TO: Sandra Simpson, Office Manager

FROM: Quentin Green, Shipping Department

DATE: September 12, 19—

RE: My Absence from Work on September 18, 19—

A memorandum, then, is a way to transmit a message to someone who is a member of your group. It can explain an event, report information, summarize progress on a project, recommend improvements, to name just a few of its purposes. Because the purpose and the reader determine the language you use in any writing, it is difficult to generalize about the level of formality appropriate to a memorandum. If you are, for example, writing (and not typing) a memo to your immediate supervisor, who has asked for a list of equipment needed for a project, you can simply write "Here's the list of equipment you asked for." On the other hand, memos may transmit to a group of executives technical, specialized information, and will thus require highly formal language. Perhaps the only generalization that can be made is this: The language should be appropriate to both the purpose of the message and the reader.

Here is a brief, informal memo Quentin wrote to his boss:

MEMORANDUM

TO: Sandra Simpson, Office Manager

FROM: Quentin Green, Shipping Department

DATE: September 12, 19—

RE: My Absence from Work on September 18, 19—

The guidance counselor at Eddington High School in Somerset wants me to participate in my high school's Career Day on September 18, so I'll be missing work that day. I've spoken to my supervisor, Mr. Trainor, about this and he said that he can cover for me, if you have no objection. I hope you will give your approval.

Memorandums that are long or have complex messages require headings—captions that tell the reader the gist of the information grouped below each heading. Headings help the writer organize the information in the memorandum, but they also are especially helpful to the reader. For example, a lengthy memo may contain sections of information of interest only to specific individuals who can then skim the facts dealing with other areas of specialization and concentrate on those sections that are relevant to their own interests. The following memo illustrates the value of headings.

TO: Virginia Patton, Communications Coordinator,
        Corporate Headquarters

FROM: Steve Henderson, District Manager

DATE: April 17, 19--

SUBJECT: Communication System at Southwestern Life In-
         surance Company in Hendrix

Here is the information you requested about the communication system within the Hendrix office and with other
Southwestern offices.

Within the Office

    Agent to Prospect:
        Graphs and charts to explain prospect's in-
            surance needs
        Telephones to call prospect to set up and
            confirm appointment
        Letters and reply cards with small free gift
            to attract new prospects
        Reply cards (Form 21-330) to request addi-
            tional information from agent
    Agent to Agent:
        Verbal agreements on best sales methods to
            use
        Weekly conferences to discuss problems and
            set weekly goals
        Discussion among agents to solve individual
            insurance problem
    Agent to Secretary:
        Messages from clients to agents relayed on
            three-copy memo (Form 44-348) or note
            card
        Dictaphone messages to be typed when agent is
            out
        Daily log of what was done and what is to be
            done
    Secretary to Client:
        Appointment verification

April 17, 19--
Virginia Patton
Communication System at Southwestern Life Insurance Company in Hendrix

Greeting of prospects when they come for appointments
Letters to clients when agent's assistance not required

To Other Offices
District Agency to General Agency:
Three-copy memos, applications for insurance, and home office inquiries to general agency
Telephone when immediate answer needed
Three-copy memos to send short messages between agencies
Weekly news bulletins to explain agents' weekly sales status
Quarterly business conferences to summarize sales and set sales goals
District Agency to Home Office:
Direct mailing information for fast response to questions
Telephone to home office personnel about applications
Transmittal letters to inform main office of changes in clients' payments or policies (Forms 37-541, 26-771, and 68-990).
Notification of policy changes and daily status of applications being processed
Monthly reports of agents' sales

Attachments (5)

Exercise

1. Imagine that you are a clerk in the credit office of a large manufacturer. On November 10 you were assigned the task of alphabetizing the company's accounts receivable records, which had been organized numerically; on November 15 you completed the job. Write a memo to the credit manager, Robert Green, describing the reorganization and telling him that it has been completed. Your task involved not only alphabetizing the records but also developing a cross-reference index organized by account numbers. The credit manager requires this information so that he and his staff can quickly find the record of an individual account.

2. Ask a local business person to describe the company's written communications. Write a memorandum to your English instructor describing the correspondence the business uses, both within its company and to its patrons. Perhaps you can attach samples of forms the company uses, such as memorandums or postcards telling customers their orders have arrived or reminders of overdue payments. Before you inquire, however, be sure to plan your interview so that you use the business person's time effectively.

WRITING PROGRESS REPORTS

Occasions may arise when you have to report on the progress of a project you are working on. For example, your advisor may ask you to report on your progress toward fulfilling the requirements of your undergraduate degree. Or the fund-raising committee of an organization to which you belong needs to know how close it is to attaining its goal. Or on the job, you may be asked to report sales progress, as in the case of the sales report on page 370, written by a student whose summer job was selling hospital supplies.

The purpose of the student's report is to document progress on sales; thus, it involves an account of his visits, the sales he made, the potential sales, a comparison with last year's sales in the same area, and a projection of sales. The report includes all of the information the reader needs to be aware of the progress of one of her representatives. Realizing that the important information, if presented in the form of a letter, would be buried in many unnecessary words and would not be organized so that the reader could see the information most useful to her—the summary of sales for the area—the student wrote the report in the form of a memo. In the memo he supplied

NATIONAL HOSPITAL SUPPLIES, INC.
MEMORANDUM

SUBJECT: Weekly Progress Report No. 7 on Sales Activities in Iowa District 17

TO: Margaret Weintraub, Iowa District Sales Manager

FROM: Ronald Symms, District 17 Sales Representative

DATE: August 9, 19—

Following are a summary of sales for District 17, a list of
my visits and sales for August 4 in the Sioux City area,
and a list of visits planned for August 11-15.

Summary of Sales

August 4-8 sales were $1778.00. Sales for District 17 are
higher than sales at this time last year. August and September sales projections are 15% above last August and
September's sales.

Visits and Sales for August 4-8

Date	Place	Sales
August 4	Maryville Hospital	$247.00
5	Harrison Hospital	865.00
6	St. Andrews Medical Center	327.00
7	Johnson Memorial Hospital	144.00
	Doctors Clinic	75.00
8	Campbell Professional Center	$120.00

Total = $1778.00

Visits for August 11-14

Date	Place
August 11	Memorial Hospital, Mill Creek
12	Huntingdon and Jackson
13	Wilson and Manning
14	Manning Rehabilitation Center
15	Mesa Memorial Hospital, Mesa

headings, eliminated words, and organized the information so that it could be understood quickly.

Because Ronald Symms knew that Ms. Weintraub would prepare a summary report to *her* supervisor using the information he and other sales representatives submitted to her, he placed a summary at the beginning of his memorandum. Usually, progress reports, which may be requested at set intervals, tell the reader what has been done, what is being done, and what remains to be done—in that order. If the progress report is a second report on a project, tie the current report to the earlier one to show continuity in the work. The second part, the most important section, discusses the work in progress, that is, the problems that have arisen, the fact that work on the project is on schedule. The final section summarizes what remains to be done.

So that you are not left with the impression that all progress reports are as brief as Ronald Symms's, consider the volumes of progress reports that would be written about a long-term defense project or a new automobile model still in the design stages.

Exercise

1. Assume that an instructor has requested three progress reports, to be submitted every two weeks, on a class project. If you are currently working on a project, write a second progress report. Otherwise, create a situation about which you can write a second report.

2. In an earlier exercise (page 357), you requested local businesses to contribute toys and money for a children's hospital. Assume that it is a month before the toy drive is to end. As the chairperson of the toy drive, report your committee's progress in a memo that will be read at the next executive meeting of the organization.

A Guide to Research

C HAPTER 6 discussed exposition, writing that is used to explain ideas, explore them, or demonstrate them through data or logic or both. The typical "research paper" demonstrates. It states a problem, discusses it (with necessary "facts and figures"), and draws a conclusion. If the evidence presented is adequate and the conclusion logically follows from the evidence, the reader will be convinced.

However, any kind of writing might call for research: a report (explanatory writing) might be based totally on research; research into a problem might not yield a conclusion, and the result could well be a piece of exploratory writing. In order to persuade readers (to vote for a given candidate, for example), it is often necessary to provide reliable background data that comes from research.

There are, of course, many kinds of research: a chemist might well do most of his or hers in the laboratory, while anthropologists frequently use whole cultures or societies as their "laboratories." Public opinion polls are another kind of research, as are personal interviews of the kind published in *Playboy* and other magazines. But this chapter will concern library research. It surveys library resources and outlines procedures for gathering information and for documenting sources within the paper (that is, footnoting).

THE RESEARCH SITUATION

Much of this book has been a discussion of problem-solving. (For example, all of Chapter 3, on prewriting, concerned that.) And this chapter will not repeat what has been handled in detail else-where, but will attempt to give you some guidance with the kinds of problems that research can solve.

Notice how common it is to encounter a problematic situation that demands research. In your reading, you come across a word that you don't know the meaning of, so you go to the dictionary. That's research of a sort. Your old car finally gives out. Now you have a problem: What kind of car should you buy to replace the old one? You decide that you want a compact, but don't know which kind. So you go to *Consumer Reports* for evaluations, you visit dealers and take test drives, you talk with people who own the various types of compacts. You have done research.

The first of these two problems would not provide the basis for a research paper. To solve it, you simply look up a small piece of in-formation (the meaning of the word). But the second problem— what kind of new car to buy—could well provide the basis for an interesting paper, which in outline might look like this:

I. Background of problem
   A. The reason for a new car
   B. Factors affecting the choice of a new car
      1. Need for a car that will accommodate four passengers
      2. Financial restrictions, limiting the initial purchase price
      3. Considerations of fuel economy
II. Formulation of problem [Taking passenger space, purchase price, and fuel economy into consideration, you decide to buy a compact. Thus the problem is: Which compact should you buy?]
III. Investigation of problem
   A. *Consumer Reports*
   B. Opinions of current owners of various makes of compacts
   C. Test drives of various makes
IV. Conclusion based on investigation

The third section of the paper is the one that embodies the results of your research, and the reader will be asking, "Where did the writer get this information? Are the sources reliable? Does the writer let me know what the sources are so that I can verify the paper's accuracy?" You would need some way of referring your reader to the proper issue of *Consumer Reports*, you probably would want to give some background about the owners whose opinions you cited, and you would want to report fully on the results of your test drives. All of this amounts to *documentation*, about which we will be talking as the chapter progresses.

A BRIEF SURVEY OF LIBRARY RESOURCES

Once you have formulated a problem, how do you find printed materials (articles, book, monographs, charts, tables, government reports, newspaper articles, and so on) that bear on it?

We assume that you have a general familiarity with the card catalogue, that you know how to navigate in the library. If you do *not* have that knowledge, then you must get it immediately. Chances are, your college library conducts orientation tours or has prepared a free guide. In any case, you need to know how to use a library. What follows is a general guide to the types of sources that you can find in a library.

General Encyclopedias

When you must do research in a field that is unfamiliar, you need some kind of introduction, or overview. The best source for this is a general encyclopedia. The five standard encyclopedias are:

The Encyclopaedia Britannica. Noted for the excellence of its articles concerning the humanities. Contains selected bibliographies that can be useful to a person who is just beginning to do research on a given topic.

The Encyclopedia Americana. Usually considered the best source for articles concerning the sciences. References will lead the researcher to other standard discussions of topics.

Chambers's Encyclopedia. Provides standard references on topics. A British publication.

Collier's Encyclopedia. The bibliography is centralized in the twenty-fourth volume.

Columbia Encyclopedia. Articles are not as extensive as those in the other encyclopedias. Useful for quick reference.

Unabridged Dictionaries

If the research in question involves the meanings of words, the unabridged dictionaries are invaluable sources. The three that you ought to be aware of are these:

A Dictionary of American English on Historical Principles. This four-volume work, edited by Sir William A. Craigie and James R. Hulbert, gives the histories of meanings of words in American English.

The Oxford English Dictionary. Available as a thirteen-volume work or in a two-volume, reduced-print edition that must be read with a magnifying glass. A reissue of *A New English Dictionary on Historical Principles,* this work is the most complete source for the histories of word meanings in English.

Webster's Third New International Dictionary. This is the most widely used unabridged dictionary of English, the huge book that you find in the reading rooms of most libraries.

Other unabridged dictionaries are *Funk & Wagnall's New "Standard" Dictionary of the English Language, The Random House Dictionary of the English Language,* and *Webster's New Twentieth Century Dictionary.*

General Indexes

Suppose your research involved the eruption of Mount St. Helens in 1980. Your library would probably contain books about volcanos in general, but none about Mount St. Helens specifically. Your primary source would be magazines and newspapers. Fortunately, a variety of general indexes direct you to specific newspaper and magazine articles. Most of these indexes are arranged like the card catalogue in your library; that is, each entry is listed by author, title, and subject.

Book Review Digest. Appears monthly (except February and July). As its name indicates, it is a guide to reviews of books.

International Index. In April of 1965, the title was changed to *Social Sciences and Humanities Index,* and beginning in April of 1974, the volume was split so that *Social Sciences Index* and *Humanities Index* appear separately. Both of these now appear quarterly, with yearly cumulative issues. As the names imply, they are indices to journals that publish articles in the social sciences and humanities.

New York Times Index. An author-subject-title listing of articles in the *New York Times.* Since newspapers all over the country deal with the same national and international news events, this index also serves as a rough index to other newspapers.

Nineteenth Century Reader's Guide to Periodical Literature, 1890–1899. An author-subject index covering some fifty periodicals that were published during the period concerned.

Poole's Index to Periodical Literature, 1802–1881. Index to British and American periodicals of the period covered.

Reader's Guide to Periodical Literature. An author-subject-title listing of articles in about 125 periodicals of general interest. Issued semimonthly, with annual and five-year cumulative editions.

Biographical Sources

Should your research involve biographical questions, you can go to

Biography Index: A Cumulative Index to Biographical Material in Books and Magazines.

Current Biography: Who's News and Why. Fairly extensive biographies of people in the news.

Who's Who. Brief biographies of notable people, chiefly in the British Commonwealth.

Who's Who in America. American counterpart of *Who's Who.*

Dictionary of American Biography. Excellent and fairly extensive biographies of dead Americans.

Dictionary of National Biography. British counterpart of *Dictionary of American Biography.*

Specialized Sources

Our purpose is to survey the kinds of sources available to the researcher, not to provide a complete bibliographical list of everything that a good library contains. Therefore, it is enough to say that there are specialized reference works (including indexes) for virtually every subject. For example, if your question involves mythology, you will find the *Larousse Encyclopedia of Mythology,* or if your question concerns physics, you may want to turn to *International Dictionary of Physics and Electronics.* To get some idea of the range of sources that are available, just glance through the following list: *Dictionary of Modern Ballet, Art Index, Cambridge Bibliography of English Literature, Encyclopedia of the Social Sciences, The New Schaff-Herzog Encyclopedia of Religious Knowledge, Van Nostrand's Scientific Encyclopedia, Education Index.* And the list could go on and on.

Your college or public library undoubtedly has trained people in its reference room who can guide you to exactly the sources that you need.

A SYSTEMATIC APPROACH TO RESEARCH AND WRITING

The following outline is a sort of recipe for a research paper. None of the steps are sacred, and you will undoubtedly develop your own methods as you become a sophisticated researcher. Meanwhile, however, following the steps that are about to be explained will get you under way with a minimum of turmoil and wasted time.

Survey of Materials

Once you have stated your problem, you need to survey the materials that are available concerning it. A good first step is to get an overview of the subject by reading pertinent articles in general and specialized encyclopedias. But the actual research will probably begin at the card catalogue. (What books, pamphlets, and other materials concerning the subject are in your college library?) Probably the next step will be to survey the periodical literature concerning the subject; therefore, you'll go to indexes, such as the *Reader's Guide* or the *New York Times Index,* or others, depending on your subject.

Bibliography Cards

Obviously, you need some way of keeping track of the possible sources that you find. Therefore, you will want to make a bibliography card for each source. Listing each source separately on either a 3″ x 5″ or a 4″ x 5″ card will allow you to shuffle entries, alphabetize them, and locate them more quickly. Another tip: make absolutely certain that the information on your bibliography card is accurate and complete. You will be using this information to find the sources in the library, and later you will be using it as the basis for your footnotes.

For Books

The following is a useful and convenient form for a bibliography card for a book:

(a) *Merill, Thomas F.*

(b) *Allen Ginsberg*
(c) *New York:* (d) *Twayne Publishers,* (e) *1969*

(f) *PS 3513 I7428*

Key: (a) author's name, last name first; (b) full title of the book; (c) place of publication; (d) publisher; (e) date of publication or copyright; (f) library call number for the book. You will need items (a) through (e) for your footnotes and for the bibliography that you append to your paper. You will need item (f) in order to find the book in your library.

For Journal Articles

The following model of a bibliography card can be used for journal or magazine articles:

(a) Dickstein, Morris

(b) "Allen Ginsberg and the 60's," (c) *Commentary*, (d) 49 (e) (Jan. 1970), (f) 64-70

Key: (a) name of the author of the article, last name first; (b) title of the article; (c) name of the magazine or journal in which the article appeared; (d) volume number of the issue in which the article appeared; (e) date of the issue; (f) pages on which the article appeared. (If the magazine is assigned a call number, it should be entered in the right-hand corner.)

These are the two basic forms, and they will cover about three-fourths of the sources that you normally encounter. If you encounter sources that pose special problems, you should speak to your instructor, or turn to *A Manual for Writers of Term Papers, Theses, and Dissertations,* by Kate L. Turabian. The thing to remember, however, is that you need full information on your bibliography card.

When we come to the discussion of footnotes, you will see forms for a variety of sources, and these will guide you to the information that you will need to include on your bibliography card. For example, you might read an article by one author that is included in a collection edited by another author. In that case, your card would look like this:

(a) Jakobson, Roman

(b) "Linguistics and Poetics,"

(c) *Style in Language*.

(d) Ed. Thomas A. Sebeok.

(e) Cambridge, Mass.   (f) M.I.T. Press,

(g) 1960. (h) Pp. 379-386

(i) 808
C748's

Key: (a) name of the author of the article; (b) title of the article; (c) title of the volume in which the article appears; (d) name of the editor—the abbreviation *ed.* means "edited by"; (e) place of publication; (f) publisher; (g) date of publication; (h) pages on which selection is found; (i) library call number.

Note-Taking

After your survey of the available materials is completed, you are ready to start your reading—though much of what you do will not be reading at all, but scanning. In other words, your initial survey has provided you with possible sources for information; now you must go to those sources to see if they contain materials that will be useful to you.

Once again, 3" x 5" or 4" x 6" cards are essential. When you find useful information, you need to record it; by recording it on cards, you can order the items according to the aspect of your subject that they deal with. Let's take a concrete example.

Your subject is the poetic development of Allen Ginsberg. You have done a complete survey of possible resources and have a large stack of bibliography cards that will guide you to those resources. Among the cards is this one:

> *Roszak, Theodore*
>
> *The Making of a Counter-Culture*
> *Garden City, New York: Anchor*
> *Books, 1969*
>
> HN
> 17.5
> R6

In this book, on page 126, you find a passage claiming that Ginsberg's early poems are tighter and more formally satisfying than the later ones. The passage reads like this:

> There is the willingness to be brief and to the point—and then to break off before the energy has been dissipated. By the early fifties, however, Ginsberg has abandoned these conventional literary virtues in favor of a spontaneous and unchecked flow of language. From this point on, everything he writes has the appearance of being served up raw, in the first draft, just as it must have come from his mind and mouth.[1]

You decide to incorporate this opinion into your paper, for it seems to be important. You have two choices: either you can transcribe it verbatim onto a note card, making sure that you do not miscopy, or you can paraphrase it. In most instances, you will want to paraphrase, for transcribing the exact words of your sources would be far too tedious a job and wouldn't be useful anyway, since you are looking for concepts and information, not quotes. Suppose, then, that you decide Roszak's opinion will be useful to you, but that you don't want to quote him exactly. In that case, you will make a note card that looks something like this:

[1] Theodore Roszak, *The Making of a Counter-Culture* (Garden City, N.Y.: Anchor Books, 1969), p. 126.

> *Roszak*   *poetic technique (crits.)*
>
> *126. As G. progressed through the 1950s he became more undisciplined, did not revise or tighten. R. says that by the early 50s everything that G. writes has "the appearance of being served up raw, in the first draft."*

At the top of your note card, in the left-hand corner, you have written the last name of the author of the book. Therefore, you can refer back to your bibliography card and find exactly where the material came from. (If in your bibliography you had more than one work by Roszak, you would include a key word of the title after his name, to indicate which of your sources this note had come from.) In the upper right-hand corner, you have put a key phrase, to indicate to yourself the general subject of the note. The *126* is the exact page on which the material was found. This information is extremely important for footnoting. Finally, you have paraphrased the material, but in so doing, you have used some of Roszak's phrases. Whenever you have quoted Roszak directly, you have put the material in quotation marks so that you will know which words are your own and which are Roszak's.

Let's pause to give an illustration that will clarify the process being discussed. You are writing your paper, and in one section of it you want to discuss the supposed artistic deterioration of Ginsberg. One passage in this section of your paper reads like this:

> Ginsberg's work has changed through the years, but has it deteriorated? One critic claims that Ginsberg's earlier poems are tighter and more formally satisfying than the later ones. As Ginsberg progressed through the 1950s, he became more undisciplined, did not revise or tighten. In fact, says this critic, by the early 1950s, everything that Ginsberg writes has "the appearance of being served up raw, in the first draft." [5]

Notice, first, that the information on your note card has been incorporated into this passage; then observe that the passage ends with superscript 5. That number is the key to a footnote that will appear either at the bottom of the page or at the end of the paper, depending on the format that you choose to follow. In order to obtain the information for the footnote, you turn to the bibliography card for the Roszak source, and the footnote reads this way:

⁵Theodore Roszak, *The Making of a Counter-Culture* (Garden City, N.Y.: Anchor Books, 1969), p. 126.

Now the reader of the paper will know the exact origin of the opinion that you have taken from a source, including the page on which the material is found.

This example illustrates the interactive use of bibliography and note cards.

We have gotten a little ahead of ourselves; basically, we are discussing the gathering of material, not the actual writing of the paper. To recapitulate: we began our research task by making a list of sources available—that is, we compiled a working bibliography. Now we are looking at those sources, reading some in detail, scanning others, and rejecting those that do not suit our purpose. Every bit of data, information, or opinion that we take from a source appears on its own note card, with the name of the author, a subject key, and the page or pages from which the material was taken.

Organization

Now the reading for the paper is done. All the notes have been taken. It is time to organize. Suppose that your paper is titled "Ginsberg and the Critics"; its purpose is to find out and report what Ginsberg says he's been trying to do in his poetry and what the critics say he's actually done. It turns out that your note cards can be arranged into five groups, according to the key phrases in the upper right-hand corners. The five key phrases are these:

poetic technique (Gins.)
poetic technique (crits.)
content (Gins.)
content (crits.)
G's reputation

That is, you have cards that bear on five subject areas: Ginsberg's statements concerning his poetic technique; statements by critics concerning his poetic technique; Ginsberg's statements about his content; statements by critics concerning his content; and statements that bear on Ginsberg's general reputation as a poet. Here are note cards that give examples of each:

282-3. G. says that his meters are "choriambic-Greek meters, dithyrambic meters." He says that he does not sit down to use a preconceived meter but uses his own physiological movements to arrive at a pattern. The key is arriving at a pattern organically rather than synthetically.

56. Ginsberg and Holmes had long talks about the need for "a new literalness, and thus a new prosody." Studying Pound, Lanier, and W. C. Williams, Ginsberg became dissatisfied with the mechanical forms of most poetry.

88. G comments on his anal erotic poetry. At first (and uncharacteristically), he was afraid to read it, but he did. "When I get to a barrier of shame like the one I felt when writing this poem, I know it's the sign of a good poem, because I'm entering new public territory. I write for private amusement and for the golden ears of friends who'll understand and forgive everything from the point of view _humani nihil a me alienum puto._ – 'Nothing human is foreign to me' – but it's fearsome to make a private reality public."

Fiedler content (Crits)
244. Fiedler puts Ginsberg in the Whitman
tradition, but while Whitman viewed himself
as a mystical healer, "Ginsberg celebrates
himself as an angel of death and derangement.
He is a prophet not of the beginnings of
man, but of his end; and if, like Whitman,
he tries to write first poems, they are the
first poems of the next evolutionary stage
beyond us, anticipating the verse of
meta-humans."

Trilling, Diana G's reputation

Trilling's essay was one of the first
estimates of Ginsberg's value as a poet,
and Trilling attacked him roundly.
Her point is that Ginsberg is merely a
barbarian who would like, in his
secret soul, to be respectable and
respected.

These are merely samples from a whole stack of note cards that have been gathered and organized under the five topics listed. Now the organization for your paper appears obvious. It will look something like this:

I. Ginsberg's place in modern poetry
II. The critics on Ginsberg
   A. His poetic technique
   B. His content
III. Ginsberg's own theories
   A. Poetic technique
   B. Content
IV. Conclusion

An alternate arrangement might be this:

I. Ginsberg's place in modern poetry
II. His poetic technique
   A. The critics
   B. Ginsberg
III. His content
   A. The critics
   B. Ginsberg
IV. Conclusion

Now the paper is ready to be written.

Footnote Form

Here is a list of commonly used footnote forms:

Book with One Author

[1]Truman Capote, *In Cold Blood* (New York: Random House, 1965), p. 65.

Book with Two Authors

[2]Alan C. Purves and Richard Beach, *Literature and the Reader* (Urbana, Ill.: National Council of Teachers of English, 1972), pp. 131–32.

Book with More Than Two Authors

[3]Albert C. Baugh et al., *A Literary History of England* (New York: Appleton-Century-Crofts, 1948), pp. 1021–22.

No Author Given

[4]*Psychology Today: An Introduction* (Del Mar, Cal.: CRM Books, 1970), p. 153.

Edited Collection

[5]Jack Davis, ed., *Discussions of William Wordsworth* (Boston: D. C. Heath, 1964), p. ix.

Second or Later Edition

[6]James M. McCrimmon, *Writing with a Purpose,* 5th ed. (Boston: Houghton Mifflin, 1972), p. 289.

Work of One Author Edited by Another

[7]Thomas Hardy, *Tess of the d'Urbervilles,* ed. Scott Elledge (New York: W. W. Norton, 1965), pp. 82–83.

Work of One Author in a Collection Edited by Another

   [8] John W. Gardner, "Tyranny Without a Tyrant," in *A Preface to Our Times*, ed. William E. Buckler (New York: American Book Company, 1968), p. 87.

Magazine or Journal Article

   [9] John Fraser, "Evaluation and English Studies," *College English*, 35 (Oct. 1973), 2.

Anonymous Article

   [10] "L.B.J. and His Dollar," *Life*, 19 Jan. 1968, p. 4.
   [11] "Sitting Bull," *The Encyclopedia Americana*, 1962, XXV, p. 48.

Newspaper Article

   [12] "Aussie, Russian Stars Compete in Times Games," Los Angeles *Times*, 21 Jan. 1968, Sec. D1, p. 1.

The following list of footnotes illustrates a couple of important principles:

   [1] Leslie A. Fiedler, *Waiting for the End* (New York: Stein and Day, 1964), p. 109.
   [2] Ibid., p. 112.
   [3] John Hollander, "Poetry Chronicle," *Partisan Review*, 24 (Spring 1957), 300.
   [4] Ibid., p. 302.
   [5] Fiedler, p. 111.
   [6] Hollander, p. 303.

The principles that the above illustrates are: (1) The first mention of a work in footnotes should be a full citation, as are 1 and 3. (2) The abbreviation *Ibid.* means "in the same place" and refers to the footnote directly above it. Thus, footnote 2 refers the reader back to footnote 1, and footnote 4 refers the reader back to footnote 3. (3) As footnotes 5 and 6 illustrate, full information concerning a source needs to be cited only once in the paper. After the first citation, shortened forms are preferred.

In-Text Citations

   Another method of documentation, used extensively in the social sciences, is becoming increasingly popular in all fields. It consists of citing sources within the text, not in footnotes. The basic principle is very simple: wherever you would put a superscript indicating a footnote, you put instead key information about the source in parentheses within the text, thus:

> One critic says that Allen Ginsberg is a prophet of the end of man (Fiedler, p. 244).

The information in parentheses refers the reader to the bibliography at the end of the paper, where full information about the work by Fiedler appears.

Often the dates of works are included in the parentheses, giving the reader an idea of how current the source is. The dates also allow differentiation of two works by the same author that may be used in the paper. If the source is an article rather than a book, page numbers are normally not given.

Here is an example of this form of documentation:

> A higher incidence of left-handedness has long been reported in clinical populations than in the general population (Bingley, 1958; Gordon, 1920; Hecaen & Ajuriaguerra, 1964; Hicks & Barton, 1975; Hildreth, 1949). In the mentally retarded the incidence of left-handedness is usually reported to be between 17 and 20%, a greater than twofold increase over that found in a normal population (Bingley, 1958; Brain, 1945; Gordon, 1920). Hicks and Barton (1975) have recently reported that left-handers are more prominent among the severely and profoundly retarded than among the mildly or moderately retarded.

When more than one source is mentioned in the parenthesis, arrangement can be alphabetical or chronological. Note in particular the citation of Hicks and Barton in the last sentence. Since the names of the authors are given in the text, the citation contains only the date.

Bibliography Form

If you use the sort of documentation explained above, you must append a bibliography to the paper. Sometimes, of course, a bibliography is called for regardless of the method of documentation. The following forms of entries are widely used:

Book

> Abrams, M. H. *The Mirror and the Lamp.* New York: Oxford University Press, 1953.

Magazine or Journal Article

> Chapman, Jewell A. "The Prose Portrait." *College Composition and Communication,* 18 (Dec. 1967), 252–54.

Edited Collection

> Dean, Leonard F., and Kenneth G. Wilson, eds. *Essays on Language and Usage.* New York: Oxford University Press, 1963.

Magazine Article, No Author Given

> "L.B.J. and His Dollar." *Life,* 19 Jan. 1968, pp. 4–5.

Encyclopedia Article

> "Sitting Bull." *Encyclopedia Americana.* 1962 ed.

Finally

This chapter has thrown a great many details at you, and you may feel overwhelmed. But the real problem in research writing is to gather significant data and to make sure that the reader will know your source in every instance; getting the footnotes and bibliography entries just right is important, but secondary.

Once you have put the paper together in a logical fashion, you can worry about the mechanical details. Guides such as Turabian's *Manual for Writers of Term Papers, Theses, and Dissertations* or *A Manual of Style,* published by the University of Chicago Press and popularly known as the *Chicago Style Manual,* will help you, and you can always get advice from your instructor.

The main point is this: enjoy the adventure of research, and enjoy the art of presenting your findings to a reader. If you do that, the mechanical details will take care of themselves.

THE RESEARCH PAPER: A MODEL

The following selection by the American historian Oscar Handlin will give you an idea of how a professional scholar uses documentation. You will notice that the footnotes do not follow either of the two forms explained in this chapter, yet they are clear and authoritative; you will also find that footnotes can be used to give explanations and make comments. (For another example of foot-noting, see the essay by Richard H. Fogle, on pages 308–21.)

The Historical Background

Oscar Handlin

The settlement of strangers in New York was never an easy mat-ter. But the newcomers who arrived after 1870 were slightly better off than the immigrants of the 1840's and 1850's. The later arrivals too were unskilled; 80 per cent of them between 1880 and 1890 had no trade. They too lacked capital and found it necessary to adjust to a difficult new economic environment. Like their predecessors they were compelled to struggle for a livelihood by unskilled labor and petty artisanry. But their struggle was eased by the growth of indus-try. They found positions not only in construction work and in the building trades but also in the expanding manufacturing enterprises. Although there were some tendencies toward concentration—as of Jews and Italian women but not men in the garment industries or of Germans and Bohemians in cigar-making—all labor received a meas-ure of relief by the absorption of some in manufacturing.[1]

For want of alternative, the immigrants took the lowest places in the ranks of industry. They suffered in consequence from the poor pay and miserable working conditions characteristic of the sweat-shops and homework in the garment trades and in cigar-making. But they were undoubtedly better off than the Irish and Germans of the 1840's for whom there had been no place at all.[2]

The community paid a considerable social price in the damaging effects of the low wages on which these branches of manufacturing thrived. Yet without the presence of an abundant supply of cheap labor these industries could not have expanded as they did. The 100,000 hands employed in the clothing trades were almost all recent immigrants. Such occupations were open to newcomers because the older residents and their children abandoned them as soon as pos-sible. The sons and daughters of the Irishmen and Germans who had been tailors in the 1850's and 1860's or of the Swedes who had en-tered that trade in the 1880's did not take up the needle or the iron;

[1] John R. Commons, "Immigration and Its Economic Effects," U.S. Industrial Com-mission, Reports on Immigration (Washington, 1901), XV, 298, 385; John H. Mariano, Second Generation of Italians in New York City (Boston, 1921), 32 ff.; Jane E. Robbins, "Bohemian Women in New York," Charities, 13 (1904), 194 ff.

[2] See U.S. Industrial Commission, Reports on Immigration, 15, xxiv ff., xxxii; Com-mons, "Immigration and Its Economic Effects," 316 ff., 345, 368. There are interesting pictures in Harper's Weekly, February 9, 1895, p. 136.

THE HISTORICAL BACKGROUND   Oscar Handlin. Reprinted by permission of the publishers from *The Newcomers: Negroes and Puerto Ricans in a Changing Metropolis*, by Oscar Handlin, Cambridge, Mass.: Harvard University Press. Copyright © 1959 by the Regional Plan Association, Inc.

and that made employers dependent upon the fresh hands from Italy or Russia.[3]

Escape from the ranks of unskilled labor was, however, not easy and became steadily more difficult. The want of skill and capital was always a handicap. But, in addition, discrimination against the newer ethnic groups grew ever more intense, especially after the turn of the century. These handicaps were particularly burdensome to the second generation. The crucial limitations appeared in the middle ranks of big business as that became more institutionalized.

On the other hand, economic expansion created some channels of upward mobility along which some immigrants and their children could ascend to more desirable places. As earlier, petty trade remained an important avenue of progress. In many neighborhoods the local merchant who sold food his neighbors desired or spoke their language and understood their habits had an advantage even over the emerging chain store. Other immigrants found opportunities in kinds of businesses from which natives withdrew because of the social odium attached to them. Among the Italian, Jewish, and Syrian peddlers of ice, fruit, clothing, dry goods, and junk, who passed along the crowded downtown streets, were some who accumulated the funds to open shops and develop thriving businesses.[4] The independent service trades also offered a start to Italian and Greek barbers and shoemakers and to Jewish tailors.[5] There were, in addition, some means of rising in industry. Wherever contracting was the predominant form of organization, the immigrant—whether an Irish or Jewish boss or an Italian or Greek *padrone*—had an advantage in his access to the labor supply.[6]

A few professional men—doctors, lawyers, pharmacists, clergymen, and politicians—also catered to the needs of the people they understood and who trusted them. The children of the newest arrivals had no more desire to follow their parents' occupations than had earlier generations of Americans.[7] In escaping from the immigrant callings to the professions, they found ties to their ancestral groups, supplemented by education and skills acquired in America, particularly advantageous. The ability to depend upon the support of the group made careers in government and, to a lesser extent, in the church especially attractive to the second generation who in this respect were sometimes better off than the children of the natives.[8]

[3] Commons, "Immigration and Its Economic Effects," 293 ff., 318, 325.

[4] U.S. Industrial Commission, *Reports on Immigration,* 15, 442 ff.

[5] Kate H. Claghorn, "The Foreign Immigrants in New York City," U.S. Industrial Commission, *Reports on Immigration* (Washington, 1901), XV, 473.

[6] U.S. Industrial Commission, *Reports on Immigration,* 15, 430 ff.; Edward Fenton, "Immigrants and Unions. A Case Study: Italians and American Labor, 1870–1920" (Harvard University Ph.D. thesis 1958).

[7] Commons, "Immigration and Its Economic Effects," 369.

[8] Caroline F. Ware, *Greenwich Village 1920–1930* (Boston, 1935), 67 ff.; Oscar Handlin, *Al Smith and His America* (Boston, 1958), 18 ff.

There were also some small but significant areas of employment in which talent was absolute and surmounted all distinctions of origin. On the stage, in the athletic arena, and in the scientific laboratory, the Irishman or Italian or Jew could demonstrate his worth and establish himself without serious impediment.[9]

Finally, there were opportunities for advancement in businesses of marginal morality, in which immigrants were not restrained by the inhibitions that excluded natives concerned with respectability. Europeans who did not attach to gambling the opprobrium that Americans did quickly took over the policy wheels and other games of chance. Prohibition created the bootlegger; and manpower shortages and hostility to unions, after 1915, made room for the labor racketeer. The logic of the use of violence and of gang organization led the participants in these enterprises into other forms of crime as well and also established an uneasy relation to local politics. But illegality nonetheless provided an attractive means of social advancement, if not always a permanent one.[10]

There were significant differences in the ability of various groups to move out of the ranks of unskilled labor. Although precise measurements are difficult, there is evidence that the mobility of the Jews—given the recency of their arrival—was exceptionally rapid; and that of the Irish—given the length of their residence—was exceptionally slow.[11]

A complex of factors influenced the differences in the rate of social mobility. A comparison of the Irish and the Jewish extremes shows that both groups started low and both were originally limited to such business opportunities as peddling afforded. But the Irish moved upward much more slowly than the Jews. The latter had some experience in trade before emigration, the former did not. The Jews found coreligionists on the spot who were able to help them get established; the earlier Irish immigrants had been peasants no better off than the later. Jewish patterns of family expenditure emphasized the value of saving and eased the process of capital accumulation; Irish surplus earnings were either unprofitably hoarded or expended on higher living standards and on houses which produced no income. With few exceptions, Irish fortunes came from speculative ventures in real estate and from contracting. But beyond these particular factors—important as those were—lay a more general cultural difference

[9] See, for example, Eddie Cantor, *My Life is in Your Hands* (New York, 1928); Michael Pupin, *From Immigrant to Inventor* (New York, 1923).

[10] Ware, *Greenwich Village*, 56 ff., 71, 273. There is a good deal of material relevant to this point in 81 Congress, [Kefauver] Senate Special Committee to Investigate Organized Crime in Interstate Commerce, *Hearings*, Part 7.

[11] See, on the general problem, Thomas, *Migration and Economic Growth*, 141 ff.; Oscar Handlin, "Ethnic Factors in Social Mobility," *Explorations in Entrepreneurial History* (1956).

which enabled the Jews to orient themselves more purposefully and more quickly to the terms of their new life.[12]

Differential mobility rates became even more important to the second generation. The influence of the initial differences was compounded, as family values shaped the life goals of young people and gave them the means of making a better or worse start. To some degree, family standards influenced attitudes toward education and that in turn was reflected in the extent to which the public school, to which all children were subjected, was stimulating. If the children of Italians in the 1890's and 1920's were inattentive in class, it was not because of want of intelligence but because of lack of incentive; and that proved more of a problem in their studies than unfamiliarity with English. Those who accepted the public school not only acquired valuable skills from it but also values which stressed the importance of the climb upward. For such there were more opportunities to penetrate into the professional and managerial ranks than were open to their contemporaries who either left the school early or were segregated in ethnic parochial schools.[13]

The occupational adjustment of the immigrants was reflected in the nature of their settlement in New York. The newly arrived discovered a residential pattern already in existence; and, in distributing themselves through the city, largely accepted the conditions imposed by that pattern, complicated, however, by the rise in total population and the consequent increase in density of residence.

As earlier, speculators in real estate found it advantageous to allow marginal properties to deteriorate. The rise in the level of taxation made investment in such holdings preferable to that in vacant land so long as there was enough rental income to cover current charges. There was consequently still a rapid change in the character of neighborhoods. Within that context, in general, a combination of income and ethnic factors dictated the choice of a domicile. The poorest elements in the population had the least mobility and were confined to the center of the city; the wealthier moved outward, in a direction shaped by ethnic considerations.[14]

There was, it was true, a large floating population of unaffiliated individuals and families. Such men and women, whatever their origin,

[12] For data on the percentage of various groups in the high schools, see Mariano, Second Generation Italians, 62, 63. See also Claghorn, "Foreign Immigrant," 477; Ware, Greenwich Village, 68; Handlin, Al Smith, 146 ff.

[13] For a discussion on vocational ambitions, see Mariano, Second Generation Italians, 35, 36; Leonard Covello, The Heart Is the Teacher (New York, 1958), 29, 128 ff. See also Claghorn, "Foreign Immigrant," 475; Ware, Greenwich Village, 337 ff.

[14] There is an informative discussion, together with helpful maps, in Claghorn, "Foreign Immigrant," 470 ff. These may be compared with the maps for 1860, 1890, and 1894 prepared for the Tenement House Commission and reproduced in Harper's Weekly, January 19, 1895, pp. 60–62. See also G. B. L. Arner, "Land Values in New York City," Quarterly Journal of Economics, 36 (1922), 545.

had dissolved their ties with the ethnic group; and they selected their homes primarily on the basis of personal convenience and income. They took advantage of opportunities for anonymity supplied by the large and growing number of boarding houses and apartments in districts like Greenwich Village; and their number was constantly being replenished by members of the second generation who wished to escape their immigrant affiliations. Yet in a sense even these people constituted a group for whom ethnic considerations had an import, although a negative one. In avoiding Irish, Jewish, or German neighborhoods, they constituted themselves a group of the unaffiliated.

For most New Yorkers, ethnic affiliation remained significant to the third generation and beyond. Even in the 1920's, the great-grandchildren of the German or Irish immigrants of the 1830's or 1840's and the great-great-grandchildren of the Yankees of 1800 still had meaningful ties to the groups of their ancestors. Those ties established the character of the group's identification. The wish to live close to people of similar backgrounds was fed by the desire to share common religious and cultural resources; and the ability to shop in familiar stores and to attend a familiar church strengthened ethnic links and established the character of a neighborhood whether that extended over one block or many. Children who grew up within the same environment tended to marry within the group so that the ethnic ties passed from generation to generation; and, even when circumstances compelled a group to change its residence, those ties continued to influence the direction of their movement.[15]

The developing lines of settlement can therefore best be traced in ethnic terms. The descendants of the original settlers were by the 1880's usually identified as Anglo-Saxons, a term defined by contrast with the immigrants of the period after 1820. The common element that held this group together was its Protestantism and the absence of any other affiliation. It included not only the old Dutch and English families, but also the New Englanders and Quakers of the first half of the nineteenth century and occasional Scots, English, Welsh, and even Germans and Frenchmen who arrived later but attached themselves to it.

The poor and unsuccessful in this group were generally lost in characterless enclaves scattered throughout the city, in part of the West Side, of Greenwich Village, in Brooklyn, and later in Queens, where they were surrounded by communities of foreign-born. The very poorest were left behind, immobilized by their failure, and swamped beneath the successive waves of immigrants. In the notorious "Big Flat" tenement on Mott Street, for instance, lived 478 residents, of whom 368 were Jews and 31 Italians, who were just entering the neighborhood. But there were also 31 Irish, 30 Germans, and 4 natives, a kind of sediment left behind when their groups

[15] Ware, *Greenwich Village*, 82 ff.; Mariano, *Second Generation Italians*, 27.

departed. However, among the Anglo-Saxons, these were a small minority as compared with the families of wealth or of moderate incomes.[16]

The very wealthiest segments of this group were able to maintain a high degree of freedom of choice as to residence. They entrenched themselves in the good sections of Greenwich Village and built their town houses up the East Side of Manhattan with Fifth Avenue and Central Park providing a protective barrier against the fringe of unwelcome neighbors. They could take refuge also in country estates scattered across the two hundred miles between Southampton, Long Island, and Tuxedo Park—this in addition to vacation homes and resorts more remote still.

The less wealthy, although by no means poor, were not so fortunate. Such people were small proprietors or held managerial, clerical, and professional positions. But they were anxious to make the most of their incomes and wished, above all, to preserve their status, threatened by contact with the foreigners. The desire to do so was not merely a matter of sentiment. Identification with good family, neighborhood, churches, schools, and societies could open valuable opportunities for mobility upward for themselves and their children. The wrong identifications could create serious obstacles.

That anxiety was the dynamic element in their situation. These people could not remain where they were when their neighborhoods were threatened. As immigrants moved in, the Protestant churches found their Sunday schools, attendance at services, and membership dwindling so that the costs for those who remained mounted astronomically.[17] The old shops lost patronage and the public schools changed in character. Anyone who stayed was engulfed in a new ethnic community. It was therefore essential to move and wisest to do so at the first hint of a change.[18]

Hence the persistent concern about desirable places of residence. The boarding house and hotel life of the earlier period was no longer feasible except for the newly married, for the costs rose rapidly after the Civil War. Yet the range of permissible choices for an independent household was most limited. Those who were willing to live in apartments built in the 1880's and 1890's after the French fashion could find space on the upper West Side of Manhattan. The area above 59th Street had still been mostly vacant in 1881.[19] It was to fill up quickly with such inhabitants in the next two decades.[20]

But the apartment house was slow to take hold and at first

[16] Claghorn, "Foreign Immigrant," 476.
[17] Ware, Greenwich Village, 293 ff., 467.
[18] Ware, Greenwich Village, 82 ff.
[19] Map Showing the Condition of Buildings in New York City from the Battery to 135th Street (Survey of February, 1881, otherwise unidentified, HCL, Map 3585.21.2).
[20] The settlement of the west side in the last two decades of the century is described in Harper's Weekly, July 25, 1896, pp. 730 ff.

received only those who had no alternative. "The Stuyvesant," built in 1869, had been regarded with distrust; and a persistent prejudice nagged most people with aspirations toward respectable status in the conviction that they must be property owners and live in single-family dwellings, whatever the cost. The one-family house and garden—though it be a plot but 20 × 100—became a symbol of their Americanism and drove them steadily outward toward the suburban fringes of the city.

It was impossible to hold on to space of this sort near the center. The rapid spread of cheap transit facilities in Manhattan and the rise in passenger volume were signs of the intrusion throughout the island of the masses of the poor willing to accept high-density housing. In 1890 the good single-family house survived only in the northernmost reaches of Manhattan and on the edge of Brooklyn. Those who sought such residences then had to look outward to Flatbush, Flatlands, Bensonhurst, Queens, the Bronx, and New Jersey where promoters were converting farms into lots. For those who could afford the time and the carfare, these areas were brought within reach of the central city by a network of trolley lines and commuting railways; yet their remoteness and expense isolated them from the poor.[21]

[21] Map, *Harper's Weekly,* August 1, 1896, p. 755: Richard Barry, "How People Come and Go in New York (illus.)," *ibid.,* February 26, 1898, pp. 204 ff.; New York Chapter, American Institute of Architects, Committee on Housing, *Riverside, a Study of Housing on the West Side of Manhattan* (New York, 1954), II, 5 ff.; Syrett, *Brooklyn,* 17. There is a political history of the surface lines in Carman, *Street Railway Franchises,* 108 ff., 143 ff., 175. Passenger figures are given *ibid.,* 145. See also W. C. Clark, "Some Considerations Affecting the Long-Term Trend of the Building Industry," *Review of Economic Statistics,* 8 (1926), 47 ff.

Review

For some of the following exercises you will need specific answers, so you will have to go to the proper sources in the library to obtain them. Others involve only common sense or a bit of logic.

1. Give several reasons why footnotes are important in research writing.
2. George B. Griffenhagen of the American Pharmaceutical Association wrote a brief general discussion of cod-liver oil. Where did it appear?
3. Name a general reference source that deals with matters concerning Jews.
4. What is probably the best source for a relatively brief overview of the history of Greece?
5. Where would you find a list of magazine articles concerning Queen Victoria's accession to the throne of Great Britain?

6. Where would you find a reliable and relatively brief biography of Robert E. Lee?

7. Give the date of birth of George Cecil Winterowd, a well-known architect and a professor of architecture at the University of Minnesota. Where did you find this information?

8. Where would you find a complete list of all the periodicals that your library subscribes to?

9. What is the first recorded use of the word *screwy* meaning "tipsy"? Where did you find this information?

10. How would you go about locating the author and source of a magazine article entitled "Mother's Love"? Give the author, magazine, and date.

11. If your library has a microfilm collection, go to the microfilm room and become acquainted with these resources. For instance, the *New York Times* is available on microfilm, and you might want to run through some issues just to see how the equipment works.

12. Take a self-guided tour of the reference room in your library. List ten reference sources that you had not previously been aware of.

13. Find out whether your library catalogues its books according to the Dewey decimal system or the Library of Congress system. (Perhaps it uses both systems.) Explain these systems.

14. List three reviews of *Someday, Maybe,* by William Stafford (New York: Harper & Row, 1973). Where did you find this information?

15. A relatively brief biography of Henry A. Kissinger begins with the words, "President Nixon's innovative approaches to international relations . . . ." Where does that biography appear?

16. Suppose that you want to find out how a local newspaper such as the *Salt Lake City Tribune* handled some national or international event from the 1940s. Where would you go to get a rough idea of the dates on which items concerning this event appeared in the *Tribune?*

17. Approximately how many volumes are in the library (or libraries) on your campus? On the basis of that figure, can you determine the approximate number of cards that must be in the card catalogue?

18. Explain the use and usefulness of bibliography cards. Why is it better to enter each bibliography item on a separate card than to list all of them sequentially on notebook paper?

19. Do you know what an *abstract* is? If not, find out. Name some of the abstracts in your college library. What is the usefulness of collections of abstracts?

20. If in a research paper you stated, "Richard Nixon was the first President of the United States to resign," would you need a footnote? Explain.

11

Style

DICTION AND USAGE

Words are symbols that convey concepts and, therefore, are basic to the thought process. In fact, words and their functions in sentences are topics that ought to interest the intellectually curious, and some knowledge of words is necessary to the writer.

This much said, let us turn for a second time to a little tale composed by Jonathan Swift, who told of the marvelous adventures of Gulliver during his travels. Everyone knows about Gulliver's voyage to Lilliput, where he met the little people, but not everyone knows about his voyage to Balnibarbi, where he visited the great Academy of Lagado. In the academy, all sorts of learned and scientific projects were under way. One scientist, for instance, was attempting to distill sunbeams from cucumbers so that they could be used on gloomy days, and another was working at turning ice into gunpowder. Gulliver's tour of the academy progresses:

> We next went to the School of Languages, where three Professors sat in Consultation upon improving that of their Country.
> The first Project was to shorten Discourse by cutting Polysyllables into one, and leaving out Verbs and Participles; because in Reality all things imaginable are but Nouns.
> The other, was a Scheme for entirely abolishing all Words whatsoever: And this was urged as a great Advantage in Point of Health as well as Brevity. For, it is plain, that every Word we speak is in some Degree a Diminution of our Lungs by Corrosion; and consequently

contributes to the shortening of our Lives. An Expedient was therefore offered, that since Words are only Names for *Things,* it would be more convenient for all Men to carry about them, such *Things* as were necessary to express the particular Business they are to discourse on. And this invention would certainly have taken place, to the great Ease as well as Health of the Subject, if the Women in Conjunction with the Vulgar and Illiterate had not threatened to raise a Rebellion, unless they might be allowed the Liberty to speak their Tongues, after the Manner of their Forefathers: Such constant and irreconcilable Enemies to Science are the common People. However, many of the most Learned and Wise adhere to the new Scheme of expressing themselves by *Things;* which hath only this Inconvenience attending it; that if a Man's Business be very great, and of various Kinds, he must be obliged in Proportion to carry a greater Bundle of *Things* upon his Back, unless he can afford one or two strong Servants to attend him. I have often beheld two of those Sages almost sinking under the Weight of their packs, like Pedlars among us, who when they met in the Streets, would lay down their Loads, open their Sacks, and hold Conversation for an Hour together; then put up their Implements, help each other to resume their Burthens, and take their Leave.

But, for short Conversations a Man can carry Implements in his Pockets and under his Arms, Enough to supply him, and in his House he cannot be at a Loss; therefore the Room where Company meet who practice this Art, is full of all *Things* ready at hand, requisite to furnish Matter for this kind of artificial Converse.

Another great Advantage proposed by this Invention, was, that it would serve as a universal Language to be understood in all civilized Nations, whose Goods and Utensils are generally of the same Kind, or nearly resembling, so that their uses might easily be comprehended. And thus, Embassadors would be qualified to treat with foreign Princes or Ministers of State, to whose Tongues they were utter Strangers.

In this piece, Swift is poking fun at those who hold oversimplified views of how language works. Words, of course, denote *things,* as *table, book, mountain; concepts,* as *democracy, honesty, guilt; states of mind,* as *happiness, sadness, glee.* But words, obviously, do not gain their total meaning from what they refer to—even concrete words such as *book* or *table.* On the contrary, words gain much of their meaning from other words, through definition. Our understanding of the term *God,* for instance, depends upon the other words that make up the "definition."

In any case, all words have shades of meaning.

Denotation and Connotation

Consider the word *man* in the following two sentences:

A man is a male human.
Keith is a real man.

The first means something cut and dried, almost like this: male + adult + human = man. But the meaning of the second sentence is harder to make clear: Keith is strong and virile; he is courageous and trustworthy; there is nothing soft or effeminate about him.

In these two kinds of meaning can be seen the difference between *denotation* and *connotation*. The core of meaning—the sort of thing that we can define with features such as "male," "adult," "human" or with the kind of statement found in a dictionary—is *denotation*. The associations that words carry with them, either in context or out of it, are called *connotation*.

The denotation of all these phrases is the same: *to die, to kick the bucket, to pass away.* But to illustrate the power of connotation, let's make up a little story.

A teen-age girl is deeply attached to her grandmother, who becomes ill and is hospitalized. One afternoon, the girl goes to the hospital and meets her grandmother's physician in the hall. "How's Grandma today?" she asks. The physician replies with *one* of the following:

Your grandmother died this morning.
Your grandmother kicked the bucket this morning.
Your grandmother passed away this morning.

If the physician made the first reply, we might assume that he was a callous sort of person, for *to die* is a bit harsh in its connotative value. The second reply is utterly tactless, for *to kick the bucket* has humorous connotations. Undoubtedly the physician gave the third reply, for the connotation of *to pass away* is not as harsh as that of *to die*.

Many terms with unfavorable connotations can be replaced: *garbage man–sanitary engineer, toilet–water closet, mortician–funeral director, shit–feces, dirty underwear–soiled linen, to lie–to fib, to vomit–to upchuck.*

The word *toilet* is interesting. Here is the *American Heritage Dictionary* definition of the word:

1. A disposal apparatus consisting of a hopper, fitted with a flushing device, used for urination and defecation. 2. A room or booth containing such an apparatus and often a washbowl. 3. The act or process of grooming and dressing oneself. 4. A dressing table. 5.a. Dress: attire. b. A costume or gown. —make one's toilet.

Thus, in *The Rape of the Lock,* Alexander Pope wrote,

> And now, unveiled, the Toilet stands displayed,
> Each silver Vase in mystic order laid.
> First, robed in white, the Nymph intent adores,
> With head uncovered, the Cosmetic powers.

But, of course, in modern English it is highly unlikely that one would hear, "Gloria is at her toilet, making herself beautiful." The word *toilet* simply has picked up too many unfavorable connotations. In the attempt to avoid these, *ladies' room* was substituted, and when that term picked up too many unfavorable connotations, *powder room* was substituted—a powder room being, presumably, where one goes to take a powder.

Here are some interesting sets of terms, each set having roughly the same denotations, but varying broadly in connotations:

UNFAVORABLE	NEUTRAL	FAVORABLE
legal murder	euthanasia	mercy killing
birth control	contraception	family planning
spying	surveillance	intelligence
peddling	selling	marketing
farting	flatulation	breaking wind
crazy	psychotic	mentally unbalanced
cancer	carcinoma	lingering illness
soggy (day)	rainy (day)	misty (day)

And, of course, to the residents of Los Angeles, *smog* is often *haze.*

The practice of substituting a word with favorable connotations for one with unfavorable connotations is known as *euphemism,* and the word so substituted is also known as a euphemism. Thus one might substitute *fibber* for *liar* (*Mike is a liar/Mike is a fibber*) because *fibber* has much less harsh connotations than *liar.* In the preceding list all the words in the "favorable" column might be viewed as euphemisms for the equivalents in the "unfavorable" column.

Levels of Usage

To the delight of most people who think about language, speakers and writers are gaining freedom from the strictures that society imposed so rigidly in the past. There was a time, for instance, when contractions (*isn't, haven't, don't,* and so on) were found only in extremely informal writing, and much fuss was made about the usage of *shall* and *will* (*shall* with the first person, as in *I shall return,* but *will* with the other persons, as in *you, he, they will return*). No sensible person nowadays would raise an eyebrow at finding an *isn't,* let alone an *I will,* even in publications, such as scholarly journals, that typically demand a great deal of formality.

On the other hand, society does impose boundaries on usage, reacting against or proscribing certain features of so-called nonstandard English. (See p. 405 and pp. 417–23.)

Unwritten, tacitly accepted dress codes provide a good analogy with language usage. Not many years ago, the better restaurants in, say, Atlanta demanded that male patrons wear ties and jackets, and not many years before that, suits were demanded. Now only the most exclusive restaurants expect men to wear ties and jackets, and one would have to search for a restaurant that demanded suits. In short, dress codes are becoming much more flexible.

But there are regional variations in this permissiveness. For instance, in San Francisco, dress tends to be a good deal more formal than in Los Angeles, while in Las Vegas anything goes.

From my point of view, in the best of all possible worlds, we would dress just as we pleased, but we do not live in the best of all possible worlds. For this reason, I sometimes break down and put on a tie and a suit, either because I could not gain admittance to a certain place without such dress or because I would feel conspicuous and uncomfortable if I did not conform to the expectations that the situation imposed.

Dress codes and language codes are alike in that they result from custom, and they are socially imposed. The individual is quite free (*most* of the time) to conform to them or to ignore them, but ignoring them has its consequences.

To divide language into levels of usage is, to a certain extent, artificial. Nonetheless, such a division is instructive in that it allows one to grasp very real differences in language use.

Formal and Informal Usage

At one end of the usage scale is what might be called *formal,* both written and spoken. As was pointed out in Chapter 6, formal

written English might well contain fewer contractions than informal, and it avoids slang.

Here is an example of formal writing from a respected publication:

> It is easy to grasp why stringed instruments make the sounds they do.
> When the strings are struck or plucked, they vibrate at different natu-
> ral frequencies in accordance with their tension and diameter. The
> energy of the vibration is then transferred to the air by way of a
> vibrating plate of wood and a resonating air chamber, with the sound
> eventually dying away. The musician can vary the pitch, or fre-
> quency, of individual strings by changing their vibrating length with
> the pressure of his fingers on the frets or the fingerboard.
>
> —Arthur H. Benade, "The Physics of Brasses," *Scientific American.*

And here is an example of informal usage. A woman writes to
Abigail Van Buren, "Dear Abby." The letter explains that the writer
must pick her boyfriend up and drive him home because he doesn't
have a car, and to add insult to injury, the woman must also pay a
toll to cross a bridge to get to her boyfriend's house. Abby answers:

> Thirty minutes in an automobile beats two and a half hours in a
> subway, no matter who does the driving. If he hasn't offered to pay
> for the toll, suggest it. If he can't or won't pay for it, you will have to
> decide whether dating him is worth the portal to portal service you're
> providing.

The characteristics of this informal usage, as opposed to the formal,
are obvious. First are the contractions: *hasn't, can't, won't, you're.*
In fact, Abby's failure to contract *you will* is almost jarring. The
slang is also a feature of informality: "Thirty minutes in an automobile *beats* two and a half hours in a subway. . . ."

Here is an example of formal spoken English:

> I don't look at aggression in such traditional terms as Reich or
> Lowen. I don't make the assumption that there is any one right way
> to reach out to the world, nor any single correct pattern for sexual
> expression. In a primitive culture if a man couldn't be aggressive, kill
> and rape a little, he wouldn't survive. But that has all changed. Civili-
> zation has allowed some of us to become artists and poets, to assert
> our existence in soft ways.
>
> —Stanley Keleman, interview in *Psychology Today*

The contractions, the double negative ("I don't make the assumption . . . *nor* any single correct pattern"), the relative brevity of the

sentences—all these features mark the passage as spoken. Indeed, this example demonstrates that the line between formal written and formal spoken is thin.

Informal written and spoken English differ from formal largely on the basis of the words that they allow. For instance, in formal English, one might speak of being very *fond* of sherry; in informal English, one might be *crazy about* sherry. In informal English, one might *get a job,* but in extremely formal English, one would probably *obtain a position.*

Nonstandard Usage

Nonstandard usage has nothing to do with good or bad, and nonstandard usage is *not sub*standard. In fact, every society contains a power elite—the group of people who control the economy, who set educational policy, who determine the program content of the media, who edit the newspapers—and the concept of standard is derived from the usage that this power group finds acceptable.

It would be wrong to assume that there is a monolithic, well-defined entity called standard English. But standard can be defined by the usages that it does not allow, if not by a complete description of what it permits. For instance, standard allows midwesterners to sit on the *stoop* while westerners sit on the *front porch.* It doesn't matter whether you carry a *bucket* or a *pail* in standard, but you can't *tote* either one. In standard, you are perfectly free to say either *I know WHO you gave it to* or *I know WHOM you gave it to,* but you can't say *HIM and ME went.*

The concept of levels of usage is no great mystery. The importance of usage is a social condition that we might deplore, but that we nonetheless must recognize. Both *Sandy ain't been here for an hour* and *Sandy hasn't been here for an hour* convey the same meaning, so from one point of view it's silly to prefer one form over the other. On the other hand, the second of those sentences is more acceptable than the first to the power elite in society.

A Word about Slang

Slang terms can be characterized as follows. They are used to produce an effect, such as humor, hipness, or cynicism. They are markedly excluded from formal usage. And they frequently are *nonce words,* or terms appearing in the language briefly and then fading away, even though some slang persists for decades or even centuries. As an illustration of how short-lived most slang is, think about the following terms: *twenty-three skiddoo, bundling, petting, necking, hubbahubbahubba, skirt* (for "woman"), *frail*. On the other hand, some slang terms last forever, it seems: *bones* (for "dice"); *shake a leg; nuts, screwy; rod* (for "pistol").

Sometimes, interestingly, a slang term appears to have no nonslang equivalent. When a child runs with a sled and then slams it down and jumps on it face down to ride downhill, he is doing a *belly-flop*. In his *Linguistic Atlas of the Upper Midwest,* Harold B. Allen lists these synonyms for belly-flop, all of them slang: *belly-bump, belly-gut, belly-buster, belly-bust, belly-booster, belly-bunt, belly-wopper, bellity-bumper, belly-butting, belly-coaster, belly-down, belly-slam, belly-slide.*[1] Allen also lists *slamming,* which is unfamiliar to me.

The big problem with slang in writing, of course, is that it is so rapidly dated, and nothing sounds so trite as yesteryear's or yesterday's slang. Another problem with slang is its vividness. Writing that uses slang is likely to sound as if the author is straining for effect.

Jargon

Jargon refers to those words and expressions that are used by members of an occupation, profession, or social set. Thus, physicians speak of a *sphygmomanometer*, not of a *blood pressure machine*. A patient has *phlebitis,* never inflammation of a vein. Every physician would much prefer to mention *iatrogenic* disease than to talk about diseases that are caused by the treatments that physicians administer.

Modern linguistics has its own, virtually impenetrable jargon: *suprasegmental phonemes* for intonation patterns in speech; *deep structure* for meaning; and a whole array of such exotics as *phoneme, morpheme, complementation,* and *deletion transformation.*

Subcultures also develop their own jargons. One example is the vernacular of jazz, as described by Robert S. Gold in an extremely interesting article.[2] Gold calls the language of the jazz world *jive.* Like jazz, it was developed by black Americans as a unique form of expression, creating a social identity. It has been said that the word *jive* itself was derived from the standard English word *jibe,* "to scoff at, to sneer at, to ridicule." A brief jazz glossary lists these items: *apple:* the earth, the universe, New York City; *balling:* having a

[1] Harold B. Allen, *Linguistic Atlas of the Upper Midwest,* I (Minneapolis: Univ. of Minnesota Press, 1973), pp. 390–92.
[2] Robert S. Gold, "The Vernacular of the Jazz World," *American Speech,* 32 (Dec. 1957), 271–82.

good time (but in current slang this term means something quite different); *beat:* tired (this bit of jive has been adopted as slang in general usage); *benny:* overcoat; *capped:* excelled; *cat:* a musician, a man; *chick:* a girl; *conk:* the head; *dicty:* snobbish; *dig:* understand; *dims and brights:* days and nights; *drape:* a suit; *groovy:* great; *hep, hip:* aware of; *juice:* liquor; *kick:* a pocket; *kill:* thrill, fascinate; *mad:* fine, capable, able, talented; *nod:* sleep; *ofay:* white person; *pad:* house, apartment, room; *scoff:* food; *sky:* hat; *troll:* street, avenue; *trey:* three; *twister:* key.

There is nothing inherently wrong with jargon. One physician talking to another would be deemed naive if he spoke of the blood pressure machine, rather than *the sphygmomanometer;* one plumber speaking to another is quite justified in talking about *P-traps, U-joints,* and *nipples;* literary critic to literary critic, there's nothing at all wrong with the terms *affective fallacy* and *objective correlative.*

It's all a matter of audience. When one specialist is addressing another, the jargon of the group is useful and informative, but when a specialist (a jazz musician or a plumber or a linguist) is addressing a layman, jargon is simply confusing.

Gobbledygook

Stuart Chase had this to say about gobbledygook:

Said Franklin Roosevelt, in one of his early presidential speeches: "I see one-third of a nation ill-housed, ill-clad, ill-nourished." Translated into standard bureaucratic prose this statement would read:

> It is evident that a substantial number of persons within the Continental boundaries of the United States have inadequate financial resources with which to purchase the products of agricultural communities and industrial establishments. It would appear that for a considerable segment of the population, possibly as much as 33.3333 percent of the total, there are inadequate housing facilities, and an equally significant proportion is deprived of the proper types of clothing and nutriment.

This rousing satire on gobbledygook—or talk among the bureaucrats—is adapted from a report prepared by the Federal Security Agency in an attempt to break out of the verbal squirrel cage. "Gobbledygook" was coined by an exasperated Congressman, Maury Maverick of Texas, and means using two, or three, or ten words in the place of one, or using a five-syllable word where a single syllable would suffice. Maverick was censuring the forbidding prose of executive departments in Washington, but the term has now spread to windy and pretentious language in general.

—Stuart Chase, *Power of Words*

Here is another example of gobbledygook:

> Due to the fact that hydro-electric generation of electrical current now involves costly materials and operations, it is respectfully requested that personnel be assiduous in ascertaining that all electrical appliances, particularly those used for illumination, are turned off if not in use.

That sloggy sentence means nothing more than this: Since electricity is expensive, please turn off the lights.

Abstractness

Closely related to the disease called gobbledygook is another, just as frustrating: abstractness. Here is an example:

> Objective consideration of contemporary phenomena compels the conclusion that success or failure in competitive activities exhibits no tendency to be commensurate with innate capacity, but that a considerable element of the unpredictable must invariably be taken into account.

The preceding example is George Orwell's rewrite of a glorious passage from the Bible:

> I returned and saw under the sun, that the race is not to the swift, nor the battle to the strong, neither yet bread to the wise, nor yet riches to men of understanding, nor yet favour to men of skill; but time and chance happeneth to them all.

Orwell wrote his parody in order to illustrate what happens to prose when it becomes totally abstract. In the Bible passage, concrete images not only convey but also reinforce the idea; the reader is given specific examples of what the passage means. In the Orwell parody, the reader has nothing specific to grasp, nothing to peg ideas on.

The best prose is concrete and imagistic, even when it is dealing with abstruse subject matter. Here is a brilliant example. The American thinker William James is discussing habit, certainly an abstract subject, but notice how he handles it concretely:

Habit is thus the enormous fly-wheel of society, its most precious conservative agent. It alone is what keeps us all within the bounds of ordinance, and saves the children of fortune from the envious uprisings of the poor. It alone prevents the hardest and most repulsive walks of life from being deserted by those brought up to tread therein. It keeps the fisherman and the deck-hand at sea through the winter; it holds the miner in his darkness, and nails the countryman to his log-cabin and his lonely farm through all the months of snow; it protects us from invasion by the natives of the desert and the frozen zone. It dooms us all to fight out the battle of life upon the lines of our nurture or our early choice, and to make the best of a pursuit that disagrees, because there is no other for which we are fitted, and it is too late to begin again. It keeps different social strata from mixing. Already at the age of twenty-five you see the professional mannerism settling down on the young commercial traveler, on the young doctor, and the young minister, on the young counselor-at-law. You see the little lines of cleavage running through the character, the tricks of thought, the prejudices, the ways of the "shop," in a word, from which the man can by-and-by no more escape than his coat-sleeve can suddenly fall into a new set of folds. On the whole, it is best he should not escape. It is well for the world that in most of us, by the age of thirty, the character has set like plaster, and will never soften again.

—William James, *The Principles of Psychology, I*

James starts off with a metaphor: habit is the flywheel of society, the force that keeps all the other parts moving. He then gives a number of examples of how habit keeps people in their appointed places. Next, he points out that members of given professions adopt the habits of those professions. Finally, he ends with two wonderful figures of speech: it is as unlikely that people will change their habits as that a coat will suddenly change its folds, and the character sets like plaster.

Review

1. Characterize the following passages as nonstandard, informal, or formal. Indicate the features that led you to make your characterization.

   a. *What about the young dissenters?*
      If you gave 'em a push, they'd turn into homosexual. When the German hordes fifty years ago surrounded Paris, Marshall Petain brought out the pimps, whores, thieves, underground operators, he says: Our playground is jeopardized by the German Hun. Well, all Paris, every thief,

burglar, pimp, he come out and picked up a musket. Stopped the German hordes.

—Quoted in Studs Terkel, *Hard Times*

b. My recall is nearly perfect, time has faded nothing. I recall the very first kidnap. I've lived through the passage, died on the passage, lain in the unmarked, shallow graves of the millions who fertilized the Amerikan soil with their corpses; cotton and corn growing out of my chest, "unto the third and fourth generation," the tenth, the hundredth. My mind ranges back and forth through the uncounted generations, and I feel all that they ever felt, but double. I can't help it; there are too many things to remind me of the 23½ hours that I'm in this cell. Not ten minutes pass without a reminder. In between, I'm left to speculate on what form the reminder will take.

—George Jackson

c. Now about Yolanda is a good friend to me all my friend is very nice to me, but Yolanda is the most good friend to me. In my class Yolanda and me we are always talking about people especially about boy and a teacher the teacher is a nice teacher he teach me and Yolanda in a school called ———— Junior High School it is located in Los Angeles, California. Yolanda has a brother name Orlando she has two more brother but I do not know their name but if Yolanda is a good friend to me well I guess her brothers are nice but one of them had got kick out of school.

—A junior high school student

d. An abundant and increasing supply of highly educated people has become the absolute prerequisite of social and economic development in our world. It is rapidly becoming a condition of national survival. What matters is not that there are so many more individuals around who have been exposed to long years of formal schooling—though this is quite recent. The essential new fact is that a developed society and economy are less than fully effective if anyone is educated to less than the limit of his potential. The uneducated man is fast becoming an economic liability and unproductive. Society must be an "educated society" today—to progress, to grow, even to survive.

—Peter F. Drucker

2. Make an inventory of the slang that is current on your campus right now. Define the words and terms now in use. Do any of them seem to have been around for some time? (For example, *flunk* is a slang term that has had great staying power.)

3. Are you familiar with the jargon of any particular field or group? If so, list and explain the words and terms that appear.

4. Revise the following sentences to eliminate the gobbledygook:

a. Return with the utmost haste.

b. Before he retires for the night, Paul scrupulously observes a regimen of oral hygiene.

c. Do not enumerate your domestic fowls before they emerge from the ovarian state.

d. Feathered vertebrates of the same genus show a decided tendency to congregate.

e. George always set aside a portion of his earnings so that he would be prepared in the event that inclement weather should precipitate unforeseen circumstances which would necessitate his having extra coin of the realm.

f. The domestic canine is frequently *Homo sapiens'* most devoted ally.

THE BASIC WORD STOCK OF ENGLISH

To put the English language in perspective, we will draw a thumbnail sketch of the development of the vocabulary.

In about the middle of the fifth century, three Germanic tribes—the Angles, the Saxons, and the Jutes—invaded the island of Britain, driving out the native Celts. The invaders isolated themselves from their native lands (now Germany), and one of the results of isolation (either geographical or social) is the development of new linguistic forms. The first English language, often called Old English, was Anglo-Saxon, a dialect of German.

In 597, Saint Augustine of Canterbury and some forty monks arrived in England, their mission to bring Christianity to the island. They soon converted King Ethelbert, and the church was established in the British Isles. Since Latin was the language of the church, the Latin vocabulary soon began to appear in Old English.

Toward the end of the eighth century, Danes (the Vikings) began to attack England, conquering all of the northern and most of the eastern parts of the island. Because King Alfred expelled the Danes a century later, Scandinavian did not become the language of the ruling classes, but many Scandinavian words came into English.

The most famous date in English history is, perhaps, 1066 —when the Norman French conquered England. Because the language of Normandy was that of the power elite, English changed drastically, adjusting itself to the language of the conquerors. So it is fair to say that modern English is basically a Germanic language with a heavy overlay of French.

The point is this: our basic word stock is Anglo-Saxon and French, with an admixture of Latin, Scandinavian, and other languages.

Before we go on, we ought to wring the moral from this brief historical sketch: All varieties of language aspire toward that of the power elite. If the president of the United States, his cabinet, and the members of Congress today spoke French, anyone who wanted to be successful in the system would attempt to master that language. If the urban black dialect were the language of the power elite, everyone who wanted to enter the power structure would attempt to master the phonetic and grammatical characteristics of black English.

According to Edward L. Thorndike,[3] English is composed of these elements:

Words of	
Old English origin	61.7%
French	30.9
Latin	2.9
Scandinavian	1.7
Mixed	1.3
Uncertain	1.3
Low German and Dutch	.3

French has had a double influence, because English speakers first got vocabulary items from the Normans, and then picked up many French words when that language became an international means of communication among the elite.

Words Borrowed from French

By about 1154, Norman French words began to appear in English writing: *castel* ("castle"), *tur* ("tower"), *justice, pais* ("peace"). By the time Geoffrey Chaucer started writing, late in the fourteenth century, French had really taken hold, and it is estimated that about thirteen percent of his words are of French origin. Some of the words from French that ultimately established themselves in English: *contract, import, debt, felony, criminal, judge, ointment, medicine, surgeon, chamber, lodge, chapel, buttress, portal, vault.*

The following list will give you some idea of the influence that French has had on English since about 1500. The words are categorized by general subject to which they apply, and the first date of their appearance in print is indicated in parentheses.

Military and naval   colonel (1548), dragoon (a doublet of *dragon,* 1622), reveille (1644), corps (1711 in the military sense; *corpse,*

---

[3] Edward L. Thorndike, "The Teacher's Word-Books," in Stuart G. Robertson, ed., *The Development of Modern English,* rev. Frederic G. Cassidy (Englewood Cliffs, N.J.: Prentice-Hall, 1954), p. 155.

"body," is from 1325), sortie (1795), barrage (1859 "dam"; 1917 in the sense of "bombardment").

People   viceroy (1524), bourgeois (1564), coquette (1611), chaperon (1720, used earlier to mean "hood"), habitué (1818), chauffeur (1899).

Buildings and furniture   scene (1540), parterre (1639), attic (1696), salon (1750), chiffonier (1806), hangar (1902).

Literature, art, music   rondeau (1525), hautboy (1575; later spelled *oboe*), burlesque (1656), tableau (1699), connoisseur (1714), brochure (1756), carillon (1803), renaissance (1840), matinée (1880).

Dress, fashion, and materials   grogram (1562; borrowed again as *grosgrain,* 1869), cravat (1656), denim (1695), chenille (1738), corduroy (1787), blouse (1840), cretonne (1870), suede (1884).

Food and cooking   fricassee (1568), table d'hôte (1617), soup (1653), croquette (1706), aspic (1789), restaurant (1827), chef (1842), mousse (1892).[4]

Etymology

Etymology is the history of a word's derivation. It is interesting to discover that English is truly an international language in that it has borrowed words from every part of the world. The following is a sample of English words and their etymologies. You might like to use this list for a game, the rules for which are simple: cover the right-hand column, and then guess the language from which the word came. Only the language from which the word came into English is the right answer. For instance, suppose that a word came from Latin into French and then into English from French; French would be the right answer. (The source here is *The American Heritage Dictionary of the English Language.*)

1. alcohol   New Latin. Latin got the word from the Arabic *al-kuhl* or *al-kohl*. In Medieval Latin, the word meant a fine powder of antimony used to tint the eyelids. By the way, we adopted the Arabic definite article along with the word, for *al* means "the."

[4] W. Nelson Francis, *The English Language: An Introduction* (New York: W. W. Norton, 1965), p. 144.

2. assassin
French. The first source of the word was the Arabic *hashshashin,* meaning "hashish addicts." You might look up the fascinating story of this word in an encyclopedia.

3. basenji
Bantu, an African language.

4. Bible
Old French. The word was adopted during the Middle English period. The ultimate source was *Byblos,* the name of the Phoenician port from which papyrus, used for making paper, was shipped to Greece.

5. blitzkrieg
German. It means "lightning war."

6. booze
Dutch. It came into Middle English and originally meant "to carouse."

7. brougham
Scotch. From Henry Peter Brougham, Baron of Brougham and Vaux (1778–1868), a Scottish jurist. (Along the same lines, you might want to look up *sandwich.*)

8. burlesque
French. From the Italian *burlesco.* The *-que* ending should tip you off.

9. cigar
Spanish *cigarro,* possibly taken from the Mayan word meaning "tobacco."

10. didactic
From Greek *didaktikos,* "skillful in teaching."

11. egg
Old Norse. It came into Middle English.

12. flak
German *Fl(ieger)a(bwehr)k(anone),* "aircraft defense gun." Thus, the word is an acronym, like *NASA, NATO,* and countless others that are derived from the initial letters of their words.

13. gin
From Dutch *jenever,* which came from the Latin word *juniperus,* "juniper."

14. goulash
Hungarian.

15. goy
Yiddish.

16. gumbo
Bantu. The Louisiana French adopted it.

17. hamburger
From the German city Hamburg; short for *hamburger steak.*

18. jazz
The origin is uncertain, so you can give yourself credit for this one.

19. junk (ship)   From Portuguese *junko* and Dutch *jonk*. The Portuguese and Dutch took the word from Malay *jong*, "sea-going ship." Give yourself credit if you said either Portuguese or Dutch.

20. khaki   From Urdu (a language of India), "dusty" or "dust-covered." Urdu borrowed it from Persian.

21. kimono   Japanese.

22. lariat   From Spanish *la reata*.

23. lemon   Old French. The French borrowed it from Arabic, and Arabic borrowed it from Persian.

24. marijuana   Mexican Spanish. If you said Spanish, give yourself credit.

25. moose   From Natick, an American Indian language.

26. mukluk   Eskimo.

27. obnoxious   Latin.

28. papoose   Algonquian. If you said American Indian, give yourself credit.

29. polka   French and German. Borrowed from Polish.

30. ranch   From the Mexican Spanish *rancho*.

31. robot   From Czech.

32. rodeo   Spanish.

33. safari   Arabic.

34. samovar   Russian.

35. sauerkraut   German, "sour cabbage."

36. sauna   Finnish.

37. schlemiel   Yiddish.

38. schmaltz   German.

39. smorgasbord   Swedish.

40. stucco   Italian, but the Italians got it from Old High German.

41. syphilis   Latin. Syphilis was the title character of a poem (1530) by Girolamo Fracastoro, a Veronese physician who supposedly had the disease.

42. tamale	Mexican Spanish.
43. tavern	Old French. The French took it from the Latin *taberna*, "hut." It is interesting to note that *tavern* and *tabernacle* come from the same source.
44. thug	From Hindi, a language of India.
45. tomato	Spanish. The Spanish borrowed it from Nahuatl, the language of the Aztecs and other related tribes.
46. totem	From Ojibwa, an American Indian language.
47. verandah	From Hindi.
48. vodka	Russian. It is the diminutive of *voda*, "water," so *vodka* literally means "little water."
49. whiskey	From the Irish *usquebaugh*.
50. xenophobia	Made up of *xeno* from the New Latin, meaning "stranger" and adopted from the Greek, plus the Greek *phobos*, "fearing."

Other Sources for the English Vocabulary

It should now be obvious that borrowed words make up a great portion of our word stock, but there are other interesting ways in which new words enter the language.

Many English words are derived from an existing word to which a prefix or suffix is added. That was the process used to make the word *passive* into a verb by the addition of the suffix *-fy*: *passify*. The corresponding adjectival form would be *passific*, the noun would be *passification*. Once the word *telegraph* came into the language by the process of combining the Greek root *tele*, meaning "far," with the Greek root *graph*, meaning "write," the words *telegraphy*, *telegrapher*, and *telegraphic* were easily derived.

Compounding is a common source of new words: *air-plane*, *free-loader*, *light-house-keeper*.

Words also undergo *functional shift*; that is, they move from one category to another. The noun *freak* is now used as a verb: "Gloria *freaked* Tony." Or perhaps it would be better to say that the categories of English words are to some extent fluid. The noun *head*, for instance, is also used as an adjective:

The *head* man is the president.

a verb:

Thompson *headed* the investigation.

Here is another example of functional shift:

A secretary says, "I didn't back-file the letter; I waste-basketed it." [5]

In the process of *back-formation,* a new word is created by removing a suffix from an existing word: *editor/edit, burglar/burgle, lazy/laze,* and many more. *Clipping* is much like back-formation, but does not limit itself to the deletion of suffixes: *dormitory/dorm, omnibus/bus, examination/exam, laboratory/lab.*

In the etymologies, we saw a word that entered the language from a proper name: *brougham.* There are many more such words: *sandwich, pasteurization, pander* (from the character Pandarus in Chaucer's *Troilus and Cressida*), *calico* (from Calcutta), and *bowdlerize* (from Thomas Bowdler, who produced a "cleaned-up" edition of Shakespeare).

Some words are simply *coined. Kodak* is one such word that was made up, and more recently Standard Oil coined *Exxon* as a trade name.

These are only some of the sources of words in English. If this discussion has aroused your interest in words and their nature, it has served its purpose. To be a good writer, you should be interested in—even fascinated by—words and their ways, and in your writing you must make careful choices of words.

WHAT ARE DIALECTS?

A *dialect* is a version of a language spoken by a group of people—for example, the Brooklyn and Southern dialects in American English and Cockney in Britain. Dialects are mutually intelligible; that is, the speaker of one dialect of a language can understand the speakers of other dialects. *And everyone in the language group speaks a dialect,* whether it be the dialect of the majority or a minority, of a limited geographical area or as widespread as what is sometimes called *standard,* the dialect of Walter Cronkite and other television newscasters.

Even an untrained observer can recognize dozens—if not hundreds—of dialects of English. From one point of view, at least, there is no such thing as the English language, but merely a number of mutually intelligible dialects.

---

[5] Francis, p. 157.

No two people—even those in the same dialect group—speak exactly alike, which is to say that we all have our own *idiolects*. So we can look at language this way:

> A *language* is a collection of dialects (and dialects of a language are mutually intelligible).

> A *dialect* is a collection of idiolects with certain features in common.

> An *idiolect* is the language used by the individual speaker.

It is possible, therefore, to say that *idiolect* reflects the speaker's personal identity in speech. *Dialect* represents his or her social or geographical identification.

Development of Dialects

Dialects develop, it seems, because of either cultural or geographical isolation. For example, the West Indies have been relatively isolated, and they have developed and maintained their own dialects, such as that spoken in Jamaica. Similarly, the social isolation of blacks in the United States undoubtedly contributed to the development of the urban black dialect that one hears in large cities from coast to coast.

The following chart makes this point vividly:

	NORTHERN	SOUTHERN
EDUCATED	you (men, women)	you all
UNEDUCATED	youse	you all

The Northern *you* and *youse* mark a cultural distinction; the Southern *you all* is a regional usage. Therefore, when we consider dialect, we must think of the cultural and geographic variations of speech.

Prestige Dialects

As we have seen, every speaker of every language belongs to a dialect group—that is, all of us speak dialects. However, not all dialects in a language have equal prestige. The most common prestige dialect in America is standard, which is the kind of language spoken by most newscasters.

Since there is a standard dialect, we can say that any other dialect is *nonstandard,* but the word "nonstandard" does *not* imply "substandard." Nor should you assume that the only prestigious dialect in America is standard. For instance, there is considerable evidence that a certain kind of British accent confers an advantage in America—namely, the accent used by announcers of the British Broadcasting Corporation. To a great many Americans, this dialect sounds refined, cultured, while a dialect such as that spoken by some Brooklynites sounds uncultured, even crude.

A Look at a Nonstandard Dialect

The differences among dialects of a language are always fairly superficial. To give you some idea of how dialects differ from one another, I would like to present a brief description of Sanpete, spoken in central Utah where Sanpete County is located. Like other dialects, Sanpete can be identified by certain of its *vocabulary items,* by *pronunciation,* and by some ways in which words are put together in sentences.

A vocabulary difference: the word *husband* is practically non-existent in spoken Sanpete, so that one might speak of "Mary and her *man,*" whereas standard would use "Mary and her *husband.*" In Sanpete, the noun *drink* means almost exclusively a carbonated beverage other than cola. Therefore, if a Sanpeter asks you if you want a drink, he does not mean water, nor does he mean a martini, but rather root beer, orange soda, or something of the kind.

Sanpete has one noticeable *phonetic* variation from standard: the pronunciation of the sequence of letters *or* as in *horse.* The San-peter pronounces *horse* as a speaker of standard would pronounce *harse,* if there were such a word. Thus, "fork" is /fark/, and "corn" is /carn/.

The structural variations that differentiate Sanpete from standard are limited. The phrase *and them* means something like "and the others." Thus, "Let's go visit Ken and them" means something like "Let's go visit Ken and the other members of his family." Also the phrase *to home* is used for *at home:* "I wonder if Evelyn and them are *to home.*"

Let's go on briefly to discuss the Sanpete dialect, for we can learn some important lessons from it. People who have lived in San-pete all their lives and have become respected members of the community have pronounced nonstandard dialects, that is, they speak Sanpete. They have no cultural reason to change, and they have maintained their relative geographical isolation. However, when young people move from Sanpete into other societies, they tend to lose their native dialect, for they often enter communities in which Sanpete is not a prestige dialect. Therefore, they change their speech patterns in order to avoid the sneers and snickers that their non-standard dialect would arouse in the standard-speaking community.

Dialect and Social Mobility

The next point to be made is fairly complex, but it is interesting and important. Take a look at the following graph:[6]

Class stratification of /r/ in *guard, car, beer, beard*, etc., for native New York City adults.

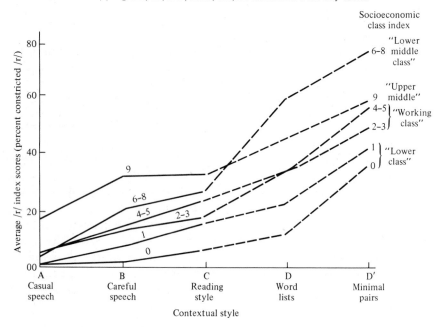

As is generally known, many New Yorkers tend to suppress the /r/ sound in such words as *guard, car,* and *beard,* pronouncing them something like this: /guahd/, /cah/, /behd/. From the point of view of standard English, this pronunciation is, of course, "improper." In casual speech, none of the groups of speakers pronounces the /r/ more than twenty percent of the time, but as the types of usage change from casual speech to careful speech to reading sentences to

[6] From William Labov, *The Study of Nonstandard English* (Urbana, Ill.: National Council of Teachers of English, 1969). Copyright © 1969 by the National Council of Teachers of English. Reprinted by permission of the publisher and the author.

reading word lists and finally to reading minimal pairs (such as *car* and *far*), all groups increase the percentage of pronounced /r/'s. But notice which group increases most dramatically: the lower middle class, even more than the upper middle class.

The explanation for this fact is most interesting. As Labov says, "This 'hypercorrect' behavior, or 'going one better,' is quite characteristic of second-ranking groups in many communities." The more motivated a group is toward upward social mobility, the harder that group will try to speak the power dialect. Therefore, it would seem, change in dialect is intimately connected both with one's place in the social-economic hierarchy and with one's aspirations to move upward. No group will change its dialect as long as the members of the group feel that they have no chance to improve their lot in the economic and social system that prevails.

> In highly stratified situations, where society is divided into two major groups, the values associated with the dominant group are assigned to the dominant language by all. Lambert and his colleagues at McGill University have shown how regular are such unconscious evaluations in the French-English situation in Quebec, in the Arabic-Hebrew confrontation in Israel, and in other areas as well. When English-Canadians heard the same person speaking Canadian French, on the one hand, and English, on the other, they unhesitatingly judged him to be more intelligent, more dependable, kinder, more ambitious, better looking and taller—when he spoke English. Common sense would tell us that French-Canadians would react in the opposite manner, but in fact they do not. Their judgments reflect almost the same set of unconscious values as the English-Canadians show. This overwhelmingly negative evaluation of Canadian French is a property of the society as a whole. It is an omnipresent stigma which has a strong effect on what happens in school as well as in other social contexts.[7]

In other words, the social stratification of dialects is tragic, not only because the speakers of prestige dialects look down on the speakers of nonprestige dialects, but also because the speakers of nonprestige dialects *look down on themselves*. It is hard to estimate the damage that this linguistic arrogance causes, but any American can look around and sense the devastation that whole classes and races have undergone because of attitudes toward dialect.

Two points are worth repeating. By definition, the dialects of a language are mutually comprehensible. When a dialect becomes incomprehensible to other speakers of a language, that dialect has

[7] Labov, p. 31.

become another language, as is the case with Dutch, which drifted so far away from High German as to become a separate language.

The second point is equally important. All the evidence indicates that no language or dialect is inferior to any other language or dialect. Every language and dialect will do everything that its speakers want it to do. The idea that you can "think better" in one language or dialect than in another is simply a destructive myth.

Switching Dialects

Now a significant problem arises—one that you must solve for yourself: Should the individual speaker make an effort to change his or her dialect? Though it is very difficult, if not impossible, for some people to change their pronunciation, every normal speaker of English can master the grammatical and structural niceties of standard spoken and written English. Let's take a representative structure from urban black dialect as an example of the insignificant differences between urban black and standard.

A typical urban black sentence is

Didn't nobody see it.

At first glance, it may seem to be far removed from standard

Nobody saw it.

Both sentences are in past tense. In the urban black sentence it is the auxiliary verb *didn't* that shows this tense, while in the standard version of the same idea tense is carried by *saw.* In this case, then, nonstandard can be changed to standard simply by changing the tense carrier. (No speaker of urban black would say *Didn't nobody saw it.*)

Another characteristic of urban black is the omission of the possessive -*s,* so that a typical sentence would be

Fido is John dog.

rather than

Fido is John's dog.

There are other differences between urban black and standard, but the point is this: surely a child or young person who can master the complications of surviving in a modern city can, *if he or she wants to,* also master the negatives, possessives, tense systems, and other features of standard English.

In my own opinion, the best solution to the problem of dialect change is this: don't do it. We should change society's attitudes toward dialects and leave the dialects alone. America avowedly honors its cultural diversity, and certainly one of the most important aspects of a culture is its dialect. Why should people give up so important a part of themselves as the way in which they and the other members of their culture speak?

But, sadly, until society's attitudes do change, I honestly believe that the ability to speak and write standard can well mean money in your pockets and power in your hands.

Exercise: Watch Your Language

1. Find someone who speaks a minority dialect, and do an informal study of it, recording its features in notes. How does it differ from standard in vocabulary, pronunciation, and structure? You may want to report on your "field work" in class discussion or in a brief essay.

2. What seem to be the outstanding features of your idiolect?

3. Listen to and think about the language of someone who speaks your dialect. What are the features of that person's idiolect?

4. Do some features of a person's idiolect or dialect annoy you? What are they? Why are they annoying?

5. In a standard encyclopedia, look up "Gullah." What did you learn about dialect? Discuss your findings.

FIGURATIVE LANGUAGE

Meanings can be expressed either literally or figuratively. For instance, here is an idea expressed literally:

Nature is holy and mysterious, and can be understood only dimly by man.

The French poet Charles Baudelaire (as translated by R. G. Stern) expressed that idea figuratively in this way:

Nature is a temple from whose living pillars
Confusing words are now and then released.

Comparison of these examples raises a question: Why express ideas figuratively at all? The answer is complicated and will take up the rest of this chapter, but to get our discussion under way, a couple of tentative answers might be advanced.

First, the figurative statement is more imagistic; it presents something for the reader's mind to "see." As has been pointed out again and again in this book, concrete, specific language has a special power that general, abstract language does not. For total comprehension of ideas, the mind often seems to need images.

Second, as if by magic, a great deal more meaning can usually be compressed into a figurative statement than into a literal one. Everyone would agree, I think, that the second example is a good deal more suggestive than the first—which is simply another way of saying that figurative language compresses meaning and is thus economical. The figure *Nature is a temple* is a good example. The word *temple* implies the whole history of humanity's veneration of something higher than itself: a magnificent structure (for a temple is not a mere church), a holy place, the concept of worship, the notion of the universality of worship (for all religions have temples), the smallness of the individual in relation to the structure (for a temple is not the Little Brown Church in the Vale), the concept of deity, a sense of quietness and wonder, mystery and awe—and on and on. So, everyone would grant, figurative language has considerable power. But not everyone—in fact, almost no one—wants to write poetry.

It turns out, however, that figurative language is not only vivid and useful, but absolutely essential in most kinds of writing.

For example, explaining how an airplane flies, the author of the following passage first states Bernoulli's theorem in literal terms and then explains it with an *analogy,* a form of comparison you are already familiar with. (See pp. 34–37.)

> The ordinary airplane is held up by air pressure on its wings and this is explained by a very strange theorem first propounded by the Swiss mathematician Bernoulli. Bernoulli's theorem states that when a fluid flows past a fixed object the pressure exerted sideways on the object decreases as the velocity of flow increases.
>
> For example, start a water hose spurting a jet of water straight up in the air, then place a Ping-pong ball on top of the jet. The ball bounces and twists but manages to stay on top of the stream of water—defying all apparent logic. What actually happens as the water flows around the ball? First it tends to slip to one side, say to the left. The water divides around the ball, much of it shooting straight up on the right side of the ball: some of it forced to take the long way around to the left. The detour makes the water slow down and as it slows its sidewise pressure builds up. Simultaneously the pressure of the high-speed water shooting up the right side of the ball

has lowered, and so the ball moves toward the low-pressure side, away from the high-pressure side and back into the center of the jet.

The shape of an *airfoil* (wing section) is so designed as to increase the pressure of passing air on the underside and decrease it on the upper surface of the wing. This is accomplished in two ways—by tilting the wing slightly up at the front so that the incoming air hits the underside of the wing and slows down (increasing the pressure), and by forcing the air to travel a longer path over the upper surface than it travels along the lower surface of the wing.

—Richard Korff, "How Does It Work?—The Airplane"

This passage draws an analogy between what happens when a ping-pong ball dances at the top of a stream of water and the function of an airplane's wing, the purpose being to clarify Bernoulli's principle. The analogy clearly has made understanding easier.

Much like analogy, in that they draw comparisons, are metaphor and simile.

Metaphor

The meaning of the term *metaphor* will become obvious as this section progresses. For the moment, let's take a look at metaphors that present different views of human beings:

Humans are machines.
Humans are biochemical systems.
Humans are gods.

The first example implies that human beings do not have free will, but respond to the laws of mechanics as do machines such as pulleys or gears; in the next one, humans are only a collection of chemicals, such as might emerge from a laboratory; and in the last, humans assume the qualities of divinity. In a real sense, we can think of metaphors as instruments whereby we generate and organize our knowledge of the world. If we view humans as machines, our conclusions about them will be quite different from those that are based on a view of humanity as a divine image of God.

The following passage is metaphoric because we do not believe that people on New York sidewalks actually dance, and yet we sense that their movements can be viewed as if they were a ballet company in a theater:

The stretch of Hudson Street where I live is each day the scene of an intricate sidewalk ballet. I make my own entrance into it a little after eight when I put out the garbage can, surely a prosaic occupation, but

I enjoy my part, ~~my little clang~~, as the droves of junior high school students walk by the center of the stage dropping candy wrappers.

—Jane Jacobs, "Sidewalk Ballet"

Verbs frequently carry the metaphorical sense of a passage:

Headstones *stagger* under great draughts of time. . . .

—John Berryman

Literally, the line would read something like this:

The headstones stand at odd angles. . . .

Drunks stagger, carriers stagger under heavy loads, and even dogs can stagger; only animate, human-like beings can literally stagger.

Adjectives can also carry the metaphorical burden:

.   After great pain a *formal* feeling comes—
The nerves sit *ceremonious* like tombs;
The *stiff* Heart questions—was it He that bore?
And yesterday—or centuries before?

—Emily Dickinson

In what sense is a feeling formal? We know of formal statements, dress, dinners. But feelings? The adjective *formal* seems to apply only to nouns that are in some way tangible; we can hear the formality of a speech and see the formality of a dinner, but there is no direct way for us to experience someone else's feelings. The adjective *ceremonious* seems to have the same quality; it will not apply literally to that which cannot be experienced directly in some way. And, of course, the adjective *stiff* applies only to substances like rubber that have varying degrees of flexibility.

Finally, adverbials can create metaphorical sense:

When men were all asleep the snow came flying,
In large white flakes falling on the city brown,
Stealthily and perpetually settling and loosely lying. . . .

—Robert Bridges

The point here is that only humans or animals can be stealthy: a cat or a burglar, for instance. Snow, rain, and soot can merely fall.

As these explanations have pointed out, metaphor arises when meanings don't quite add up. If I say that *Herman is a young Greek god,* you will undoubtedly take my statement to be metaphorical, for you will assume that I don't really believe that Herman is an immortal living on Mount Olympus, but I intend something like this: Herman is extremely handsome and well proportioned.

However, not every break in meaning creates metaphor. For instance, if I encountered the following, I would be puzzled by it and interpret it as nonsense, not as a metaphor:

A carrot is a revolution.

The meaning of *carrot* is simply too far removed from the meaning of *revolution* for me to make any connection.

Metaphor, then, depends on some kind of interpretability, the exact nature of which is especially hard to explain. This is why the sentence

Colorless green ideas sleep furiously.

is taken to be not metaphorical, but surrealistic.

The "poems" that computers write have this enigmatic, surreal quality:

Poem No. 078

THOUGH STARS DRAINED SICKLY UPON IDLE HOVELS
FOR LIFE BLAZED FAST UPON EMPTY FACES
WHILE BLOOD LOOMED BITTER ON IDLE FIELDS
NO MARTIAN SMILED

Even the most sophisticated computers are unable to make the intricate decisions necessary to create metaphors. For, as should now be apparent, it takes knowledge of the world to create and interpret metaphors. If a reader believes that Greek gods exist and that Herman might well be one, then *Herman is a young Greek God* will not be a metaphorical statement for that reader; it will be literal.

Four Types of Metaphors

In an extremely interesting discussion, Laurence Perrine sheds further light on the nature of metaphor. Here is his definition:

A metaphor . . . consists of a comparison between essentially unlike things. There are two components in every metaphor: the concept actually discussed, and the thing to which it is compared. I shall refer to these, ordinarily, as the literal term and the figurative term. The two terms together compose the metaphor.[8]

POEM NO. 078, RCA 301, RCA *Electronic Age.* Reprinted with permission of RCA *Electronic Age.*
[8] Laurence Perrine, "Four Forms of Metaphor," *College English,* 33 (Nov. 1971), 125–38.

Keeping in mind that a metaphor always consists of a literal term and a figurative term, we can identify four classes of metaphors: (1) those in which both terms are named; (2) those in which only the literal term is named, the figurative term being supplied by the reader; (3) those in which only the figurative term is named, the literal term being supplied by the reader; (4) those in which neither the literal nor the figurative term is named, both being supplied by the reader. Let's see how this works, using mostly Perrine's examples.

Type 1

Shakespeare provides an example of the first type, in which both literal and figurative terms are named:

> All the world's a stage,
> And all the men and women merely players.

This metaphor is "equational": *world* (literal term) = *stage* (figurative term). But the linking need not take place with the copula ("literal term *is* figurative term"). Prepositions can establish the link:

> Too long a sacrifice
> Can make a stone *of* the heart.   —William Butler Yeats

Here the literal term is *heart* and the figurative term is *stone*. The link can be established through a variety of other grammatical relationships.

> Come into the garden, Maud,
>   For the black bat, night, has flown.   —Alfred, Lord Tennyson

In this case, the metaphorical link between the literal term *night* and the figurative term *bat* is established through grammatical apposition. In the next example, the demonstrative *that* establishes the link between *beauty*, the literal term, and *lamp*, the figurative term:

> Be watchful of your beauty, Lady dear!
> How much hangs on that lamp, you cannot tell.
>   —George Meredith

Type 2

In metaphors that state only the literal term, the reader must supply the figurative term.

> Sheathe thy impatience; throw cold water on thy choler.
>   —William Shakespeare

To understand these two metaphors the reader must supply the figurative terms *sword* and *fire,* for one *sheathes* a sword and *throws cold water on* a fire. Indeed, the metaphorical equation comes out something like this: *impatience = sword* and *choler = fire.*

> The tawny-hided desert crouches watching her.
>
> —William Butler Yeats

Here, the reader makes the equation *desert = lion,* because the adjective *tawny-hided* and the verb *crouches* suggest that animal.

Type 3

Here is an example of a metaphor in which the figurative term is given and the literal term must be supplied by the reader:

> Night's candles are burnt out.   —William Shakespeare

The reader makes the inevitable equation *night's candles = stars.* Riddles often take this form:

> In spring I look gay
> Decked in comely array,
> In summer more clothing I wear;
> When colder it grows,
> I fling off my clothes,
> And in winter quite naked appear.

A child might ask, "What am *I?*" And the answer is the equation *I = tree.*

Type 4

The most difficult type of metaphor to interpret is that in which neither the literal term nor the figurative term is expressed.

> Let us eat and drink, for tomorrow we shall die.   —Isaiah 22:13

The literal meaning of this is *Life is very short.* But the word *tomorrow* gives the clue to the proper figurative term: *day.* The quote from Isaiah means *Life is only a day. Life* is the literal term, and *day* is the figurative one.

Metaphor in Prose

Metaphor does not occur only in poetry; it can often be found in prose also, as the following example illustrates.

The thesis which these lectures will illustrate is that this quiet growth of science has practically recoloured our mentality so that modes of thought which in former times were exceptional are now broadly spread through the educated world. This new colouring of ways of thought had been proceeding slowly for many ages in the European peoples. At last it issued in the rapid development of science; and has thereby strengthened itself by its most obvious application. The new mentality is more important even than the new science and the new technology. It has altered the metaphysical presuppositions and the imaginative contents of our minds; so that now the old stimuli provoke a new response. Perhaps my metaphor of a new colour is too strong. What I mean is just that slightest change of tone which yet makes all the difference. This is exactly illustrated by a sentence from a published letter of that adorable genius, William James. When he was finishing his great treatise on the *Principles of Psychology,* he wrote to his brother Henry James, "I have to forge every sentence in the teeth of irreducible and stubborn facts."

—Alfred North Whitehead, *Science and the Modern World*

Simile

Simile is really a variety of metaphor, but one in which the equation between the literal and the figurative is expressed, usually by *like* or *as.* Examples:

The inflated style is itself a kind of euphemism. A mass of Latin words falls upon the facts *like* soft snow, blurring the outlines and covering up all the details.

—George Orwell, "Politics and the English Language"

I ran, I shouted, I climbed, I vaulted over gates, I felt *like* a schoolboy let out on a holiday.

—Vita Sackville-West

So Elvis Presley came, strumming a weird guitar and wagging his tail across the continent, ripping off fame and fortune as he scrunched his way, and, *like* a latter-day Johnny Appleseed, sowing seeds of a new rhythm and style in the white souls of the white youth of America.

—Eldridge Cleaver

A simile from John Donne's "A Valediction: Forbidding Mourning":

> Our two souls therefore which are one,
>   Though I must go, endure not yet
> A breach, but an expansion,
>   *Like* gold to airy thinness beat.

Irony

The tapestry of language is richly woven with figurativeness, not only metaphor and simile, but a variety of other nonliteral ways of conveying meaning.

Suppose I want to convey the notion that I disapprove of cheating on tests. I can state this idea literally:

Cheating on tests is bad.

I can also convey my attitude through a metaphor or a simile:

Cheating on tests is assassination of academic integrity.

Cheating on tests is like playing cards with a marked deck.

I might also use irony:

Cheating on tests is obviously an extremely noble thing for students to do.

For the last example to have an ironic effect, the reader must somehow see that I intend something quite different from what I say literally.

Metaphor comes about because of a mix of semantic features. Another way of saying this is that metaphor is a function of the denotations of words. Irony can result from a mix of *connotations*.

For example, the connotative value of *emperor* is one of glory, magnificence, and power. *Ice cream* suggests the common and everyday. Therefore, when Wallace Stevens titled a poem "The Emperor of Ice-Cream," he created verbal irony. The irony is reinforced by the opening of the poem:

Call the roller of big cigars,
The muscular one. . . .

What does an emperor have to do with ice cream or rollers of big cigars?

Another example of this sort of irony:

Rod McKuen is the poet laureate of the pimpled generation.

The phrase *poet laureate* is elevated in connotation, but *pimpled generation* is just the opposite. The clash of connotations between these two terms conveys irony, which reveals a highly unfavorable attitude toward Rod McKuen.

An Example of Irony

The following is an ironic passage, and the irony stems largely from the word *momma* applied to America, for *momma* has a richly (perhaps overly) sentimental connotation, and the writer's attitude toward America is hardly sentimental:

> Now that I am a man, I have "given up childish ways." I realize that America is my momma and America was Momma's momma. And I am going to place the blame for injustice and wrong on the right momma. Even today, when I leave my country to appear on television and make other public appearances in foreign countries, I find it difficult to speak of the injustices I experience in this country. Because America is my momma. Even if Momma is a whore, she is still Momma. Many times I am asked if I would go to war if drafted. I always answer, "Yes, under one condition; that I be allowed to go to the front line without a gun. Momma is worth dying for, but there is nothing worth killing for. And if I ever change my opinion about killing, I will go to Mississippi and kill that Sheriff who spit in my wife's face."
>
> America is my momma. One fourth of July, I want to go to the New York harbor and talk to Momma—the Statue of Liberty. I want to snatch that torch out of her hand and take her with me to the ghetto and sit her down on the street corner. I want to show her the "tired, the poor, the huddled masses yearning to breathe free." I want to show Momma what she has been doing to her children. And Momma would weep. For the grief of the ghetto is the grief of the entire American family.
>
> —Dick Gregory, *The Shadow That Scared Me*

The passage is not, of course, unrelieved irony. It is a mixture of the ironic and the straightforward. In particular, the last sentence in each paragraph is completely straight.

A Second Example

In this passage, Lenny Bruce attacks Americans' homogenized version of themselves and their country:

> I credit the motion picture industry as the strongest environmental factor in molding the children of my day.
>
> Andy Hardy: whistling; a brown pompadour; a green lawn; a father whose severest punishment was taking your car away for the weekend.
>
> Warner Baxter was a doctor. All priests looked like Pat O'Brien.
>
> The superintendent of my school looked like Spencer Tracy, and the principal looked like Vincent Price. I went to Hollywood High, folks. Lana Turner sat at the next desk. Roland Young was the Eng-

lish teacher and Joan Crawford taught general science. "She's got a fabulous body, but she never takes that shop apron off."

Actually, I went to public school in North Bellmore, Long Island, for eight years, up until the fifth grade. I remember the routine of milk at 10:15 and napping on the desk—I hated the smell of that desk—I always used to dribble on the initials. And how enigmatic those well-preserved carvings were to me: BOOK YOU."

—Lenny Bruce, *How to Talk Dirty and Influence People*

The irony in this passage comes from the fact that the reader knows what Bruce's attitude is, even though he does not specify it. He is saying something like this: Americans' vision of themselves is false and callow and unthinking. The last paragraph, where Bruce begins to tell it like it really was, is the tip-off to the irony of what goes before.

The effect of irony is powerful, for it makes the reader a conspirator with the writer. The reader says unconsciously, "I know what this guy is getting at; I'm in on the secret of his meaning—even though he doesn't give that meaning directly, in so many words."

Other Figures

Literally hundreds of kinds of figures of speech have been identified and given such tongue-twisting names as *aposiopesis, diacope, epitimesis, hypozeuxis, poiciologia,* and so on. We will let most of these rest in peace, but a few of them are useful enough to deserve brief mention.

Metonymy and Synecdoche

Metonymy is a kind of metaphor in which a term that is closely associated with the literal term is substituted for it. Thus

He lived by the sword and died by the sword.

substitutes the word *sword* for *force* or *violence,* the sword being closely associated with force and violence.

Closely related to metonymy is *synecdoche,* the figure of speech in which a part stands for the whole.

At least fifty sails set out for the race.

The sails are only parts of the racing yachts, but they stand for the whole.

Oxymoron

An *oxymoron* joins two contradictory terms to create a paradox. When this device is used unintentionally, it can produce confusion and seem foolish. But when it is used well, as for example by
Shakespeare in *Romeo and Juliet* ("O heavy lightness! serious vanity!"), an oxymoron can convey additional insights through its startling combinations. "Holy devil" and "Hell's Angels" are two
contemporary examples of oxymoron.

Overstatement and Understatement

Overstatement and *understatement* (*hyperbole* and *litotes* in
the jargon) also are figurative devices. The figurative effect arises
when the reader understands that the writer is overstressing or un-
derstressing a statement. In other words, there is a disjunction between the importance that the writer *seems* to put on a statement
and its actual importance. Here is an example of overstatement:

> He [a lion] roared so loud, and looked so wonderous grim,
> His very shadow durst not follow him.
>
> —Alexander Pope

And here is an example of understatement:

> God loves his children not a little.

This means, of course, that God loves his children a very great deal.

Review

The following passages use a variety of kinds of figurative language.
Underline the figurative elements, and name them if you can. Try to restate
the ideas, eliminating the figures. What is lost? What is gained, if anything?
Why?

1. Madison Avenue frequently exaggerates the importance of new features
   and encourages consumers to dispose of partially worn-out goods to
   make way for the new.

   —Alvin Toffler

2. Nobody knows how many people in America moonlight. . . .

   —Peter Schrag

3. In the magazines and newspapers, top management, formerly so autocratic (think of Henry Luce), now casts itself at the feet of the publicity intellectuals, seeking their intercession with the youth-worshiping public. One picks up *The New York Times* and reads on the front page that the posthumous homosexual novel of E. M. Forster is about to appear in England. Why not simply Forster's posthumous novel, on page 40? No, the word is HOMOSEXUAL and it is on the front page. The *Times* still keeps up its statesmanlike and grave appearance, but its journalism is yellower than ever. It has surrendered without a fight to the new class.

—Saul Bellow

4. The bridge by which we cross from tragedy to comedy and back again is precarious and narrow.

—Christopher Fry

5. Miss Nims, take a letter to Henry David Thoreau. Dear Henry: I thought of you the other afternoon as I was approaching Concord doing fifty on Route 62. That is a high speed at which to hold a philosopher in one's mind, but in this century, we are a nimble bunch.

—E. B. White

6. Sex is dead. Nobody seems to have noticed its passing, what with the distraction caused by recent reports of the death of God, the death of Self, the death of the City, the death of Tragedy, and all the other cultural obituaries of the past few years. Yet is is a fact: sex is dead and we must begin to learn how to live in a world in which that is an incontrovertible fact.

—Earl H. Brill

7. I have been told to "look down from a high place over the whole extensive landscape of modern art." We all know how tempting high places can be, and how dangerous. I usually avoid them myself. But if I must do as I am told, I shall try to find out why modern art has taken its peculiar form, and to guess how long that form will continue.

—Kenneth Clark

8.   I am the daughter of earth and water,
    And the nursling of the sky:
I pass thro' the pores of the ocean and shores;
    I change, but I cannot die.
For after the rain when with never a strain,
    The pavilion of heaven is bare,
And the winds and sunbeams with their convex gleams,
    Build up the blue dome of air,
I silently laugh at my own cenotaph,
    And out of the caverns of rain,
Like a child from the womb, like a ghost from the tomb,
    I arise and unbuild it again.
      —Percy Bysshe Shelley, "The Cloud"

APPENDIX

Sentences: Readability and Emphasis

Sentences can often be made more readable without losing the ideas intended by them:

> That Norman thought that Lillian had eaten the dumpling was not surprising.
> It was not surprising that Norman thought Lillian had eaten the dumpling.

The second example is far more readable than the first. As a general rule, there is no reason to write sentences that are hard to read when other versions of those same sentences are easier. There are times, however, when you will want to write the more difficult version, as when I constructed the nearly unreadable sentence above just to show that some sentences are indeed difficult to read and that they usually can be revised to improve readability.

This appendix is about readability. It will help you write sentences and paragraphs that do not obscure your ideas because of bad construction or faulty emphasis.

COMBINING SENTENCES: TOWARD FLUENT WRITING

When you read the following passage, you will probably have the sense that something is wrong, that the expression of ideas is out of kilter:

The core of the good ole boy's world is with his buddies. It is the comfortable, all-male camaraderie. It is hyperhearty. It is joshing. It is drinking. It is regaling one another with tales of assorted, exaggerated prowess. Women are outsiders. Some social events are unavoidably mixed. Then the good ole boys cluster together at one end of the room. They leave wives at the other. The GOB's magic doesn't work with women. He feels insecure. He feels threatened by them. In fact, he doesn't really like women. He likes them only in bed.

You might say that the passage is choppy or even a bit incoherent. As a reader, you probably had some trouble determining how the ideas related to one another. The passage is simply not fluent.

It is a mangled version of a passage written by Bonnie Angelo, London bureau chief for *Time* magazine. Here is the original version:

The core of the good ole boy's world is with his buddies, the comfortable, all-male camaraderie, joshing and drinking and regaling one another with tales of assorted, exaggerated prowess. Women are outsiders; when social events are unavoidably mixed, the good ole boys cluster together at one end of the room, leaving wives at the other. The GOB's magic doesn't work with women; he feels insecure, threatened by them. In fact, he doesn't really like women, except in bed.

—Bonnie Angelo, "Those Good Ole Boys"

You will probably agree that this fluent version just sounds better—seems to have been produced by a more skilled writer and, perhaps, even a more intelligent person. Furthermore, the fluent version is much easier to read, for the relationships among the ideas are shown by the sentence structure, the writer having done the grouping that the reader must do for him- or herself in the choppy first version.

Here is an interesting experiment that you can easily perform. Show passages *1* and *2* below to ten of your fellow students (who are not in your English class and thus have not been tipped off). Tell them that two writers answered the question "What does the gesture of tapping the temple mean?" After your subjects have read the passages, ask them the following questions: (1) Which passage "sounds" better? (2) Which passage is easier to read? (3) Which writer is more intelligent?

1. *Tapping the Temple*

Many people understand this as a sign of stupidity. You might instead twist your forefinger against your temple. This makes the meaning more precise. It indicates "a screw loose." You might rotate your forefinger close to your temple. This signals that the brain is going round and round. But even these actions would be confusing to some people. In Saudi Arabia stupidity can be signaled by touching the lower eyelid with the tip of the forefinger. Other local stupidity gestures include tapping the elbow of the raised forearm. They also include flapping the hand up and down in front of half-closed eyes. Also, they include rotating a raised hand or laying one forefinger flat across the forehead.

2. Tapping the Temple

Many people understand this as a sign of stupidity. To make the meaning more precise, you might instead twist your forefinger against your temple, indicating "a screw loose," or rotate your forefinger close to your temple, signaling that the brain is going round and round. But even these actions would be confusing to some people. In Saudi Arabia, for example, stupidity can be signaled by touching the lower eyelid with the tip of the forefinger. Other local stupidity gestures include tapping the elbow of the raised forearm, flapping the hand up and down in front of half-closed eyes, rotating a raised hand, or laying one forefinger flat across the forehead.

The second passage is by the zoologist and author Desmond Morris, from *Manwatching*. As some of the subjects in your experiment might realize, the first passage is a mangled rewrite of the second.

If the experiment works as it is intended, most subjects will say that the second passage sounds better, is easier to read, and is written by the more intelligent author. However, both convey exactly the same information about gestures. The essential difference—as you will see if you compare the two passages—is in the style.

In general, then, fluent prose is more effective than prose that stops, starts, and stutters—though sometimes, for specific reasons, you may want your prose to lack fluency. You should, however, have the ability to write the kind of prose that best fits your purpose in communicating with a given audience.

Exercise

Most people have a great deal of skill in writing fluent prose, an ability that perhaps they are unaware of. You can make a rough test of your own ability to create fluent prose. Below are examples of how short sentences can be combined into single well-formed sentences. Following the examples are groups of sentences that you can combine into single sentences.

Here are the examples:

a. The typewriter spills words onto the page. It clatters on. Its operator is in a trance. He does not care what comes out.
(Spilling words onto the page, the typewriter clatters on, its operator in a trance, not caring what comes out.)

b. The clouds massed below us. They were in great billows. They looked almost solid. We could jump from the plane. We could land safely in them. It would be like jumping from the barn into a huge feather bed.
(Massing below us in great billows, the clouds looked almost solid, as if we could jump from the plane and land safely in them, like jumping from the barn into a huge feather bed.)

c. Of one thing we are certain. We are certain that writing is hard work. It is hard. It is rewarding. A well-written essay says something. It says just what we want it to. It conveys our exact meaning to our readers.
(Of one thing we are certain: that writing is hard work, hard but rewarding, for a well-written essay says just what we want it to and conveys our exact meaning to our readers.)

d. The wind normally dies down. It dies down during the afternoon. That creates a peaceful interlude. During the interlude students stroll along the river. They sit under the elms on campus. They read. They chat. They just daydream.
(During the afternoon, the wind normally dies down, creating a peaceful interlude during which students stroll along the river or sit under the elms on campus, reading, chatting, or just daydreaming.)

e. The professor was a fascinating lecturer. He was an expert on the early lyrics of Christopher Smart. He was a fascinating lecturer for anyone interested in his subject. Few people are interested in his subject, as a matter of fact.
(The professor, an expert on the early lyrics of Christopher Smart, was a fascinating lecturer for anyone interested in his subject, which, as a matter of fact, few people are.)

Now you combine the following sentences:

1. The book has been in print for fifty years. It is utterly boring to most readers.
2. The assignment was given. The class asked the professor something. They asked when the paper was due. The professor was a kindly old duffer.
3. You do not know how to punctuate. You must go to the writing lab. It is located in the basement of Phillips Hall. You must learn that important skill. You must work with exercises until you have mastered it.
4. Students often discover something. They discover that they

haven't left themselves enough time to do the essay question. They discover this toward the middle of the test.

5. The furniture was lovely to look at. Nevertheless, it was not awfully sturdy. The legs of the chairs often snapped under the weight of hefty occupants.

6. The wind was blowing at twenty miles per hour. It created a chill factor of $-20°$. This was enough to keep most of us indoors. Some hardy adventurers explored the fields and streams. The fields and streams were around the lodge.

7. Ethan Hatch claims something. It is easier to learn Chinese than English. I find this idea totally ridiculous. I know that young children learn all languages with equal speed and ease.

8. The second edition of the book was a great improvement over the first. The second edition appeared in 1975. It gave a more complete explanation of the history of typography. It included a full index. This feature is essential if the book is to be used as a reference source.

9. The computer is fast but dumb. It makes astronomical numbers of decisions in fractions of a second. Its speed allows it to complete infinitely complex problems in the wink of an eye. The programmer must know how to ask the right questions.

10. The day is ending. The sun is sinking in the west. It gives the sky and ocean a bronze sheen.

Purposes, Audiences, Situations

Below are two passages conveying essentially the same ideas:

Opera is a great art form, combining music and drama, providing a visual as well as aural spectacle, which is one reason fans prefer opera to any other art form.

Opera is a great art form. It combines music and drama. It provides a visual as well as aural spectacle. This is one reason fans prefer opera to any other art form.

The first is, of course, more fluent, but is it for this reason better? The only answer is this: Better for what? *No language form is good or bad out of context.* A skilled writer will be able to produce either version, but to determine which is best, we would need to know

the writer's purpose,
the audience,
and the situation.

Depending on these considerations, one or the other version might be preferable. In other words, neither example can be judged until it is in context.

This much seems obvious, but what might not be so clear is the value of being able to write fluent sentences when the occasion demands. If the writer is capable of producing only the kinds of sentences in the second example, then he or she is severely limited— like the mechanic who has only a monkey wrench and a hammer, when, in fact, auto repairs demand a well-stocked toolbox. As an old saying goes, if the only tool you have is a hammer, then you treat everything like a nail.

A Theory of Sentence Combining

Perhaps a bit of theory will be helpful at this point. The grammar of a language is nothing other than an instrument of mind. In this instance, we do not mean the grammar that you studied in high school when you learned to find the subjects and predicates of sentences or defined *noun* as "the name of a person, place, or thing." Grammar, as we are using it here, refers to the structures which carry ideas or meaning. One can say that the brain invented grammar, and, this being the case, obviously grammar must be important to thought and certainly to the expression of that thought. The writer who has not mastered grammar—in the sense of the structure of sentences—will have some difficulty getting his or her ideas down on paper, will fumble about, use more words than necessary, and find writing to be enormously frustrating. To convey your ideas, you must be a fluent writer—that is, you must be able to call upon the grammatical resources of the language when you need them. Lack of this ability is a severe handicap to writing.

We can push this subject just a bit further. Every sentence contains one proposition or more than one, and we can define *proposition*, roughly, as a minimal sentence, carrying a single idea. The following is an example of a one-proposition sentence:

The man bites the dog.

The next example, however, is a two-proposition sentence:

Being vicious, the man bites the dog.

Why do we say that this sentence contains two propositions? Well, *the man bites the dog* is obviously a proposition in our sense, but what about *being vicious?* In the first place, note the following:

The man is vicious. The man bites the dog.

Doesn't that convey essentially the same information as the second example? Furthermore, in "Being vicious, the man bites the dog," we must know who it is that is vicious, or we won't understand the sentence; so when we read the sentence, it is as if we were reading "[*The man*] Being vicious, the man bites the dog."
Or take the following:

The dog, a German shepherd, yelped with pain.

We can express these ideas in two sentences:

The dog yelped with pain. The dog was a German shepherd.

So in the first of these, we actually have two propositions that could be expressed as two sentences.
Here are some further examples:

1. Strong tea, which is easy to make, revives the spirits.
   (Strong tea revives the spirits. Strong tea is easy to make.)
2. We smelled the aroma of coffee, pungent in the cold of the mountain cabin.
   (We smelled the aroma of coffee. The aroma was pungent in the cold of the mountain cabin.)
3. It is strange that a ham sandwich always tastes good.
   (It is strange. A ham sandwich always tastes good.)
   That a ham sandwich always tastes good is strange.
   (*Something* is strange. A ham sandwich always tastes good.)
4. Watching the embers glow in the fireplace, I felt completely at peace with the world.
   (I was watching the embers glow in the fireplace. I felt completely at peace with the world.)
5. The fire having nearly died out, we decided it was time to crawl into our bunks.
   (The fire had nearly died out. We decided *something*. It was time to do *something*. We crawled into our bunks.)

The last example has four propositions, yet the meaning of the sentence remains clear.

Exercise

If you gain the meaning of a sentence that contains more than one proposition, then you have gained the meanings of all of the propositions in that sentence. In other words, when you read, you isolate propositions, even though you are not consciously aware that you do this. Each of the following sentences contains more than one proposition. What are they?
Here are some examples:

a. People who live in glass houses shouldn't throw stones.
   (People shouldn't throw stones. People live in glass houses.)

b. Being careful not to break the yolk, I let the egg slide from the shell into the pan.
   (I was careful not to break the yolk. I let the egg slide from the shell into the pan.)

c. The omelette, a tasty dish, pleased my son, his appetite having been whetted by the smell of cooking.
   (The omelette pleased my son. The omelette was a tasty dish. His appetite had been whetted by the smell of cooking.)

d. Too hot for tennis, the weather kept us from taking any exercise and drained us of energy.
   (The weather was too hot for tennis. It kept us from taking any exercise. It drained us of energy.)

Now separate the propositions in the following sentences:

1. Thus he fought his last fight, thirsting savagely for blood.
                                                    —H. L. Mencken

2. Walking through the fields, we learn quite a number of things about snails.
                                                    —Danilo Dolci

3. I am injected into this enormous silver monster, floating gently on a sea of Muzak, the sweet Karo Syrup of existence.   —Jean Shepherd

4. My own house faced the Cambridge world as a finely and solidly constructed mansion, preceded by a large oval lawn and ringed with an imposing white-pine hedge.   —e. e. cummings

5. To snare a sensibility in words, especially one that is alive and powerful, one must be tentative and nimble.   —Susan Sontag

6. Heads up, swinging with the music, their right arms swinging free, they stepped out, crossing the sanded arena under the arclights, the cuadrillas opening out behind, the picadors riding after.
                                                    —Ernest Hemingway

7. When the notion of man as machine was first advanced, the machine was a very simple collection of pulleys and billiard balls and levers.
                                                    —Wayne C. Booth

8. The babies were all under one year old, very funny and lovable.
—Grace Paley

9. Under the changes of weather, it may look like marble or like sea water, black as slate in the fog, white as tufa in the sunlight.
—Saul Bellow

10. One afternoon the previous May, a month when the fields blaze with the green-gold fire of half-grown wheat, Dewey spent several hours at Valley View, weeding his father's grave, an obligation he had too long neglected. —Truman Capote

---

By now, you should be convinced of two points: the ability to write fluent sentences is a great advantage, sometimes an absolute necessity; if you are not fluent at present, you can learn fluency.

Learning to write fluent prose is not difficult, and there are some excellent aids available. If you need to develop your fluency, get one of the following books, and work with it regularly for a month or six weeks.

William Strong, *Sentence Combining: A Composing Book* (New York: Random House, 1973).

Michelle Rippon and Walter E. Meyers, *Combining Sentences* (New York: Harcourt Brace Jovanovich, 1979).

Your composition instructor can undoubtedly help you with your problem.

SENTENCE STRATEGIES

The grammar of English gives the writer many techniques for producing different effects with sentences. For example, the following all convey essentially the same information, but are quite different in effect.

Most people enjoy peace and quiet.
Peace and quiet are enjoyed by most people.
What most people enjoy are peace and quiet.
Peace and quiet—that's what most people enjoy.
Most people enjoy this: peace and quiet.

If you understand and can use some of the important sentence strategies, you will be able to make your point in just the way you want to, with the right emphasis at the right time.

The following pages will give you practice in using various sentence strategies.

Periodic and Loose Sentences

A sentence "base" is the main clause of a sentence. In the following, the bases are printed in italics:

> *We decided not to take our vacation* because the price of gasoline had skyrocketed.
> Although our car gets excellent mileage, *we feel that we should conserve energy by not driving.*
> A *large park is near our house,* giving us the chance to get outdoors without using gasoline.
> The weather having been sunny and warm, *the park was crowded all weekend.*

As you can see, modifiers sometimes follow the base and sometimes precede it. When the modifiers follow the base, the sentence is called *loose;* when they precede it, the sentence is called *periodic.*

Here are two examples of loose sentences, printed to show how the modification works.

> 1. *Life disappears or modifies its appearances so fast that everything takes on an aspect of illusion—*
>   a momentary fizzing and boiling with smoke rings,
>   like pouring dissident chemicals into a retort.
>
> —Loren Eiseley
>
> 2. *We caught two bass,*
>   hauling them in briskly
>   as though they were mackerel,
>   pulling them over the side of the boat
>   in a businesslike manner
>   without any landing net
>   and stunning them with a blow on the back of the head.
>
> —E. B. White

The indentations in examples *1* and *2* indicate what modifies what. For example, "hauling them in briskly," "pulling them over the side of the boat," "and stunning them with a blow on the back of the head" all modify the base, but "as though they were mackerel" relates to "hauling them in briskly," and "without any landing net" refers to "in a businesslike manner."

Here are two periodic sentences, the modifiers preceding the bases:

3.   As the least drop of wine tinges the whole goblet,
      so the least particle of truth colors our whole life.

—Thoreau

4.   Instead of a squad of Nazi supermen in shiny boots, and pack-
      ing Lugers,
      *we were confronted by five of the most unkempt, stunted, scrubby
      specimens I have ever had the pleasure of capturing.*

—Donald Pearce

Compare the effect of the following periodic sentence, example 5, with its loose version, example 6:

5. Having entered the House of Commons in the customary manner
    for peers' sons, from a family-controlled borough in an uncon-
    tested election at the age of twenty-three, and, during his fifteen
    years in the House of Commons, having returned unopposed five
    times from the same borough, and having for the last twenty-
    seven years sat in the House of Lords, *he had little personal expe-
    rience in vote getting.*

—Barbara Tuchman

6. *He had little personal experience in vote getting,* having entered
    the House of Commons in the customary manner for peers' sons,
    from a family-controlled borough in an uncontested election at the
    age of twenty-three, and, during his fifteen years in the House of
    Commons, having returned unopposed five times from the same
    borough, and having for the last twenty-seven years sat in the
    House of Lords.

In 5, readers are held in suspense, waiting for the main clause and thus for the sentence to resolve itself. The main predicate, *had,* is the sixty-third word in the sentence, and, of course, readers cannot organize the sentence until they reach the predicate or pivot word. In 6, *had* is the second word, and the phrases that follow its clause fall into place immediately, not needing to be held in suspension.

In 5, there is a certain force and finality that one does not sense in 6, which seems to run on and on. But this is not to say that one version is better than the other; each of the two achieves a different effect, and the value of that effect can be judged only in context, in the light of purpose, audience, and subject. Being able to perceive the different effects—and to achieve them when appropriate—is, however, important.

Here is another example of a sentence in periodic and loose forms:

> 7. In the autumn following Custer's expedition, the Sioux who had been hunting in the north began returning to the Red Cloud agency.
>
> —Dee Brown
>
> 8. The Sioux who had been hunting in the north began returning to the Red Cloud agency in the autumn following Custer's expedition.

The principles governing the use of periodic and loose sentences are fairly simple.

First, the end-of-sentence position is the most important "slot."

> Most Bostonians are prim and proper.

The first part of the sentence, "Most Bostonians," simply announces the topic; the last part, "prim and proper," gives information about the topic. The writer of that sentence has assumed that the readers would already know what "Bostonians" refers to, but that the information concerning them would be "news." In other words, sentence ends tend to carry more information than their beginnings and are thus, in general, more important.

Second, the periodic arrangement creates suspense; the reader must wait for the main clause, which will allow the meaning to be derived.

> Even in simple sentences like the following, *the end-of-sentence position is the most important "slot."*

Third, readability often determines one's choice between periodic and loose. For example, the following passage is slightly difficult to read because one does not find the subject of the second sentence immediately (and probably assumes that it is the same as that of the first):

> Since they end emphatically, periodic sentences can be more forceful than loose. Since their main clauses come first, loose sentences are usually easier to read than periodic ones.

The following version is easier to read:

> Since they end emphatically, periodic sentences can be more forceful than loose. Loose sentences are usually easier to read than periodic ones, since their main clauses come first.

Through practice, you can develop the ability to use the periodic and loose arrangements effectively.

Exercise

Some of the following sentences are loose, and some are periodic. Rearrange the periodic ones so that they become loose and the loose so that they become periodic.

1. In certain kinds of writing, particularly in art criticism and literary criticism, it is normal to come across long passages which are almost completely lacking in meaning. —George Orwell

2. The human species, according to the best theory I can form of it, is composed of two distinct races, *the men who borrow* and *the men who lend*. —Charles Lamb

3. The dog has long been bemused by the singular activities and the curious practices of men, cocking his head inquiringly to one side, intently watching and listening to the strangest goings-on in the world. —James Thurber

4. The rolling period, the stately epithet, the noun rich in poetic associations, the subordinate clauses that give the sentence weight and magnificence, the grandeur like that of wave following wave in the open sea; there is no doubt that in all this there is something inspiring. —W. Somerset Maugham

5. From the very beginning of school we make books and reading a constant source of possible failure and public humiliation. —John Holt

6. I plodded on with the lesson, trying to get the class to locate Broad and Market Streets, the site of Philadelphia's City Hall, on maps that had been passed out. —Peter Binzen

---

Parallelism and Balance

Two traditional principles involving sentences are parallelism and balance. Parallelism is a grammatical principle, and balance has to do with sentence effect.

Two or more items that are in the same sentence "slot" are usually grammatical equivalents. Thus, the sentence

    1. Barbara likes *ice cream, candy,* and *soda pop.*

is parallel, for the coordinate objects of the verb *likes* are all nouns:

    2. Barbara likes *ice cream*
                    candy
                    soda pop

But this sentence

    3. Barbara likes *ice cream, candy,* and *to dance.*

is not parallel, for *ice cream* and *candy* are nouns, but *to dance* is a verbal.

Here is another sentence that is faulty in parallelism:

    4. Robert wants to learn algebra, play tennis, and he goes to college.

The best way to explain the faulty parallelism in *4* is to analyze the sentence:

    5. Robert wants *to learn algebra* [verbal phrase]
                (to) play tennis [verbal phrase]
                he goes to college [clause]

The faulty parallelism is easily corrected:

    6. Robert wants to learn algebra and play tennis, and he goes to college.

We can analyze this as

    7. Robert wants *to learn algebra*
                    (to) play tennis
    and [conjunction]
    he goes to college

As Virginia Tufte points out in her excellent book *Grammar as Style,* some professional writers deliberately create sentences in

which parallelism is faulty, to achieve specific effects.[1] She cites
these examples:

8. Here was himself, *young* [adjective]
   good-looking [adjective]
   snappy dresser [noun phrase]
   and making dough [verbal phrase]

—John Steinbeck

9. Is there any one period of English literature to which we can
   point as being *fully mature* [adjective phrase]
   comprehensive [adjective]
   and in equilibrium [prepositional phrase]

—T. S. Eliot

10.   *Religiously* [adverb]
        politically [adverb]
        and simply in terms of the
        characters' efforts to get [prepositional phrase]
        along with one another
   this incongruity is pervasive.

—Frederick C. Crews

Closely related to parallelism, *balance* is a matter of the rhetoric of the sentence, not the grammar. As the word implies, it is a
device in which structures are balanced, for emphasis or effect.

In the following sentence, coordinated noun phrases are balanced:

11. There was a time also when in the first fine flush of
    laundries and bakeries,
    milk deliveries and canned goods,
    ready-made clothes and dry cleaning,
    it did look as if the American life was being enormously
    simplified.

—Margaret Mead

Here are three more examples of balanced sentences:

12. There is no sense in hoping
    for that which already exists
    or
    for that which cannot be.

—Erich Fromm

[1] Virginia Tufte, *Grammar as Style* (New York: Holt, 1971), pp. 207–08.

13. We go
        wherever the wind blows,
   we take
        whatever we find.

—Danilo Dolci

14. The difference
        between tragedy and comedy
   is
   the difference
        between experience and intuition.

—Christopher Fry

Most balance is not quite that perfect, however. In the following, we find phrases that *nearly* balance:

15. The view that neurosis is a severe reaction to human trouble is as
        revolutionary in its implications for social practice
   as it is
        daring in formulation.

—Jerome S. Bruner

Exercise

Using the example sentences in this section as models, write ten sentences in which balance is an obvious principle. Then rewrite those sentences so that balance is eliminated.

Active and Passive Voice

The most common definition of *passive voice* is "the form of the sentence in which the subject receives the action." Thus, example *1* is passive and example *2* is active:

1. Mary was punched by George. [passive]
2. George punched Mary. [active]

In the *active voice,* the subject (George) performs the action (punching) and the object (Mary) receives the action.

However, using the definition of the *passive* above, we could argue that

3. Mary received the blow.

is in the passive, for *Mary,* the subject, receives the action. But, as we shall see, example 3 is actually in the active voice.

To give an adequate definition of passive voice versus active voice would involve us in unnecessary complications. Perhaps the following is enough explanation for our purposes: some sentences allow you to flip-flop the subject and the object and insert a form of the verb "to be." When you do this, you change an active-voice sentence into a passive one.

ACTIVE	PASSIVE
Mary received the blow.	The blow was received by Mary.
The man had bitten the dog.	The dog had been bitten by the man.
Lyle is mowing the lawn.	The lawn is being moved by Lyle.
The reporter will write the story.	The story will be written by the reporter.

We also know that we can delete the *by*-phrases from passive sentences.

ACTIVE	PASSIVE
The technician drew five cubic centimeters of blood from the patient.	Five cubic centimeters of blood were drawn from the patient.
Someone tipped over the pickle barrel.	The pickle barrel was tipped over.
You must complete the work before you are paid.	The work must be completed before you are paid.
The mechanic replaced the sparkplugs in the auto.	The sparkplugs in the auto were replaced.

Students have often been told that the active voice is more direct, vigorous, and effective than the passive; therefore, the passive should be avoided. But once again: it all depends! In the following paragraph, the passive sentences are italicized:

4. I had a couple of close ones during this show. *On the way in, my platoon was evidently silhouetted against the night sky, and was fired on four times at a range of maybe 300 yards by an eighty-eight.* (This is a notorious and vicious gun. The velocity of the shell is so high that you hear it pass or explode near you almost at The same instant that you hear the sound of its being fired. You really can't duck. Also, it's an open-sights affair—*you are aimed at particularly: not, as with mortars, aimed at only by approximation.*) Anyway, they went past me about an arm's length above or in front of me, I don't know which. We hit the ditches. *After pointing a few more, the gun was forced off by our return tank fire.*

—Donald Pearce, *Journal of a War*

Surely this passage would not be improved if all its sentences were in the active voice.

Exercise

Some of the following sentences are in the active voice, some in the passive. Change them to their opposites and discuss the changes in emphasis that result.

1. Rats and dogs are conditioned and are usually incapable of breaking that conditioning.   —Henry F. Ottinger

2. Classroom dynamics can be described in terms of student and teacher roles.

3. The reader knows best how a productive wedding is arranged in his own field.   —William G. Perry, Jr.

4. I am using the word *image* in a wide meaning, which does not restrict it to the mind's eye as a visual organ.   —Jacob Bronowski

5. The presence of pleasure areas in the brain was discovered accidentally in 1954 by James Olds and Peter Milner in Canada.   —H. J. Campbell

6. The subject is told to administer a shock to the learner each time he gives a wrong response.   —Stanley Milgram

---

Repetition

Another interesting and useful device in sentence strategies is *repetition:*

1. He had drunk a lot of *rezina* in his time: he said it was good for one, good for the kidneys, good for the liver, good for the lungs, good for the bowels and for the mind, good for everything.
—Henry Miller

This daring extensive repetition certainly underscores the opinion about the goodness of *rezina,* a Greek wine.

In the following passage, the author uses repetition with great effect:

2. To be human, to be human, to be fully human. What does it mean? What is required?   Wayne C. Booth

Not only does Booth repeat the infinitive phrase (with a variation on the last one), but he also repeats the question form twice. To illustrate the force of repetition, I will rewrite this example, removing the repetition:

3. What is meant by and required to be fully human?

Further examples of repetition for emphasis:

4. Just as the prophets of the eighth century B.C. left their villages and carried their "thus saith the Lord" far beyond the boundaries of their home towns, and just as the Apostle Paul left his village of Tarsus and carried the Gospel of Jesus Christ to the far corners of the Greco-Roman world, so am I compelled to carry the gospel of freedom beyond my own home town.   —Martin Luther King, Jr.

5. Now what does this Let Him Be Poor mean? It means let him be weak. Let him be ignorant. Let him become a nucleus of disease. Let him be a standing exhibition and example of ugliness and dirt. Let·him have rickety children.   —George Bernard Shaw

---

Exercise

Using the example sentences above as models, write ten sentences (or passages) in which you employ obvious repetition to achieve emphasis.

Framing and Emphasis

The *frame* of a sentence is its first element. Since sentences usually begin with their subjects, the frame is also most often the subject, as in the following:

1. *Laurel and Hardy* provided laughter for millions of people in my generation.

However, sentences can be arranged so that the frame is not the subject:

2. *In my generation,* Laurel and Hardy provided laughter for millions of people.
3. *Laughter*—that's what Laurel and Hardy provided for millions of people in my generation.

Each of these three sentences achieves a different emphasis, the frame giving the sentence its direction. Indeed, any of the major elements can serve as a frame, as the following passive-voice sentence demonstrates:

4. *Millions of people* were provided laughter by Laurel and Hardy in my generation.

The point is that sentences can be manipulated so that the desired emphasis is achieved—or so that they achieve the desired emphasis. Not every sentence must begin with the logical subject. However, a word of caution: you should use restraint in departing from the normal word order. Excessive use of emphasis will defeat your purpose. If every sentence is emphatic, then none will have the force of emphasis, and your prose will seem unclear.

Look closely at how the following sentence arrangements create specific emphases:

5. *It was a heavenly place for a boy,* that farm of my Uncle John's.
   —Mark Twain

   (My Uncle John's farm was a heavenly place for a boy.)

6. *Patience, horses or a fine carriage, a widow to wive, a sloping lawn with a river at the bottom, a thriving field, an adopted daughter*—that was as far as his desire wandered.
   —William Carlos Williams

   (His desire wandered only as far as patience, horses or a fine carriage, a widow to wive, a sloping lawn with a river at the bottom, a thriving field, an adopted daughter.)

7. *To sing "Yankee Doodle"* is easy.

(It is easy to sing "Yankee Doodle.")

8. *That Mary missed the show* was a pity.

(It was a pity that Mary missed the show.)

9. *Of all virtues*, magnanimity is the rarest.   —William Hazlitt

(Magnanimity is the rarest of all virtues.)

10. *Stress* he could endure but peace and regularity pleased him better.   —William Carlos Williams

(He could endure stress but peace and regularity pleased him better.)

The point is that you don't have to begin every sentence with the subject. As the examples make clear, the frame that you choose for your sentence determines what is stressed.

Exercise

To change emphasis, rearrange each of the following sentences at least once:

1. The mail having arrived, we left for the city.
2. The students cheered, their team being seven points ahead.
3. The day, drizzlingly damp, depressed Deborah.
4. The waitress smiled toothily, artificial in her unctuous friendliness.
5. If winter comes, can spring be far behind?
6. Computer programming, though it fascinates many students, takes a long time to learn.
7. *Heart of Darkness,* a masterpiece of fiction, baffled La Wanda.
8. A spry octogenarian, my grandfather still plays golf.
9. In the morning, our whole family drinks tea.
10. Germans drink beer during the Oktoberfest.

Review

In the following sentences, various strategies are used to achieve various effects. Point these strategies out, and rearrange the sentences to achieve different effects.

1. The good fortune of the physicist—and these matters are always relative, for the material monism of physics may have impeded nineteenth-century thinking and delayed insights into the nature of complementarity in modern physical theory—this early good fortune or happy insight has no counterpart in the sciences of man.   —Jerome S. Bruner

2. Since RKO-Radio Pictures first released *King Kong,* a quarter-century has gone by; yet year after year, from prints that grow more rain-beaten, from sound tracks that grow more tinny, ticket-buyers by thousands still pursue Kong's luckless fight against the forces of technology, tabloid journalism, and the DAR. They see him chloroformed to sleep, see him whisked from his jungle to New York, and placed on show, see him burst his chains to roam the city (lugging a frightened blonde), at last to plunge from the spire of the Empire State Building, machine-gunned by model airplanes.   —X. J. Kennedy

3. I went as far as the sixth grade in school. I'm 57 now. I was 16 and didn't want to be 16 in the seventh grade so I quit.   —Linda Lane

4. What is the function of sound in music? What is the function of sound in poetry? What is the function of sound in prose composition? What is the function of sound in drama?

5. Just praise is only a debt, but flattery is a present.   —Samuel Johnson

6. And he took the pain of it, if not happily, like a martyr, at least willingly, like an heir.   —Edward Lewis Wallant

7. *Mansions there are*—two or three of them—but the majority of the homes are large and inelegant.   —John Barth

8. I am sure of this, that by going much alone a man will get more of a noble courage in thought and word than from all the wisdom that is in books.   —Ralph Waldo Emerson

9. These times—they try men's souls.

10. A sudden idea of the relationship between "lovers." We are neither male nor female. We are a compound of both. I choose the male who will develop and expand the male in me; he chooses me to expand the female in him. Being made "whole."   —Katherine Mansfield

11. Now I think—I happen to think—that those three beliefs that I speak of, the self-belief, the love-belief, and the art-belief, are all closely related to the God-belief, that the belief in God is a relationship you enter into with Him to bring about the future.   —Robert Frost

12. are you ready for the demystification of diamondback terrapins???????? they ain't nothing but salt water turtles. —Verta Mae Smart-Grosvenor

13. I was a caged panther. It was jungle. Survival was the law of the land. I watched so many partners fall along the way. I decided the modus operandi was bad. Unavailing, non-productive.   —Studs Terkel

14. Finally, one night they had Junior trapped on the road up toward the bridge around Millersville, there's no way out of there, they had the barricades up and they could hear this souped-up car roaring around

the bend, and here it comes—but suddenly they can hear a siren and see a red light flashing in the grille, so they think it's another agent, and boy, they run out like ants and pull those barrels and boards and saw-horses out of the way, and then—Ggghhzzzzzzzzhhhhhhgggggg-zzzzzzzeeeeeong!—gawdam! there he goes again, it was him, Junior Johnson! with a gawdam agent's sireen and a red light in his grille.

—Tom Wolfe

15. There are still islands where you can laze on the beach for hours and hear no sound louder than the trade winds in the palm fronds; or breakfast on a flower-decked patio and sniff the frangipani and olean-der; or wander through tumble-down towns without being jostled by cars or crowds.   —Ian Keown

---

SOME PRINCIPLES OF READABILITY

Common sense might tell you that short sentences are easier to read than long ones, but in this case, common sense turns out to be nonsense, as the structure of a sentence is more important for its readability than its length.[2] We can demonstrate this point with the following two sentences, each of which contains eleven words:

1. A good teacher explains all concepts very clearly to his students.
2. In explanation of concepts to students a good teacher is clear.

Sentence 1 is easier to read, even though both sentences convey the same idea.

Here are further examples of how sentence structure affects readability.

3. Mary turned off the lights that Jim turned on.
3a. Mary turned the lights that Jim turned on off.
4. I can write difficult sentences without even trying.
4a. Difficult sentences can be written by me without even trying.
5. It is unbelievable that Herb thinks that Bert told Mary that Helen is rude.
5a. That Herb thinks that Bert told Mary that Helen is rude is unbe-lievable.

There are a few learnable and simple principles for writing readable prose, and it is to these that we will now turn.

[2] Many of the ideas in this section derive from Joseph M. Williams, "Style: Ten Lessons in Clarity and Grace" (unpublished manuscript), and E. D. Hirsch, Jr., *The Philosophy of Composition* (Chicago: University of Chicago Press, 1978).

Closure

Both of the following sentences are difficult to read:

1. A handsome, efficiently typing, bilingual secretary can always get a good job.
2. That to talk to the people of a foreign country we must learn their language sufficiently well to convey our meanings seems perfectly obvious.

They are difficult because we must overload our short-term memories in order to gain the meaning. In sentence *1,* for instance, the words *handsome, efficiently typing,* and *bilingual* must be held in short-term memory until *secretary,* the noun that they modify, is reached. And in *2,* twenty-three words must be held in mind until the final word, *obvious.*

What has been said so far should conform to your own experience, particularly when you compare *1* and *2* with rewritten versions which are easier to read:

1a. A handsome, bilingual secretary who types efficiently can always get a good job.
2a. It seems perfectly obvious that to talk to the people of a foreign country we must learn their language sufficiently well to convey our meanings.

Because of the nature of the human mind, *1a* and *2a* are easier to read for *all* readers, not just for some.

A bit of detail about sentence *1* will clarify this point. The adjectives *handsome, efficiently typing,* and *bilingual* must relate to a noun, since adjectives modify nouns. This means that the reader must, in fact, keep three questions in mind, questions that cannot be answered until the noun is reached:

Who is *handsome?*
Who is *efficiently typing?*
Who is *bilingual?*

The adjectives cannot be totally processed for meaning until they are related to *secretary*—another way of saying that *closure is delayed.* In *1a,* however, closure is not delayed as long as in *1,* for the reader can "process" *handsome* and *bilingual* as soon as the noun *secretary* is reached and can then process the modifying clause *who types efficiently.*

The principle is this: the more a reader must keep in mind before achieving semantic closure, the more difficult the reading will be. (For this reason, periodic sentences are often more difficult to read than their loose versions. See pages 446–49).

Explaining sentence 2 is more difficult, and a completely accurate account of its difficulty would take several pages, but in general, the difficulty is this: the reader must keep everything in short-term memory until the last word of the sentence, *obvious,* which is the true predicate. What the reader must keep in mind is three complete propositions, which might be represented like this:

[we] to talk to the people of a foreign country
we must learn their language sufficiently well
[we] to convey our meanings.

The following examples give a hard-to-read sentence, an explanation of the problem, and a more readable version.

3. A snowcapped, sublime, jaggedly rising mountain peak was silhouetted against the horizon.

   EXPLANATION: We cannot "process" the modifiers *snowcapped, sublime,* and *jaggedly rising* until we reach the noun phrase that they modify: *mountain peak.*

   REVISION: A jagged mountain peak, snowcapped and sublime, was silhouetted against the horizon.

4. Whatever the family couldn't buy at the country store located at the crossroads five miles from town they did without.

   EXPLANATION: Until the reader comes to the main clause, *they did without,* he or she cannot determine how the subordinate (noun) clause will relate. The subordinate clause consists of seventeen words, putting a great strain on short-term memory: *Whatever the family couldn't buy at the country store located at the crossroads five miles from town.*

   REVISION: The family did without whatever they couldn't buy at the country store located at the crossroads five miles from town.

5. The program was a concert of relatively pleasant newly discovered Appalachian dulcimer music.

   EXPLANATION: The noun phrase *dulcimer music* is preceded by too many modifiers that must be held in suspension.

   REVISION: The program was a concert of relatively pleasant dulcimer music that had been newly discovered in Appalachia.

6. Fixing a broken dishwasher, without the proper tools, can be difficult.

EXPLANATION: The phrase *without the proper tools* interrupts the sentence and delays the process of reaching the pivot word, *difficult*.

REVISION: Fixing a broken dishwasher can be difficult without the proper tools.

7. To bake potatoes on an open bonfire, as we did when we were kids, was always a great adventure.

EXPLANATION: The interrupting clause *as we did when we were kids* delays closure.

REVISION: It was always a great adventure to bake potatoes on an open bonfire, as we did when we were kids.

All of this technical detail aside, most of us can recognize and improve difficult sentences, if we pay attention. And, of course, such attention to readability and the effort to achieve it are extremely worthwhile, for *the best style is that which expresses the writer's meaning and intention with the least effort for the reader.* If part of your intention is to write a difficult sentence, then the less readable version is better than the more readable one. But, of course, most of the time we want to express our ideas so that they can be understood with a minimum of effort. As a rule, we want our prose to be relatively straightforward rather than relatively complicated.

This is not to say that all reading can be made easy for any or all readers. Difficult ideas are hard to grasp, regardless of how well the writer constructs the sentences in which they appear. It is perverse, however, to *want* to make difficult ideas even more difficult by expressing them in unreadable sentences.

Exercise

1. All of the following sentences can be made more readable. Play around with them until you feel that you have created more readable versions *without changing their basic meaning*. You might want to test your revisions by asking the opinions of some of your classmates.

   a. That Herman thought that Hermione believed that Herbert was a thief was tragic.
   b. The child threw the mush that it had forced down up.
   c. The rapidly rising, disastrous, unnecessary rate of inflation must be controlled.

d. To learn history, a fascinating subject that most people know little about, takes time and intelligence.
e. What we once thought was necessary for the good life we have found we can do away with without any trouble.
f. The conclusively predicted spring flood was upon us.
g. Asking questions that are likely to bring productive answers in regard to any problem is a skill that can be developed.
h. Students complaining about grading standards which instructors adopt are usually those who are doing poorly in classes.
i. To write sentences that are hard to read, I am discovering, is sometimes more difficult than writing readable sentences.
j. George is eager to help when the opportunity arises anyone who is in trouble.
k. Often exemplary poorly constructed exercise sentences such as this one or the one above, which have been cooked up out of context, sound artificial.
l. Whenever the surf is up is the time when I load my surfboard in the car and head for the beach.
m. It is a custom in our family on Saturday afternoon to wash and polish our cars.
n. What, since I am the world's greatest expert on the subject, you say about fishing, people's most glorious recreation, I completely deny.
o. Over the fence to the cow some hay the farmer threw.

2. In your own writing, find ten sentences that can be made more readable. On a sheet of paper, write each one, and below it write an improved version.

Subjects and Doers

Typically, a sentence has a subject and a predicate, a concept that is more easily illustrated than explained:

SUBJECT	PREDICATE
The girl	ran ten kilometers.
She	won the race.
The Constitution of the United States of America	guarantees the principle of trial by a jury of one's peers.
Whatever you say	must be the truth.

In sentences which express an action, the doer of the action is called the *agent*, but the agent and the subject are not always the same.

Compare the following sentences, all of which mean roughly the same thing:

1. Bill hit the nail with a hammer.
2. The nail was hit with a hammer by Bill.
3. A hammer was what Bill hit the nail with.

In all three sentences, Bill is the *agent,* the person who performs the action of hitting, but only in sentence *1* is Bill the *subject.*

In general, *those sentences in which the subject and agent are identical are the most readable.* In each of the following examples, the *a* version is easier to read than the *b* version, since in the *a* versions subject and agent are identical.

4a. *Bertrand* teased Mary about her bad habit.
4b. Mary's bad habit was the reason for *Bertrand's* teasing her.
5a. *Alyosha* enjoyed caviar, a taste which was very expensive.
5b. The enjoyment of caviar by *Alyosha* was a very expensive taste.
6a. *Marvin* gave Moira a sloppy kiss.
6b. A sloppy kiss was given to Moira by *Marvin.*
7a. *Myrtle* grew petunias as a hobby.
7b. Growing petunias was *Myrtle's* hobby.

As you can see, in the *b* versions of the sentences, the agent—the doer of the action—has been displaced from the subject position, thus decreasing readability.

All of this is simple enough, but there are some complications. Finite verbs like *teased, enjoyed, gave,* and *grew* obviously have subjects: "*Bertrand* teased . . . *Alyosha* enjoyed . . . *Marvin* gave . . . *Myrtle* grew. . . ." Although less obviously, nonfinite verbs also have subjects in sentences. The nonfinite verb forms that we will be concerned with are infinitives (*to tease, to enjoy, to give, to grow*) and present participles (*teasing, enjoying, giving, growing*).

8. FINITE VERB: My friend Kyoko *makes* sushi.
8a. INFINITIVE: My friend Kyoko likes *to make* sushi.
8b. PRESENT PARTICIPLE: My friend Kyoko enjoys *making* sushi.

Why do we say that *to make* in *8a* and *making* in *8b* have subjects? Simply because we must know who is performing the action or we cannot understand the sentence. In a way, when we read the sentences we supply the subjects:

8aa. My friend Kyoko likes [Kyoko (implied subject)] *to make* sushi.
8bb. My friend Kyoko enjoys [Kyoko (implied subject)] *making* sushi.

Another example. In *9*, we know that it is Ted who is doing the pleasing, but in *10*, it is Ted who is being pleased. The implied subjects and objects are in brackets.

9. Ted is eager to please.
   Ted is eager [Ted] to please [someone].
10. Ted is easy to please.
    Ted is easy [someone] to please [Ted].

In *11*, we know that the subject of *To become* must be *you*.

11. To become a millionaire, you must be lucky.

In *12*, we know that the subject of *Fighting* must be *Naomi*.

12. Fighting the violent wind, Naomi struggled onward.

And in *13*, we know that the subject of *Having graduated* must be *Irma*.

13. Having graduated from college, Irma began to look for a job.

The problem with the following sentences is that there is momentary confusion about the subjects of the nonfinite verbs.

14. *Darting* under a mossy rock, the trout was seen by us.
    (We saw the trout *darting* under a mossy rock.)
15. *To save* time, the shortcut must be taken.
    (*To save* time, you should take the shortcut.)
16. The child was found by us *hiding* in the closet.
    (We found the child hiding in the closet.)
17. Not *to proceed* without chains was told us by the policeman.
    (The policeman told us not *to proceed* without chains.)

The principles, then, are very easy. (1) In the most readable sentences, the doers of the actions (the agents) are also the subjects. (2) If the reader cannot immediately supply the agent for a nonfinite verb in a sentence, the sentence will be confusing and hence difficult to read.

Exercise

You can improve the readability of *some* of the following sentences by revising them so that the doer of the action (the agent) and the subject coincide. If you feel that the sentence is easily readable as it stands, do not revise.

1. The cake was baked by Mary in the oven.
2. A screwdriver is what Bill opened the can with.
3. The captain of the ship hosted a reception for the passengers.
4. Playing marbles is enjoyed by the children.
5. All my friends like to attend ball games.
6. To clean chicken coops is detested by everyone I know.
7. With great enthusiasm Alvin set out on the hike.
8. To become an investment banker is the reason Lola wanted to attend college.
9. Lack of time was why the job wasn't completed by the crew.
10. A cup of strong tea is what I drink every morning.
11. Don't forget to take your pills before you go to bed.
12. To leave the key with the desk clerk should not be forgotten by guests who are checking out.
13. Taking the bus is the best way for residents to get to the park.
14. To take a taxi to the Music Center is the quickest way for concertgoers to get there.
15. Growing up in the city is found to be difficult by many youngsters.
16. Living in the country has advantages for many youngsters.
17. The members of the club, once a wild party was held by them in the Student Union Building, and to punish them they were put on academic probation by the dean.
18. Fame and fortune—that's the reason I'm studying to be an English teacher.
19. What Elvira explained to us was that we needed baking powder to make biscuits.
20. Hesitating because he was not sure which button to push, Jurgen stood before the soft drink dispenser.

Nouns versus Verbs

Many verbs have noun equivalents, for example:

VERB	NOUN
act	action
complete	completion
decide	decision
grow	growth
hate	hatred
illuminate	illumination
resolve	resolution

It is a general rule that ideas expressed with verbs are more readable than ideas expressed with nouns.

Which sentences in the following pairs do you think are most readable?

1a. I *acted* foolishly.
1b. My *action* was foolish.
2a. When we *completed* the course, we took the final test.
2b. Upon *completion* of the course, we took the final test.
3a. I hope that you *decide* to take the course.
3b. I hope that your *decision* is to take the course.
4a. Everyone knows that corn *grows* tall in Iowa.
4b. Everyone knows about the tall *growth* of corn in Iowa.
5a. Gregory tried to conceal the fact that he *hated* Mary.
5b. Gregory tried to conceal the fact of his *hatred* for Mary.

Undoubtedly, the *a* versions are easier to read, a claim that you can test by submitting them to one group of good readers and the *b* versions to another group and clocking the reading speed.

The following two passages dramatically illustrate this principle. Though both convey nearly the same information, passage 8, which uses verbs, is more readable than passage 9, which is loaded with nouns.

8. To write readable prose, you must follow certain principles. For example, express your ideas with verbs rather than nouns whenever possible; try to make subject and agent coincide; and avoid uncommon words. At times, however, the less readable version of a sentence will fulfill your purpose better than the more readable one. You must use judgment.

9. To write readable prose, *the following* of certain principles is necessary, for example, *the expression* of ideas with verbs rather than nouns, *the coincidence* of subject and agent, and *the avoidance* of uncommon words. At times, however, *the fulfillment* of

your purpose is better achieved with the less readable version of a sentence than with the more readable one. *The use* of judgment is necessary.

We have seen that finite verbs can be turned into nouns, as when we write *my failure* rather than *I failed:*

10. I knew about *my failure* on the test.
11. I knew that *I failed* the test.

Exactly the same principle applies with nonfinite verbs.

NONFINITE VERBS	NOUNS
Some farmers raise turkeys *to supplement* their incomes.	Some farmers raise turkeys for *the supplementation* of their incomes.
Fernando denied *having associated* himself with the dissenters.	Fernando denied *the association* of himself with the dissenters.
To avoid sickness, you must eat the proper food.	For *the avoidance* of sickness, you must eat the proper food.
Criticizing a play is easy, but writing one is difficult.	*The criticism* of a play is easy, but writing one is difficult.

Strangely enough, there is evidence that some readers prefer the nominal style even though it is less readable. They seem to feel that the ideas expressed with nouns are more profound than those expressed with verbs, fancier and more philosophical. This observation, of course, brings us right back to one of our main principles: when we write, we must consider our purpose and the audience for whom we are writing. Out of context, nothing in language is good or bad.

Exercise

Some of the following sentences use nouns where verbs could express the same meanings. Rewrite those sentences, changing them from the nominal to the verbal style. You will probably feel that some of the sentences do not need revision.

1. The appearance of the comet was low over the horizon.
2. Many scholars use their knowledge for the intimidation of others.

3. Marylou's success was in convincing the judge that she was innocent.
4. Because of its excitement of great interest, the new opera was a financial success.
5. Sometimes one asks whether or not all of the work to get a college degree is worthwhile.
6. Most students think that the failure of a course is tragic.
7. The construction of a good alibi is difficult.
8. Building a solid reputation for reliability is not easy.
9. Farley enjoyed the refusal of any request he received.
10. Acceptance of responsibility for your actions is a must.
11. Publication of the stories of E. M. Forster was by Knopf.
12. For the achievement of success, you must work hard unless the inheritance of your rich uncle's money happens to you.
13. Unquestionably the greatest health hazard today is cigarette smoking.
14. The Hatfields were eager in their connivance against the McCoys, for neither family wanted settlement of the feud.
15. Because Marlene planned the commission of a murder, she was saving for the purchase of a shotgun.
16. When I first made the collection of them, the stamps had only face value.
17. Because the rivers were flooding, schools were closed in Rock Island and Davenport.
18. In his attempt at proof that the language was decaying, Harvey did not fail to quote his beloved Dr. Johnson.
19. The suggestion of the committee was for the erection of a monument to honor Vronsky by the city.
20. With its abstraction and frequent angularity, modern art leaves many viewers cold.
21. It is unwise to drink the water when contamination by raw sewage has taken place.
22. Finally, the coast glimmered into view, the sandstone cliffs of Laguna rising from the blue of the calm sea.
23. The attempt at argument against a dogmatic person is a frustration to most of us.
24. The orchestration of the concerto especially for Berman was by Bernstein.
25. The milking of a wild cow by anyone takes patience and strong hands.

Sentence Sequences

So far, we have dealt with the readability of individual sentences, but readers also must easily be able to see how one sentence relates to the next. A string of clear but unrelated sentences amounts to an unreadable passage. One of the main principles in creating readable passages involves the content of sentences.

Every sentence consists of a topic and a comment on that topic (or information about it). For example, in

1. Norma brought the lunch.

Norma is the topic, and *brought the lunch* is the comment. The topic is frequently the subject of the sentence, but need not be. In

2. As to the sentence, it is the basic unit of language.

the sentence is the topic, *is the basic unit of language* is the comment, and *it* is the subject.

In the following examples, the topic is printed in *italics* and the comment is in capital letters.

3. Nowadays *farming* IS BIG BUSINESS.
4. In the *agribusiness,* THERE ARE MANY RISKS.
5. CARE by *the farmer* SHOULD BE EXERCISED IN CHOOSING WHAT CROPS HE WILL PLANT DURING THE SEASON.

As a general rule, a passage of writing is more readable if the topics of the sentences in it do not shift unnecessarily. In the following example, each sentence has a different topic, with the result that the passage is somewhat difficult to read:

6. As their name implies, *structural linguists* analyze the structure of language. *Transformational generative grammar* attempts to explain how the human brain creates language. *The control of language* is not the purpose of the science of linguistics.

Without loss of essential meaning, this passage can be rewritten so that it is more readable:

7. As their name implies, *structural linguists* analyze the structure of language. *Transformational generative linguists* attempt to explain how the human brain creates language. Neither *structural* nor *transformational generative linguists* presume to control language.

In passage 6, the topics are *structural linguists, transformational generative grammar,* and *the control of language.* But in passage 7, all of the topics have *linguists* as their main element.

Example *8* is easier to read than *9*, for the topics in *8* are all related in meaning:

8. *The writer* does not need a theoretical knowledge of grammar, but often must have a sure command of language to avoid offending readers. *He* must be able to produce well-edited texts that contain no serious errors in such matters as verb agreement and pronoun reference. However, if he pays too much attention to these matters during the writing process, *the beginner* may find that the well of ideas dries up.

9. *The writer* does not need a theoretical knowledge of grammar, but often must have a sure command of language to avoid offending readers. *The well-edited text* contains no serious errors in such matters as verb agreement and pronoun reference. However, *too much attention* to these matters during the writing process may dry up the well of ideas.

In *8*, all of the topics relate to "the writer," but in *9*, the topics do not have this close relationship: *the writer, the well-edited text, too much attention.* This diversity makes *9* more difficult to read than *8*.

The topic-comment principle is not an absolute, but it is a concept worth paying attention to. Especially in paragraphs, if topics shift unnecessarily from sentence to sentence, coherence disappears, and "incoherence" and "unreadability" are synonymous. (Pages 111–19 in this book also deal with the concept of paragraph unity.)

Subject Index

abstract-concrete sentences, journal
    writing and, 31–33
abstractness, 408–09
act, in the Pentad, 69–70
active voice, 452–53
ad hominem (against the man) fallacy,
    256–57
adjustments, requests for:
  responding to, 362–65
  writing, 352–55
advertising, persuasion in, 235–38
agency and agent, in the Pentad, 70
analogy, 424–25
  developing expository writing with,
    202–05
  journal writing and, 34–37
  outrageous, 36–37
application letters, 340–46
argument (argumentation), 239–52
  data, link, and claim in, 243–48
  grounds for, 241–42
  logic and, 252–67
    deduction and induction, 254–56
    fallacies, 256–59
    formal and material truth, 253–54
  model for, 243–48
  reservation and qualification in,
    247–48
  substance of, 239–41
attitude, *see* tone
audience (readers), 87, 88
  composing process and, 20–23
  defining your, 4–5

exposition and, 48–50
intention or purpose of writing and,
    173
rhetorical stance and, 217–21
specialized, 220
universal, 218–20

balance, 449–52
bandwagon fallacy, 257
begging the question, fallacy of, 257
bibliography, 388–89
bibliography cards, 378–80
biographical sources, 377
books, bibliography cards for, 378–80
brainstorming, 58–65
business letters and communications,
    335–71
  job search letters, 340–51
    application letters, 340–46
    recommendations, requests for,
      346–47
    resumés, 348–51
    thank-you's for interviews, 347–48
  memorandums, 365–69
  progress reports, 369–71
  requests
    responding to, 357–65
    writing, 351–57
  tone in, 337–39

characters, in prose fiction, 303–04
checklist, writer's, 187–88

473

Author Index

B 1
C 2
D 3
E 4
F 5
G 6
H 7
I 8
J 9